Curiosity and the Aesthetics of
1770–1840

Curiosity and the Aesthetics of Travel Writing, 1770–1840

'From an Antique Land'

NIGEL LEASK

OXFORD
UNIVERSITY PRESS

OXFORD
UNIVERSITY PRESS

Great Clarendon Street, Oxford OX2 6DP

Oxford University Press is a department of the University of Oxford.
It furthers the University's objective of excellence in research, scholarship,
and education by publishing worldwide in

Oxford New York

Auckland Bangkok Buenos Aires Cape Town
Chennai Dar es Salaam Delhi Hong Kong Istanbul Karachi
Kolkata Kuala Lumpur Madrid Melbourne Mexico City Mumbai Nairobi
São Paulo Shanghai Taipei Tokyo Toronto

Oxford is a registered trade mark of Oxford University Press
in the UK and in certain other countries

Published in the United States
By Oxford University Press Inc., New York

British Library Cataloguing in Publication Data
Data available

Library of Congress Cataloging in Publication Data

Leask, Nigel, 1958–
Curiosity and the aesthetics of travel writing, 1770–1840 : from an antique land/Nigel Leask.
p. cm.
Includes bibliographical references and index.
1. Travelers' writings, English—History and criticism. 2. English prose literature—19th
century—History and criticism. 3. English prose literature—18th century—History and
criticism. 4. British—Foreign countries—History. 5. Ethiopia—Description and travel.
6. Mexico—Description and travel. 7. India—Description and travel. 8. Egypt—Description
and travel. 9. Antiquities in literature. 10. Curiosity in literature. 11. Travel in literature.
12. Aesthetics, British. I. Title.

PR756.T72 L43 2002   820.9'355—dc21   2001036762
ISBN 0-19-924700-5
ISBN 0-19-926930-0 (pbk.)

1 3 5 7 9 10 8 6 4 2

Typeset in Bulmer MT
by Best-set Typesetter Ltd., Hong Kong
Printed in Great Britain
on acid-free paper by
T. J. International Ltd,
Padstow, Cornwall

To my daughters, Isabel (b. 1997) and Flora (b. 2000),
and in memory of my mother, Anne Leask (1928–2001)

Acknowledgements

Thanks to all those friends and colleagues who read and commented on this book, either as work in progress or in its final stages: John Barrell, Peter de Bolla, Michael Bravo, Gordon Brotherston, Steve Clark, Eivind Kahrs, Neil Kenny, Martin Ruehl, Simon Schaffer, Nicholas Thomas, and my anonymous third reader for Oxford. Thanks also to the many others in Cambridge and beyond who have made writing this book such an enjoyable and interdisciplinary project. To name but a few: Chris Bayly, Carlos Lopez Beltrán, Gautam Chakravarty, Phil Connell, Stefan Collini, Mike Dettelbach, Brian Dolan, Jas Elsner, Patricia Fara, Tim Fulford, Indira Ghose, Charlotte Grant, Sudeshna Guha, Anita Herle, Simon Jarvis, Patrick Leech, Ruth Morse, Jackie Phillips, Ato Quayson, Michael Rossington, Jim Secord, Kate Teltscher, and Carl Thompson. Thanks also to Nicholas Rupke for inviting me to participate in the International Humboldt Symposium at Göttingen in May 1997.

I owe an enormous debt of thanks to my wife, Evelyn Arizpe: if she unintentionally inspired this project in the first place, as the rationale for my own long-distance travel, she has nobly borne the consequences and been a tremendous support throughout. She will doubtless be greatly relieved to see it completed! Much of the actual writing was done during a term's sabbatical leave in 1998, and subsequently during two university summer vacations, in Tepoztlan, Mexico, thanks to the warm hospitality of Lourdes Arizpe and other members of my Mexican family. The 'curious' mountain landscape of the Tepozteco offered constant inspiration, strenuous walking, and mysterious rock paintings. At home, my thanks are due to the patience of the librarians in the Rare Books Room, and to the Syndics of Cambridge University Library, for permission to reproduce visual material. Thanks also to the President and Fellows of Queens' College, Cambridge, for a grant to cover photographic costs. I am also grateful to Sophie Goldsworthy, Frances Whistler, and Sally McCann at Oxford University Press for all their work in the various stages of production.

Nigel Leask

Contents

Illustrations

Introduction:
Practices and Narratives of Romantic Travel

> I met a Traveller from an antique land.
>
> (P. B. Shelley, 'Ozymandias', 1818)

> [In the late Middle Ages] the interest attached to the narratives of travels was . . . wholly dramatic, and the . . . admixture of the marvellous, gave them almost an epic colouring . . . They had that character of unity which every work of art requires; everything was associated with one action, and made subservient to the narration of the journey itself . . . In the midst of the obscurity in which the East and the interior of Asia were shrouded, distance seemed only to magnify the grand proportions of individual forms. This unity of composition is almost wholly wanting in most of our recent voyages, especially where their object is the acquirement of scientific knowledge. The narrative in the latter case is secondary to observations, and is almost wholly lost sight of . . . this partial disadvantage is fully compensated for by the increased value of the facts observed, the greater expansion of natural views, and the laudable endeavour to employ the peculiar characteristics of different languages, in rendering natural descriptions clear and distinct.
>
> (Alexander von Humboldt, *Cosmos* 1849)[1]

This book is a study of European travel writing about Ethiopia, Egypt, India, and Mexico in the years between 1770 and 1840: countries situated within the 'torrid zones' of Africa, Asia, and America, which, despite their cartographic and cultural distance from one other, shared the fate of being considered 'antique lands' by Europeans. Unlike most recent studies of extra-European travel writing in these decades, I am principally concerned with aesthetic and archaeological (in contemporary terminology, *antiquarian*) discourses of travel rather than with science or natural history. Of course, one of the attractions of travel writing in the period is the uninhibited energy with which it ranges across modern disciplinary boundaries, as the shaping itinerary narrative is

---

[1] Alexander von Humboldt, *Cosmos: A Sketch of a Physical Description of the Universe*, 5 vols., trans. by E. C. Otte (London, Henry Bohn, 1849), ii. pp. 434–6. Hereafter *C*.

punctuated with reports on botany and zoology alongside ancient ruins and monuments, mineralogy alongside modern manners, ancient history alongside contemporary politics. Nevertheless, most travel narratives are shaped by the dominant intellectual concerns of their authors, and whilst I will keep an eye on the broader range of travellers' interests, my decision to focus on 'antiquarian' travel has to some extent determined the approach and choice of material in the present book.

In contrast to the ruin-strewn 'marble wilderness' of Italy, and later Greece, the destination of the seventeenth and eighteenth century Grand Tour, the antique lands discussed here to some extent lacked the rich texture of literary and cultural associations which distinguished Greco-Roman topography in the minds of educated eighteenth- and nineteenth-century Europeans. Nevertheless, as exemplified by Shelley's famous sonnet 'Ozymandias', Egypt (like India or Mexico) had particular resonance for romantic sensibility, attracted as it was to the antique, the picturesque, and the exotic, even when (as in Shelley's case) that attraction was qualified by political and moral critique of the past or present inhabitants of the antique lands. Because of the associative vacuum, European travellers constantly 'temporalized' the antique lands (and especially their modern inhabitants) by comparing them with more familiar classical, biblical, or medieval worlds, at the same time as they incorporated them into a 'universal' grid of geographical orientation based in Europe. A recurrent theme of the present book is thus the dialectical relationship between antiquity and modernity in travel writing situated on the threshold of the modern era.

Shelley's usage in 'Ozymandias' of the word 'antique' (the sonnet is discussed in some detail in Chapter 3) is overdetermined in its punning reference to the etymologically unrelated term 'antick', sometimes also spelt 'antique', which the *OED* defines as 'grotesque, in composition or shape; grouped or figured with fantastic incongruity; bizarre'.[2] Whilst travellers frequently found it possible to 'temporalize' peoples and topographies with reference to Europe's classical past, Shelley's veiled pun on 'antick' perfectly captures contemporary notions of Egyptian (or Hindu or Mexican) monuments and antiquities as 'curious' rather than beautiful, 'colossal' rather than sublime. In the decades under consideration this discrimination was still not based primarily on 'racial science' but rather on a comparison with the perceived naturalism and humanistic scale of classical Greek art, considered as the foundation-stone of European civilization. In the decades after 1790 the antique lands were increasingly caught up in a power struggle between Britain and post-revolutionary

[2] Kelvin Everest points out that in 1817 the first syllable of 'antique' would still have been stressed, just as 'antic' still is. '"Ozymandias": The Text in Time, in *Shelley Bicentenary Essays*, ed. K. Everest (Cambridge: The English Association, 1992), pp. 24–42, 28.

France for ideological control of the meanings of antiquity. As the century progressed, and in a manner rather different from Italy or Greece, the extra-European antique lands became increasingly subject to the quantifying and typifying scrutiny of colonial surveillance, as well as to European aesthetic judgement. Hence the conjunction between romanticism and colonialism which is a central concern of what follows.

In contrast to the dominant navigational mode of eighteenth-century exploration—exemplified in Bougainville and Cook's Pacific voyages—the characteristic mode of romantic exploration, and of the travellers studied in this book, was the penetration of continental interiors, a practice institutionalized in Britain by the foundation of the African Association in 1788.[3] (Although I shall devote a lot of space to the consideration of non-British travel writing, my main focus will be on texts by British travellers, or the reception of French, German, and Italian travelogues in the British context.) Intra-continental exploration was a practice which, especially beyond the sphere of European colonial power, exposed land travellers like James Bruce or Mungo Park to intimate (although in this period rarely *first*) contact with local peoples and alien topographies, and vulnerability to kinds of danger, especially tropical diseases, unknown to sea-borne travellers in their floating fortress/laboratories.[4] In such regions the traveller needed to disguise himself (seldom herself) in local costume and master diverse cultural languages and health regimes if he was to avoid attack, imprisonment for espionage, or death by tropical disease. The defeat of British forces in Europe, Asia, and (most damagingly) America in the 1770s and 1780s, with the loss of her first empire, exacerbated the difficulties faced by British travellers in these continents. The global outreach of the European wars of 1793–1815 (a substantial proportion of the period with which I am concerned) brought about substantial changes as travellers exchanged cultural disguise for military uniforms, exemplified by the French invasion of Egypt and the British counter-attack in 1799–1802, discussed in Chapter 3. The acquisition of Britain's 'second empire' after 1815, the fruit of global victory over Napoleonic France, further changed the situation of British travellers in distant lands. With the exportation of a Christian, capitalist, ethic and an ideology of bourgeois domesticity to Britain's Asian and African colonies, male—and now increasingly also female—travel writers celebrated their emancipation from the necessity of cultural disguise alongside an increased sense of separation from indigenous peoples.

---

[3] This is not to deny the importance of earlier land exploration like La Condamine's 1735 expedition to South America, nor of later navigational expeditions such as Ross, Parry, and Franklin's voyages to the Arctic in the years 1818–27, which had a profound impact on late Georgian culture.

[4] See Alan Bewell, *Romanticism and Colonial Disease* (Baltimore: Johns Hopkins University Press, 2000) for a wide-ranging study of tropical illnesses in the literature of the period.

The recent polemic between Marshall Sahlins and Gananath Obeyesekere over the 'apotheosis of Captain Cook' has highlighted some of the difficulties in studying eighteenth- and nineteenth-century European explorers and travellers without either simply restating exploded myths of empire, on the one hand, or else subscribing to post-colonial blame, on the other.[5] Although this book does deal largely with individual cases such as James Bruce, Giovanni Belzoni, or Alexander von Humboldt, it seeks to avoid either unequivocal praise of the traveller's heroism in surmounting unforeseen dangers or else a rhetoric of blame which presumes that all European travellers were uniformly racists, jingoists, or imperialists. For a start I attempt to situate each traveller within highly particularized, performative parameters of class, gender, and nationality, rather than presupposing any essential 'European' identity. Moreover, I have chosen James Bruce rather than Captain Cook as my starting point for a particular reason. In contrast to the European-wide apotheosis of his exact contemporary Cook, Bruce's account of the 'antique land' of Abyssinia was widely ridiculed and disbelieved by the British public. Bruce simply failed to win credit, a fact which throws a question mark over the supposedly irrefragible authority of eighteenth-century travel narratives in the construction of a European 'orientalist' archive.[6] European travellers could be written off as myth-mongers in their own cultures, in a rather different understanding of the word 'myth' from that employed by Obeyesekere.[7]

I am, however, less concerned with the practices or politics of distant travel than with travel *writing* in the decades stretching from 1770 to about 1840. Or, more precisely, with travel accounts motivated by antiquarian and (as we shall see, often the same thing) ethnological curiosity, which distinguishes the texts studied here from other forms of travel writing current in the same period, such as works exclusively focused upon missionary activity or botanical collecting, or else captivity and slave narratives. The 'curiosity' signalled in my title actually embraces two increasingly distinct senses of the word as it was employed in eighteenth- and nineteenth-centuries discourses of travel, which I shall discuss at more length in Chapter 1. The first is bound to a negative account of the wonder aroused by distant lands, associated with a socially exclusive desire to possess the 'singular' object or else (especially in the later part of the period) a vulgar, popular interest in exotic objects for commercial profit. The second—employed more positively—denotes an inclination to knowledge which will lead the observer to a rational, philosophical articulation of foreign singularities.

---

[5] See Gananath Obeyesekere, *The Apotheosis of Captain Cook: European Mythmaking in the Pacific With a new afterword* (Princeton, NJ: Princeton University Press, 1997), and Marshal Sahlins's *How 'Natives' Think: About Captain Cook, For Example* (Chicago and London: Chicago University Press, 1996).

[6] I refer, of course, to Edward Said's 1978 study *Orientalism* (Harmondsworth: Penguin 1985).

[7] See e.g. *The Apotheosis*, p. 12, where Obeyesekere argues against Sahlins that Cook's apotheosis was a European, rather than a Polynesian, phenomenon.

The term 'curiosity' (to an even greater extent than 'wonder') appears with almost mechanical regularity in travel writing throughout the period, well after its eclipse in natural philosophy and other branches of knowledge. I shall suggest that travel writing remained yoked to the negative as well as to the positive senses of curiosity, inasmuch as it is (almost by definition) linked to fleeting, superficial accounts of foreign lands and peoples, and to the novelty, singularity, and dazzle of the traveller's 'first impressions'. This compromised its epistemological prestige after the eclipse of empiricism in the early nineteenth century, whilst enhancing its value as a 'literary' genre according to the new conception of literature emergent in the early nineteenth century (although, as I shall indicate below, this was not necessarily equivalent to the literary canon of 'high romanticism'). Because of its generic dependence on reported experience rather than imagination, I have preferred the notion of a 'curious' rather than a 'romantic' tradition of travel writing, notwithstanding my purpose of exploring the transformation of curiosity in negotiation with romantic aesthetics, such as the sublime and picturesque.

In her influential study of illustrated travel accounts, *Voyage into Substance*, Barbara Maria Stafford argued that the empiricist and objectivist bias of the enlightenment travelogue was superseded by a 'romantic quest which [leads] ultimately, not unidirectionally out into the blank plains, dense forests, or nebulous skies of a beckoning or unknown land, but back into the tangled self'.[8] Stafford privileges the enlightenment 'voyage into substance' over a romantic predilection for metaphor, associationism, and picturesque 'seeing as' (*enargeia* over *energeia*). In contrast to the enlightenment traveller, Stafford argues, the romantic tourist 'felt the landscape without precisely seeing it', a shift which she sees as having put paid to the heroic age of scientific travel.[9] George Parks, Charles Batten, and Roger Cardinal have likewise discerned a shift from the objective to the subjective in romantic travel writing, with metaphorical or metaphysical travelling replacing an enlightenment fascination with the unknown outer world.[10] Beyond the self-conscious imaginative paradigms of Coleridge's

---

[8] Barbara Maria Stafford, *Voyage into Substance: Art, Science, Nature, and the Illustrated Travel Account 1760–1840* (Cambridge, Mass., and London: MIT Press, 1984), p. 444.

[9] Ibid., p. 443. Stafford defines *energeia* ('forceful writing') as 'the metaphoric habit of ensouling nature through the power of the imagination . . . the projection of psychic dynamism that supplements what the external signs indicate only in part', enargeia ('vivid description') as 'the creation of illusion' (p. 48). She problematically represents *enargeia* as an unmediated and transparent representation of phenomena which ignores rhetorical convention. Stafford's focus on the visual rather than narrative aspects of travel books is understandable in the work of an art historian; her apparent endorsement of the 18th century view of the traveller as (like the genius) 'the embodiment of the great and exemplary man . . . a modern Ulysses' (p. 384) is more questionable.

[10] George Parks, 'The Turn to the Romantic in the Travel Literature of the 18th Century', *Modern Language Quarterly*, 25 (March 1964); Charles Batten *Pleasurable Instruction: Form and Convention in 18th Century Travel Literature* (Berkeley, LA, London: University of California Press, 1978); Roger Cardinal, 'Romantic Travel', in *Rewriting the Self: Histories from the Renaissance to the Present*, ed. Roy Porter (London and New York: Routledge, 1997).

Ancient Mariner or Byron's *Childe Harold*, the residue of romantic travel writing proper is rather hastily apportioned by these scholars into the 'purely entertaining travel book and the instructive guide (the ancestor of the Baedecker volumes)'.[11]

Although many of the travel accounts discussed in the present book are unquestionably marked by a new emphasis on the subjectivity of the traveller and a corresponding scepticism about purely objective description, I believe that the standard account of 'romantic travel writing' is in need of serious revision. By ignoring the complexity and diversity of the literary and epistemological fields in the romantic period, it elevates the importance of one, self-consciously literary, strain of travel writing at the expense of other discourses of travel which were of equal importance. Humboldt's reflections on travel writing from *Cosmos* (quoted above) should sound a note of caution in accepting the standard account. Humboldt—surely the paramount traveller of the period, and a constant point of reference throughout this book—conceives of the historical development of the genre in terms of an economy of gains and losses with regard to the relative importance of literary narrative versus objective description. The popular format of *Cosmos: A Sketch of a Physical Description of the Universe* (based on public lectures given in Berlin in the 1820s and 1830s) itself embodied Humboldt's struggle against what he considered to be the deleterious effects of purging aesthetics from scientific discourse, and equally of relegating scientific content from literature increasingly construed in terms of the 'romantic ideology'.[12] Yet, as we shall see in the case of Humboldt's own *Personal Narrative* in Chapter 6, the equilibrium between aesthetic and scientific discourses was fragile and difficult to sustain. The modern 'descriptive' travelogue praised in *Cosmos* was itself premised on the abandonment of literary and aesthetic qualities which Humboldt admired in earlier 'unscientific' travel writing.

Humboldt testifies to the fact that by mid-century the rise of scientific disciplinarity, the emergence of geography, anthropology, natural history, and archaeology (among other disciplines), betokened the need to evacuate the anecdotal, interactive 'personal narratives' of travel in order to establish a more objective epistemological authority.[13] The discourse which Matthew Edney has termed

---

[11] Stafford, p. 442. This glosses Batten's argument on pp. 29–30 of *Pleasurable Instruction*.

[12] See Jerome McGann, *The Romantic Ideology: A Critical Investigation* (Chicago and London: Chicago University Press, 1983).

[13] James Clifford has argued that the suppression of dialogue, diegesis, and narrative (as well as the grammatical temporal shift from the past historic to the 'ethnographic present') were essential to the achievement of ethnographical authority' differentiating modern anthropology from its pre-disciplinary forebear, the travel narrative. 'On Ethnographic Authority', in *The Predicament of Culture: 20th Century Ethnography, Literature and Art* (Cambridge, Mass., and London: Harvard University Press, 1988), pp. 21–54.

'geographical narrative', the 'representation of observed facts, of truth portrayed in various graphics and texts', anxiously sought to 'obscure the production of those representations'.[14] Or else, in the words of Michel de Certeau, the 'map' as 'a plane projection totalizing observations' was gradually winning out over the tour/story which had initially represented its condition of possibility.[15] *Topicality* thus replaced a vectoral *tropology*, just as (in narratological terms) mimesis overcame diegesis, in 'scientific' discourse at least.[16] Conversely, the rise of mass readerships and 'popular curiosity', twinned with the social phenomena of widespread travel in the service of empire and the rise of commodified tourism, wrought powerful changes in the nature of travel narrative. Travel books were evacuated of scientific or scholarly specificity, and increasingly came to privilege authorial 'egotism' and entertaining reflections, often motivated by pious, patriotic, and imperialistic ideologies.[17] By the 1820s the consolidation of Europe's global power and improved technologies of travel increasingly disenchanted distance; in consequence, the traveller's subjective reflections often seemed more interesting than descriptions of the lands through which they travelled, so that travel narratives became *more* rather than less 'literary' in the modern sense of the term.[18]

Where my account principally differs from Stafford, Batten, and Cardinal, then, is the fact that I locate this disjuncture between scientific and literary travel writing in the decades *after* 1790–1820 (decades which saw the retrospective construction of 'romantic ideology'), rather than seeing it as essentially constitutive of the genre in the period itself. In the earlier decades travel writing struggled to integrate (with greater or lesser success) anecdotal personal narrative with 'curious' or 'precise' observation, often in the form of lengthy digressions

[14] Matthew Edney, *Mapping an Empire: The Geographical Construction of British India, 1765–1843* (Chicago and London: Chicago University Press, 1998), p. 79. Edney also comments that geographical narrative 'focused on not the new and novel but the everyday and common in order to classify all aspects of a region . . . pass[ing] beyond the "primary discoveries" that fill the explorer's account' (p. 66).

[15] Michel de Certeau, *The Practice of Everyday Life*, trans. by Stephen Rendall (Berkeley, LA, London: University of California Press, 1984), pp. 120–1. See also Edward S. Casey's magisterial *The Fate of Place: A Philosophical Study* (Berkeley, LA: University of California Press, 1997), which lucidly articulates the philosophical suppression of *place* in favour of absolute *space* in the period with which I am concerned.

[16] Ibid., p. 129. Gerard Genette, *Narrative Discourse: An Essay in Method*, trans. by James Lewin (Ithaca: Cornell University Press, 1980), pp. 166–7.

[17] This countered the suppression of the vectoral travel narrative by the 'map' in scientific discourse; as de Certeau points out, 'the organisation that can be discerned in stories about space in everyday culture is inverted by the process that has isolated a system of geographical places' (ibid., p. 121).

[18] As James Buzard argues in *The Beaten Track: European Tourism, Literature, and the Ways to 'Culture'* (Oxford: Clarendon Press, 1993), tourism in the modern sense first emerged in the 1820s, a decade which saw thirteen new Italian tour-books from British publishers alone (pp. 69–70). Buzard argues that the binary opposition between 'travel' and 'tourism' is 'fundamental to and characteristic of modern culture' (p. 18). Many of the texts studied in this book—exploratory, imperial, or antiquarian—provide the model against which the later tourist narrative defined itself, often with an acute sense of belatedness.

or dissertations. To generalize travel writing in the romantic period as merely 'subjective' is to ignore not only the majority of travelogues produced during the period but also the testimony of contemporary commentators. Humboldt was not alone in seeing the nineteenth-century travel account as superior to those of former periods in terms of its descriptive or 'objective' adequacy (the very reverse of Stafford's contention about 'romanticism'). In an essay appended to the Scots antiquarian and geographer John Pinkerton's seventeen-volume compilation of travel literature published in 1808–14 (arguably the most important British collection of the early nineteenth century), the editor noted that travel accounts written before 1768 are 'rather to be regarded as *curious*, than useful . . . The old catalogues of pictures and statues, with trifling adventures by sea and land, which were called books of travels, have sunk into obscurity before the new and important works, which illustrate the phenomena of nature, and display the politics and ethics, the agriculture and commerce, the state of the arts and sciences'[19] [italics mine]. Ultimately objectivity and utility, rather than curiosity and the entertainment value of 'first impressions', were Pinkerton's main priorities. Casting off his earlier reputation as antiquarian forger, Pinkerton now championed the objectivist values of the nineteenth-century exploration establishment exemplified by John Barrow at the Admiralty and, after its foundation in 1832, by the Fellows of the London Geographical Society.

In contrast, an entry in the poet S. T. Coleridge's *Table Talk* for 12 March 1827 lavished praise upon William Bartram's *Travels in . . . Florida* (1791), a work of descriptive natural history whose veracity had been called into question by some contemporary commentators: 'The latest book of travels I know, written in the spirit of the old travellers, is Bartram's account of his tour in the Floridas. It is a work of high merit every way.'[20] I have argued elsewhere

---

[19] John Pinkerton, ed., *A General Collection of the Best and Most Interesting Voyages and Travels*, 17 vols. (London 1814), xvii. pp. xxviii, xxix. 'A Retrospect of the Origin and Progress of Discovery, by Sea and Land, in Ancient, Modern, and the most Recent times'. Although Pinkerton adhered to scrupulous philological standards which eschewed the common practice (initiated in Samuel Purchas's re-editing of Hakluyt) of abridging and recasting earlier narratives in the third person, his work was nevertheless intended to be a kind of source book for his influential *Modern Geography* (1802). See G. R. Crone and R. A. Skelton, 'English Collections of Voyages and Travels 1625–1846', in Edward Lynam (ed.), *Richard Hakluyt and his Successors* (London: Hakluyt Society, 1946), pp. 65–140, p. 132. According to Crone and Skelton, 'A Retrospect' was actually the work of Sir Walter Scott's German 'secretary', Henry Weber, rather than Pinkerton. Weber also published a compilation entitled *Popular Romances: Consisting of Imaginary Voyages . . . Including Gulliver's Travels . . . and the Adventures of Robinson Crusoe* (Edinburgh, 1812), thereby reinforcing the distinction between 'useful' factual travels and entertaining fictional ones. Pinkerton, like the French geographer Conrad Malte-Brun, was engaged in the characteristic concern of 18th-century geography, to describe, by both cartographic and textual means, the 'unity and coherence of the world'. See Anne Godlewska, *Geography Unbound: French Geographic Science from Cassini to Humboldt* (Chicago and London: University of Chicago Press, 1999), p. 21.

[20] *Table Talk*, ed. by Carl Woodring, 2 vols. (Princeton, NJ and London: Princeton University Press, 1990), ii. p. 57.

that Coleridge's counter-enlightenment interest in the aesthetic achievement of those archaic, 'marvellous' travelogues dismissed by Pinkerton as merely 'curious' is manifest in his suppression, in the celebrated preface to 'Kubla Khan', of Macartney, Barrow, and Bruce's modern travelogues in favour of Marco Polo's account of China as redacted in *Purchas his Pilgrimage* (1613).[21] But the point to be made here is that Coleridge's 'romantic' predilection for early narratives cannot easily be enlisted as evidence for prioritizing 'subjective' over 'objective' styles of travel writing. This is clear from another *Table Talk* entry for 4 September 1833, in which Coleridge 'wish[ed] the naval and military officers who write accounts of their travels would just spare us their sentiment. The Magazines introduced this cant. Let these gentlemen read and imitate the old captains and admirals, as, Dampier &c.'[22] Critical of the ostentatious egotism of popular travel writing, Coleridge singles out for praise the earlier combination of narrative drama and empirical curiosity. But as Coleridge's response to James Bruce (discussed in Chapter 2) goes to show, the 'visionary' exoticism of travel narrative clearly had the edge over either its veracity or utility.

Further reflection on Humboldt's (wishful) economy of gains and losses, and the contradictory opinions of Pinkerton and Coleridge, suggests that travel writing in the romantic period still struggled to integrate literary and scientific discourses, rather than embodying the achieved triumph of imagination over knowledge. The moment that travel writing rid itself of this integrative impulse, it perhaps forfeited some of the dramatic intensity and epistemological inclusiveness which constitute the generic charm of narratives by Bruce, Denon, Belzoni, or Graham studied in the chapters which follow. For Coleridge, at least, omission of personal narrative and what I shall call the 'aesthetics of distance' in the interest of purely objective description left one with a geographical or statistical gazetteer, but not a travel book as such. Conversely (as the second *Table Talk* entry makes clear), the substitution of 'curious' description by authorial egotism also risked banalizing the genre, offering sentiment, wit, or retro-irony in the place of the narrative project of representing the foreign.

A balance between the two extremes was evidently hard to achieve, judging from the animadversions of reviewers throughout the period, who were rarely satisfied that a travelogue was entertaining and instructive in equal degrees. For example, in his 1813 review of E. D. Clarke's *Travels in Greece, Egypt and the*

---

[21] Nigel Leask, 'Kubla Khan and Orientalism: The Road to Xanadu Revisited', in *Romanticism*, 4.1 (1998). On the medieval and renaissance tradition of 'marvellous' travel writing, see Mary B. Campbell, *The Witness and the Other World: Exotic European Travel Writing, 400–1600* (Ithaca, NY, and London: Cornell University Press, 1988) and the editors' introduction to *Voyages and Visions: Towards a Cultural History of Travel*, ed. by Jas Elsner and Joan-Pau Rubiés (London: Reaktion Books, 1999).

[22] *Table Talk*, ii. 265. See also i. 444 n., in which the editor indicates that Coleridge was referring specifically to the contemporary Indian travel accounts of the 'military tourists' Skinner, Mundy, and Archer studied in Chapter 5.

Holy Land, Reginald Heber (whose own Indian travelogue is discussed in Chapter 4), wrote that

we have still to complain of a reliance on first impressions, which is not altogether compensated by an acuteness of observation undoubtedly more than common . . . we have sometimes perceived a want of that previous knowledge, without which, to travel is but to wander, and we have suspected that he has rather read to illustrate his tour, than journeyed to illustrate his reading.[23]

The 'first impressions'-type literary narrative is acceptable here as long as it is mediated by epistemological preparation; otherwise, (as Heber wrote of another 'purely entertaining' literary travelogue) it 'will seldom find a place in the library, but may lie without offence on the parlour table'.[24] Conversely, even when authorial reflection of a literary nature did overbalance 'instruction', the placement of travel books within the literary canon of high romanticism influentially described by Thomas De Quincey as 'the literature of power' (which he opposed to the 'literature of knowledge') was dubious. As De Quincey wrote in 1823, 'even books of much higher pretensions must be excluded [from the category of the 'literature of power']—as, for instance, books of voyages and travels, and generally all books in which the matter to be communicated is paramount to the manner or form of its communication'.[25]

   The whimsicality of much modern travel writing—and the genre *is* now firmly situated on the parlour table rather than in the library—suggests nostalgia not just for an imperial age of travel 'before' tourism but also for an epoch of 'integrated' travel narrative when literary representation of the foreign was at the cutting edge of emergent discourses both of the self and of scientific knowledge.[26] The twentieth-century predilection for the sort of travel book that sits on the parlour table has perhaps been detrimental to our sense of the importance of the *other sort* in the period covered here. At the same time, a De Quinceyan scruple about the literary value of travel writing has placed it on the margins of the academic literary canon: often the study of the genre has only

---

[23]   *QR*, 9 (March 1813), 162. For an excellent (and more sympathetic) account of Clarke, see Brian Dolan, *Exploring European Frontiers: European Travellers in the Age of Enlightenment* (Basingstoke: Macmillan, 2000), *passim*.

[24]   Review of Robert Ker Porter's *Travelling Sketches in Russia and Sweden*, *QR*, 2 (November 1809), 301.

[25]   'Letters to a Young Man whose Education had been Neglected. No. III On Languages'. *The London Magazine*, 7 (1823), 332.

[26]   The most damning indictment of modern travel writing (in a work which none the less bears a close relationship to the genre) is surely Claude Lévi-Strauss's at the beginning of *Tristes Tropiques* (1955) trans. by J. Weightman and D. Weightman (New York: The Modern Library, 1997), pp. 3–5. See also Patrick Holland and Graham Huggan, *Tourists with Typewriters: Critical Reflections on Contemporary Travel Writing* (Ann Arbor: University of Michigan Press, 1998). In their study of Bruce Chatwin, Eric Newby, and Redmond O'Hanlon, the authors point out how 'the contemporary travel writer's (melo)dramatic aspirations—as itinerant aesthete, jackdaw sage, pseudo-explorer, reporter, biographer—are ideally served by that most self-consciously theatrical of figures, the dandy' (pp. 39–40). Thanks to Graham Huggan for the gift of a copy of this book.

been countenanced when it is thought to have provided source material for properly 'imaginative' literature, as in the celebrated case of Jonathan Livingstone Lowe's *The Road to Xanadu*. Part of my aim in writing this book has therefore been to make these *estranged* travel narratives (many of them thousands of pages long) better known on their own terms, rather than as merely providing documentary evidence for historians of exploration, or source material for the study of literary or poetic fictions.

The popularity of travel books during the decades with which this study is concerned, although universally acknowledged, is hard to quantify. Charles Batten's claim that by the end of the eighteenth century travel books were the most widely read division of literature, second only to novels and romances, seems credible.[27] P. J. Marshall and Glyndwr Williams describe the publication of travel books in the eighteenth century—whether in the form of published journals, reprints, translations from foreign works, abridgements and compilations—as 'reaching flood-tide proportions'.[28] French, Spanish, Italian, and German travel books were translated rapidly into English and reviewed in British periodicals, a process reciprocated in Europe and America. This cultural permeability underlay my decision not to confine myself to British travel literature here but to include study of translated foreign writers like Denon, Volney, Jacquemont, and Humboldt, whose works were of great importance for the development of the genre in Britain.

G. R. Crone and R. A. Skelton (focusing on published collections of voyages and travels, only one of the many outlets for travel writing in the period) note that 'by the middle of the 18th century the vogue for travel collections created amongst the landed gentry and merchants by the imposing works [of Churchill, Osbourne, Harris, and Astley] . . . had spread to the large middle-class reading public at a lower economic level, and the booksellers were not slow to exploit it'.[29] Illustrated travel accounts, more than other genres of literature, could be very expensive; in 1803 Arthur Aikin complained that Denon's *Voyage dans la basse et la haute Égypte* was selling for 21 guineas in London, at a time when an artisan family was living on an income of about 1 pound a week.[30] This, admittedly, represents an extreme case, as Denon's was a lavishly illustrated

[27] Batten, *Pleasurable Instruction*, p. 1. Batten perhaps overlooks the enormous currency of popular theology.

[28] *The Great Map of Mankind: British Perceptions of the World in the Age of Enlightenment* (London and Melbourne, J. M. Dent and Sons, 1982), p. 45. See Edward G. Cox, *A Reference Guide to the Literature of Travel*, 3 vols. (New York, 1935–49) (which unfortunately stops at 1800), and the useful catalogue *of English Travel Literature in the Micro-Edition of the Fürstliche Bibliothek Corvey* (Olms Neue Medien, 1998) largely focused on the romantic period.

[29] Crone and Skelton, p. 109. Thomas Astley's collection (1745–7) already divided the traveller's 'personal narrative', contained in his journal, from his remarks on the country observed, 'mark[ing]a stage in the evolution of descriptive geography from the raw material provided by travellers' (p. 101).

[30] Preface to his translation of Denon's *Travels in Upper and Lower Egypt*, 3 vols. (London, 1803), i. p. viii. See also Brian Dolan, *Exploring European Frontiers*, p. 19.

book published during wartime in enemy Paris, and therefore extremely scarce. On the evidence of extensive research in publishers' archives and trade catalogues, William St Clair has indicated that a more typical pricing for quarto travel books in this period was between 2 and 5 guineas, already a high price in relative terms, as is evident from their limited print runs of between 500 and 750 copies. As exemplified by Aikin's abridged translation of Denon, these expensive quartos were reprinted in cheaper octavo editions if demand was high. For many travel books, however, a small expensive edition in quarto was often as much as could be expected.[31] Nevertheless, the plundering of travel accounts in popular periodicals (such as the *London Magazine*'s 'prepublication' of Bruce and Cook's travels discussed in Chapter 2), lengthy quotations in prestigious 'high-brow' reviews such as the *Edinburgh* and *Quarterly Reviews*, the enduring popular success of fictional travelogues such as Defoe's *Robinson Crusoe* or Swift's *Gulliver's Travels*, and, at the bottom end of the market, the chapbooks' mingling of romance with popular exoticism,[32] ensured that travel writing permeated all levels of eighteenth- and nineteenth-century literary culture. By the 1830s bowdlerized texts of the travels of Bruce, Park, or Belzoni provided Samuel Smiles-type manuals of self-help and enterprise aimed at artisan and lower class readers, presaging the rise of 'Boy's Own' literature in the imperialist Victorian era.

This process of cultural permeation was furthered by the institution of circulating and subscription libraries in the second half of the eighteenth century, which made expensive illustrated travel books in quarto or folio accessible to a wider public. Paul Kaufmann's analysis of the borrowing figures from the Bristol library in the years 1773–84 (figures which have uniquely survived) reveal that John Hawkesworth's *Account of the Voyages undertaken by the Order of his Present Majesty for making Discoveries in the Southern Hemisphere* (1773) was borrowed 201 times,[33] compared to 180 borrowings of Hume's *History of England*, 127 borrowings of *Tristram Shandy*, and 92 of Johnson's *Lives of the*

---

[31] I am grateful to William St Clair for making some typical print runs and pricings available to me, upon which these remarks are based, to be published in his forthcoming study *The Reading Nation* (Cambridge University Press).

[32] *Great Map of Mankind*, p. 54. See also Elizabeth Hagglund, 'Reviews of Travel in the Monthly Review, 1749–1758: An Introductory Survey', in *Studies in Travel Writing*, 2 (Spring 1998), 1–45. In her sample decade, Hagglund finds 35–43 travel-related books being published annually, the largest proportion concerned with Britain and Europe rather than more exotic destinations. No works by women appear in this sample.

[33] Paul Kaufmann, *Borrowings from the Bristol Library, 1773–1784: A Unique Record of Reading Vogues* (Charlottesville: Bibliographical Society of the University of Virginia, 1960). Patrick Brydone's *Tour through Sicily and Malta* (1774) was borrowed 192 times, making it the second most popular travel book, and one which extended the 'beaten track' of the Grand Tour narrative to the exotic sites of southern Italy and Malta. See also W. H. Pearson, 'Hawkesworth's "Voyages"', in R. F. Brissenden (ed.), *Studies in the 18th Century*, ii. (Canberra: ANU Press, 1973), pp. 239–57; and Jonathan Lamb, 'Circumstances Surrounding the Death of John Hawkesworth', *18th Century Life*, 18 (November 1994), 97–113.

Poets. Hawkesworth's *Account* was thus the most widely borrowed individual book in the library, whilst titles in the 'History, Antiquities and Geography' section, including Travel, were far in the lead in the overall borrowing figures.[34]

Despite its popularity (it was the first official account of Cook's first Pacific voyage), Hawkesworth's book flouted many of the conventions of eighteenth-century travel writing, given that it was the work of a literary compiler who had not personally witnessed the events that he described. Chosen by the Earl of Sandwich, First Lord of the Admiralty, to 'ghost-write' the journals of Byron, Wallis, Carteret, Banks, and Cook into a single continuous narrative, Hawkesworth received the huge sum of 6,000 pounds sterling for the completed manuscript from the booksellers Strahan and Cadell. 'It was determined', he wrote in his Preface, 'that the narration should be in the first person, and that I might notwithstanding intersperse such sentiments and observations as my subject should suggest.'[35]

The fact that, in order to obtain credit, travel books had to satisfy a freight of generic and moral expectations, is illustrated by the furore which accompanied (and doubtless fed) the unprecedented popularity of Hawkesworth's *Account*. This seems to have been caused largely by Hawkesworth's interpolated philosophical reflections, such as his rejection of the doctrine of a particular providence in describing the *Endeavour*'s escape from shipwreck on the Great Barrier Reef, or his 'indelicate' treatment of Tahitian sexual mores and their freedom from a sense of shame.[36] The author's prefatory appeal to Samuel Richardson's novel *Pamela* as a precedent (in his analysis of Tahitian manners) for the 'enumeration of particulars in themselves so trifling, that we almost wonder how they could occur to the author's mind'[37] hardly helped. Reference to a novel which had itself instigated a moral panic proved a dangerous hostage to fortune. The Anglican moralist Vicesimus Knox, in his influential 1778 essay 'On the Manner of Writing Voyages and Travels' noted that 'Few books have succeeded better of late than voyages and travels' but regretted that the genre had been vitiated by Hawkesworth's licentious descriptions as well as Laurence Sterne's 'subtile poison' in the *Sentimental Journey*.[38] Knox censured

[34] Kaufman, p. 121. The figures may, of course, be slightly inflated given that Bristol was a centre of commerce and navigation, but figures for other libraries elsewhere in the country do not exist for this period.
[35] John Hawkesworth, *An Account of the Voyages Undertaken by the Order of his Present Majesty for Making Discoveries in the Southern Hemisphere, and successively performed by Comm. Byron, Capt. Wallis, Capt. Carteret, and Capt. Cook . . . Drawn up from the Journals which were kept by the several Commanders, and from the Papers of Joseph Banks, Esq.*, 3 vols. (London: W. Strahan and T. Cadell, 1773), i., p. iv.
[36] Lamb, 'The Death of John Hawkesworth', 98–100.
[37] Hawkesworth, i., p. vii.
[38] Vicesimus Knox, *Essays, Moral and Literary* (1778) A New Edition, 2 vols. (Dublin, 1786), XXIV, I, 113, 115.

Hawkesworth's 'lamentable error' in invalidating 'some of the most comfortable parts of the creed of his countrymen', adding sententiously, 'but who can wonder at what was written, when a Sandwich was the patron?'[39] (The Earl of Sandwich was a notable libertine.)

Instead Knox reaffirmed the commonsensical Johnsonian norms for travel writing:

the style of voyages and travels should be plain, simple, perspicuous, and unaffected. I think they seldom appear to great advantage, but when written in the words of the traveller or voyager, at the very time at which the circumstances which he relates occurred.[40]

Knox here underscores the conventions of 'naïve empiricism', autoptic witness, and 'writing to the moment' expected of travel writing in the eighteenth century. When purged of superfluous adulterations, as well as anything 'injurious to the morals or the political principles of one's own country', Knox knew 'of no books of amusement whatever so well adapted to young people . . . They interest the mind as much as a novel; but, instead of rendering it effeminate and debauched, they make it usefully inquisitive, and furnish it with matter for reflection'.[41] (Knox felt that travel books made improving reading for young women as well as men; his presupposition that most writers in the genre were men is reflected in the relative scarcity of eighteenth-century travelogues by women, in comparison to their high nineteenth-century profile.) As we shall see in Chapter 1, the educative and moralizing qualities of 'novelty and curiosity' were frequently taken to be more problematic than appears to be the case in Knox's account. Like the eighteenth-century novel, travel writing could transgress social norms, but inasmuch as it represented a 'literature of fact'—and of heroic endeavour— it was considered to be at least potentially improving in a way that no purely fictional narrative could be.

---

[39] Vicesimus Knox, i., p. 114.   [40] Ibid., i., p. 117.   [41] Ibid., i., p. 118.

1

Cycles of Accumulation, Aesthetics of Curiosity, and Temporal Exchange

The eighteenth-century popularity of books of voyages and travels reflected the rise of European commercial and colonial expansion. It is appropriate that the contemporary wave of scholarly interest in travel writing should follow in the wake of Edward Said's pathbreaking *Orientalism* (1978) and the interest in the discourses of colonialism which it stirred up, especially in literary studies. Ironically, as Steve Clark points out, 'because of post-colonial scholarship, travel writing . . . has become interesting for us again; but usually as a kind of love that dare not speak its name'.[1] Said's constructivist notion of 'orientalism' is acknowledged in the present study to the extent to which the voices and descriptions of indigenous peoples reported by travellers are read as mirrors of their own cultures, and their insistence on 'objectivity' is understood as being at least partly rhetorical in function. Michel de Certeau warns of the futility of 'set[ting] off in quest of this voice that has been simultaneously colonised and mythified by recent Western history. There is . . . no "pure" voice, because it is always determined by a system . . . and codified by a way of receiving it'.[2]

Nevertheless, I am wary of underestimating the degree to which eighteenth- and early nineteenth-century travellers were bound by empirical protocols which demanded rigorous practices of description and notation, however distorted these reports now seem to us. In this respect Edward Said is only partially correct in describing travel writing as 'a textual attitude'.[3] Representations that appeared to be merely 'textual' stereotypes were refused credit, just as representations that—to quote Vicesmus Knox again—were 'injurious to the morals or political principles of one's own country' (that is, were *inadequately*

---

[1] 'Introduction' to *Travel Writing and Empire: Postcolonial Theory in Transit*, ed. by Steve Clark (London and NY: Zed Books, 1999), p. 3. See John Mackenzie, *Orientalism: History, Theory and the Arts* (Manchester and New York: Manchester University Press, 1995) for a historian's critique of Said.
[2] *The Practice of Everyday Life*, pp. 132, 134. See also Gayatri Spivak 'Can the Subaltern Speak?', in *Marxism and the Interpretation of Cultures*, ed. by Cary Nelson and Lawrence Grossberg (Urbana and Chicago: University of Illinois Press, 1988), p. 294.
[3] Said, *Orientalism* (Harmondsworth: Penguin, 1985), pp. 92–3.

textual inasmuch as they threatened ethical and literary norms) were equally unacceptable. The following chapters are written in the spirit of Anthony Pagden's subtle point that 'the process by which this "other" is constructed is not, as has so often been claimed, a rather simple act of political appropriation . . . For however much we may . . . fabricate rather than find our counter-image, we do not fabricate it out of nothing. We cannot think counter-factually about less than whole worlds.'[4]

In this chapter I seek to provide some theoretical orientation for the more empirical readings that follow. In the first section I examine the (by no means inevitable, or uncontested) dynamics of Europe's appropriation of distant peoples, knowledges, and objects, which provides the material context for the travel narratives and exotic displays studied in this book. In the second I consider the aesthetics of curiosity as a phenomenology of distant travel, troubling to many enlightenment commentators to the extent that it seemed to undermine a rational and 'philosophical' appropriation of the foreign. In the final section, I turn (with specific reference to the 'antique lands' of my title) to the temporalizing metaphor which interpreted geographical in terms of historical distance, but which also came increasingly under attack from 'modernizing' critics who sought to replace a hermeneutic with a scientific framework for representing distant places and peoples. How did 'modern' European travellers represent their own relation to 'antique lands', I ask, and to what extent was the 'temporal exchange' (whereby European modernity was exchanged for the archaic, the curious, and the picturesque) constitutive of travel writing in this period?

I take as my starting point, however, the *vulnerability* rather than self-sufficiency of European travellers, in relation to the lands and peoples in which they travelled, and the instability rather than authority of their published narratives, in the eyes of metropolitan readerships. (One might note here Felix Driver's remark that even in a later era of high imperialism, 'attitudes towards both exploration and empire were far more diverse than has often been recognised'.[5]) Rather than represent Europe's encounter with its 'others' as a manichaean opposition of power and innocence, a uniform global plot resulting in 'fatal impact', I follow Nicholas Thomas in stressing the contingency (and often confusion) which determined the 'cultural entanglements' of European travellers in diverse times and places.[6] Particularly in the light of the pressing global inequalities of our own time, there is an urgent political need to contest

[4] Anthony Pagden, *European Encounters with the New World, From Renaissance to Romanticism* (New Haven and London: Yale University Press, 1993), p. 184.

[5] Felix Driver, 'H. M. Stanley and his Critics: Geography, Exploration and Empire', *Past and Present*, 133 (November 1991), 134–66, 136.

[6] Nicholas Thomas, *Entangled Objects: Exchange, Material Culture, and Colonialism in the Pacific* (Harvard University Press, 1991) and *Colonialism's Culture: Anthropology, Travel and Government* (Princeton, NJ: Princeton University Press, 1994). See also the editors' introduction to *Voyages and*

the tendency (ironically enough, often manifested by post-colonial critics them-selves) to exaggerate the historical and geographical reach of European hege-mony, and its power over different cultures.

Notwithstanding the barbarities of the eighteenth-century Atlantic slave tri-angle, and the subsequent historical record of European imperialism, the rela-tive weakness of Europe's global power in the period addressed in this book will perhaps surprise modern readers. The 1770s and 1780s, for instance, saw the defeat of British forces by well-equipped modern Maratha and Mysorean armies in India, as well as by her colonists in America. Of the other regions studied in this book, Abyssinia remained independent of colonial rule until the twentieth century, destroying an invading European army as late as 1895,[7] whilst both Egypt and Mexico actually rid themselves of European colonial *rule* by military means (if not an increasing dependence upon European *capital*) in the early decades of the nineteenth century. If European power on a global scale was considerably weaker around 1800 than it was to be a century later, then con-comitantly Asian and African societies beyond the boundaries of European rule were much stronger.[8] If the narratives studied in this book are to make any his-torical sense, it is this global balance of power which must be acknowledged as a context for European travel, rather than a projection back in time of the *modern* globalized world-order.

One major achievement of Mary Louise Pratt's seminal *Imperial Eyes: Travel Writing and Transculturation*, beyond its scrupulous attention to the literary conventions of European travel writing,[9] has been to question the notion of colonial discourse as a 'closed system' which efficiently suppressed (or merely ventriloquized) indigenous voices, thereby granting European colonialism a ret-rospective authority which in effect it never possessed. Pratt's use of notions like 'transculturation' and 'autoethnology' permit a more nuanced account of 'the interactive, improvisational dimensions of colonial encounters so easily ignored or suppressed by diffusionist accounts of conquest and domination'. Although acknowledging that these encounters were often characterized by

Beaches: Pacific Encounters, 1769–1840, ed. by Alex Calder, Jonathan Lamb, and Bridget Orr (Honolulu: University of Hawaii Press, 1999), pp. 1–25.

[7] The Italians lost 70 per cent of their army to the Emperor Menilek at the Battle of Adwa. See George Marcus, *A History of Ethiopia* (Berkeley and LA: University of California Press, 1994), pp. 98–9.

[8] As C. A. Bayly has indicated, this fact has tended to be overlooked partly because powerful indige-nous states like Ranjit Singh's Punjab or Muhammad Ali's Egypt *did* lose their independence in later decades, between 1830 and 1880. See C. A. Bayly, *Imperial Meridian: The British Empire and the World 1780–1830* (London and New York: Longman, 1989), p. 234.

[9] Generic questions are deliberately put aside in two influential recent studies, Denis Porter's *Haunted Journeys: Desire and Transgression in European Travel Writing* (Princeton, NJ: Princeton University Press, 1991), and Tim Youngs' *Travellers in Africa: British Travelogues, 1850–1900* (Manchester and New York: Manchester University Press, 1994).

'radically asymmetrical relations of power',[10] Pratt commendably side-steps a totalizing neo-imperialist teleology. In so doing she punctures the myth of an unassailable history of European global supremacy and acknowledges the historical agency of those peoples who were in constant (and often effective) struggle against the imposition of colonial subalternity.

Nevertheless, it seems to me that Pratt does not go far enough in breaking up and discriminating the grand historical narrative of European global dominance. Discourses of eighteenth-century travel are still to some extent read retrospectively in terms of the hawkish imperatives of Victorian high imperialism. Although she derives her notion of the 'contact zone' from the linguistic study of 'contact languages' such as pidgin and creole, it is hard to avoid the semantic resonance of the imperialist 'combat zone' (intentionally?) underlying her nomenclature.[11] By the same token, scientific travel writing in the eighteenth century is denominated 'anti-conquest' in order to evoke 'the strategies of representation whereby European bourgeois subjects seek to secure their innocence in the same moment as they assert European hegemony'.[12] But until eighteenth-century travellers exchanged cultural disguise for military uniform (a transition studied in Chapters 3 and 4 of the present book) they were often more concerned with survival than with rationalizing their curiosity as a form of 'anti-conquest'. If they were lucky enough to return home (many were not) to publish their travel accounts, they were perhaps more concerned to convince sceptical readers of the truth of their claims than to feed a triumphalist discourse of empire. Even in an age of sensibility, the rhetoric of vulnerability in travel writing was not merely feigned.

How can we gain a purchase on the historical particularity of the traveller's encounter with foreign cultures without subscribing to an essentializing binary model of 'otherness'? How might one theorize the material relations between Europe's 'centre' and 'peripheries' whilst relativizing the epistemology of travel writing in relation to those non-European knowledges upon which it was often dependent? In tackling these questions, I have found a useful resource in Bruno Latour's actor/network model of exploration as a 'cycle of accumulation', out-

[10] Mary Louise Pratt, *Imperial Eyes: Travel-Writing and Transculturation* (London and New York: Routledge 1992), p. 7.

[11] James Clifford has since deployed Pratt's term to theorize the 'overlapping, discrepant histories' of the post-colonial museum, in which, given the tempo of recent debates about repatriation, the sense of cultural contact as combat seems perfectly appropriate. See 'Museums as Contact Zones', in *Routes: Travel and Translation in the late-20th Century* (Cambridge, Mass.: Harvard University Press, 1997), chapter 7, p. 208.

[12] Pratt, pp. 7, 39. Although Pratt claims that her coinage 'anti-conquest' seeks to disassociate enlightened exploration from 'older imperial rhetorics of conquest associated with the absolutist era' (p. 7), it might just as well serve to define 18th-century travel *by negation* as precursor of the grand narrative of later 19th-century imperial conquest.

lined in his 1987 *Science in Action*.[13] Although like all sociological models it has
its limitations for the purposes of literary analysis, Latour's understanding
of 'science in action' as the progressive mobilization and accumulation of distance makes it extremely suggestive for thinking about the relations between
eighteenth-century travel accounts, the worlds they describe, and the metropolitan institutions and readerships which determined their reception. The
economic allusion which resonates in Latour's use of the term 'accumulation'
also indicates the manner in which exploration networks stood in an asymp-
totic relationship with those of European commerce and capital. Complemen-
tary, of course, but not identical: eighteenth-century travel was required to be
both curious and useful.

Latour's chapter 'Centres of Calculation' begins by considering the exemplary case of the French explorer La Pérouse, who, in July 1787, landed in a
little-known region of the north-west Pacific coast called Sakhalin. Like most
eighteenth-century sea-borne explorers, La Pérouse was primarily concerned
with collecting latitudinal and longitudinal measurements and coastal profiles
in order to map unknown regions of the world. La Pérouse wanted to know
whether Sakhalin was an island or a peninsula, but, because he had no time
to find out for himself, he engaged some Sakhalinese Ainu people (Latour
erroneously calls them 'Chinese savages')[14] to draw him a map of the area on
the sand of the beach. On the evidence of a map sketched by one obliging old
man, La Pérouse understood that Sakhalin was indeed an island: the map
revealed its spatial position *vis-à-vis* the Chinese mainland, although it was of
limited use in other respects and was of course washed away by the next tide.
Bad weather prevented La Pérouse from verifying this information, but nevertheless the old man's cartography was taken to be correct. At Kamchatka, La
Pérouse sent one of his officers, De Lesseps, overland back to France carrying
the maps, notebooks, and bearings gathered over two years of exploration,
including the information about Sakhalin. The next year, 1788, La Pérouse's two
ships disappeared in the Pacific and none of the crew was ever seen again. The
only trace ever found was a piece of the ship's stern bearing the image of a fleur-
de-lis that had become the door of a native hut, and the hilt of a sword, found
on the island of Vanikoro in the Santa Cruz group in 1826.

Latour elicits from this episode the mechanism by which the implicit
geography of the inhabitants of Sakhalin was made explicit by European

[13] Bruno Latour, *Science in Action: How to Follow Scientists and Engineers through Society* (Milton
Keynes: Open University Press, 1987). See also Michael Bravo's essay 'Ethnographic Navigation and
the Geographic Gift' in *Geography and the Enlightenment*, ed. by David N. Livingstone and Charles
W. J. Withers (pp. 199–235), which finds some problems with Latour's model, not least his historical
grasp of what was at stake in La Pérouse's encounter with the natives of Sakhalin.

[14] See Bravo, p. 228.

geographers, as local knowledge was translated into the universal grid of European cartographers. Unlike Pratt, however, Latour denies that this transition from ethnogeography to geography reflects anything more than a difference of degree (not a difference of kind) between European and native knowledges. In fact, when La Pérouse's ship *L'Astrolabe* first arrived on the coast of Sakhalin, La Pérouse's knowledge is described as being 'weaker' than that of the natives whom he met, given his ignorance of the lie of the land and his dependence upon indigenous information.[15] Latour does not need to interpret the vulnerability claims of early travellers as merely rhetorical statements which mask imperatives of imperial conquest. If the traveller disappears, or more importantly, if he fails to gather information (publication may itself be seen in this light as a kind of rite of passage), then his enterprise will have been completely unproductive, except in so far as his failure might serve to stimulate other explorers. Latour insists that the traveller

will always be weaker than any one of the peoples, of the lands, of the climates, of the reefs, he meets around the world, always at their mercy. Those who go away from the lands in which they are born and who cross the paths of other people [can] disappear without trace.[16]

However, the traveller *will* gain an advantage over the native peoples he meets if he is able to bring back information and objects which will allow them to be seen for the first time 'so that others might be sent back again to bring other things back. How to be familiar with things, peoples and events, which are *distant?*'[17] Had La Pérouse not dispatched De Lesseps on his long overland journey with the notebooks, his disappearance in the Pacific would have meant that European knowledge would have remained in a weaker position than that of the Sakhalinese in the Western Pacific region. The power of the centre to act at a distance upon unfamiliar events, places, and peoples lies in its prior ability to bring them back home. Distant places, events, and objects must be rendered *mobile, stable* (so that they can be moved back and forth without decay or distortion resulting from decontextualization), and *combinable*, 'so that whatever stuff they are made of, they can be cumulated, aggregated, or shuffled like a pack of cards'.[18] Whilst the morphology of land masses has to be translated into cartographic symbols in order to be rendered mobile, material objects such as rocks, birds, plants, and artefacts can be directly extracted from their contexts, preserved (stabilized), dispatched (mobilized), and combined in European

---

[15] This is especially likely to be the case if, in an eventuality not adequately developed by Latour, native knowledge is already inscribed within the networks of another powerful, non-European cycle of accumulation, such as Mogul India, Ottoman Western Asia, or Manchu China.

[16] Latour, p. 219.   [17] Ibid., p. 220.   [18] Ibid., p. 223.

museums, libraries, and universities. Transverse relations can then be established between them and objects collected and accumulated from other points
on the network so that a representation of the distant world can be constructed
in the metropolis. The same can be said, of course, for the experience of the
travellers themselves as narrated in the travel account, with the proviso, as
Anthony Pagden points out, that 'the traveller's narrative is . . . the most
complex and least stable thing which he can bring back with him. Taken from
their contexts, words, too, lose their certainty just as objects do.'[19]

Accordingly, when the English ship *Neptune* landed in the same bay of
Sakhalin a decade later, in 1797, the European navigators were now 'stronger'
than the natives because they were in possession of the 'mobiles' gathered by
La Pérouse and conveyed overland to the Parisian 'centre of calculation' by De
Lesseps. The epistemological asymmetry which had developed between the
inhabitants of Sakhalin (orientated—*for Europeans*—'on the periphery'), and
European geographers and cartographers at the 'centre of calculation' is a
consequence of the latter's accumulation of mobiles 'bearings, clocks, diaries,
labels, dictionaries, specimens, herbaries', many of which translated indigenous
knowledge.[20] Latour is at pains to emphasize that this asymmetry is not constituted by a qualitative opposition of 'knowledge' to 'ignorance', or even 'oral'
to 'written', but rather needs to be considered in relation to the whole cycle of
accumulation which historically favours the Europeans as natives of a 'centre of
calculation . . . act[ing] at a distance on many other points'.[21] Rejecting a binary
opposition between Western scientific realism versus Sahkilinese 'local knowledge', Latour posits instead 'two local knowledges, one of them having the
shape of a network transporting back and forth immutable mobiles to act at a
distance'.[22] To illustrate this, he makes the challenging assertion that 'botany is
the *local knowledge* generated inside gathering institutions like the Jardin des
Plantes or Kew gardens'.[23]

Latour's model should not be interpreted as a celebration of the inexorable
advance of Western exploration networks over global space. Rather than
enjoying uncontested movement, he insists, Europeans and their mobiles
'travel[led] inside narrow and fragile networks, resembling the galleries termites
build to link their nests to their feeding sites'.[24] (This is especially true of land-
travellers like Bruce, Mungo Park, or Burckhardt, entirely dependent upon
indigenous routes and caravans, compared to sea-borne explorers.) There were
frequent opportunities for leakage along the way, and the networks of accumulation were far from being entirely dependable, even by sea. Mobilization—the
collection of objects and information—could fail due to linguistic incompre-

[19] Pagden, p. 48.   [20] Latour, p. 218.   [21] Ibid., p. 222.
[22] Ibid., p. 229.   [23] Ibid., p. 229.   [24] Ibid., p. 232.

hension, incompetent selection on the part of ill-prepared travellers, or resistance on the part of indigenous peoples (interference by the networks of other cultures).[25]

In relation to the texts studied in this book, however, Latour's notion of 'combination' pays insufficient attention to the problem of credit facing eighteenth-century travel writers, although (as I shall argue in Chapters 2 and 3) the early nineteenth-century stabilization and disciplining of traveller's subjectivity, combined with the rise of the 'museum order' as a means of organizing physical mobiles, made this less of a problem in the later decades. Thus travellers describing unknown regions faced the problem that, in the words of William Browne (the first European to visit the Sudanese kingdom of Dar-fur in the 1790s): 'the praise of fidelity, the only one to which the writer lays claim, cannot be received until another shall have traced his footsteps'.[26] Objects collected by travellers, as well as journal entries recorded 'to the minute', could too easily lose their 'original' meaning when removed from their original context and redacted in travelogue form, and this fragility of credit partly explains the currency of epistolary or journal-based travelogues based on the convention of 'writing to the moment'. Questions of literary form and style (including the vexed question of plagiarism and intertextuality) were key factors here, problematizing the reception of travel narratives and their efficacy as 'combinables' in the accumulation cycle.

The starting point for all the chapters in the present book is the manner in which mobiles were returned to the centre (hence my title '*from* an antique land')[27] rather than the 'primary' experience of the traveller on the periphery. It might not be an exaggeration to claim that the accumulation of knowledge in the travel *narrative* (usually based on the redaction of field journals) was seen to provide the sole philosophical justification for the moral and physical risks of distant travel. Whatever the romantic appeal of the heroic traveller/explorer in an imperial culture, the contribution made 'to visions of empire and to imperial expansion depended crucially on seemingly mundane tasks undertaken in

[25] Latour's model is apposite for the travellers discussed in the present book. But, as Steve Clark indicates, travellers do not always move along Latourian networks: 'in principle travel may be from the periphery to a stronger, if none the less exotic culture . . . and in a more contemporary guise, to the metropolitan centre: the post-war immigrant to London . . . the European to New York . . . the American to Tokyo', *Travel Writing and Empire*, p. 5. For an account of 'reverse travels' in the 18th century, see Michael Harbsmeier, 'Early Travels to Europe: Some Remarks on the Magic of Writing', in *Europe and its Others*, ed. by Francis Barker et al., 2 vols. (Colchester: University of Essex, 1985), i. 72–88.
[26] William G. Browne, *Travels in Africa, Egypt and Syria, from the year 1792 to 1798* (London, 1799), p. viii.
[27] In contrast, Amitav Ghosh's marvellous travelogue/novel *In an Antique Land* (London: Granta Books, 1992) appropriately misquotes Shelley's line to evoke the experiences of an Indian anthropologist doing field work in Egypt.

centres of calculation',[28] including the travel writer's rhetorical success in encompassing distance in the published travel account.

Curiosity and the Aesthetics of Distance

Curiosity is seldom so powerfully excited, or so amply gratified, as by faithful Relations of Voyages and Travels. The different Appearances of Nature, and the various Customs of Men, the gradual Discovery of the World, and the Accidents and Hardships of a naval Life, all concur to fill the Mind with Expectation and with Wonder. (Samuel Johnson, Advertisement to John Newbery's *The World Displayed*, 1759)[29]

Whilst Bruno Latour's sociological theory of 'the mobile' offers an excellent purchase on the spatial dynamics of travel writing, it ignores the aesthetics of distance—the traveller's *desire* for the distant—which is crucial to the literary interest of travel writing.[30] Fortunately, such an aesthetic theory was well developed in the eighteenth century in terms of the notion of 'curiosity', and its cognate terms 'novelty', 'singularity', and 'wonder'.[31] Samuel Johnson's linkage of curiosity, travel, and wonder illustrates this configuration, highlighting the fact, remarked upon above, that the term 'curiosity' is coterminous with the practices and representations of travel throughout the whole period. 'Curiosity' was, of course, by no means limited to travel: as Hans Blumenberg and (more recently) Krzysztof Pomian have demonstrated, the term has a long and ambivalent history in European culture as the disposition of mind which desires knowledge of the world, but one which easily oversteps the boundaries set by God in a Faustian show of intellectual pride.[32] Assailed by Aquinas and the

---

[28] David Miller, 'Joseph Banks, Empire, and "Centers of calculation" in late-Hanoverian London', in *Visions of Empire: Voyages, Botany and Representations of Nature*, ed. by David Miller and Peter Reill (Cambridge University Press, 1996), p. 33. See this endorsed by Dr Johnson's remarks in the *Idler* no. 97, quoted in Thomas Curley, *Samuel Johnson and the Age of Travel* (Athens, Georgia: Georgia University Press, 1976), p. 73.

[29] Newbery's was a collection of travels and voyages; quoted by Curley, p. 50.

[30] Denis Porter offers a psychoanalytical explanation of the desire for distance in *Haunted Journeys*, interpreting travel as an Oedipal 'flight from repressive paternal power' (p. 149). However, he seems to admit a problem with this approach in acknowledging the danger of being 'both ahistorical and apolitical' (p. 14). See also Yi-Fu Tuan, *Space and Place: The Perspective of Experience* (London: Edwin Arnold, 1977), chapter 5.

[31] For an illuminating study of these and other cognates, and the semantic fluctuations of the term 'curiosity' itself, see Neil Kenny, *Curiosity in Early Modern Word Histories*, Wolfenbütteler Forschungen, Band 81 (Wiesbaden: Harrassowitz Verlag, 1998).

[32] Hans Blumenberg, *The Legitimacy of the Modern Age* (1966), (English trans. by R. Wallace, Cambridge, Mass.: MIT Press, 1983); Krzysztof Pomian, *Collectors and Curiosities: Paris and Venice, 1500–1800* (1987), trans. by Elizabeth Wiles-Porter, (Cambridge: Polity Press, 1990). Blumenberg's grand narrative of the triumph of 'theoretische Neugierde' (theoretical curiosity) in the modern age is contradicted by more recent, historically localized work on curiosity by Pomian, Benedict, Daston and Park, and Kenny. As Kenny indicates, this is because Blumenberg's 'theoretische Neugierde' *sometimes*

Church Fathers, 'blind' curiosity again came under censure with the rise of the scientific revolution, condemned by Descartes in favour of 'research carried out in accordance with the rules of method'.[33] But, as Pomian writes, from the early seventeenth to the eighteenth centuries at least, curiosity as 'a science of miracles, exuberant, incoherent, muddled, assailed by contradictions, and pulling in all sorts of different directions, enjoyed a temporary spell in power, an interim rule between those of theology and science'.[34]

The role of wonder in Renaissance travel writing has been the focus of attention in some of the best recent scholarship, exemplified by De Certeau, Pagden, and Greenblatt's discussions of Jean de Léry's narrative of his wonder-struck reaction to the singing of the Brazilian Tupinamba Indians in his *Histoire d'un voyage fait en la terre de Bresil* (1578).[35] In an important recent study (although one not primarily concerned with travel literature), Lorraine Daston and Katherine Park have described how wonder briefly allied itself with curiosity in the early modern period, so that whilst wonder (as it were) caught the attention of the inquirer, curiosity riveted it. The alliance was however short-lived: in the eighteenth century, they argue, curiosity and the knowledge that it provoked were more often conceived as a *cure* for 'vulgar' wonder than its product.[36]

On the evidence of the texts studied in this book, it would seem, however, that concepts of wonder and curiosity survived longer in the discourse of distant travel than in many other fields. Arguably a general overemphasis on the enlightenment rhetoric of *enargeia*, and a narrowly epistemological understanding of eighteenth-century empiricism, have obscured the continuing importance of curiosity and wonder in later travel accounts. As Pinkerton's slighting remark about the mere 'curiosity' of pre-1768 travelogues (cited in the Preface) indicates, by 1814 the term had assumed a highly ambivalent meaning for British geographers at least. On the other hand, its currency in contemporary travelogues and exhibition culture suggests that the 'official' critique of curiosity was unrepresentative. Coleridge's arch apology for publishing his exotic fragment 'Kubla Khan' 'rather as a psychological curiosity, than on the grounds of any supposed *poetic* merits' (in the poem's 1816 Preface) suggests *both* the distance of curiosity from polite aesthetics *and* the extent to which romantic poets

coincides with historical uses of the word 'curiosity' and its cognates, but 'does not do so systematically or necessarily' (Kenny p. 47).

[33] Pomian, p. 62.

[34] Ibid., p. 64.

[35] Michel de Certeau, 'Ethno-Graphy: Speech, or the Space of the Other: Jean de Léry', in *The Writing of History*, trans. by Tom Conley (New York: Columbia University Press, 1988), pp. 209–43); Anthony Pagden, *European Encounters with the New World* (pp. 42–7); Stephen Greenblatt, *Marvellous Possessions: The Wonder of the New World* (Oxford: Clarendon Press, 1991), pp. 16–17.

[36] L. Daston and K. Park, *Wonder and the Order of Nature, 1150–1750* (New York: Zone Books, 1998), pp. 305, 311, 321.

sought to recuperate the discredited discourse of curiosity in justifying exotic and orientalist literature.[37]

Henry Home's, Lord Kames's, extended treatment of the aesthetics of curiosity in his influential *Elements of Criticism* (1762) reveals not only the semantic complexity which the term had come to bear in the second half of the eighteenth century but also illustrates the bifurcation in its meaning observed by Daston and Park. Because Kames's treatment is at once typical of, and yet more extensive than, those of his near-contemporaries (like David Hume, Edmund Burke, Samuel Johnson, Adam Smith, Sir Joshua Reynolds, or Richard Payne Knight, not to mention French commentators like Furetière, La Bruyère, Diderot, or Grimm discussed by Pomian), I shall limit my analysis to it alone.[38] Kames formulated the aesthetics of distance in terms of a rhetorical question which illustrates the dynamic relationship between curiosity and its cognates such as novelty, singularity, and wonder:

men tear themselves from their native country in search of things rare and new; and novelty converts into a pleasure the fatigues and even perils of travelling. To what cause shall we ascribe these singular appearances? To curiosity undoubtedly, a principle implanted in human nature for a purpose extremely beneficial, that of acquiring knowledge; and the emotion of wonder, raised by new and strange objects, inflames our curiosity to know more about them.[39]

Kames here posits a sequential relationship between novelty, curiosity, and wonder: novelty 'invariably raises' wonder, which in turn 'inflames' curiosity to know more; this affective chain converts the pains into the pleasures of travel as otiose wonder is converted into a desire for knowledge. But wonder/novelty, the motivating impulse of travel (like surprise, from which it differs in other respects)[40] is marked by the 'shortness of [its] duration' as novelty 'degenerates' into familiarity.[41] In this respect wonder differs from the sublime (discussed in

---

[37] S. T. Coleridge, *Poetical Works*, ed. by E. H. Coleridge (Oxford University Press, 1912), p. 295. The distinction between romantic 'retro' curiosity and the vestiges of 18th-century patrician curiosity is exemplified in William Hazlitt's essay 'Fonthill Abbey', which contrasts William Beckford's effeminate and patrician curiosity as a collector of tacky *chinoiserie*, with a more appealing version of orientalism set in 'the marble baths of the Moorish Alhambra, or amidst the ruins of Tadmor, or in barbaric places, where Bruce encountered Abyssinian queens!' *Complete Works of Hazlitt*, ed. by P. P. Howe, 21 vols. (London and Toronto: Dent, 1930–4), xviii., pp. 173–80.

[38] Stafford misreads Kames's account of wonder as the equivalent of enlightenment empiricism, ignoring his subsequent critique of its primitivism and puerility. *Voyage into Substance*, p. 409.

[39] Lord Kames, *Elements of Criticism*, (1762), 11*th edition with the author's last corrections and additions* (London, 1839), p. 112.

[40] Kames, p. 113.

[41] The most celebrated 18th-century account of the somatic disturbance wrought by wonder is Adam Smith's 1774 (?) essay 'The Principles which lead and direct Philosophical Enquiries; illustrated by the History of Astronomy'. Smith concludes that '[the subject] must find out some resemblance or other, before he can get rid of that Wonder, that uncertainty and anxious curiosity excited by its

the preceding chapter of Kames's *Elements*), which, although sharing wonder's effect of 'transport', is not dependent upon novelty but can also be elicited by familiar objects.[42] The discourse of wonder/novelty is likewise distinct from the rhetoric of sublime inarticulacy ('words cannot describe . . .') in that it generates precise and paratactic description, the attempt to articulate verbally or visually *exactly* what was singular and remarkable about an object, motivated by desire but often issuing in pedantry.[43]

For Kames the 'curious', fast-burning desire for novelty, by an association of ideas, can be attached to persons or objects encountered at home, as well as stimulating the desire to brave the hazards of travel. Distance in space can also substitute for distance in time (a substitution which will be further explored in the next section), so that 'a friend . . . after a short absence in a remote country, has the same air of novelty as if he had returned after a longer interval from a place near home: the mind forms a connection between him and the remote country, and bestows upon him the singularity of the objects he has seen'.[44] For Kames, distance itself becomes a scale for measuring value in the appetitive economy of wonder: if two 'new and singular objects' are offered to the spectator, he equivocates; but 'when told that one of them is the product of a distant quarter of the world, he no longer hesitates, but clings to it as the most singular'.[45]

Kames's association of novelty and wonder with woman's fashions[46] and 'foreign luxuries' as well as 'foreign curiosities, which appear rare in proportion to their original distance',[47] suggests a link between curiosity and the rise of eighteenth-century consumer culture in the mercantilist economy of imported 'luxuries'. Nicholas Thomas argues that 'curiosity was deeply, almost causally, linked with commerce—the desire for novelties being postulated as the stimulus to trade—and with the moral ambiguities and latent corruption of commer-

singular appearance . . . Philosophy, by representing the invisible chains which bind together all these disjointed objects, endeavours to introduce order into this chaos of jarring and discordant appearances, to allay the tumult of imagination' (*The Essential Adam Smith*, ed. by Robert L. Heilbroner and Lawrence J. Malone (Oxford University Press, 1986), p. 31). Daston and Park point out that wonder was entirely absent from Hume's analysis of the passions in the *Treatise*, and that Smith was almost unique among 18th-century theorists in treating it at such length (*Wonders*, p. 327). As we shall see, this should not be taken to mean that it was insignificant in contemporary travel accounts.

[42] This may explain why the sublime tends to assume less importance than curiosity and wonder in exotic travel accounts. Chloe Chard, writing of the hyperbolic language of the Grand Tour narrative, suggests that the sublime invests the topography with a wonder that is not dependent upon novelty: 'this topography of the not-so distant foreign is, in some ways, at a disadvantage, when compared with more exotic regions . . . by invoking the sublime, the traveller is able to insist that the Alps and Italy offer an effect of strangeness that is undiminished by familiarity', *Pleasure and Guilt on the Grand Tour* (Manchester and New York: Manchester University Press, 1999), p. 113.

[43] Katie Whitaker, 'The Culture of Curiosity', in *Cultures of Natural History*, ed. by N. Jardine, J. A. Secord, and E. C. Spary (Cambridge University Press, 1996), p. 82. Whitaker writes that in the late 17th century 'This accurate reporting of wonders formed a new style of natural history' (ibid.).

[44] Kames, p. 116.   [45] Ibid., p. 116.   [46] Ibid., p. 113.   [47] Ibid., p. 116.

cial society'.[48] Selling off 'curiosities' collected *en route* (as well as publishing a travel narrative) could, of course, help the traveller to recoup some of the expenses of the voyage.[49] At the same time we need to remember that, despite their 'unconsecrated' aesthetic status, objects of curiosity were still in Pomian's term 'semiophores',[50] that is to say, their value as collectibles depended upon their removal from the economic circuit, so that their link with the 'invisible' and distant endowed their possessors with symbolic capital. The distinction is extremely fragile, however: eighteenth-century travels are frequently described as being 'both curious and useful', distinguishing between a disinterested and an interested (commercial, colonial) motivation which qualifies their complementarity in respect to the 'cycle of accumulation', but the two types of motivation easily collapse into one another.[51] One thread of the present book reveals an increasing commodification and popularization of curiosity as it was exorcized from scholarly and scientific discourse and associated with popular wonder and the commercial profit deriveable from it, illustrated in my concluding comparison between Humboldt and William Bullock. At the same time, by an apparent contradiction, curiosity continued throughout the period to describe the traveller's 'disinterested' motive for braving the hazards of travel, as well as frequently providing an ethnological *cordon sanitaire* dividing him from the 'native', who, although maybe possessing a sense of wonder, appeared *incapable* of curiosity.[52]

Kames's linkage of the effect of wonder/novelty with verbs like 'inflame' and 'swell'[53] prepares the reader for the critical tone introduced later in his chapter, supporting Thomas's contention that the eighteenth-century discourse of curiosity (he is discussing responses to ethnographic objects) was 'not fixed but morally slippery . . . the legitimacy of curious inquiry is uncertain'.[54] This is perfectly demonstrated in Kames's rhetorical question:

the love of novelty . . . prevails in children, in idlers, and in men of shallow understanding: and yet, after all, why should one be ashamed of indulging a natural propensity? A distinction will afford a satisfactory answer. No man is ashamed of curiosity when it is indulged in order to acquire knowledge. But to prefer any thing merely

[48] 'Licenced Curiosity: Cook's Pacific Voyages', in John Elsner and Roger Cardinal (eds.), *The Culture of Collecting* (London: Reaktion Books, 1994), p. 123.

[49] See Dolan, *Exploring European Frontiers*, pp. 153–88.

[50] *Collectors and Curiosities*, p. 30.

[51] As Simon Schaffer writes in his afterword to *Visions of Empire*, 18th-century commentators 'were able and willing to discriminate between philosophical curiosity and commercial or imperial purposes' (p. 338).

[52] Hawkesworth's *Account of the Voyages* famously describes the episode when a group of Tierra del Fuegans boarded the *Endeavour*, commenting 'curiosity seems to be one of the few passions which distinguish men from brutes; and of this our guests appeared to have very little' (ii. 45).

[53] Kames, p. 114.   [54] Thomas, p. 122.

because it is new, shows a mean taste, which one ought to be ashamed of: vanity is commonly at the bottom, which leads those who are deficient in taste to prefer things odd, rare, or singular, in order to distinguish themselves from others. And, in fact, that appetite . . . reigns chiefly among persons of a mean taste, who are ignorant of refined and elegant pleasures.[55]

Kames's distinction will be extremely useful in distinguishing positive and negative, rational and vulgar, valences for 'curiosity' as they occur throughout this book, as well as locating the yawning gulf between curiosity and polite taste.[56] As a discourse of connoisseurship and collection, it is clearly cognate with seventeenth- and eighteenth-century practices of virtuosity (and, as we shall see, antiquarianism)[57] but quite distinct from gentlemanly discourses of taste in the Shaftesburyan tradition. Like Adam Smith, Kames sought to salvage a rational, philosophical, and progressive sense for curiosity, whilst reserving an archaic, negative, and merely vulgar definition for the term inasmuch as it applied to novelty, wonder, singularity, or rarity. In the seventeenth and eighteenth centuries 'curiosity' was often used in a positive sense meaning 'careful', precise empirical investigation (actually its etymological sense, from the Latin *cura* meaning 'attention'), as in Robert Boyle's 1691 treatise *Curiosities in Chemistry: Being New Experiments and Observations Concerning the Principles of Natural Bodies*.[58] But curiosity in Kames's 'vulgar' sense is arrested in a vain, exclusive, and infantile desire to possess the irreducible, decontextualized, 'distant' object. As Daston and Park observe, like Aesop's Ant and Grasshop-

---

[55] Kames, p. 117. See Harriet Guest 'Curiously Marked: Tattooing, Masculinity, and Nationality in 18th-century British Perceptions of the South Pacific', in *Painting and the Politics of Culture. New Essays on British Art, 1700–1850*, ed. by John Barrell (Oxford University Press, 1992), p. 313. The terms of Kames's critique survive in Hazlitt's remarks on Beckford's collection at Fonthill: 'The motive for the production of such toys is mercenary, and the admiration of them childish or servile. That which pleases merely from its novelty . . . cannot be expected to please twice' *Complete Works*, xviii. 175.

[56] Barbara Benedict in her essay 'The "Curious Attitude" in 18th-Century Britain: Observing and Owning' (*Eighteenth-Century Life*, 14 (1990), 3, 59–98) also draws attention to the moral and aesthetic ambivalence attached to 'curiosity', from Alexander Pope's attack on 'Criticks, of less *Judgement* than *Caprice*, | *Curious*, not *Knowing*, not *exact* but *nice*' in the *Essay on Criticism*, to Dr Johnson's laudatory remark in *Rambler* 103 that 'Curiosity is one of the permanent and certain characteristics of a vigorous mind' (p. 59). Benedict notes that in the *Dictionary*, Johnson none the less distinguishes the 'inclination to enquiry' from an 'act of curiosity', or 'nice experiment', and from 'an object of curiosity', a 'rarity'; yet cites nine varied definitions of 'curious', including 'accurate', 'artful', and 'rigid' [ibid.].

[57] Johnson's *Dictionary* allows for both definitions of a 'virtuoso' as 'A man skilled in antique or natural curiosities; a man studious of painting, statuary, or architecture'. In the Augustan quarrel of the ancients and the moderns, antiquarians were paradoxically on the side of (pedantic) moderns rather than 'tasteful' classics, given that the figure of the antiquarian had no equivalent in classical culture.

[58] Michael Bravo points out that 'curiosity' and 'precision', although often combined in 18th-century scientific discourse, also marked a difference of social register, curiosity being considered a gentlemanly virtue, whilst precision belonged more squarely to the world of instrument-makers, engineers, architects, artisans, and astronomers. 'Precision and Curiosity in Scientific Travel', in *Voyages and Visions*, p. 164.

per, 'noble curiosity worked hard and shunned enticing novelties [whilst] vulgar wonder wallowed in the pleasures of novelty and obstinately refused to remedy the ignorance that aroused it'.[59] For curiosity in this 'noble' and rational sense, Kames went on to argue in his next chapter, was 'a vigorous propensity, which never is at rest . . . [it] attaches us to every new object; and incites us to compare objects, in order to discover their differences and resemblances'.[60] Kames's own polygeneticist *Sketches of the History of Man* (1774) demonstrated this kind of philosophical curiosity in relation to the 'four stages' theory of social development axiomatic to eighteenth-century Scottish enlightenment sociology.[61]

The Scottish 'conjectural historians' discovered in the synchronic comparison of cultures and the stadial model of historical progress a methodological improvement upon the unsystematic absorptiveness of mere wonder or vulgar curiosity. But although Kames, William Robertson, Adam Ferguson, and John Millar drew heavily on travel accounts in comparing diverse cultures, in the end their systematic mapping of the world on the axes of 'absolute' time–space coordinates, and their construction of an ascending scale of civilizations ('from savages to Scotsmen')[62] made the existential and aesthetic discourse of 'curious' travel narrative—in the 'vulgar' sense—seem utterly redundant. Edward Casey argues in *The Fate of Place* that enlightenment philosophers 'assume that places are merely momentary subdivisions of a universal space quantitatively determined in its neutral homogeneity. Places are at best convenient and expedient pockets in the vast intact fabric of what Newton called "absolute space" in 1687'.[63] This neutralization of locality implies the erasure of an 'aesthetics of distance' as a phenomenology of proximity and remoteness. The very 'emplacement' and temporal specificity of travel writing, with its narrative of the traveller's personal travail and interaction with foreign peoples, and its reliance on superficial 'first impressions', always risked a damaging proximity to curiosity in Kames's negative sense. The unshackling of wonder from 'rational' curiosity

[59] Daston and Park, p. 328.
[60] Kames, p. 120. In this respect, Kames's 'rational' sense of curiosity foreshadows Blumenberg's 'theoretische Neugierde'.
[61] See Ronald Meek, *Social Science and the Ignoble Savage* (Cambridge University Press, 1976), pp. 155–60. Meek points out that interest in the four-stage theory peaked in the final two decades of the 18th century (p. 177).
[62] Walter Bagehot, quoted by John Gascoigne, *Joseph Banks and the English Enlightenment: Useful Knowledge and Polite Culture* (Cambridge University Press, 1997), p. 168. See also Andrew Sharp, 'Scots, Savages and Barbarians: Humphry Clinker and the Scots Philosophy', *Eighteenth-Century Life*, 18 (November 1994), 65–79.
[63] Edward S. Casey, *The Fate of Place*, p. 134. Casey's 'place' is closely related to my phenomenological notion of 'distance'. In discussing the Scots philosophers' reading of travel narrative, Andrew Sharp writes 'it was not the detail of savage and barbarian lives that mattered . . . but rather the situation of those lives in a narrative illustrating the progress of society through its various stages'. 'Scots, Savages, and Barbarians', p. 70.

may for this reason have contributed to the demotion of travel writing from the status of 'philosophical' discourse to the realm of *belles-lettres* in the period under consideration.

One major site for the display of 'curiosity' in eighteenth-century culture was the pre-modern museum, or 'cabinet of curiosities', descendant of the renaissance *Kunst- und Wunderkammer*.[64] Since Stephen Bann's pathbreaking work on the 'poetics of the museum' in *The Clothing of Clio*, it has become easier to discern the syntagmatic parallels between museums and literary texts.[65] The present book proposes an affinity between museology and travel accounts, focused on travel writer/collectors like Giovanni Belzoni in Chapter 3, Colin Mackenzie in Chapter 4, Fanny Parks in Chapter 5, and William Bullock in the Conclusion. (Belzoni's and Bullock's travel accounts served as commercial plugs for their popular exhibitions, and vice versa.) Museums, and to a greater extent popular exhibitions, shared with travel narratives the aspiration to make distant lands present; given that 'spatial and temporal distance are forms of absence, for which the presentness of the artifact [or narrative] itself must compensate'.[66] I shall argue that the relationship between élite and popular travel writing thus has its equivalent in the difference between the imperial 'museum order' and the popular exoticism of the 'shows of London' during the nineteenth century.[67]

In the pre-modern museum 'curiosities' were displayed without much consideration of whether they were 'natural' (objects of natural history) or 'artificial' (objects of antiquarian, aesthetic, or ethnological provenance). In contrast to nineteenth- and twentieth-century display practices, they were exhibited (often in the closed drawers of custom-built cabinets rather than open display cases) with the purpose of eliciting wonder at their rarity, singularity, or ingenuity as objects, rather than for any quality of typicality which might lend them

---

[64] Pomian argues that in the 17th century such cabinets 'were sufficiently numerous . . . to constitute in themselves an important socio-cultural phenomenon . . . by the 18th century, they were already on the wane . . . and after the 1750s they became very few and far between indeed' (*Collectors*, p. 48). On the evidence of many of the museums and collections discussed in this book, this terminal date seems premature, at least in Britain. Fanny Parks's 'amateur' cabinet (dating from the 1840s–50s) discussed in Chapter 5 essentially conforms to the principles of Pierre Borel's collection described in ch. 2 of *Collectors and Curiosity*, rather than to the taxonomic principles of the 'new' British Museum.

[65] *The Clothing of Clio: A Study of the Representation of History in 19th-century Britain and France* (Cambridge University Press, 1984), ch. 4 'The Poetics of the Museum: Lenoir and Du Sommerard'. See also Kenny, p. 169 on the metaphorical transfer from cabinets of curiosities to texts.

[66] Frederick N. Bohrer, 'The Times and Spaces of History: Representation, Assyria, and the British Museum', in *Museum Culture: Histories, Discourses, Spectacles*, ed. by Daniel Sherman and Irit Rogoff (London: Routledge 1994), p. 199.

[67] For the related question of colonial museums, see Gyan Prakash's discussion of Victorian India in *Another Reason: Science and the Imagination of Modern India* (Princeton, NJ: Princeton University Press, 1999), ch. 2, 'Staging Science'. Prakash discusses how for indigenous élites at least (and contrary to the intentions of imperial hegemony), the exhibition of the European 'sciences of classification and function instituted themselves in curiosity and wonder', creating an 'ambivalent zone of power and agency' (p. 47).

pedagogic meaning.[68] In Stephen Greenblatt's terms, the 'wonder' of such objects was more significant than their 'resonance'.[69] Until its nineteenth-century modernization, the British Museum (founded in 1757) was still a cabinet of rarities in this sense, based on the donation of Sir Hans Sloane's collection in 1753. In the 1760s, a visitor described how

the [visiting] party was conducted into a handsome salon, furnished with a curious selection of miscellaneous objects, for the most part the Egyptian antiquities presented by the Lethieullier family, including the first of the Museum's famous collection of mummies, various specimens of coral, a vulture's head in spirits, and the stuffed flamingo.

Juxtaposed with these antiquarian and natural objects were the *lusus naturae*, like the one-eyed 'cyclops pig' or a horn that grew out of the head of the unfortunate Mary Davies, whose portrait, complete with the obtruding horn, hung on the wall above.[70] Little attempt was made to label specimens, given the frequent presence of guides or 'docents' who conducted eighteenth-century visitors around the collection, seeking to elicit wonder rather than instruction, an attitude antithetical to that of the Victorian curator who described the ideal museum as 'a collection of labels illustrated by well-selected specimens'.[71] In Latourian terms, the pre-modern museum represented an inadequate realization of the 'centre of calculation'. Its curiosities were indeed mobilized and stabilized, but were not combinable in any systematic sense, representing merely anecdotal glimpses of incommensurable worlds, as philosophically insignificant as the freaks of nature with which they shared cabinet space.

Wonder responded to the superficiality rather than to the intrinsic or contextual meaning of the curiosities on display, either (when 'artificial') to their 'elegant, neat, laboured, finished' qualities,[72] or (when 'natural') to frivolous, rococo resemblance with works of art, a sort of visual punning between nature and culture.[73] Despite the similarities between such museums and the popular

[68] See Tony Bennett, *The Birth of the Museum: History, Theory, Politics* (London and New York: Routledge, 1995), p. 2.

[69] 'Resonance and Wonder', in *Learning to Curse: Essays in Early Modern Culture* (New York and London: Routledge, 1990), pp. 161–83.

[70] Edward Miller, *That Noble Cabinet: A History of the British Museum* (London: Andre Deutsch, 1973), pp. 65–6.

[71] Bennett, p. 42.

[72] Definition number 8 of 'curiosity' in Johnson's *Dictionary*. James Bunn describes curious collections as the expression of 18th-century mercantilist accumulation, in which artificial or natural curiosities exist as a singularities, irrevocably removed from their original context, 'The Aesthetics of British Mercantilism', *NLH*, 11, 2 (Winter 1980), 303–21, 304.

[73] See Barbara Benedict, 'The Curious Attitude', p. 78. Cf. the 17th-century collector John Bargrave's description of a piece of rock crystal from the Rhaetian Alps 'One would wonder that nature should so counterfett [*sic*] art. There is no man but [that] seeth it but would veryly believe that by tools and art it had binn put into that figure.' Quoted in Stephen Bann, *Under the Sign: John Bargrave as Collector, Traveler, and Witness* (Ann Arbor: University of Michigan Press, 1994), p. 90.

exhibition order in a common dedication to wonder and rarity rather than 'reso-nance', private collections and public museums (such as the British Museum or the Napoleonic Louvre) were associated with the social power of private or state ownership which dared to collect the heterogeneous meanings of the world within the enclosing and totalizing walls of the cabinet.[74] Although the state's appropriation of the 'museum order' in the romantic period brought with it a new form of legitimacy (as well as a new, systematic form of display), private collecting practices often continued to embody the values of élite curiosity or virtuosity of the kind attacked by Kames, values mimicked and transculturated in the popular, commercialist exhibition order. After the purchase of an expen-sive collection of minerals in 1809, Sir Joseph Banks (a trustee of the British Museum) suggested that two different displays be created 'the one for the man of science, and the other for the stupid gaze of the visiting vulgar'.[75] Despite the durability of this kind of intellectual snobbery, the boundaries between virtuo-sity, scientific display, and commercial exhibitions were perhaps more perme-able than they seem at first glance.

A risible incongruity between the totalizing ambition and a perceived entan-glement in minor detail, resulting in '[an absolute ignorance] of all facts and principles'[76] determined the common eighteenth-century caricature of the vir-tuoso, the antiquary, or the curioso. He is represented (as in Gillray's caricature of Sir William Hamilton) (Ill. 1) as a wealthy, licentious, yet impotent old man bent over an object of curiosity (often symbolized as a scantily-clad female bust of antique provenance), which he scrutinizes with the aid of a magnifying glass, the very negative of polite 'distanced' viewing practices in the period. Diderot's definition of a 'curieux' in the Encyclopédie exemplifies the dominant style of such satire: 'Not every one who indulges in [curiosity] is a connoisseur; and this is why enthusiasts are so often figures of fun . . . However, curiosity, this desire for possession, which is almost always without limits, is almost always deleterious to one's pocket.'[77]

It is beyond the scope of the present study to chart the neglected discourse of curiosity in the wider literary field (as championed, for example, in Isaac Disraeli's Curiosities of Literature (1792) and Dissertation on Anecdotes (1793))

---

[74] The British Museum, like Sir Ashton Levere's museum, the Duchess of Portland's cabinet, and the India Museum, restricted public access by the sale of tickets, thereby maintaining the 'secretive and cultic' nature of earlier princely cabinets. As late as the 1810s, when attendance had risen from 13,406 visitors in 1807–8 to 27,479 in 1833, Cobbett denounced the British Museum in the House of Commons as a place 'intended only for the amusement of the curious and the rich, and not for the benefit or for the instruction of the poor' (quoted in Miller, p. 136). Tony Bennett argues that the birth of the modern museum was in part based upon a desire to differentiate its principle of display from the popular exhi-bition order.

[75] Dolan, Exploring European Frontiers, p. 155.

[76] Pomian, Collectors, p. 62. The quotation is from La Bruyère.

[77] Quoted ibid., p. 132.

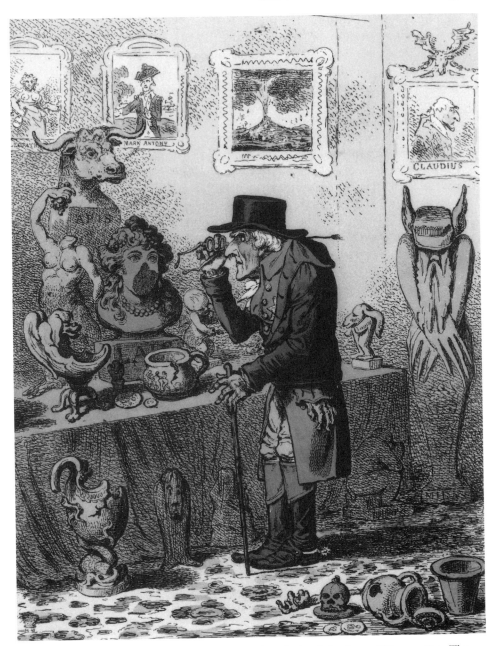

1. 'A Cognoscenti contemplating ye Beauties of ye Antique', by James Gillray, *c*.1801. The 'curioso' satirized, Sir William Hamilton, is peering at a cracked bust of his wife Emma, labelled 'Lais' after a celebrated Greek courtesan.

and the conflict between curiosity and what Coleridge called 'method'.[78] However, the miscellaneous, anecdotal structure of travel writing in this period exemplifies a tension between 'curious' aesthetics and an antithetical project of reordering the world according to a philosophical systematics of time and space. The critique of patrician curiosity common in the later enlightenment tended to target it either on the grounds of *pedantry* or *licentiousness*, or both together, as in Gillray's cartoon. In the remainder of this section I shall briefly illustrate the rationale of such charges in two exemplary eighteenth-century travel texts, in order to provide a context for my discussion of James Bruce in Chapter 2. I discuss the charge of 'curious pedantry' in relation to the antiquarian Richard Pococke's 1743 travelogue *A Description of the East*, and 'licentious curiosity' with reference to the Pacific travel account of the naturalist Joseph Banks, as redacted by John Hawkesworth. I conclude by considering George Forster's reformist and modernizing *Voyage Round the World* by way of contrast with the 'curious' travel account.

Pococke's *Description of the East* still in many respects conforms to the seventeenth-century idiom of John Bargrave's catalogue of curiosities, described by Stephen Bann in *Under the Sign*: '[it] *itemizes*, in the literal sense of the word, and exposes the object to a relentless view . . . desire follows the logic not of a greater whole completed by the imagination, but, rather, of an intricate structure revealed by intensive study'.[79] Based on the extended 'architectural' Grand Tour which Pococke made to Egypt, Syria, and Greece in the late 1730s, the *Description* is partly modelled on Joseph Addison's influential travel book *Remarks on Several Parts of Italy* (1705).[80] Pococke's lavishly illustrated folio, true to the aims of the Royal Society (of which he was a member) with its motto '*nullius in verba*', was largely concerned with the business of classical topography, checking classical descriptions of Egyptian antiquities by means of careful empirical observation. Pococke measured the Sphinx in order to assess the accuracy of Pliny's measurements:

I found by the quadrant that it is about 27 feet high, the neck and head only being above ground; the lower part of the neck, or the beginning of the breast is 33 feet wide, and it is 20 feet from the fore part of the neck to the back, and thence to the hole in the back it is 75 feet, the hole being 5 feet long, from which to the tail, if I

[78] See Phil Connell, 'Bibliomania: Book Collecting, Cultural Politics, and the Rise of Literary Heritage in Romantic Britain', *Representations*, 71 (Summer 2000), 24–47, for a suggestive starting point.

[79] Bann, *Under the Sign*, pp. 102–3. Cf. also Chard, *Pleasure and Guilt*, pp. 26–30.

[80] Batten points out that later readers had lost the key to Addison's generic conventions, Dr Johnson in 1773 considering it 'tedious' (p. 19). Pococke, a Whig clergyman and future Bishop of Ossory, was a friend of the Earl of Sandwich and Edward Wortley Montagu, both of whom had visited Egypt, and with them a co-founder of the short-lived Egyptian Society in 1741 dedicated to the Freemasonic project of promoting and preserving 'Egyptian and other ancient learning'. See John Gascoigne, *Joseph Banks and the English Enlightenment*, p. 128.

mistake not, it is 30 feet long; which something exceeds Pliny's account, who says that it is 113 feet long.[81]

The omission of any iconographic interpretation, affective or emotional response to the Sphinx is particularly striking when compared with A. W. Kinglake's description in *Eothen*, written a century later: 'comely the creature is, but the comeliness is not of this world . . . those lips, so thick and heavy, were fashioned according to some ancient mould of beauty'.[82]

Pococke (like James Bruce, who visited the Nile thirty-odd years later) exemplifies 'curiosity' in the sense of nice or 'careful' empirical examination of singular phenomena, without any attempt at aesthetic evaluation or contextualization. The *Description of the East*, predominately concerned with ancient monuments and architecture, is itself organized like an arrangement of singular objects in the cabinet of curiosities. The fact that it is published as a travel account at all is a result of 'the persuasion of some friends, to give an account of his travels, and of several accidents, that might give an insight into the customs and manners of people so different from our own, in order to render the work more acceptable to the generality of readers'.[83] Pococke is here forced to acknowledge that he is writing for two audiences: one private, learned, antiquarian, and 'curious'; the other public, unlearned, in search of personal narrative and entertaining descriptions of 'men and manners' rather than dry architectural description. Such personal narrative as there is is sparsely distributed throughout the book as a whole, confined to the last paragraph or two at the end of each chapter. One feels that personal adventures, including Pococke's grudging account of his transactions with native Egyptians, are represented as so many obstructions to the fulfilment of his 'curious' antiquarian project. Dr Johnson placed Pococke's *Description* low on the scale of travel writing 'because of its poor style and emphasis upon ancient architecture, a subject that he considered less important than the manners of foreign people'.[84]

In many respects British exploration and travel writing in the period with which this book is concerned is inextricably connected with the figure of Sir Joseph Banks.[85] Although principally celebrated for his role as the leading

---

[81] Richard Pococke, *A Description of the East, and Some Other Countries*, 2 vols. (London, 1743), i. 46.

[82] A. W. Kinglake, *Eothen; or, The Traces of Travel, brought home from the East* (London, 1844), p. 323.

[83] Pococke, p. iii.

[84] Quoted in Curley, p. 76. By contrast Johnson thought very highly of Patrick Brydone's *Tour through Sicily* (ibid., pp. 77–8) with its rejection of 'pedantic' antiquarian measurement and lively account of the author's transactions with local peoples.

[85] Banks, a wealthy Lincolnshire landowner, was a pivotal figure in the clubbable, gentlemanly 'culture of curiosity' of late 18th-century London: a member and later president of the Royal Society from 1778 until his death in 1820, a member of the council of the Society of Antiquaries 1785–7, and

impresario of British (and European) natural history, pioneering Linnaeus's botanical taxonomy in England, Banks was also a committed antiquarian, comparative linguist, and anthropologist, a highly significant congeries of interests upon which I shall touch again in the next section. Banks was himself also a famous traveller, having accompanied Captain Cook on his first, *Endeavour* voyage of 1768–72. 'Every blockhead [travels to Italy]' he is reported as saying; 'my Grand Tour shall be one round the whole globe'.[86] Upon his return from the Pacific in 1773 Banks's travel journals—along with half a dozen others by Cook and other members of the expedition—were 'ghosted' by John Hawkesworth in his *Account of the Voyages*, although the work was apparently overseen by Banks himself, who had paid Hawkesworth 1,000 pounds for the inclusion of his journal.[87] Banks was himself reticent about venturing into print, preferring the gentlemanly role of collector and impresario, but he would pay a high price for this reticence in more than just a financial sense.

Despite his earlier criticism of travel writing in which 'no passion is stongly excited except wonder', in which the traveller 'is rarely discovered to have any excellencies but daring curiosity',[88] Hawkesworth's attempt (writing in the character of a polite essayist) to refine his sources had severely backfired. Jonathan Lamb attributes his inability to universalize the singularities and wonders described by the voyagers to a

failure to locate a principle of relation between events . . . the unmediated and unprecedented encounter with the [particular] incline[s] him, who is impersonating it, to concentrate not upon the needs of the reader but on the agitations of the adventurer. The stress of shocks and miracles induce a non-justifying, particularizing, egoistic language of the moment that Hawkesworth had defined as savage, but which he is increasingly willing to elaborate and inhabit.[89]

Curiosity in Kames's negative sense is exemplified by Hawkesworth's nine-page discussion of the 'Patagonian giants' recorded in Commander Byron's nar-

again 1813–20, founder of the African Association in 1788, as well as a member of the Royal Academy, the Dilettanti Society, the Athenian Club, and Dr Johnson's famous literary circle (Gascoigne, p. 121).

[86] Quoted in Gascoigne, p. 61. Banks dignifies the artisanal practice of nautical exploration by affording it the patrician dignity of the Tour, at the same time as implying that Grand Tourists following the Italian 'beaten track' are lacking in curiosity and enterprise.

[87] For Hawkesworth's 'raw material', see *The Endeavour Journal of Joseph Banks*, ed. by J. C. Beaglehole, 2 vols., (Sydney: Angus & Roberston, 1962): 'it was true that Banks had handed [his *Endeavour* journal] over to Hawkesworth to use as he thought fit; but if Banks had wished to put it into shape and publish it as a separate entity, there was nothing to stop him' (p. 121). See also W. H. Pearson, 'Hawkesworth's Voyage', in *Studies in the 18th Century*, ed. by R. F. Brissenden, p. 240 *et passim*.

[88] *Adventurer*, No. 16, 30 Dec. 1752 and No. 4, 18 Nov. 1752, quoted in W. H. Pearson, *Hawkesworth's Voyages*, p. 253.

[89] 'Circumstances Surrounding the Death of John Hawkesworth', *Eighteenth-Century Life*, 18 (November 1994), 97.

rative, excused on the grounds that they were objects 'both of popular and philosophical curiosity'.[90] Despite the novelty of its lavish ethnographic illustrations and painstaking translation of previously unknown flora and fauna into the language of Linnaean genus and species, Hawkesworth's *Account* is in many respects a 'curious' rather than a philosophical travel narrative in Kames's pejorative sense, a 'relation of little circumstances' (i., p. vii) which did nothing to justify the voyages in a providential or patriotic fashion. His landscape descriptions (in contrast, say, to Patrick Brydone's immensely popular *Travels in Sicily and Malta*, published the following year in 1774, replete with 'affective realism' and landscape aesthetics) are generally more concerned with topographical and botanical singularities than with conveying typicalities of exotic nature. When a landscape feature is detailed, it is often because it represents 'a very extraordinary natural curiosity', like the rock on the coast of New Zealand which, 'perforated through its whole substance, so as to form a rude but stupendous arch or cavern . . . produced an effect far superior to any of the contrivances of art' (ii., pp. 317–18).[91] Barbara Maria Stafford has argued that this sort of description represents an emergent 'romantic' landscape vision 'bound up with a sentient earth that finds expression in specific vital forms, in singularities'.[92] On the contrary, it seems to me more representative of a residual discourse of 'curious' perception in which the singular landscape feature is privileged for its superficial analogical qualities (nature copying art, as in the rococo visual pun) rather than for any 'typical' relationship to its geographical context. As Bernard Smith argues in discussing the work of William Hodges, artist on Cook's second, *Resolution* voyage, it is the emergence of the 'typical landscape' as a dialogue between scientific and aesthetic interpretations of exotic nature (topographical versus picturesque) which marks the real challenge of the Pacific voyages to traditional European modes of seeing and representing.[93]

[90]   Hawkesworth, i., p. xvi. It is noteworthy that Banks's *Journal* actually denied that the Tierra del Fuegans were giants (*Endeavour Journal*, i. 227). Percy Adams goes so far as to argue that 'much of the popularity of travel literature [in the 1770s] can be attributed to the universal interest in the South American giants', *Travellers and Travel Liars 1660–1800* (New York: Dover Publications, 1980), pp. 28, 38. Swift had already satirized this popular interest with his Brobdingnagians in *Gulliver's Travels*. Gigantism, as well as other distortions in the dynamics of scale, was a common feature of pre-modern travel accounts, the hyperbole which figured distance. It had been a serious concern of the early 18th-century culture of curiosity. (See Frederik N. Smith, 'Science, Imagination, and Swift's Brobdingnagians' in *Eighteenth-Century Life*, 14 (1990), 1, 100–14). As I shall argue in Chapter 3, there is a fine irony in the fact that G. B. Belzoni began his career as a fairground strongman whose stage name was the 'Patagonian Sampson'.

[91]   See Smith's discussion of this in *European Vision*, pp. 28–34, which somewhat overstates the 'empiricism' of such views, rather than linking them to a tradition of 'curious' representation.

[92]   Barbara Maria Stafford, 'Toward Romantic Landscape Perception: Illustrated Travels and the Rise of "Singularity" as an Aesthetic Category', in *Art Quarterly*, (1977), 89–124, n.s. i, p. 112.

[93]   Smith, *European Vision*, p. 4. Although the Pacific travelogues differ from those concerned with 'antique lands' on account of the lack of specifically antiquarian interests, there are exceptions, such as

Jonathan Lamb has described how in redacting the *Endeavour* journals Hawkesworth 'oriented his first person [voice] towards Banks rather than Cook' in order to gild the plain sailor's narratives with the 'much more full and particular' (ii., p. xiv) record of Banks's patrician curiosity. Although Hawkesworth may have attempted to tone down Banks's 'soft primitivism' and cultural relativism[94] his 'indelicate' account of Tahitian sexual habits (and Banks's keen interest in them) led to Banks's public stigmatization as the 'Maca-roni of the South Pacific', a botanizing, foppish *curioso* who had spent more time making love to Tahitian women than in scientific exploration and collection. The fact that the *Endeavour* had set out with the intention of observing the Transit of Venus from the South Pacific was grist to the satirist's mill. In his account of the licentious 'Spectacle at Point Venus', which caused a particular furore among English readers,[95] Hawkesworth wrote 'this incident is not mentioned as an object of idle curiosity, but as it deserves consideration in determining a question which has been long debated in philosophy; whether the shame attending certain actions . . . is implanted in Nature, or superinduced by custom' (ii., p. 128). The pseudo-philosophical gloss of course rendered this all the *more* curious 'in the idle sense'.[96] Banks's flirtations with Purea ('Queen Oberea') and other Tahitian women, his 'effeminate' botanizing, and his 'creo-lized' fascination with Tahitian culture led him dangerously near the brink of decorous behaviour. For example, after he was robbed of his clothes while asleep, Purea dressed him in 'some of her country clothes' so that 'when he came to us he made a most motley appearance, half Indian and half English' (ii., p. 134). Commenting on Banks's 'great curiosity' to see a Tahitian funeral, Hawkesworth also described how he was

stripped of his European clothes, and a small piece of cloth being tied round his middle, his body was smeared with charcoal and water . . . till it was as black as that of a negroe: the same operation was performed upon several others, among whom

---

Hawkesworth's interest in Tahitian 'Morais' and the 'singular curiosity' of the 'Manioe' (giant basket-work human figure described at ii. 165). Cf. also George Forster's description of the Easter Island statues, which he compares with Egyptian antiquities in *A Voyage Round the World*, 2 vols. (London, 1777), i. 567.

[94] W. H. Pearson, 'Hawkesworth's Voyages', 242–7. Bridget Orr argues that Hawkesworth's account of Tahitian infanticide further qualified Banks's 'Arcadian' view of Tahiti; 'Stifling Pity in a Parent's Breast: Infanticide and Savagery in late 18th-Century Travel Writing', in *Travel Writing and Empire*, ed. by Steve Clark, pp. 140–1.

[95] This passage was actually based on Cook's rather than Banks's account. See J. C. Beaglehole, *The Endeavour Journal of Captain Cook* (Sydney, 1962), i. 93–4; and Neil Rennie, *Far-Fetched Facts: The Literature of Travel and the Idea of the South Seas* (Oxford: Clarendon Press, 1995), p. 99.

[96] The episode was excerpted in *The Covent Garden Magazine; or, Amorous Repository* and other semi-pornographic journals, lending some credibility to the commentator who complained 'Our Women may find in Dr Hawkesworth's Book stronger excitement to vicious Indulgences than the most intriguing French novel could present to their Imaginations'. Cited in Rennie, p. 101.

2. 'Joseph Banks', *c.*1772, by Benjamin West.

were some women, who were reduced to a state as near to nakedness as himself.   (ii., p. 146)[97]

Benjamin West's 1772 portrait of Banks appears at first glance perfectly to illustrate Banks's 'amphibious' nature as both a systematic, Linnaean naturalist and an effeminized, creolized 'curioso' (Ill. 2). Nicholas Thomas writes that the portrait of an exotically costumed Banks suggests 'vanity and personal acquisitiveness with respect to the curiosities that surround the subject', but this 'implication is counterbalanced by the presence of the strictly scientific image of the plant [in the folio of botanical drawings at Banks's feet], which is obviously a specimen, not an ornament'.[98] The ambivalent relationship between the 'curious' and the 'useful' touched on above is perfectly exemplified here by the fact that in his portrait Banks is conspicuously fingering the flax from which the New Zealand cloak is woven, as if to indicate its utility as a material to provide much-needed sail-cloth for Britain's ships. It is no coincidence that the book of botanical drawings at his feet is open at the flax plant.[99] It was the 'useful' botanical specimen rather than the 'curious' Tahitian curios which won out in the end in the career of Joseph Banks, as in British natural history over the next half-century. As John Gascoigne comments,

Banks's work represented a transformation of the collecting mentality of the gentlemanly virtuoso in that he ordered collections along systematic lines. To foreshadow the public/private issue, it was significant too, that Banks made such collections publicly available—again moving away from the private-collecting mentality of the virtuoso.[100]

In the years after 1780 Banks became the hub of what David Miller has termed a 'learned empire', based on his own 'centre of calculation', his house at 32 Soho Square, although he also exercised a profound influence on the public domain of knowledge as represented by the Royal Society, the Board of Longitude, Kew Gardens, and the British Museum, of which he became a trustee in 1813.[101]

---

[97] On the sexual connotations of curiosity, see Kenny, pp. 167–8; and Benedict, 86–92.

[98] 'Licensed Curiosity', p. 130. See also Harriet Guest's account of the West portrait in 'The Great Distinction: Figures of the Exotic in the Work of William Hodges', *New Feminist Discourses: Critical Essays on Theories and Texts*, ed. by Isobel Armstrong (London and New York: Routledge, 1992), pp. 308–9; and 'Curiously Marked', pp. 101–34.

[99] I am grateful to Dr Patricia Fara for this point. See her 'Images of Men of Science', in *History Today* (October 1998), 42–9. In a longer, unpublished version, Fara also indicates Banks's effeminization in this portrait, as well as the fact that it was becoming more common for women than for men to be portrayed in costume . . . 'like a woman, Banks has been transformed into a seductive allegorical image'.

[100] John Gascoigne, '"The Ordering of Nature and the Ordering of Empire": A Commentary', *Visions of Empire*, p. 109.

[101] David Miller, in 'Joseph Banks, Empire, and "Centers of Calculation"', *Visions of Empire*, pp. 30–3. But see Gascoigne's doubts about the applicability of the Latourian model to the early, 'curious' Banks, ibid., p. 108.

In the preface to his 1777 *Voyage Round the World*, the young German naturalist George Forster commented on the 'universal censure, I had almost said contempt' with which Hawkesworth's *Account* had been received. What Forster called the 'ill-success' of the work had been attributed to the 'frivolous observations, the uninteresting digressions, and sophistical principles' of Hawkesworth himself, although he was not entirely sure that the compiler, rather than the authors of the journals (like Banks) upon which he had based his narrative, deserved to take all the blame.[102] George Forster's *Voyage*, although less impressive in ethnographic terms than his father, J. R. Forster's, *Observations Made During the Voyage Round the World*, is in many ways a milestone for romantic period travel writing, establishing the principles which would increasingly be demanded from scientific travel writers over the next half-century. It is also a sustained attack on the type of 'vulgar' curiosity underpinning Hawkesworth's narrative. Forster—like his compatriot Immanuel Kant—attacked the requirement that the traveller be merely a collector of facts.[103] (Kant, needless to say, had only contempt for the *Wunderkammern*; 'a taste for all that is rare, little though its inherent worth otherwise might be . . . a spirit of minutiae [is] the opposite of the sublime', he wrote dismissively.)[104] Contesting the notion of the purely empirical observer, Forster believed that 'two travellers seldom saw the same object in the same manner, and each reported the fact differently, according to his sensations, and his peculiar mode of thinking'.[105] 'It was therefore necessary', he continued, 'to be acquainted with the observer, before any use could be made of his observations'.[106]

---

[102] George Forster, *A Voyage Round the World, in his Brit. Majesty's Sloop Resolution, commanded by Capt. Cook, during the years 1772, 1773, 1774, and 1775*, 2 vols. (London, 1777), i., p. ix. George's father, J. R. Forster, the cantankerous German naturalist aboard Cook's *Resolution*, the next year published his strictly philosophical account *Observations made during the Voyage round the World, on Physical Geography, Natural History, and Ethic Philosophy* (London, 1778). Because of a dispute between Forster and the Admiralty, the work was published without any of its plates. Much aggrieved, Forster had decided that the original agreement limiting the nature of his travel account was binding only upon him, but that it need not prevent his son George from publishing a narrative of the voyage under his own name. Thus the very conception of *A Voyage Round the World* was linked to the Forster's disaffection with the official monopoly on travel writing. See the editors' introductory essays in the new edition of *Observations*, ed. by N. Thomas, H. Guest, and M. Dettelbach (University of Hawaii Press, 1996).

[103] As an organicist and a follower of Herder, George Forster nevertheless disagreed with Kant's anthropological theories, which he attacked in the Oct.–Nov. 1786 issue of the *Teutsche Merkur*, in an article entitled 'Noch etwas über die Menschenrassen'. See Frederick C. Beiser, *The Fate of Reason. German Philosophy from Kant to Fichte* (Cambridge, Mass. and London: Harvard University Press, 1987), 154–7. Kant's reply to Forster's article became the preparatory sketch for his critique of teleological judgement in the *Critique of Judgement* (1790).

[104] *Observations on the Feeling of the Beautiful and the Sublime* (1764), trans. by John T. Goldthwait (Berkeley, Los Angeles, Oxford: University of California Press, 1991), p. 71.

[105] Forster, i., pp. xi–xii. See also Margarita Bowen, *Empiricism and Geographical Thought* (Cambridge University Press, 1981), pp. 211–12.

[106] Forster, i., p. xii.

Forster insisted that new discoveries should not be made happenstance, but rather be deduced from transcendental inquiry in such a way that might indicate a disciplined programme for future research. At the same time, his privileging of the traveller's affective response to nature appears more akin to Rousseau's cult of sensibility than to Kant's stoic rationality:

I have sometimes obeyed the powerful dictates of my heart, and given voice to my feelings; for, as I do not pretend to be free from the weaknesses common to my fellow-creatures, it was necessary for every reader to know the colour of the glass through which I looked.[107]

The new importance of 'affective realism' in prose narrative—most fully developed in the literature of sensibility—had been recognized by Adam Smith under the rubric of 'indirect discourse' in his *Lectures on Rhetoric and Belles Lettres* (1751–63). This involved not 'direct' objective description but rather 'the passion or affection [the speaker] is poss⟨ess⟩ed of and intends, by sympathy, to communicate to the reader'.[108] As Ian Duncan comments, 'the author places a figure within the scene as the reader's mirror or proxy, serving to situate and integrate the rhetorical effect'.[109]

Smith's desideratum is exemplified in the the new style of 'personal narratives' by travellers like Patrick Brydone and George Forster, although conspicuously absent from Hawkesworth's *Account*, despite the latter's adoption of a first-person narrative voice. In the chapters that follow I shall chart the uneven deployment of 'affective realism' in the travel writing of James Bruce and Giovanni Belzoni, and its stabilization in the discourse of picturesque travel writing, where 'curious' singularities are *objectively* organized within 'typical landscape', and *subjectively* disciplined in relation to the traveller's associative sensibility. Thus, for Uvedale Price writing in 1794 (in a significant reformulation of curiosity), 'the effect of the picturesque is curiosity', the latter propensity now described as an affective *via media* which 'gives play to the mind', mediating between the 'violent stretch' of the Burkean sublime and the lassitude of beauty.[110]

It is likely that Forster's remarks on the traveller's sensibility in the *Voyage* influenced Mary Wollstonecraft when she wrote in her *Short Residence in Sweden* (1796) 'I perceived that I could not give a just description of what I saw, but by relating the effect different objects had produced on my mind and feel-

---

[107] Forster, i., pp. xii–xiii.

[108] Adam Smith, *Lectures on Rhetoric and Belles Lettres*, ed. by J. Bryce (Oxford: Clarendon Press, 1983), p. 25.

[109] Ian Duncan, 'Adam Smith, Samuel Johnson and the Institutions of English', in Robert Crawford (ed.), *The Scottish Invention of English Literature* (Cambridge University Press, 1998), pp. 46–7.

[110] Uvedale Price, *An Essay on the Picturesque, as Compared with the Sublime and the Beautiful*, new edn. (London, 1796), pp. 105–6.

ings, whilst the impression was still fresh'.[111] Although it is by no means predictable from Wollstonecraft's remarkable travelogue, the link between 'affective realism' and a sensibility regulated in the direction of nostalgic *amor patriae*
and the domestic affections ensured that the picturesque became the approved
(although not uncontested), idiom for women travel writers, the subject of
Chapter 5. My sixth chapter discusses Alexander von Humboldt's representation of the traveller's 'transcendental self' as a critique of curiosity (George
Forster, we should remember, was the young Humboldt's tutor and intellectual
mentor), paradoxically leading to the failure of 'personal narrative'.

Although, as I shall argue, Humboldt's failure was symptomatic of a
nineteenth-century division between scientific and literary travel writing, it
would be a historical oversimplification to say that 'affective realism' as discussed here represented any simple shift from 'objective' to 'subjective' travel
writing. According to Forster's transcendental principle, the aesthetic sensibility of the traveller must unify the manifold of sense experience which is his (or
her) 'objective' task to describe, with the proviso that the traveller's affective
reactions to phenomena are a part of their 'objective' description. This sensibility is communal, disciplined, and morally self-conscious,[112] in contrast to the
'curious attitude' with its indiscriminate passion for superficialities and singularities. On this account, the increased 'inwardness' of romantic travel writing
(at least as anticipated in Forster's text) was not conceived, *pace* Charles Batten
and Barbara Stafford, as the eclipse of the *utile* by the *dulce* foreshadowing a
trivialization of the genre, but rather an attempt at their synthesis. Following
Forster's lead, travel writers increasingly sought to express a holistic relationship between social and natural factors in diverse geographical environments,
while parading sensibility as the marker of a 'modern' Western self, capable
of at once empathizing with and transcending the 'antique land' and its
inhabitants.

Temporalization and the Comparison of Cultures

Suppose Greek literature to be known in modern Greece only, and there
to be in the hands of priests and philosophers; and suppose them still to
be worshippers of Jupiter and Apollo; suppose Greece to have been

---

[111] *A Short Residence in Sweden*, ed. with introduction and notes by Richard Homes
(Harmondsworth: Penguin, 1987), p. 62. Wollstonecraft cites J. R. Forster's *Observations* in her
Vindication of the Rights of Woman (1794).

[112] George Forster's attitude to the 'sexual curiosities' of Polynesian cultures was far less indulgent
than Banks's or Hawkesworth's, whose lubricious description of native women is transformed into
sexual disgust (i. 211–13). Forster's philosophical attitude to Cook's 'confirmation' of cannibalism
among the Maoris also contrasts with Hawkesworth's macabre 'curiosity' (see i. 517–18).

conquered successively by Goths, Huns, Vandals, Tartars, and lastly by
the English; then suppose a court of judicature to be established by the
British parliament, at Athens, and an inquisitive Englishman to be one
of the judges; suppose him to learn Greek there, which none of his countrymen knew, and to read Homer, Pindar, Plato . . . Such am I in this
country; substituting Sanscrit for Greek, the *Brahmans*, for the priests
of *Jupiter*, and *Valmic*, *Vyasa*, *Calidasa*, for Homer, Plato, Pindar.

(Sir William Jones)[113]

In his study of the spatio-temporal codes of romantic historicism, James
Chandler has discerned in the literature of the period 'a new preoccupation with
the dating of the cultural place, the locating of the cultural moment'.[114] In this
final section I shall complete my consideration of the 'curious' travel account by
discussing the role of 'temporalization', an aesthetics of *time*, which compli-
mented the aesthetic of distance discussed above. One of the main concerns
of eighteenth-century exploration (as we saw in Latour's account) was the filling
up of spaces on the map by frequent and repeated latitudinal and longitudinal
measurements, the employment of *time* to measure *distance*. But the standard-
ization of global time for longitudinal measurements was not the only time-scale
of importance to travellers. In studying texts from a period 'newly preoccupied'
with the relationship between history and the location of cultures, we also need
to consider the relationship of personal or 'phenomenological' time and historical time, in relation to travellers' itineraries in antique lands. For when travellers
moved from the centre to the periphery, or their mobiles moved back from the
periphery to the centre, they were frequently represented—or represented themselves—as moving in 'deep' historical time as well as cartographic space. The
congruence is well illustrated by David Hume's intriguing metaphor in the *Treatise*, when he observes that 'a great traveller, 'tho in the same chamber, will pass
for a very extraordinary person; as a *Greek* medal, even in our cabinet, is always
esteem'd a valuable curiosity'.[115] We might denominate this 'curious time' to differentiate it from 'universal' time in the rational Cartesian sense.

One dominant form of temporalization in the travel accounts studied in this
book is the discourse of classical topography, the mapping of a modern land-

[113] *The Letters of Sir William Jones*, ed. by Garland Cannon, 2 vols. (Oxford, 1970), ii. 755–6.
[114] James Chandler, *England in 1819: The Politics of Literary Culture and the Case of Romantic Historicism* (Chicago and London: University of Chicago Press, 1998), p. 108.
[115] *A Treatise of Human Nature* (1739–1740), Bk II, Pt III, section viii, 2nd edn., with an analytical index by L. A. Selby-Bigge, rev. by P. H. Nidditch (Oxford: Clarendon Press, 1978), p. 433. In contrast to Kames, the point of Hume's metaphorical connection between the traveller and the antique coin is to inculcate the former with some of the charisma of the latter, given his belief that 'a distance in time has a more considerable effect than that in space'. Hume explained this in purely mechanical, associ- ationist terms: the imagination moves with more difficulty in passing from one portion of time to another, than in a transition through the parts of space, given the equation between 'difficulty' and sublime 'affect' (ibid., p. 436).

scape in terms of its classical geography, mentioned above in relation to the eighteenth-century Egyptian traveller Richard Pococke. With the rise of 'affective realism' discussed in the previous section, travel writers increasingly sought to solicit readerly identification with their sensitive, modern, and disciplined selves, as mirrors which might reflect the 'antick' shapes of distant places and peoples. In describing the ruins of Taormina in his *Tour through Sicily*, Patrick Brydone needed to differentiate himself from the Pococke-style antiquarian and curioso: 'I shall . . . content myself (I hope it will content you too) with endeavouring to communicate, as entire as possible, the same impression I myself shall receive, without descending too much to particulars, or fatiguing myself or you with the mensuration of antique walls.'[116] The traveller's emotional sensitivity here inteferes with a 'curious' antiquarian evocation of the past, thus (in the words of Chloe Chard) 'convert[ing] historical time into personal time, a task that travel writing of this period constantly sets itself, and defines as crucial to the efficient appropriation of the foreign'.[117]

The point is further illustrated by Byron's tremendously popular 'poetic travelogue' *Childe Harold's Pilgrimage* (1812–18), where the Childe's melancholy contemplation of the ruins of Greece and Rome has almost entirely eclipsed antiquarian curiosity. In Canto II, the theme of *sic transit gloria mundi* is favourably contrasted with the despoliation of the Parthenon by Lord Elgin and other British antiquaries. In an 1811 review of the classical topographer William Gell's *Geography of Ithaca* and *Itinerary of Greece*, Francis Hodgson (assisted by his friend Byron) mocked Gell's extreme temporalization of the modern Greek landscape and people, and his pedantic designation of the modern 'Mainotes' by their classical name of 'Eleuthero-Lacones'.[118] Acknowledging that 'there have been tourists and "strangers" in other countries, who have kindly permitted their readers to learn rather too much of their sweet selves' (perhaps referring to Byron's forthcoming poem), Hodgson complained that Gell has gone to the other extreme in suppressing the traveller's *modern* subjectivity: 'we like to know that there is a being yet living who describes the scenes to which he introduces us; and that it is not a mere translation from Strabo or Pausanius which we are reading, or a commentary on those authors'.[119]

The triumph of sensibility and imagination over erudition in such discourses

---

[116] Patrick Brydone, *A Tour Through Sicily and Malta*, 2 vols. (Dublin, 1774), i. 70.

[117] Chard, p. 133.

[118] *Monthly Review*, lxv (May–Aug. 1811), pp. 371–85, 382. Although Tom Moore attributed this review to Byron (partly on the poet's own evidence), the editor's copy preserved in the Bodleian Library clearly attributes it to Hodgson. It was probably a collaboration between the two men. See Andrew Nicholson (ed.), *Lord Byron: The Complete Miscellaneous Prose* (Oxford: Clarendon Press, 1991), pp. xxvi–xxvii, justifying its non-inclusion.

[119] Ibid., p. 380. Cf. also Carolyn Springer's account of Byron's 'anti-archaeological' poetry ('what is gained for erudition is lost to the imagination') in *The Marble Wilderness: Ruins and Representation in Italian Romanticism, 1775–1850* (Cambridge University Press, 1987), p. 6.

of the Grand Tour may have been in part a response to the traveller's belated-ness, the sense that classical topography was all too familiar to readers, had been described too many times. By contrast, early explorers and travellers who ven-tured beyond the 'beaten track' of Italy and the Mediterranean littoral often tended, by a reverse logic, to convert personal into historical time. This is most famously expressed in the French ideologue J.-M. Degérando's ethnographical manual *The Observation of Savage Peoples*, written for Baudin's expedition to Australia in 1799 (which Humboldt sought, unsuccessfully, to join): 'The philo-sophical traveller, sailing to the ends of the earth, is in fact travelling in time; he is exploring the past; every step he makes is the passage of an age.'[120] Degérando's typically 'ideological' project of understanding civilized man through his 'decomposed' *alter ego*, the savage, clearly partook of the systematizing imperative of the late enlightenment rather than the culture of curiosity (in fact Baudin followed hard on the heels of La Pérouse, Latour's exemplary case of 'scientific' travel). None the less, Degérando's criticism of the superficiality of earlier European travellers, and his Rousseauvian sympathy with the savage, is less often commented upon. His remark that 'the first means to the proper knowledge of the Savages, is to become after a fashion like one of them; and it is by learning their language that we shall become their fellow cit-izens' has been considered to anticipate the practice of participant observation in modern anthropology.[121]

Degérando's account of space/time travel highlights a *temporalization of space* (or rather, given the phenomenological orientation of travel writing, *dis-tance*) still recognizably located within the paradigms of Hume's metaphor of the antiquarian numinosity of the 'great traveller'. Despite a superficial resem-blance, the traveller's temporalization of distance needs to be distinguished from an antithetical discourse which might be described as the *spatialization of history*, emergent in the same period and best summed up by Hegel's dictum 'World history travels from east to west; for Europe is the absolute end of history, just as Asia is the beginning.'[122] This latter discourse was destined to triumph over the traveller's 'curious' time in nineteenth-century evolutionist anthropology.[123] Its anticipation in the comparativist 'conjectural history' of the

[120] J.-M. Degérando, *The Observation of Savage People*, trans. by F. C. T. Moore, Preface by E. E. Evans-Pritchard (London: RKP, 1969), p. 63. Degérando's memoir was presented to the Société des Observateurs de l'Homme, whose members included Volney, Millin, Cuvier, Pinel, Jussieu, and Jaufrett, Europe's first insititutionalized anthropological body.

[121] Degérando, p. 70. See Evans-Pritchard's Introduction to Degérando, cited above. Had it been widely read in England, it would doubtless have provided ammunition for British counter-revolutionary propaganda which sought to associate French materialism with savagery and primitivism.

[122] Hegel, *Lectures on the Philosophy of World History. Introduction*, trans. by H. B. Nisbet with an Introduction by Duncan Forbes (Cambridge University Press, 1975), p. 197.

[123] See Johannes Fabian, *Time and the Other: How Anthropology Makes its Object* (New York: Columbia University Press, 1983), pp. 11–21.

Scottish enlightenment is well illustrated by Edmund Burke's letter to the historian William Robertson in 1777:

I have always thought with you, that we possess at this time very great advantages towards the knowledge of human Nature. We need no longer to go to History to trace it in all its stages and periods. History from its comparative youth, is but a poor instructour . . . But now the Great Map of Mankind is unrolld at once; and there is no state or Gradation of barbarism, and no mode of refinement which we have not at the same instant under our View.[124]

In his concern with the 'the savage' in a state of nature, Degérando exemplifies an enlightenment anthropology which adopted its goals and methodology from botany and other natural sciences.[125] By contrast, the dominant orientation of the travellers studied in the present book is *antiquarian*, concerned with the ruin-strewn continental interiors of Egypt, India, and Mexico rather than the Edenic archipelagos of the Pacific. As I mentioned in my Introduction, the focus on archaeology rather than herbaria distinguishes my book from recent studies of exotic travel writing by Mary Louise Pratt, Barbara Stafford, and Bruno Latour, all of whom (quite properly) designate natural history in general, and Linnaean botany in particular, as the dominant epistemological paradigms of the period.[126] Pomian's quantitative study of the transformation of eighteenth-century French cabinets in his chapter 'Medals/Shells = Erudition/Philosophy' confirms this trend in the parallel instance of collecting, revealing the increasing prestige of natural history collections (such as shells) over 'curious' antiquarian collections (notably numismatics) in the later enlightenment.[127]

Yet there has perhaps been a danger here, particularly evident to a student of romantic orientalism, of neglecting the 'residual' discourse of antiquarianism

[124] 9 June 1777, *The Correspondence of Edmund Burke*, vol. iii. ed. by George H. Guttridge (Cambridge University Press, 1961), pp. 350–1. See also Meek, *Social Science and the Ignoble Savage*, p. 173.
[125] 'What science does not aspire to be a natural science? . . . The natural sciences are in a way no more than a series of comparisons', Degérando proclaimed at the beginning of his manual. Degérando, p. 62.
[126] Fabian cites the example of Linnaeus's *Institutio Perigrinatoris* (1759) (instructions for scientific travellers), one of the precursors of Degérando's text, and also notes 'the roots of the new science of travel in natural-historical projects of observation, collection and classification, and description'. *Time and the Other*, p. 8. Stafford goes to the extreme of almost completely ignoring the ethnographic aspects of romantic travel narratives in *Voyage into Substance*.
[127] Pomian argues that the reason for this was not just the fact that shells were cheaper than medals, although the financial accessibility of natural history specimens did reflect the *embourgeoisement* of collectors. Rather, the medals sought after by Pomian's patrician collectors embody the object of curiosity as discussed above, attractive on account of their rarity, value, and superficial legibility. They were, however, 'incapable of integrating the facts . . . amassed into a meaningful whole' (Pomian, *Collectors*, p. 128). In contrast, collectors of shells (or any other objects of natural history) 'facilitated observation by bringing together nature's creations in these same cabinets which grow daily in number', according to Diderot (ibid., p. 138).

in favour of the 'emergent' discourse of natural history in travel writing of this period. As John Gascoigne reminds us in his account of Joseph Banks's intellectual development 'from antiquarian to anthropologist', in seventeenth- and eighteenth-century Britain antiquarianism and natural history had developed as cognate branches of intellectual inquiry and shared common institutional sites. (Joseph Banks was a member of the Dilettante Society and the Society of Antiquaries as well as President of the Royal Society, a shared membership so common that the two societies scheduled their meetings specially so that members could attend both.)[128] It is doubtless true that the prestige of Linnaean taxonomy in natural history increasingly left the study of antiquarianism (which failed to develop any equivalent systematics) high and dry. Developments in philosophical aesthetics, following the seminal *History of Ancient Art amongst the Greeks* (1764) of the German critic J. J. Winckelmann (paralleled in Britain by the theories of Sir Joshua Reynolds, Archibald Alison, and Richard Payne Knight), offered an alternative evaluation of antique art in the discourse of Taste.[129] As we saw in the previous section, travel writing's focus on 'first impressions' rather than philosophical comparison rendered it hospitable to wonder and curiosity long after these discourses had been rationalized out of existence in other areas of knowledge. In many of the travel narratives studied below, the systematic protocols of natural history, antiquarian curiosity, and Taste (reflected in the 'indirect discourse' of the traveller's response to people and places) coexist in loose solution, reflecting the 'predisciplinary' nature of the genre itself.[130]

In justifying my focus upon antiquarianism rather than natural history in romantic travel writing, it is necessary to say a general word about the temporalizing tropes adopted by writers like Bruce, Volney, Denon, Belzoni, Graham, and others studied in the chapters that follow. The discourse of these 'travellers

---

[128] Gascoigne, p. 121. See also Martin Rudwick's chapter on the study of fossils in the late Rennaissance, which he entitles 'Natural Antiquities', *The Meaning of Fossils: Episodes in the History of Palaeontology*, 2nd edn. (New York: Neal Watson Academic Publications, 1976), pp. 49–100.

[129] On Winckelmann, see Suzanne L. Marchand's useful discussion in *Down from Olympus: Archaeology and Philhellenism in Germany, 1750–1970* (Princeton, NJ: Princeton University Press, 1996), pp. 7–16. Thanks to Martin Ruehl for this reference. See also John Brewer, *The Pleasures of the Imagination: English Culture in the Eighteenth Century* (London: HarperCollins, 1997), ch. 6 'Connoisseurs and Artists'.

[130] Gascoigne points out that Banks's own attempts to systematize his antiquarian projects 'did not extend much beyond organizing his material around specific topics, particularly those which impinged upon his native Lincolnshire' (*Joseph Banks*, p. 125). By the late 18th century antiquarians sought to professionalize their practice as a branch of history or aesthetics, although without achieving much success. See Phillipa Levine, *The Amateur and the Professional: Antiquarians, Historians, and Archaeologists in Victorian England, 1838–1886*, (Cambridge University Press, 1986), p. 70. Joseph Levine suggests that Winckelmann provided a 'Linnaean' method for antiquarians in relation to the genesis of artistic styles. *Dr Woodward's Shield: History, Science and Satire in Augustan England* (Ithaca and London: Cornell University Press, 1991), p. 280.

from antique lands' is better designated 'orientalist' than 'primitivist', to distinguish it from the enlightenment discourse of the Pacific. Sir William Jones's extraordinary mapping of modern Hindu and ancient Greek culture (quoted above) perfectly exemplifes the style of temporalization with which I am concerned. Egyptian, Hindu, or Mexican 'high cultures' were temporalized not as proto-historical, Arcadian sites but rather by analogy with later stages in the historical trajectory of the West, most notably its classical and feudal epochs.[131] In Chapter 6 I shall explain why Mexico can be considered 'oriental' rather than occidental in these terms, and why the '*New* World' should feature so prominently in a book concerned with 'antique lands'.

Edward Said describes temporalization as simply one European 'orientalizing strategy' among others: 'faced with the obvious decrepitude and political impotence of the modern Oriental, the European Orientalist found it his duty to rescue some portion of a lost, past classical Oriental grandeur in order to "facilitate ameliorations" in the present Orient'.[132] Whilst this seems valid in relation to the 'modern' orientalism which is Said's real subject, it ignores the fact that in the earlier period—since the renaissance at least—temporalization had represented a sole secular resource for rendering alien cultures commensurable, and therefore intelligible, to European travellers and colonizers.[133] In contrast to the arrested fascination of 'wonder', temporalization represented a 'principal of attachment' which provided the basis for description and cultural interpretation. This remained the case even when the modern inhabitants of an 'antique land' were represented as abject survivors of former greatness, and despite the constant tendency to stereotype cultural diversity involved in temporalization. A historically based model of classical or feudal 'antiquity', rather than evolutionary biology and its concomitant 'racial science', still provided the dominant matrix by which cultures could be understood and compared in this period.[134] The metaphorical structure of temporalization worked in both directions: in a period of massive historical nostalgia in Europe it was very far from being simply a mechanism for denigrating the 'antique' in relation to 'the modern'. Classical or feudal tropes frequently served to highlight the corruption or social disaggregation of the traveller's own native

---

[131] *The London Magazine* (August 1774), 390, commented that both Banks in the Pacific and Bruce in Abyssinia had discovered 'feudal' societies, demonstrating 'the universality of the Feudal System'.

[132] Edward Said, *Orientalism*, p. 79.

[133] See Pagden, *European Encounters*, pp. 148–9.

[134] Although, of course, many scholars have discovered the roots of 'racial science' in earlier periods. See Sipe Stuurman, 'François Bernier and the Invention of Racial Classification', *History Workshop Journal*, 50 (Autumn 2000), 1–22; Richard Popkin, 'The Philosophical Basis of 18th-Century Racism', in H. E. Pagliaro, *Racism in the 18th Century* (Cleveland and London, 1973), pp. 245–62; Alan Richardson and Sonia Hofkosh, *Race, Romanticism and Imperial Culture, 1780–1834* (Bloomington and Indianopolis: Indiana University Press, 1996); Robert Young, *Colonial Desire: Hybridity in Theory, Culture and Race* (London and New York: Routledge, 1969).

modernity when applied to 'antique lands', as well as (in a more familiar imperialist version) privileging that modernity in relation to oriental stasis and
'underdevelopment'.

As long as the hermeneutic and historical (*civic* rather than naturalistic) paradigm survived, the distant and different could not be written off as irreducibly
'other' by European commentators. As Norbert Peabody has argued in his
study of the discourse of feudalism in the historiography of early nineteenth-
century British India, the 'relational or segmented mode' of social representations characteristic of the Scottish enlightenment (still the dominant historical
mode in British romanticism) 'is not tied to the assumption of opposed essences
in which East is ontologically different from West, [but] permits a unified ana-
lytic framework for the social construction of difference that is simultaneously
applicable to Oriental and Occidental contexts'.[135] Differences there
undoubtedly were between the West and the rest in this period, and differences
which were increasingly premissed upon unequal commercial and political relations, but they were still theorized as differences of degree not of kind. Caution
is therefore necessary in ascribing notions of ontological difference (and its
methodological expression, the binary oppositions of alteritist criticism) to
romantic travel narratives and the discourse of early colonialism.

Nevertheless, many of the texts studied in the following chapters do reveal
an increasing tendency to undercut the 'civic' trope of temporalization either
by denying the antiquity of exotic high cultures, by establishing a pejorative
comparison with Hellenic culture, or (often the same thing) 'fossilizing' extra-
European antique lands and their inhabitants into a non-progressive past. James
Mill exemplified the first of these tendencies when he wrote that 'rude nations
seem to derive a particular gratification from pretensions to remote antiquity',
his target just as much the temporalizing rhetoric of European antiquarians and
travellers as the alleged hyperbole of oriental nations themselves.[136] Mill's rationalist alternative hardly offered a more benign picture of 'rude nations', and it
comes as no surprise to encounter his severe critique of 'curious' travel narratives and the distorting power of distance ('*ex longinquo reverentia*'), discussed
in Chapter 4 below. The second and third tendencies are revealed in the cases
of travellers (such as Maria Graham, Reginald Heber, or Humboldt, studied in
Chapters 4, 5, and 6 below) who either qualified the 'temporalized' classical

---

[135] Norbert Peabody, 'Tod's *Rajast'han* and the Boundaries of Imperial Rule in 19th-Century India',
Modern Asian Studies, 30, I (1996), 185–220. Peabody does, however, show that both Henry Hallam in
his *View of the State of Europe during the Middle Ages* and the anonymous reviewers of James Tod's
Annals of Rajast'han argued that European and Indian feudalism were profoundly different, signalling
the breakdown of temporalization as a vehicle of cultural commensurability by the mid-19th century
(pp. 196–200).

[136] James Mill, *The History of British India* (1817), ed. by John Clive (Chicago: University of Chicago
Press, 1975), p. 27.

paradigm or made negative comparisons between the aesthetics of Hindu, Egyptian, or Mexican antiquity and the Hellenic model.

As I mentioned above, Winckelmann and his followers had established a Hellenic aesthetic which 'conceived the progress of art—and, therefore of civilisation—in terms of a rise and fall, with classical Greece representing the paramount, pivotal point', a hierarchy of styles which became the foundation-stone of the new nineteenth-century 'museum order'.[137] For most of the period with which this book is concerned Greece was part of the Ottoman Empire, and therefore in cultural and geopolitical terms 'oriental' no less than Turkey, Egypt, or India (in contrast to the Italian states visited by eighteenth- and early nineteenth-century Grand Tourists). But the fact that 'Greek art was the norm and appealed because its supposed purity provided a model of western, even British, moral values'[138] sets Greece apart from the distant cultures represented in travel accounts which I have chosen to study in this book. Romantic Hellenism embodied a norm for gauging the space dividing 'antique/antick lands' from the standard of ideal beauty and of progressive civilization.

As organicist and evolutionary models derived from the natural sciences gradually came to dominate thinking about history and aesthetics (in the romantic period partly spurred on by Kant's account of organicism as a shared regulative ideal for aesthetics and biology in the *Critique of Judgement*) 'oriental' cultures were temporalized in increasingly negative, inferior terms. In the case of Humboldt, for example, Cuvier's distinction between extinct and living species in natural history provided the Prussian traveller with an invidious model for discriminating between the *vital* aesthetics of Hellenism and the 'extinct' monuments of oriental high cultures, which had resulted in the historical fossilization of the latter. The discourse of romantic travel marked not only a *genre* in transition, as I argued in my Introduction, it also marked a critical epistemic threshold in the relations between hermeneutic and scientific modes of apprehending the world, albeit heralding the eventual triumph of the latter over the former.[139]

---

[137] Ian Jenkins, *Archaeologists and Aesthetes in the Sculpture Galleries of the British Museum 1800–1839* (London: British Museum Press, 1992), p. 63.

[138] Ian Jenkins, p. 10. The British emphasis on Hellenic 'purity' (focused on the Elgin Marbles, which arrived in London in 1807) in the period covered by Jenkins replaced an earlier taste for Romano-Grecian sculpture associated with the 18th-century Italian Grand Tour, of which the Apollo Belvedere and the Medici Venus were the privileged exemplars. See Nicholas Penny and Francis Haskill, *Taste and the Antique* (New Haven and London: Yale University Press, nd). But Romano-Grecian art served the same normative function as Greek in relation to the Egyptian, Indian, and Mexican artworks discussed here.

[139] See Fabian, 'It is not the dispersal of human cultures in space that leads anthropology to "temporalise" (something that is maintained in the image of [Degérando's] "philosophical traveller" whose roaming in space leads to the discovery of "ages"); it is naturalised–spatialised Time which gives meaning . . . to the distribution of humanity in space. The history of our discipline reveals that such use of Time almost invariably is made for the purpose of distancing those who are observed from the Time of the observer' (*Time and the Other*, p. 25).

'The tropics are less exotic than out of date', Lévi-Strauss wrote famously in the 1950s.[140] The 'antique lands' discussed in this book are now more often referred to as 'developing countries', except in the tourist brochures where the romantic picturesque still reigns supreme as the prospective tourist is invited 'to step back into the past' (all mod cons included). As the adjective 'developing' suggests, temporalization has survived the fall of the European empires, as the pace of modernization has been vastly accelerated by economic globalization, the revolution in information technology, and jet tourism. Distance as an imaginative dimension for contemplating the rich diversity of human emplacement has been superseded by uniform space in the sentimentalized community of the global village, an experiential loss of incalculable dimensions. Despite the resilience of diverse cultural traditions and socialist and nationalist resistance, some of those countries once known to Europeans as 'antique lands' found themselves high and dry in the new world order. Like their expropriated labour and raw materials, returning in the phantom form of the commodity, the (plural) knowledges which had been wrested from them, mobilized, and combined at the centre, were returned to Europe's colonial peripheries in the form of universal reason, science, progress: the 'homogeneous, empty time' of modernity.[141]

After the struggles of the independence era, many new post-colonial nations (given the radical inequality of the global distribution of wealth) had little choice but passively to accept their roles as clients for Northern capital, or recipients of Northern arms and aid in a *neo-colonial* world order. In some cases, the discourse of temporalization was taken over wholesale from the colonial order to justify the continued suppression of indigenous 'tribal' or ethnic minorities whose worlds are considered to be 'frozen in the past' by modernizing bourgeois élites. The emergence of a multicultural, migrant aesthetic which has sought to resist the homogenizing, market-driven logic of globalization by creating an 'interstitial time and space' represents a hopeful counter-weight. (Although it is largely located within social margins and/or diasporic élites in metropolitan urban centres, rather than the *ci-devant* 'antique lands' themselves.)[142] The question remains how far multiculturalist critique can challenge the seemingly triumphant march of multinational corporatism in the globalized economy.

Romanticism played a unique and distinctive role in the 'temporal exchange' of global capitalism, whereby the antique, the curious, and the picturesque were imported to the metropolis, as modernity, technology, rationalism, and 'univer-

[140] *Tristes Tropiques*, p. 89.

[141] Walter Benjamin, 'Theses on the Philosophy of History', *Illuminations*, ed. with intro. by Hannah Arendt (London: Fontana, 1970), p. 263.

[142] Homi Bhabha, *The Location of Cultures* (London and New York: Routledge, 1994), p. 235. ('How Newness Enters the World').

salist' aesthetics were exported to the periphery.[143] One aim of the present book, beyond charting the development of a particular literary genre, is to rethink the spatial co-ordinates of European romanticism in these global and historical terms. To do so via the fragile, soon-to-be eclipsed, 'curious' tradition of travel writing permits an understanding of European discourse in a more contingent, exploratory, and transitive relation to distant cultures. In his uncompleted 'Arcades project', the Marxist/modernist *curioso* Walter Benjamin conjured with the concept of 'dialectical images' to allegorize the 'petrified' commodities of early capitalism in the direction of a utopian meaning.[144] It is hoped that the 'curious' travel narratives studied here might offer an analogous resource for imagining how difference might be differently conceived.

---

[143] But for an illuminating account of how modernist aesthetics were appropriated for nationalist ends in British India, see Partha Mitter, *Art and Nationalism in Colonial India 1850–1922* (Cambridge University Press, 1994), esp. ch. 9.

[144] See Susan Buck-Morss, *The Dialectics of Seeing: Walter Benjamin and the Arcades Project* (Cambridge, Mass., and London: MIT Press, 1989).

2

Curious Narrative and the Problem of Credit: James Bruce's *Travels to Discover the Source of the Nile*

Curiosity and the Dynamics of Scale

> A great traveller, 'tho in the same chamber, will pass for a very extraordinary person; as a *Greek* medal, even in our cabinet, is always esteem'd a valuable curiosity.
>
> David Hume, *Treatise of Human Nature*, 1739–40

In the late summer and autumn of 1774 London society was gripped by a mania for curiosity. Writing in her journal in that year, the young novelist Fanny Burney noted that 'the present *Lyon* of the Times . . . is Omy, the Native of Otaheite;—& next to him, the present Object is Mr Bruce, a Gentleman who has been Abroad 12 years, & spent 4 of them in Abyssinia, & places in Africa, where no English man before has gained admission. His adventures are very marvellous.'[1] Mai (or Omai as his name was incorrectly transliterated) was a young Polynesian brought back from the Pacific on board Captain Furneaux's *Adventure,* which had accompanied Cook on his second voyage. He was indeed lionized in England, being presented to the king and queen at Kew, dining with the members of the Royal Society, painted by Sir Joshua Reynolds, and entertained by Lord Sandwich at his country seat at Hinchinbrook. English high society considered Mai to be the embodiment of the noble savage, but with the emphasis upon the 'noble' rather than the 'savage'.

The second 'lyon' mentioned by Burney was the Scots traveller James Bruce of Kinnaird, who, just prior to the arrival of the *Adventure,* had returned to England after ten years' travelling in North Africa, including a three-year sojourn at the unknown court of Gonder in Abyssinia, in which country he claimed to have discovered the true source of the Nile, veiled in obscurity since

---

[1] *The Early Journals and Lettes of Fanny Burney*, Vol. II (1774–7), ed. by Lars E. Troide (Oxford: Clarendon Press, 1990), p. 44.

ancient times. Bruce, a scion of the minor Scottish aristocracy, had used his political connections in London to obtain the post of British consul in Algiers, where he had improved his Arabic and prepared himself for an expedition into the African interior. His initial purpose (like Cook's first *Endeavour* voyage) had been to observe the 1769 Transit of Venus and study and draw classical ruins; later he was persuaded—in part by the French naturalist Buffon—to undertake a search for the source of the Nile. Unlike most of the other travellers discussed in this book, with the notable exception of Humboldt, Bruce's travels were self-funded. Despite his landed background, Bruce's family wealth was based on new capital: in November 1760 he had signed a lucrative contract with the directors of the Carron Iron Foundry (one of the first modern industrial plants, situated near Larbert, in Central Scotland) to supply them with coal from the rich seams under his estate at neighbouring Kinnaird.

Bruce arrived in London just as the dust was settling from the scandal surrounding Hawkesworth's *Account* of Cook's first voyage, published the previous year. On the strength of initial public acclamation, Bruce was elected a member of the Royal Society, and (like Mai) was presented to the king and fêted by polite society. Bruce temporarily stole the fire of the Pacific navigators (although the return of Furneaux's *Adventure* in turn overshadowed his fame); as Horace Walpole wrote in July 1774:

Africa is, indeed, coming into fashion. There is just returned a Mr Bruce, who has lived three years in the court of Abyssinia, and breakfasted every morning with the maids of honour on live oxen. Otaheite and Mr Banks are quite forgotten . . . Oh yes, we shall have negro butchers, and French cooks will be laid aside.[2]

In a sense, Walpole's irony encompassed the whole Bruce phenomenon. In August and September 1774 James Boswell, writing for the *London Magazine*, scooped Bruce's 'marvellous' adventures, praising the Scots traveller's 'curiosity and spirit of adventure [which] prompted him to undertake a series of travels, which must be contemplated with astonishment'.[3] The August issue accepted Bruce's 'sublime' claim to have discovered the true source of the Nile, quoting Lucan and adding that 'Mr Bruce may exult in having attained to what imperial Caesar so ardently wished for in vain'.[4] The *London Magazine* 'temporalized' both Bruce's Abyssinia and Banks's Tahiti in terms of the European

[2] To Sir Horace Mann, 10 July 1774. *The Yale Edition of Horace Walpole's Correspondence*, ed. by W. S. Lewis, 48 vols. (London and New Haven, CT: Oxford University Press and Yale University Press 1937–83), 24, viii. 21.
[3] *London Magazine or Gentleman's Monthly Intelligencer*, xliii (August 1774), 388 (henceforth LM). Boswell 'interviewed' Bruce in Edinburgh in August 1774; Bruce was, in fact, his distant relative. J. M. Reid, *Traveller Extraordinary: The Life of James Bruce of Kinnaird* (London: The History Book Club, 1968), p. 288.
[4] LM, 389.

feudal system,[5] implying, not without a hint of satire, that Bruce, who claimed descent from Robert Bruce, the medieval victor of Bannockburn, had found himself quite at home in such a feudal world. It detailed the various campaigns in which he had fought in the service of the crumbling Ras Mikail Sehul's regime before his defeat by rebel forces at the battle of Sarbakusa in 1771.

It was, however, the September 1774 issue of the *London Magazine* that first published the 'breakfasting on live oxen' story reported by Walpole. Abyssinia and Tahiti might be comparable as 'feudal' societies but what disturbed the English public was the fact that the religion of the former (unlike the naturalistic 'deism' of the latter) 'is a kind of a coarse Christianity, with a considerable mixture of Judaism'.[6] Nevertheless, the article continued,

the light of the gospel beams upon them very faintly, for they are a fierce and a cruel people: a strong instance of which is their manner of eating. Not satisfied with devouring raw flesh, their custom is to eat collops cut from live animals, which they tear to pieces with their teeth while warm, and palpitating with vital motion.

The *London Magazine* followed this up with a revolting narrative of the Abyssinian 'Brinde feast' or 'savage repast [which] puts one in mind of Virgil's description of the Cyclops' (ibid.), an account considerably elaborated in Bruce's own *Travels* published sixteen years later, in 1790.[7]

Initial excitement about Bruce's account of Abyssinia rapidly gave way to scepticism about the truth of his claims, focused bizarrely enough upon the raw beef story. The refusal to accept this particular thread in Bruce's account seems to have unravelled the credibility of the whole fabric, collapsing his 'astonishing' sublimity into empty hyperbole. It is hard to explain exactly why this should have been so, although in the eighteenth-century dietary customs were heavily overdetermined as indices of savagery, civility, or corruption, and the 'raw/cooked' opposition traditionally served to distinguish the savage state from the civil. It was evidently easier for the public to credit the account of New Zealand cannibalism brought back by the *Resolution* and *Adventure* the same year, particularly after what James Burney described as Cook's 'horrid and undeniable proofs' of anthropophagy.[8] Cannibalism was the *antipodes* of civilized diet, but at least cannibals carefully cooked their meat. Perhaps what concerned the public was the fact that the Abyssinian dietary custom reported by

---

[5] LM, 390.

[6] LM (Sept. 1774), 429. The dominant religious party in Ethiopia adhered to the Monophysite theology that Christ's human nature had become perfect through union with the divine.

[7] Ibid.

[8] Neil Rennie, *Far-Fetched Facts*, p. 130. Fanny Burney's brother James had served as an officer on the *Adventure*. See Gananath Obeyesekere, '"British Cannibals": Contemplation of an Event in the Death and Resurrection of Captain James Cook, Explorer', *Critical Inquiry*, 18 (Summer 1992), 630–54 for a thoughtful account of the incident which suggests that 'large-scale anthropophagy was a reaction to the European presence' (p. 653).

Bruce (who strongly denied that Abyssinians were cannibals) was, like their religion, a 'curious' parody, rather than an antithesis, of civilized—and particularly English—eating habits. In the decade of the rebellion of the American colonies this was particularly problematic, the failure of English virility being frequently represented in terms of the luxurious refinements of an imported French and Italian culinary regime.[9] As 'A New Song, to the Tune of the Roast-Beef of Old England' nostalgically put it (published in the same August number of the *London Magazine* as the account of Bruce's travels): 'When mighty roast-beef was the Englishman's food, | It ennobled our veins, & enliven'd our blood, | Our soldiers were brave, & our courtiers were good'.[10] Bruce's own brand of Abyssinian medievalism seemed to parody rather than reinforce this English ideal by its grotesque literalism (the fact that he was a Scotsman can hardly have helped). Rather than metaphorically 'enlivening their blood' by consuming roast beef, the Abyssinians quite literally gorged the 'tepid blood of the miserable animals, whose lowings and groanings, through violence of anguish, served for a dinner bell'.[11] At the beginning of a decade which saw the loss of Britain's first empire this seems to have played on the collective anxieties of the travel reading public.

I shall have more to say about Bruce's live beefsteaks later in the chapter; my remarks here are intended only as reflections upon the growing scepticism concerning his initial claims in the mid-1770s. Quite apart from the immediate historical circumstances of Britain's imperial crisis, the public's response to Bruce exemplifies the 'paradox of attachment', as if realizing David Hume's speculation (in the *Enquiries)*, that 'should a traveller, returning from a far country, bring us an account of men, wholly different from any with whom we were ever acquainted . . . we should immediately . . . prove him a liar, with the same certainty as if he had stuffed his narration with stories of centaurs and dragons, miracles and prodigies'.[12] Vicemisus Knox—as we have seen—preferred to recommend that 'incommensurable' reports of this kind should be simply suppressed inasmuch as they were subversive of public morals. As an instance of eighteenth-century ethnography, what is interesting about the 'live beef' story is the fact that, faced by an account of an exotic custom which they found

---

[9] The link with foreign diet is evident in the contemporary use of the term 'macaroni' to denote an effeminate man.

[10] LM (Aug. 1774), 400.

[11] LM (Sept. 1774), 429. For a contrasting interpretation, see Tim Youngs, *Travellers in Africa*, pp. 63–4, who reads Bruce's account as 'a parody of cultural consumption, [which] has the result of normalising British customs'.

[12] *Enquiries Concerning Human Understanding and Concerning the Principles of Morals, reprinted from 1777 edition, with intro and analytical index by L. A. Selby-Bigge*, 3rd edn., with text revised and notes by P. H. Nidditch (Oxford: Clarendon Press, 1975), p. 84 (*Enquiry*, sec.8, pt.1, par.65). Hume's example, however, concerns a utopian rather than a dystopian traveller's account.

morally unacceptable, the public preferred to condemn the reporter as a travel liar than turn their disgust upon the Abyssinians themselves (presumably Bruce's detractors argued that the Abyssinians roasted, broiled, or stewed their beef, having butchered their cattle first like everybody else). What the public's disbelief reveals is both the fragile credit afforded to eighteenth-century travellers, and the strength of the enlightenment's belief in universal moral norms.

It had been relatively easy for critics to reject the morally unacceptable truths reported on Cook's first voyage by blaming Hawkesworth, who had not been an eyewitness to the events he described (although, as we saw in Chapter 1, Banks came in for his share of ridicule). As Boswell put it, in conversation with Cook himself: 'Why Sir,' said I, 'Hawkesworth has used your narrative as a London tavern keeper does wine. He has *brewed* it.'[13] An outraged John Wesley was of the opinion that Hawkesworth's subversive fables of savagery might be acceptable to a Hume or a Voltaire, but that he could 'not but rank this narrative with that of Robinson Crusoe'.[14] Wesley's complaint that Hawkesworth 'read like a novel' may have been disingenuous, given that, as Lennard Davis has pointed out, eighteenth-century novels no less than eighteenth-century travel accounts (both of which anxiously distinguished themselves from 'fables and romances') were expected to fulfil two quite different criteria of truthfulness, simultaneously satisfying the demands of what Davis calls 'actual' and 'ethical' verisimilitude.[15] Whilst readers of *Robinson Crusoe* or *Pamela* needed to believe that they were reading 'actual' narratives (true stories rather than fables, their veracity based upon a rhetoric of 'naive empiricism'), 'ethical' verisimilitude demanded that the world they represented conformed to universal moral norms.

Given that Bruce, unlike Hawkesworth, was at once the sole protagonist, witness, and narrator of his own adventures, his personal veracity was directly impugned by this public refusal of credit (although Hawkesworth allegedly died of shame following the reception of the *Account of the Voyages*). Writing to his friend the poet William Mason, Horace Walpole described a dinner party at which 'somebody asked Mr Bruce if the Abyssinians had any musical instruments? "Musical instruments! said he, and paused—yes, I think I remember one—lyre." George Selwyn whispered to his neighbour, "I am sure there is one less since he came out of the country." '[16] Dr Johnson was likewise unimpressed by Bruce: as the *Gentleman's Magazine* reported tartly in 1789, 'when [Dr Johnson] first conversed with Mr Bruce, the Abyssinian traveller, he was very much inclined to believe that he had been there; but that he had afterwards

---

[13] Quoted in Rennie, p. 108.   [14] Ibid., p. 101.

[15] Lennard Davis, *Factual Fictions: The Origins of the English Novel* (New York: Columbia University Press, 1983), pp. 111–13.

[16] Quoted in Percy Adams, *Travellers and Travel Liars*, p. 211.

altered his opinion'.[17] In fact, Johnson was no more inclined to believe Bruce than his compatriot James Macpherson, putative 'translator' of the ancient Gaelic epic *Ossian*: in some respects the reputation of Bruce's *Travels* and Macpherson's *Ossian* ran a parallel course, as we shall see. The fact that Johnson's first published work had been a translation of Father Jerome Lobo's *Voyage to Abyssinia*, in 1735 (Abyssinia had also, of course, provided a setting for Johnson's oriental tale *Rasselas*, which portrayed the country in a very different light from Bruce), and in consequence he was regarded as an 'Abyssinian expert', added weight to Johnson's harsh judgement of Bruce. Bruce sought revenge on Johnson when he finally got round to publishing the account of his travels in an attempt to clear his name.

In a facetious article in the *London Magazine* in February 1775 entitled 'On the Advantages which *Great-Britain* may derive from the Discoveries of Travellers' James Boswell, whose initial interest in Bruce had also now turned to incredulity, ridiculed what he regarded as merely 'curious' travel narratives on the grounds that they could not compete with fables and romances: 'surely the *Arabian Nights Entertainment*, and the *Adventures of Jack the Giant Killer*, are as entertaining as *Hawkesworth's Collection of Voyages*, or the *Travels of Mr Bruce*'. Authors of such accounts might do just as well in a 'snug apartment in London, with pen, ink and paper' as risking their necks by field and flood. 'Utility therefore is required' Boswell continued, 'and how much has been, or may be of that, I would humbly consider'.[18] Utility was, of course, also being required of the mid-eighteenth-century novel by Dr Johnson in his famous *Rambler* essay, and in his remarks on *Ossian*: '[the novel's] province is to bring about natural events by easy means, and to keep up curiosity without the help of wonders'.[19] At the same time, however, imaginative literature in the 1760s was renegotiating its relationship with romance, signalled by Horace Walpole's gothic tale *The Castle of Otranto* (1764). In fact Walpole indulged both gigantism and 'wonder' (particularly as the first edition passed itself off as an 'authentic' medieval document) to a far greater extent than either Hawkesworth or Bruce. Walpole's Preface declared defiantly, contra the demands of utility, that 'the great resources of fancy have been dammed up, by a strict adherence to common life' and proposed in his gothic romance to let them flow free.[20]

[17] Quoted in Percy Adams, p. 211. See also Thomas M. Curley, *Samuel Johnson and the Literature of Travel* (Athens, Georgia: Georgia University Press, 1976), pp. 23–4.
[18] LM, XLIV (Feb. 1775), 74. The article was signed 'Numicius'. On Boswell's own travel journals, see Denis Porter, *Haunted Journeys*, ch. 1 'Uses of the Grand Tour: Boswell and his Contemporaries'.
[19] *Yale Edition of the Works of S. Johnson*, ed. by W. J. Bate and A. B. Strauss, 16 vols. (New Haven and London: Yale University Press, 1969), iii. 19.
[20] Horace Walpole, Preface to the 2nd edn. of *The Castle of Otranto, Three Gothic Novels*, ed. by E. F. Bleiler (New York: Dover Publications, 1966), p. 21.

Boswell, in identifying the merely curious travel account as a form of romance, satirically conflated all the recent 'wonders' of the genre and imagined them being turned to practical use (in a manner reminiscent of Swift's satire on the projectors in the third book of *Gulliver's Travels*). Captain Byron's Patagonian giants would be enlisted as London night-watchmen; the Tahitian ignorance of metal might result in the abolition of metal coinage and the inauguration of 'banks of air'; the practice of eating raw meat might save on coal consumption; and British cavalry regiments might be mounted on bulls, which could provide the soldiers with victuals as well as transport. (In a revealing comment, Boswell added that the bull-cavalry might also serve as a secret weapon against the rebellious Bostonians.)[21] Boswell's extraction of use-value from the 'curious' idiosyncrasies of recent travelogues was, of course, intended as a literary joke, but, as we shall see, it also participated in the demand for the rationalization and professionalization of travel writing in order to conform with the demands of the Latourian 'cycle of accumulation' discussed in Chapter 1. At the same time, it perhaps helps to explain the fascination of the curious travel account for the romantic generation, Walpole's heirs, as in Coleridge's comment on Bartram's *Travels*. Writers like Coleridge would appreciate precisely the *inutility* of the curious travel account as a model for the autonomous imagination, as the romantic aesthetic struggled to free itself from the didacticism of neo-classical, Johnsonian, precept.

Despite his concern with precise territorial measurement, Bruce's failure to stabilize his 'immutable mobiles' by rendering them commensurable with European norms resulted in a grotesque distortion of scale in which the world of myth and magic—in generic terms, of romance—usurped rational credibility. Bruce, by his own account, was perceived to have exchanged his civil identity for that of a savage, and moreover a gigantic savage. This is evident in Fanny Burney's burlesque description of the man she satirically dubbed 'his Abyssinian majesty'. (Related to a certain Mrs Strange, a family friend of the Burneys, Bruce was a regular visitor at their household while residing in London in the mid-1770s.) Both Bruce's claim of royal descent, and his height of 6 foot 4 inches mark Burney's hyperbolic description 'His Figure is almost Gigantic! He is the Tallest man I ever saw' (in another version, Burney inserted the word 'gratis' here, comparing Bruce to a fairground attraction) '& exceeding well made, neither too fat or lean in proportion to his amazing height' [*sic*].[22] Whilst Burney consistently represents Mai as a paragon of 'domesticated' noble savagery, particularly dressed up in his 'suit of Manchester velvet, Lined with white satten, a *Bag*, lace Ruffles, & a very handsome sword which the King had given to him', Bruce by contrast manifests civility in a feral condition.[23] As she noted in March

[21] LM (Feb. 1775), 75–6.   [22] Fanny Burney, *Early Journals*, pp. 44–5.   [23] Ibid., p. 60.

1775: 'Haughty by Nature, [Bruce's] extraordinary Travels, & perhaps his long Residence among savages, have contributed to render him one of the most imperious of men'.[24] Although by the canons of eighteenth-century culture Bruce, in relation to Mai, represented the 'curioso' rather than the 'curiosity', the roles too easily reversed, and the two men, traveller and 'travellee',[25] came to usurp each other's identities. Appropriately enough, as the *General Evening Post* reported, Bruce was one of the first men to whom Mai was introduced, dining with him in the company of the Duke of Gloucester in July 1774.[26]

In a conversation at the Burneys' house the following year, Bruce ruefully identified Mai with his own predicament as a discredited traveller:

this poor fellow, Omai, has lost all his Time; they have taught him Nothing; He will only pass for a consummate Lyar when he returns; for how can he make them believe half the Things he will tell them? He can give them no idea of our Houses, Carriages, or any thing that will appear probable.[27]

The decontextualization suffered by the traveller makes credit no more easy of attainment in savage than in civil society. But what is striking about this comment is the straightforward manner of Bruce's self-identification with Mai, without any attempt to rescue a distinction; their common plight as discredited travellers has evidently cancelled out those cultural difference(s) which might have been thought to distinguish them.

What is even more ironic about Bruce's comment here is that, like many of his other bright ideas, it is a plagiarism from another writer, in this case from Diderot's *Supplement to Bougainville's Voyage*, serialized in Grimm's *Correspondence* in 1773 and 1774, which Bruce presumably read on his return journey through France.[28] Diderot's mouthpiece 'B' argued that the Tahitian Aotourou (Mai's French 'counterpart' brought back to France by Bougainville in 1771) would be treated as a liar if he ever returned home to tell his tale, because the Tahitians 'aimeront mieux prendre Aotourou pour un menteur que de nous croire si fous'.[29] Aotourou (like Mai) thus perfectly mirrors Bruce, except that in his case the cultural location of virtue has been reversed from civil to 'natural' society. The Tahitians prefer to brand Aotourou a liar than accept that a society as depraved as modern France or England can possibly exist, just as the English brand Bruce a liar rather than accept that a society of savages as depraved as the Abyssinians can exist. Such is his spleen against his 'civilized' detractors

[24] Ibid., p. 82.
[25] I borrow 'travellee' from Mary Louise Pratt, who, apologizing for its clumsiness, explains that it is based on an analogy with the linguistic term 'addressee' and the narratological term 'narratee'. She defines it as meaning 'persons travelled to (or on) by a traveller, receptors of travel' (*Imperial Eyes* p. 136 and note, p. 242). Mai is, of course, also a traveller as well as a travellee.
[26] Rennie, p. 126.   [27] Fanny Burney, p. 92.   [28] Rennie p. 119.   [29] Ibid., p. 124.

that Bruce (whose values are in almost every other respect quite distinct from Diderot's) is willing for a moment to identify with the viewpoint of his 'savage' *alter ego* as vicariously expressed by Diderot's 'B'.

Fanny Burney's diary goes on to describe how a possible solution to the traveller's problem of decontextualization was promptly suggested by (the aptly named) Mrs Strange;

Troth, then, they should give [Mai] a set of Doll's Things, & a Baby's House, to shew them; he should have every Thing in miniature, by way of model: Dressed Babies, Cradles, Lying in Women, & a' sort of pratty Things!

Burney found this idea replete with 'humorous ingenuity' and 'really believed that it would be well worth being tried'.[30] When the *Resolution* returned Mai to Tahiti in late 1777, he was landed on shore mounted on a charger and (in a fine instance of temporalization) wearing a suit of pseudo-medieval armour presented to him by Lord Sandwich. Rather than agonizing about his travel credit, however, according to the surgeon's mate Samwell, he 'act[ed] the part of a merry Andrew, parading about in ludicrous Masks & different Dresses to the great admiration of the Rabble'.[31] When Cook's plans for Mai on Tahiti failed to materialize, he was settled on Huanine in the nearby Society Islands, where a house was built for him 'to secure his property in'.[32] But among the useless trinkets and (more serviceable) guns and cutlasses with which he had been presented was 'a box of Toys which when exposed to publick view seemed to please the gazing multitude very much'. Rather less domestic than Mrs Strange's original conception, these miniatures included 'whole Regiments of Soldiers, Coaches, Horses and The Figure of almost Every creature we know of'.[33] The contrast with his *alter ego* Bruce is again instructive, as Bruce and Mai travesty the conventional eighteenth-century aesthetics of the sublime and beautiful. If Abyssinian savagery is metonymically represented in Georgian London by the gigantism of Bruce, then metropolitan society concomitantly presents itself on the savage periphery in the inverse form of the miniature. Moreover, if Bruce embodies a gigantic, ogre-like masculinity, Mai's credit is made to depend upon a miniaturized, feminized, and domesticated simulacrum of civility. One can clearly see here the inverted symmetry of eighteenth-century aesthetics of distance: the giant for the toy; the sublime for the picturesque; the feral European for the civilized native.[34]

---

[30] Burney, p. 92.   [31] Rennie, p. 131.   [32] Ibid., p. 132.   [33] Ibid.

[34] The dynamics of scale may not be particular to Western culture. Carsten Niebuhr described the astonishment of Arabs viewing insects magnified in his microscope: 'A servant, who saw one of those magnified insects, said that they were the growth of Europe, and that those of Arabia were, in comparison, exceedingly diminutive' [*Travels through Arabia and Other Countries in the East*, trans. by Robert Heron, 2 vols. 1792, i. 258] I have suggested that magnified scale serves in general as a metaphor for distance, in time or space.

Exaggerated dynamics of scale—what we might call 'romance' dimensional-ity—seem to replace the calibrated uniformity sought for by the 'naïve empiri-cism' of both the contemporary novel and 'geographical narrative' (The *London Magazine*, for instance, had described Bruce as 'Nec visu facilis nec dictu affa-bilis ulli'—neither easy to look at nor kindly in conversation—actually a quota-tion from Virgil's description of the gigantic Cyclops Polyphemus).[35] In this respect the parodic world of *Gulliver's Travels*, with its 'big men' and 'little men', seems to have been a more accurate comment upon eighteenth-century travel writing than the precise observation and measurement urged in 'instruc-tions for travellers' issued by the Royal Society and similar bodies. Precise measurement was an obsessive concern for eighteenth-century travel writing: not only did it constitute one paramount form of evidence for the traveller, it also stabilized the distant mobile in relation to a universal European standard, as denounced by Blake in the *Book of Urizen* (1794): 'One curse, one weight, one measure | One King, one god, one Law'.[36] As Susan Stewart argues in *On Longing*, however, ultimately 'the body is our mode of perceiving scale and, as the body of the other, becomes our antithetical mode of stating conventions of symmetry and balance on the one hand, and the grotesque and the dispropor-tionate on the other'.[37] The discourse of eighteenth-century travel writing is torn in two directions: between 'useful' observation and measurement; and a 'curious' dynamics of scale haunted by the aesthetics of distance and the (suppressed) rhetoric of wonder. For the polite readership represented by Fanny Burney, Bruce's gigantism linked him not only to the world of romance and medieval kingship but also to the carnivalesque savagery of his own Abyssinians. Gigantism (like Hawkesworth's endorsement of Byron's Patagon-ian giants) figured 'archaic' curiosity, in which the distant retained its exagger-ated scale rather than being 'mobilized' and translated into the terms of a combinable abstract standard. Bruce's gigantism conceals a hidden, mythic, agenda at odds with rationalization, for 'the giant, from Leviathan to the side-show freak, is a mixed category; a violator of boundary and rule; and over-abundance of the natural and hence an affront to cultural systems'.[38] Conversely, the 'civilizing process' of Mai works by miniaturization, childhood in the place of savagery, the domestic interior in the place of the purely public world of the savage. Bruce's 'gigantification' by contemporary society seems to have gone hand in hand with the idea that his account of Abyssinia was also a 'whopper'—a lie.

[35] Reid, *Traveller Extraordinary*, p. 290.
[36] *Blake's Poetry and Designs*, ed. by Mary Johnson and John Grant (New York and London: Norton Critical Editions, 1979) ii. 39–40, p. 145.
[37] Susan Stewart, *On Longing: Narratives of the Miniature, the Gigantic, the Souvenir, the Collec-tion* (Durham and London: Duke University Press, 1993), p. xii.
[38] Stewart, p. 73.

Publication

Embittered by the public's scepticism, Bruce retreated to his estate at Kinnaird in Stirlingshire to oversee his coal mines, lick his wounded pride, and—after the death of his second wife—to attempt to vindicate his claims by composing the narrative of his travels, published in 1790 as the 3,000 page, five-volume quarto *Travels to Discover the Source of the Nile in the Years 1768, 1769, 1770, 1771, 1772, and 1773.*[39] Bruce's *Travels*—an instance, as contemporaries noted, of textual gigantism which mirrored the mythic gigantism of its author—was probably the most widely read, cited, and anthologized travel book of the period after Hawkesworth's *Account of the Voyages*, although much more maligned.[40] The book was a massive attempt by Bruce to win back his lost credit, and as such claimed to be a 'transparent' account of his adventures in Abyssinia. (In the third edition of his *Travels*, Bruce's posthumous editor, Alexander Murray, detailed his 'dozen small [note] books of duodecimo size, suited to the pocket' as vouchers for the text's authenticity.[41]) In conformity with the norms of eighteenth-century travel writing, Bruce's Preface insisted that

the materials collected upon the spot were very full, and seldom deferred to be set down beyond the day wherein the event described happened, but oftener, when speeches and arguments were to be mentioned, they were noted the instant afterwards . . . I can assure the reader these speeches and conversations are absolutely real, and not the fabrication of after hours.   (i. lxv–lxvi)[42]

[39] 5 vols. (Edinburgh: J. Ruthven, 1790). The first edition was expensive at £5 5*s*. Bruce credited Daines Barrington (i., p. lxv) with having encouraged him to publish the account of his travels. Barrington was an antiquarian and naturalist who prompted the publication of his friend Gilbert White's *Natural History of Selborne*. He also brokered the acquisition by Sir Ashton Levere's museum of many of the 'curiosities' acquired by Cook in the Pacific. See Gascoigne, *Joseph Banks*, pp. 134–5.

[40] 'The book was immensely successful. Most of the edition was sold within thirty-two hours. It was translated into French and German. Cheap printed summaries were published', Reid, p. 305.

[41] *Travels to Discover the Source of the Nile, 3rd edition, to which is prefixed a life of the Author*, 8 vols. (Edinburgh, 1813), i., p. ccclxiii. Murray described the log-books of Bruce's Bolognese 'secretary' Luigi Balugani as 'regular, [they] may be termed diaries of the road and rates of travelling', whilst he found Bruce's to be 'more miscellaneous' (ibid.). After the Italian's death Bruce had to take over recording temperatures, longitudes, etc. himself. On his dangerous return journey across the Sennar Desert he tore out long strips of folio paper which he stitched together, and, according to Murray, 'kept his ink fixed to his girdle; and, like Caesar on a different element, carried his commentaries in his breast or hand' (i., p. ccclxviii). Remarkably enough, Bruce had drawn money in Gonder from his London bankers via the East India Company's office at Jiddah. Sounding almost like James Macpherson touting the 'authentic' manuscripts of Ossian, in the *Travels* Bruce cited the bank-draft for 1,000 crowns which financed his return journey via Sennar as evidence of his having 'been there'; 'A Bill drawn from Gondar is a very great curiosity when arrived in London; it should be now upon the file in the shop of my very worthy and honourable friends Messrs Drummond & Co at Charing Cross. It was the only piece of writing of any kind which found its way to its intended destination' (*Travels*, iv., 252).

[42] Like Richardson's heroine in *Pamela*, her journal and writing materials hidden in her underclothes, writing to the moment is the *sine qua non* of the traveller's credit. Like the 20th-century anthropologist with camera and notebook always to hand, the 18th-century European traveller was always

But the fact that it took Bruce sixteen years finally to prepare his travel notes for publication did not do him any favours in an age of 'universal scepticism', as the *Analytical Review* put it.[43] As Alexander Murray conceded, the time lag between Bruce's travels and his publication was such that his travel narrative 'resembled more that of an old veteran by his parlour fire in a winter evening, than the result of fresh and accurate observation'.[44]

Although Bruce's was the only name to appear on the title page, the book—like the travels themselves—was in fact a collaborative enterprise, notwith-standing Bruce's attempt to give the impression that he was the exclusive protagonist and author of both. Bruce had been accompanied by the Bolognese artist Luigi Balugani in the capacity of 'secretary', although the Italian had died of fever in Gonder before (or so at least Bruce claimed) the expedition to dis-cover the source of the Nile.[45] In a parallel instance, in May 1788 he hired the young Benjamin Latrobe—a Moravian minister and future premier architect of the young American republic—as amanuensis to sort through his and Balugani's notebooks and to assist with the composition of the book itself. Bruce's treatment of both his secretary and amanuensis was ungenerous to say the least, feeding subsequent charges of egotism and patrician monomania.[46]

Bruce's *Travels* opened with an extremely fulsome dedication to George III in which the author claimed the prestige of having achieved 'the first discovery attempted in your Majesty's reign' (i. np) and aligned himself with the patriotic principles of Burkean conservatism. His travels had been informed by 'that noble persuasion, the foundation of all charity, not that all men are equal, but that they are all brethren; and that being superior to the savage in every acquire-ment, it was for that very reason their duty to set the example of mildness, com-passion, and long-suffering to a fellow-creature' (ibid.). (One might detect here a belated attempt to disavow the equation between Bruce the traveller and the savages among whom he had travelled.) Bruce modestly claimed that his book would 'fill a great chasm in the history of the universe. It is not intended to

scribbling and sketching. Travel writing 'to the moment' could be as dangerous as writing letters in novels. (See, for example, George Forster, *Journey from Bengal to England* (1798), i. 212–13).

[43] *Analytical Review*, ix (March 1791), 248.

[44] Quoted in J. J. Halls, *Life and Correspondence of Henry Salt*, 2 vols. (London, 1834), i. 288.

[45] In fact Balugani died in the following year, February 1771, at Gonder. On the evidence of a nar-rative in the sixth notebook, entitled 'Viaggio alle Fontane delle Nilo, fatto nel mese di Ottob., 1770, del illustrissimo Cavaliere Signior Giacomo Bruce', Balugani accompanied Bruce on the trip to Gish, but the latter later suppressed the fact. Balugani's account could, of course, have provided the vital witness to Bruce's claim, had he been willing to share the glory. But, as J. M. Reid indicates, he 'could not use [Balugani's notebook] against London sceptics and critics because of his apparently deliber-ate misdating' (*Traveller Extraordinary*, p. 186). Cf. also Miles Bredin, *The Pale Abyssinian: A Life of James Bruce, African Explorer and Adventurer* (London: HarperCollins, 2000), pp. 163–4.

[46] Reid, p. 303. Bredin, however, questions Latrobe's probity in this matter (ibid., p. 258).

resemble the generality of modern travels, the agreeable and rational amusement of one vacant day, it is calculated to employ a greater space of time' (i. lxvii).

To its detractors, Bruce's narrative combined the qualities of pedantry and licentiousness characteristic of the 'curious' eighteenth-century travel account, quite distinct in character from the approved style of travel writing beginning to emerge in the 1790s, and exemplified by Mungo Park's highly successful *Travels in the Interior District of Africa* (1799). The 'moment' of Bruce's *Travels* is really two decades earlier, in the 1770s of Hawkesworth's *Account* or Patrick Brydone's *Tour in Sicily*. Its layout and handling of narrative development is tortuous even for a literary genre associated with the miscellaneous, anecdotal ordering of discourse. Much of Bruce's account of his transactions with the inhabitants of the regions through which he travelled is based, as we shall see, on reported dialogues,[47] making sections of the narrative read like a novel. C. F. Beckingham points out that Bruce's *Travels* actually

comprise[s] three books which might have been published separately, the story of his own travels, a history of Ethiopia from the earliest times to 1769, and a number of essays on very varied topics, such as polygamy, the origins of civilisation, the untruthfulness of Portuguese writers on Ethiopia, and the effect of the Nile on the level of the land in Egypt.[48]

In his first volume Bruce described how, under Lord Halifax's patronage, he had been appointed British consul at Algiers in 1763, where he prepared for his travels by studying Arabic and medicine, and mastering the topography and geography of North Africa. Bruce's initial plan was to conduct a picturesque tour of the Roman ruins of Algiers, Tunis, and Lybia, as well as to visit the archaeological sites of Egypt, Balbec, and Palmyra, aided by Luigi Balugani and the 'camera obscura' which he had brought from London. Like Pococke, his textual authorities were the classical geographers Diodorus Siculus and Herodotus, the Portuguese Jesuits who had visited Abyssinia in the seventeenth century, and more recent travellers like Dr Thomas Shaw, whom he treated for the most part with immoderate scorn.

---

[47] This confirms Percy Adams's point that dialogue is a form 'encountered more often than one might think', in the 18th-century travel account (*Travel Literature and the Evolution of the Novel* (Lexington: University Press of Kentucky, 1983), p. 44).

[48] *Bruce's Travels to Discover the Source of the Nile*, selected and edited by C. F. Beckingham (Edinburgh University Press, 1964), p. 18. Although Bruce and Latrobe 'processed' the narrative to the extent of excerpting the notes on natural history as an appendix, the text in most other respects conforms to the miscellaneous nature of 18th-century travel accounts which jump spasmodically between narrative and dissertation. For example, the long history of 'the line of Solomon' and the Abyssinian kings is inserted just at the point of Bruce's arrival on the coast of Abyssinia at Mits'iwa, interrupting the narrative of the journey, and the 'essays' on various subjects are scattered throughout obstructing any easy sequential movement.

After a series of lengthy dissertations on Egyptian antiquity, the history of Abyssinian commerce with India, and the 'Annals of Abyssinia' which compose the first two volumes, in the third volume Bruce finally gets down to the business of narrating his journey to Gonder in the Abyssinian interior, after travelling down the Red Sea from Egypt to the port of Mits'iwa, and his two expeditions to discover the source of the Blue Nile at Gish. Bruce proudly described his successful cultural disguise, essential to the eighteenth-century European land traveller, 'weaker' than the inhabitants of the lands through which he passed. Arriving in Cairo, he had grown a beard and adopted Egyptian clothing, working on the improvement of his already excellent Arabic 'I soon was considered as a *Fakir*, or *Dervich*, moderately skilled in magic, and who cared for nothing but study and books' (i. 24-5).[49] Unlike Mungo Park or Johann Lewis Burckhardt in the years after the formation of the African Association, Bruce did not travel as a representative of the British 'exploration establishment',[50] but was largely self-motivated as well as self-financing. Bruce and Balugani's journey would have been impossible without 'firmans' or passports from local dignitaries like the Sherif of Mecca, the Naib of Mits'iwa, the Patriarch of Cairo, and the King of Sennar, the principal ruler of the Southern Sudan. To obtain such documents, he needed to translate his 'curious' motives for travelling into terms which were acceptable in terms of indigenous culture.[51] Arriving on the coast of Abyssinia, he assumed the identity of El Hakim Yagoube (Arabic for James), an itinerant Syrian physician, a profession which would provide him with an entrée into the smallpox-afflicted family of Ras Mikail Sehul of Tigray at Gonder in 1770.

Both the persona of the wandering Dervish and the travelling physician provided a cover for the rather ostentatious practices of European 'curiosity' in the

[49] In Yemen a disguised Carsten Niebuhr boasted that 'at Dsjobla a man saluted me by the name of Hadsji Achmed, taking me for an old acquaintance'. Carsten Niebuhr, *Travels through Arabia* (i. 303). But success was by no means assured, and depended upon commanding local intelligence. William Browne (who had followed Bruce's tracks from the confluence of the Nile in 1792) was murdered in Persia in 1813 because he was mistakenly wearing Turkish, rather than Persian, garb. Often open acknowledgement of 'weakness' was safer than a show of strength; Mungo Park survived his first, solitary journey through Senegambia in 1795, but was killed in 1806 when, in Pratt's words, 'he returned to the Niger at the head of a large, highly militarised expedition that came out shooting, and disappeared to the last man' (Pratt, *Imperial Eyes*, p. 85).

[50] I borrow the term from Carl Thompson, 'The Double Voice of James Bruce', Association for the Study of Travelling in Egypt and the New East (ASTENE) Conference, Newnham College, Cambridge, 17 July 1999.

[51] Bruce's firman from the Sharif of Mecca emphasized the point (in Bruce's words) 'that I was no merchant, and had no dealings whatever with any sort of mercantile matters; and that I had no need of any man's money' (iii. 224). This was to some extent disingenuous, to say the least, for, despite the fact that, like Mungo Park in West Africa, 'trade he [did] but never for profit' (Pratt, p. 81), Bruce's informal links with British and East India Company commercial adventurism were undeniable. Like Park's book, Bruce's *Travels* frequently champions the civilizing power of commerce, echoing David Hume's essay *On Commerce* in his preference for trade over conquest (i. 367).

eighteenth and early nineteenth centuries, particularly as they licensed the scientific traveller's stock-in-trade, botanical and astronomical observation.[52] Linnean botanizing or astronomical observation to determine longitude could be transculturated as the hakim's collection of medical simples or the dervish's interest in astrology. (Antiquarianism was perhaps more dangerous as it raised the suspicion that the traveller was a 'treasure hunter.') Upon arriving in Abyssinia, Bruce claimed that he impressed his hosts at Gonder with his command of the Tigrinya and Amharic language,[53] and he quickly traded in his Syrian for an Ethiopian persona: 'My hair was cut round, curled, and perfumed, in the Amharic fashion, and I was thenceforward, in all outward appearance, a perfect Abyssinian' (iii. 210). The feminization of Bruce in Gonder (a bit like Gulliver's 'domestication' as a miniature in Brobdingnag) is the reverse of Burney's account of the exaggerated masculinity of Bruce in London, however difficult it is to imagine the tall, stout, and florid-faced Scotsman in the court costume of Gonder.

The success of Bruce's bid to ingratiate himself with the Abyssinian court lay in his display of medical skill, but his survival and the success of his sojourn was largely a result of his sentimental attachment to the elderly Ras Mikail's young wife, Ozoro Esther, whose patronage he enjoyed after he successfully treated her son for smallpox. He arrived in 1770 at the start of a period of civil chaos in Ethiopia which would last effectively until Tewodros II took power in 1855 and reinvigorated the crown. Bruce describes the rebellion against the 'king-maker' Ras Mikail (Mikail Sehul of Tigray), vizier of the puppet emperor Tekle Haimanot II, led by the chief of the Galla rebels, Fasil of Damot and his allies. Throughout the period, the powerless puppet emperors of the ancient Solomonic dynasty were at the mercy of rival war lords who appropriated revenues and commanded the loyalty of local ethnic armies.[54] Bruce's first expedition in search of the source of the Nile in the spring of 1770 was made with the protection of Mikail Sehul's army, campaigning against the Galla rebels. The outcome of the second, successful expedition depended on Bruce's skill in negotiating with Mikail's enemy Fasil, to permit him safe conduct through Galla territory towards the Nile source at Gish, above Lake Tana. But Mikail

[52] This had its disadvantages. Bruce, like Carsten Neibuhr, was asked by Ali Bey, ruler of Egypt, to display his astrological skills by forecasting the future in order to solve a problem of policy. Niebuhr, *Travels*, i. 230 and Bruce, i. 33.

[53] This was disputed. In his 1809 narrative published in *Valentia's Travels*, Salt describes meeting an old priest called Allula Lucus, who had known Bruce at Gonder and claimed that 'as he understood well neither the language of Amhara nor of Tigre' he was dependent upon interpreters' (Lord Valentia' *Voyages and Travels to India, Ceylon, the Red Sea, Abyssinia, and Egypt, in 1802–6*, 3 vols. (London, 1809), iii. 105.

[54] Harold G. Marcus, *A History of Ethiopia* (Berkeley, Los Angeles, London: University of California Press, 1994), pp. 44–52. I have followed Marcus in modernizing Bruce's spelling of Ethiopian proper names in the text, although not, of course, in quotations.

Sehul's hold on the country was beginning to crumble: the appalling massacres perpetrated by Mikail in Gonder against the followers of the pretender Susenyos and his eventual defeat at the battle of Sarbakusa [Bruce's 'Serbraxos'] by Goshu of Amhara and his allies determined Bruce's hasty departure in December 1771.

The fourth volume of *Travels* is thus mainly concerned with Bruce's sojourn in Abyssinia, which he had already represented as an 'antique land': 'we meet in Abyssinia with various usages, which many have hitherto thought to be peculiar to those ancient nations in which they were first observed' (iii. 268–9). (A sustained comparison of eighteenth-century Abyssinia with the ancient Persia of King Darius followed.) The rest of volume four details his gruelling return journey to Egypt across the Sennar and Nubian deserts. The final fifth volume is really an appendix describing the natural history of the countries visited and containing a number of natural history plates influenced by Buffon's *Natural History*. It might seem a paradox that this volume really confirms the 'antiquarian' rather than naturalistic bias of the *Travels* as a whole, Bruce's conservative predilection, in Pomian's terms, for 'coins' rather than 'shells'. His reader, Bruce insists at one point,

must be sensible how unpleasant it is to have a very rapid, well-told, interesting narrative, concerning the arts, government, or ruins of Corinth, Athens or Ephesus, interrupted by the appearance of a nettle or daffodil . . . curious and important in the eye of a botanist, but invisible and indifferent to an ordinary beholder.   (v., p. iii)

Hence the need for an appendix volume to 'contain' the natural history.

Bruce's character as virtuoso is evident in the book's piecemeal form and its concern to report 'curiosities' and 'singularities' rather than evoking contexts or typicalities of nature or culture. Apart from the ruins and obelisks of Aksum, Bruce believed that Abyssinia was devoid of antique ruins (iii. 128); nevertheless, his descriptions of natural scenery and human geography and customs were heavily influenced by his antiquarian disposition, rather than by the systematic observing habits of the natural historian. This is evident in his bizarre description of the mountains of Adowa, 'nothing resembling in shape to those of Europe, nor, indeed, any other country. Their sides were all perpendicular rocks, high like steeples, or obelisks, and broken into a thousand different forms' (iii. 114). Like his earlier suggestion that the Egyptian pyramids had been hewn out of natural rock outcrops, Bruce here exemplifies the love of visual puns, between natural and antiquarian singularities, which we have characterized as a feature of the culture of curiosity. When Henry Salt visited Abyssinia in 1804 during his travels with Lord Valentia (the first European to do so since Bruce nearly half a century before), he painted 'a more accurate view' of the same Adowan mountains, 'which certainly in no respect justifies Mr Bruce's fanciful description of their appearance. The forms are generally of an Alpine character, but certainly bear no resemblance to "slabs, obelisks, or prisms", and still less to "pyramids pitched upon their points with their base uppermost" '.[55]

Like Brydone's account of the volcanic Sicilian landscape, Bruce represents the natural history of Abyssinia and Nubia in terms of *lusus naturae*; rather than evoking 'typical landscape', he again dwells on 'singular' features such as pillars of sand (iv. 553), the poisonous simoom, or desert wind (footnoted by Coleridge in *Religious Musings*)[56] (iv. 556), and the 'twister', or desert whirlwind with the power to pick up a camel and hurl it through the air (iv. 423). The plates published throughout the 1790 edition are the visual equivalent of this kind of 'curious' description: Bruce's 'Theban harp', Abyssinian weapons, the obelisk of Aksum, and maps of the battle of 'Serbraxos'. In contrast to Salt's views published in Valentia's *Travels*, they do nothing to satisfy the fashionable taste for the picturesque description of peoples, ruins, or landscapes; there are here no representations of African landscapes, for example. Volume five features plates of botanical and zoological specimens represented in an entirely contextless fashion, after the style of Buffon's *Natural History*. All Bruce's picturesque views of classical ruins in North Africa were presented to the Royal Collection; the inconsistency between their visual idiom and that of the plates of volume five suggests that they were most probably largely the work of Balugani rather than of Bruce himself, despite the fact that he characteristically claimed sole credit.[57]

Scientific Credit

In obedience to the dictates of the Royal Society and other institutions at the 'centre of calculation', the eighteenth-century European land-traveller transformed himself into a mobile recording machine even when this was rendered difficult both by his cultural disguise and the rigours of transporting delicate instruments over rough terrain. Any contemporary reader unacquainted with the conventions of the eighteenth-century travel account might find Bruce's list

[55] Salt, *Life and Correspondence*, ed. by J. J. Halls, 2 vols. (London, 1834), i. 193. Barbara Stafford, in *Voyage into Substance*, p. 96, offers a very different interpretation of Bruce's and Salt's mountain descriptions.

[56] Coleridge, *Religious Musings*, l. 269, in *Poetical Works*, ed. by E. H. Coleridge (Oxford University Press, 1912), p. 119.

[57] The first part of Bruce's narrative does describe his attempt to render the ruins in *picturesque* style (quite different from actually representing them 'picturesquely' in his *Travels*). Bruce's camera obscuras were serviceable for 'transporting' light and shade, little vignettes and 'ornamental shrubs' 'with effect to any part [of the ruin] where they appear to be wanting' (i., pp. ix–x). He boasted that 'there is not, either in the territories of Algiers or Tunis, a fragment of good taste of which I have not brought a drawing to Britain' (i., p. xxxvi).

(in the Preface to his *Travels to Discover the Source of the Nile*) of the scientific instruments which accompanied him on his epic journey excessive, as if the instruments were intended to offer a talismanic guarantee of the veracity of his narrative. This was, of course, precisely the function of the list, although I shall suggest in this section that scientific credit was just as dependent upon rhetoric as upon precision.

Bruce's camera obscuras are perhaps the most extraordinary among the 'mimetically capacious machines' (to borrow Michael Taussig's term)[58] which accompanied him, enabling drawings to be made on the spot with 'the utmost truth and justest proportion' (i., p. ix). The first of these was a 6-foot diameter hexagon with a conical top made by Nairn and Blunt in London, in which 'as in a summer house, the draughtsman sat unseen, and performed his drawings' (i., p. ix), the other a smaller, more portable, Italian model. These bulky devices were intended to guarantee mimetic accuracy of scale and perspective while rendering the artist/observer invisible from outside. Jonathan Crary argues in *Techniques of the Observer* that the camera obscura represented a paradigm of eighteenth-century notions of vision and the relationship of the knowing subject to the external world. It also embodies a paradigm for Bruce's narrative method itself, so that it is no accident that Bruce's Preface dwelt at length on its technical capacities. On the one hand, the camera obscura represents a perfectly transparent relationship between the perceiver and his object of vision, like the 'naïve empiricism' underpinning Bruce's notion of writing to the moment. On the other, it 'necessarily define[d] an observer as isolated, enclosed, and autonomous within its dark confines. It impels a kind of *askesis*, or withdrawal from the world, in order to regulate and purify one's relation to the manifold contents of the now 'exterior' world.'[59] This corresponds to the discourse of 'affective realism' which Bruce sought to weave into his narrative; a private, enclosed, as it were 'domesticated', retreat from the public 'outwardness' of the Abyssinian world. In this respect the camera obscura becomes a kind of guarantee of Bruce's 'modern' subjectivity and a protection from excessive temporalization. Bruce can sit 'in camera'—that is to say 'in judgement'—on this atavistic primitive world secure within the dark interiority of his mimetic machine.[60]

[58] Michael Taussig, *Mimesis and Alterity: A Particular History of the Senses* (New York and London: Routledge, 1993), p. xiv. For Taussig such machines are typified by the camera.

[59] Jonathan Crary, *Techniques of the Observer: On Vision and Modernity in the 19th Century* (Cambridge, Mass., and London: MIT Press, 1990), p. 39.

[60] Crary points out this connotation of 'camera' on p. 42. Disaster could befall if a 'travellee' 'got into' the private viewing space of the camera obscura. Niebuhr described how a 'curious' Turkish merchant, upon seeing the inverted image produced by the camera obscura's lens, 'immediately spread a report, that I was come to overturn the city' (*Travels*, i. 38–9). As usual, indigenous 'wonder' at Western representational instruments has grasped a metaphorical truth often invisible to travellers themselves.

Unfortunately, the reassuring epistemological shelter of the camera obscura was jeopardized by its proximity in technological terms to the magic lantern, which, as Crary indicates, might 'subvert [the camera obscura's] operation by infusing its interior with reflected and projected images using artificial light'.[61] (The subordination of representational transparency to the aesthetic idiom of the picturesque is clear in Bruce's description of using the camera obscuras to draw the classical ruins of the Maghreb; see note 57). Like Bruce's veridical anti-romance narrative, 'the veracity of the camera obscura was haunted by its proximity to techniques of conjuration and illusion'.[62] In *Biographia Literaria*, Coleridge used the metaphor of the camera obscura in exactly this sense, as a form of epistemological hoax which exemplified the 'technology' of the popular modern novel: 'a sort of mental camera obscura . . . which *pro tempore* fixes, reflects, and transmits the moving phantasms of one man's delirium, so as to people the barrenness of an hundred other brains afflicted with the same trance of suspension of all common sense'.[63]

Particularly after he arrived in Mits'iwa, on 19 September 1769, Bruce was travelling through an area of Africa which had been practically unvisited by Europeans for over a century, and for which the data accumulated by seventeenth-century Portuguese travellers were considered unreliable, and therefore in need of constant checking. The precise measurements recorded in Bruce's *Travels* are typical of the eighteenth-century technique of inland survey-ing, which sought to build up an archive of geographical knowledge by measur-ing latitudes and longitudes at key locations, what Matthew Edney calls 'mathematical cosmography'. This allowed route surveys to be 'progressively fitted into a graticule of meridians and parallels' and thereby build up accurate maps of unknown regions.[64] The instruments listed by Bruce include a quadrant for land surveying and measuring latitude, an accurate timepiece for longitudinal readings, a 'parallactic instrument', reflecting and achromatic telescopes for celestial and terrestrial observation, as well as Caille's ephemerides and copies of the classical and modern authors and geographers whose knowledge of the region Bruce sought to follow, verify, or correct. The fourth volume of Bruce's *Travels* features an appendix of no less than ninety-four pages of barometric and thermometric measurements taken in Abyssinia. The fact that Bruce planned to participate in the international observation of the Transit of Venus in 1769

---

[61] Crary, p. 33. Carsten Niebuhr mentions that 'the magic lanthorn is a favourite amusement in the East. I was not, however, fond of such entertainments; as their scope was always to turn the dress and manners of the Europeans into ridicule' (*Travels*, i. 144).

[62] Ibid.

[63] Coleridge, *Biographia Literaria*, ed. by Nigel Leask (London: J. M. Dent, 1997), p. 32.

[64] Matthew Edney, *Mapping an Empire*, p. 18. In this case it would be more accurate to say *Balugani's* measurements, however, according to the conventional division of labour between the casual observations of the 'curious' traveller and the 'precise' climactic and celestial measurements and transcriptions of his 'artisanal' secretary. See Bravo, 'Precision and Curiosity in Scientific Travel', *Voyages and Visions*, pp. 162–83.

also accounts for the formidable array of astronomical instruments that accompanied him. Bruce boasted that it was 'an apparatus of books and instruments, which seldom accompanies the travel of an individual' (i., p. ii), despite the fact that he had 'reduced' all his books by tearing off the covers and discarding irrelevant pages to lighten their weight while in Egypt.

For Bruce, as for many of the other travellers in this book, precision instruments served as the means for accurately representing and 'mobilizing' the world in conformity with the inductive philosophy of the Royal Society and other enlightenment scientific institutions. But, as I have suggested, they also represented talismans of authorial veracity, procuring a quantitative accretion of detail which had the rhetorical effect of underwriting *qualitative* judgements about people and places which were subject to no such definitive testimony. Robert Boyle had famously stressed that 'inanimate bodies [such as laboratory or surveying instruments] are not capable of prepossessions, or giving us partial information', and Simon Schaffer has described how experimenters set out to make their own instruments count as good substitutes for personal testimony.[65] Nevertheless (and, as we shall see below, precision measurements could be regarded as fallible), the material technology of instruments needed to be underwritten by a rhetoric of 'virtual witnessing', a *'literary* technology by means of which the phenomenon produced by the [instrument] were made known to those who were not direct witnesses; and a *social* technology that incorporated the conventions experimental philosophers should use in dealing with each other and knowledge-claims'.[66] As Shapin and Schaffer argue, there was of course a distinction between the sort of credit that could be established in a laboratory and 'a report of a new species of animal . . . in the East Indies', where both the plausibility of the claim and the credibility of a single witness had to stand in for a community of witnesses.[67] All travel writers risk failure in this sense, but Bruce's *Travels* represents an exemplary case of a set of claims which failed to win credit on account of a perceived rhetorical inadequacy.

Despite the guarantees of quantitative precision associated with scientific instruments, the surveying methods practised by Bruce and Balugani were just as problematic as any other aspect of the 'naive empiricism' of contemporary travel. Michael Bravo, citing Swift's satire on the Royal Society's obsession with accurate mensuration, reminds us that 'precision, as a means of describing and representing the world, [was] simultaneously rhetorical and open to irony'.[68] An anxiety concerning the technical problems of surveying are evident

---

[65] Schaffer, 'Self-Evidence', *Critical Inquiry*, 18 (winter 1992), 327–62, 328.

[66] Simon Schaffer and Steven Shapin, *Leviathan and the Air Pump: Hobbes, Boyle, and the Experimental Life* (Princeton, NJ: Princeton University Press, 1985), p. 25.

[67] Ibid., p. 39.

[68] Bravo, 'Precision and Curiosity', p. 162. Matthew Edney points out the uncertainty of latitudinal and longitudinal measurements: 'the best that could be done was to make as many observations as possible on the assumption that the errors would cancel themselves out' (*Mapping an Empire*, pp. 18–19).

throughout Bruce's *Travels*, for example his account of 'situating' Sennar in Nubia (or rather 'resituating' it, because according to Bruce the Jesuits had incorrectly surveyed its position in 1699):

The reader . . . may implicitly rely upon the situation I have given it, being the mean result of about fifty observations, made both night and day, on the most favourable occasions, by a quadrant of three feet radius and telescopes of two, and sometimes of three feet focal length, both reflectors and refractors made by the best masters. (iv. 470)

Because no European was able to retrace Bruce's steps for at least thirty-five years, it was not possible to eliminate the inevitable margin of error by repeated measurement, so too much weight rested upon Bruce's own insistence that observations had been maximized and were guaranteed by his word as a gentleman.

In December 1807 the *Monthly Magazine* denied the veracity of Bruce's account of one of his voyages to map the Arabian Gulf and the Red Sea (in the first volume of *Travels*) and claimed that it 'was probably taken from a ship's journal', on the grounds that 'the observations are made with a Hadley's sextant or ship's quadrant . . . an instrument which Mr Bruce did not possess'. The 'large and unwieldy French quadrant which he carried to Abyssinia', it continued, 'is fit only for a very able astronomer'. Lord Valentia, citing these objections as part of his bid further to discredit Bruce, added; 'Mr Blunt, the optician, who had this instrument to repair, informs me, that it is so incorrect in its formation, that a good observation could not be made with it'.[69] This was an extremely damaging charge, although, of course, Bruce was no longer alive to take umbrage. Measuring instruments were only as reliable as the person who used them, and the harsh conditions of overland exploration rendered them especially unreliable tools of authentication. The practices of scientific observation and recording, like the transparency promised by the camera obscura, seemed no more exempt from the problems of authorial credit than the production of 'personal narrative' itself.

Observations in field notebooks and terrestrial and astronomical measurements were not the only 'mobiles' upon which Bruce sought to build his credit as a traveller. Bruce also returned to Britain laden with botanical and zoological specimens, ethnological and archaeological objects from Egypt, Abyssinia, and Nubia,[70] and rare books and manuscripts including an Ethiopic text of the

---

[69] 'On the Credit due to Bruce's Travels', *Monthly Magazine* 24 (1 Dec. 1807), 449, and Valentia's *Travels*, i. 283.

[70] Cf. Jackie Phillips, 'Seeking Bruce's Cippus', in *KMT: A Modern Journal of Ancient Egypt*, 7, 3 (fall, 1996), 32–6 on Bruce's 'cippus of Horus' brought back from Aksum and drawn by Latrobe for the *Travels*. Thanks to the author for this (and other) helpful points of information on Bruce.

apocryphal Book of Enoch. Bruce's 'curiosities'[71] both contributed to the cycle of accumulation and guaranteed his veracity. Like the latter-day souvenirs theorized by Susan Stewart, these objects 'displace[d] the point of authenticity as [they themselves] become the point of origin for narrative'.[72] Yet the fragility of 'scientific credit' is evident in Bruce's account of nearly losing his curiosities and notebooks at Saffielia in the Nubian desert, on 27 November 1772, upon his return journey. Half dead with thirst and heat-exhaustion, the small party were forced to eat their last camel and struggle on to Aswan by foot, jettisoning the camel's load. Remembering his feelings upon recovering from his desert ordeal, Bruce mournfully reflected upon the fact that, in forfeiting his curiosities, his credit would have depended upon nothing more than personal memory and writing. He could have claimed no more than the status of what Coleridge would call '*merely* a man of letters',[73] a prisoner in a world of proliferating, ungrounded textuality in an age of 'universal scepticism'. I quote the passage at some length as a fine example of Bruce's egotistical, periphrastic, and hyperbolic style:

I was now to maintain the reality of these my tedious perils, with those who either did, or might affect, from malice and envy, to doubt my veracity upon my *ipse dixit* alone, or abandon the reputation of the travels which I had made with so much courage, labour, danger, and difficulty, and which had been considered as desperate and impracticable to accomplish for more than 2000 years.

   I would be understood not to mean by this, that my thoughts were at such a time in the least disturbed with any reflection on the paltry lies that might be propagated in malignant circles, which has each its idol, and who, meeting, as they say, for the advancement of learning, employ themselves in blasting the fame of those who must be allowed to have surpassed them in every circumstance of intrepidity, forethought, and fair atchievement. The censure of these lion-faced and chicken-hearted critics never entered as an ingredient in my sorrows on that occasion in the sadness of my heart; if I had not possessed a share of spirit enough to despise these, the smallest trouble that occurred in my travels must have overcome a mind so feebly armed. My sorrows were of another kind, that I should, of course, be deprived of a considerable part of an offering I meant as a mark of duty to my sovereign, that, with those that knew and esteemed me, I should be obliged to run in debt for the credit of a whole narrative of circumstances, which ought, from their importance to history and geography, to have a better foundation than the mere memory of any man, considering the time and variety of events which they embraced; and, above all, I may be allowed to say, I felt for my country, that chance alone, in this age of discovery, had robbed her of the fairest garland of this kind she ever was to wear, which all her fleets, full of

[71]   The term used in the *London Magazine* (Sept. 1774), 430.
[72]   *On Longing*, p. 136.
[73]   *Biographia Literaria*, p. 139.

heroes and men of science, in all the oceans they might be destined to explore, were incapable of replacing upon her brow.   (iv. 598–9)[74]

This passage represents the double failure of Bruce's credit. The failure of the mobiles to make it back to the centre would invalidate the whole project of accumulation which inspired the project of eighteenth-century scientific travel in the first place. In this respect it is understandable that Bruce's dejection at Aswan should feature as a critical episode in his narrative. But more is at stake here than just the loss of mobiles: the relentless special pleading of these inter-minable sentences, the tortuous syntax which risks swamping grammatical coherence in a plethora of subsidiary clauses, instead presents an occasion for what we might call Bruce's 'egotistical overplus'. This combination of hyper-bole, invective, and self-pitying egotism (quickly rationalized as patriotic concern) underlines the *rhetorical* function of the 'curiosities' in Bruce's nar-rative. Given that the mobiles have in any case been recovered, such a rhetori-cal *tour de force* would seem to be entirely supererogatory. This passage, which is in many ways representative of the tone of Bruce's *Travels* as a whole, reveals an underlying anxiety that the epistemological priority of object to narrative has collapsed, opening up a fissure in his empiricist world-view. As we saw in Chapter 1 in discussing George Forster's programmatic remarks on travel writing, the problem of decontextualization faced by the eighteenth-century traveller could only be resolved by the rhetorical construction of a transcen-dental self as a context for reported experience. Supplementary to this (to be discussed in the next chapter) a systematic and institutionalized order of objects—the 'museum order'—needed to come into being. Its function would be to provide an alternative context in which objects (and particularly anti-quarian and ethnological, rather than natural history, specimens) could assume some meaning distinct from the status of random singularities linked to the nebulous truth-claims of curious travellers.

Bruce's misjudged egotism in this passage—his outrageous claim to have outdone all the Pacific navigators of the eighteenth century—masks his inabil-ity to make good or to systematize his credit. The abuse of his detractors and his high-handed rejection of their accusations masks an impotent rage at the conditions of literary production which determined the late eighteenth-century scene of authorship. If Bruce is 'the giant' of eighteenth-century travel writing, it is because of the immense pathos of his quixotic appeal to an archaic gentle-manly code of honour, rather than to more professional criteria of credit. And because the question of credit saturates the whole of his narrative, the 'matter

---

[74] Bruce's remarks here contain echoes of Louis de Bougainville's Preface to his *Voyage Round the World*, trans. by J. R. Forster, 2 vols. (London, 1772), i., p. xxvi, targeting Rousseau's derogatory remarks on travellers in *A Discourse Concerning the Origins of Inequality* (1754).

of Abyssinia' is presented through a distorting lens, so that the (atavistic) observer is never really distinguishable from the nightmarish world for which he vouches. Bruce's mobiles (above all his textual mobiles) were *uncombinable*, out of proportion to any acceptable notion of scale. Their rhetorical deployment appealed more to the reader's 'vulgar curiosity' than to any desire for precise knowledge of the world. Henry Salt later commented on 'the manner in which the author wrote up and embellished his original observations: in accomplishing which he has evinced a power of interesting the feelings that is almost unexampled'. But he did not mean this as a compliment; quite the contrary.[75]

At the Nile Source

In its March 1791 review of Bruce's *Travels*, *The Analytical Review* complained 'that a deluge of apparent improbabilities, inaccuracies, prejudices, conceits, contradictions, impotent witticisms, and stunning egotisms, has been poured over the mass of real information, vigorous description, sublime imagery, and pathetic scenes, we most deeply regret'.[76] This was nowhere more evident than in Bruce's account of his sublime 'discovery' of the Nile source upon which his largest claim upon posterity was grounded. (Unfortunately this claim, unlike many in the book, was completely unfounded.[77]) Although the discovery of the source of the Nile was highlighted in the book's title as Bruce's 'singular' achievement, the *Analytical*'s comment that it was 'the least interesting part of the work, perhaps only a brilliant phantom' caught the contemporary response to Bruce's

---

[75] Salt, *A Voyage to Abyssinia, and Travels into the Interior of that Country, 1809–10* (London, 1814), p. 341. Edney indicates that even in 'geographical narrative' rhetoricity was all-important in creating an illusion of objectivity (*Mapping an Empire*, p. 79). Henry Salt's back-handed 'compliment' to Bruce suggests an increasing emphasis upon *regulating* the affective subjectivity of the travel writer as picturesque sensibility (subject of my Chapter 4).

[76] AR IX (March 1791), 248. In general, however, the *Analytical Review* was favourable, as were both the *London Chronicle* and the *Critical Review*. In contrast, the *Gentleman's Magazine*, with its Johnsonian links, was hostile. In 1791 the *Travels* were translated and favourably reviewed in the *Journal des Scavans*. Hegel cited Bruce approvingly in his account of African despotism in *Lectures on the Philosophy of World History* (1823–5), p. 187.

[77] The 'fountains of Geesh' which Bruce reached on 4 November 1770 were, in fact, one of the sources of the tributary Blue Nile, rather than the White Nile, 'discovered' nearly a century later by John Hanning Speke at Lake Victoria, over 500 miles to the south. The Little Abbai river at Gish, 70 miles south of Lake Tana, had already been visited and described by Pedro Paez in 1618, as we shall see. Bruce was dead when William Browne published his *Travels in Africa, Egypt, and Syria* (1799), which correctly surmised that the 'Bahr-el-abiad' (the White Nile) was the main river, rather than Bruce's Blue Nile (p. xvi). Even if he succeeded in convincing himself that Paez was a liar, Bruce passed the junction of the White and Blue Niles at Halfaya (modern Khartoum) on his return journey to Egypt, and must have wondered about the provenance of the Blue Nile's thundering confluence. In the event, he diverted attention by commenting upon the dietary habits of the local people, who feasted upon cats, crocodiles, and 'river-horses'.

unstable combination of geographical and literary styles of narrative.[78] Both the metaphorical 'deluge' and the 'brilliant phantom' noted by the reviewer of course referred to Bruce's 'excessive' subjectivity which seemed to usurp the sublimity which had long been associated with the Nile itself, since Longinus' remarks (in *Peri Hypsos*) 'that the impulse of our nature inclines us to admire, not a little clear transparent rivulet that ministers to our necessities, but the *Nile*, the *Ister*, the *Rhine*, or still more the Ocean'.[79] This is signalled in Bruce's description of his approach to the swampy springs of the Little Abbai, where he appears to grow in sublime stature as the mighty river dwindles:

we saw, immediately below us, the Nile itself, strangely diminished in size . . . I could not satiate myself with the sight . . . the lines of the poet [Lucan] came immediately into my mind, and I enjoyed here, for the first time, the triumph which already, by the protection of providence and my own intrepidity, I had gained over all that were powerful, and all that were learned, since the remotest antiquity.   (iii. 590)

Bruce's account of his egotistical appropriation of the sublimity proper to the Nile (which now appears like Longinus' 'little clear transparent rivulet' instead of a sublime river) rapidly collapses, however, into depression and *amor patriae* which moderates his excessive 'temporalization':

Though a mere private Briton, I triumphed here, in my own mind, over kings and their armies; and every comparison was leading nearer and nearer to presumption, when the place itself where I stood, the object of my vain-glory, suggested what depressed my short-lived triumphs . . . I found a despondency gaining ground fast upon me, and blasting the crown of laurels I had too rashly woven for myself. I resolved, therefore to divert, till I could on more solid reflection overcome its progress.   (iii. 597–8)

Like the *askesis* associated with the enclosed interior of the camera obscura discussed above, Bruce's despondency prompts a retreat inwards and a corresponding detachment of the feeling self from the antique Nile which he has 'conquered'. Dealing with abysmal subjectivity thus becomes more of a problem than superseding the enterprise of kings and armies: Bruce's attempt to defer his nostalgia and depression by narrating his 'antics' at the fountains of Gish reads as one of the most bizarre episodes in a book which is not short in oddities.

For it is at this point that Bruce's hyperbolic narrative suddenly divagates into Shandeyan dialogue, as he satirizes both the sublime of discovery and the

---

[78]   AR viii (1790), 49.

[79]   *On the Sublime* (1739), trans. and edited by William Smith, 4th edn. (London, 1770), pp. 146–7. In one of the few critical studies of Bruce's *Travels*, John Whale points out that Bruce's account of the Nile is 'partially obscured by his own presence'. 'Romantic Explorers, Picturesque Travellers', in *The Politics of the Picturesque: Literature, Landscape and Aesthetics since 1770*, ed. by Stephen Copley and Peter Garside (Cambridge University Press, 1994), p. 184.

ritual of possession which, since the Renaissance, had represented the climactic achievement of European exploration and discovery:

'Strates', said I, [Strates is Bruce's Greek guide] faithful squire, come and triumph
with your Don Quixote at that island of Barataria where we have wisely and fortunately brought ourselves; come and triumph with me over all the kings of the earth,
all their armies, all their philosophers, and all their heroes—Sir, says Strates, I do not
understand a word of what you say, and as little what you mean: you very well know
I am no scholar.   (iv. 598)[80]

Perhaps echoing Hawkesworth's account of Captain Furneaux toasting George
III with a bumper of fresh river water upon 'taking possession of Tahiti' in
1766,[81] Bruce and Strates toast George III and Bruce's Scottish fiancée Margaret Murray (named 'Maria' in the 1790 text to avoid embarrassment), as well
as Catherine the Great (patroness of the Orthodox Church) with a draught of
Nile water.[82] Bruce ridicules his patriotic toast by describing the reaction of the
local inhabitants, the Agows, who look on in amazement, speculating that the
foreigners have been bitten by a mad dog.

Bruce's textual antics—his 'antick disposition'—here illustrate Chloe
Chard's account of 'self-protective irony, which acknowledges the temptation to become carried away by linguistic immoderation, and proclaims the
traveller's ability to view this temptation from a stance of critical detachment'.[83]
Such irony, virtually a commonplace in sublime discourse in travel writing
of the period, counteracts the 'grave rhetorical risks' attached to the trope
of hyperbole which 'lays the traveller open to accusations of affectation,

---

[80] Bruce reveals himself to be no more of a scholar than Strates. The literary allusion here is to the
second part of Cervantes' *Don Quixote de la Mancha*, chapter XLV, where Sancho Panza (and not Don
Quixote, as Bruce supposes) is made governor of the 'insula de Barataria' as part of an elaborate practical joke played by the Duke. (Bruce had been granted the lordship of Gish by Mikail.) The name
'Barataria' plays on the Spanish 'Barato' meaning 'cheap'—the province is a worthless possession.
Fooled by his doctor, Sancho is half-starved on a diet of water and meagre provision, which may resonate in Bruce's fresh-water toast. The identification with Quixote here is, of course, fatal for Bruce's
attempt to accrue credit as a discoverer. But for the philosophical background to Bruce's Quixotism,
see Wendy Motooka, *The Age of Reasons: Quixotism, Sentimentalism and Political Economy in 18th C.
Britain* (London and New York: Routledge, 1998).
    [81] Hawkesworth, *Account of the Voyages*, i. 446.
    [82] See J. M. Reid, *Traveller Extraordinary*, p. 170. During Bruce's long absence in Africa, and
without any communication from him, Margaret Murray gave up waiting and married the Italian
Marchese Filippo d'Accoromboni, taking up residence in his palace in Rome. Upon his return journey
through Italy in early 1774, Bruce called upon the unsuspecting marchese and demanded satisfaction.
The Italian wisely preferred to tender an apology, and was pardoned by the irascible Bruce (Reid, pp.
278–80). Bruce's amorous disappointment invites comparison with the celebrated story of Joseph
Banks's broken engagement with Harriet Blosset. Upon his return from the South Seas, Harriet discovered that 'her lover now preferred a flower, or even a butterfly, to her superior charms'. Quoted in
Alan Bewell, 'On the Banks of the South Sea', *Visions of Empire*, p. 179. Bruce, by contrast, presents
himself as the victim of female inconstancy.
    [83] Chloe Chard, *Pleasure and Guilt on the Grand Tour*, p. 6.

pretentiousness, a craven reliance on the conventional formulations of others
... or simply a general lack of discrimination'.[84] The motivation for Bruce's
sublime efflatus can easily be decoded as an anxiety about his precursor, the
Spanish Jesuit missionary Pedro Paez, who claimed to have discovered the
source of the Nile at Gish on 21 April 1618.[85] The hyperbolic rhetoric of Bruce's
own speech at Gish (part of which is quoted above) is even plagiarized from
Paez's, and oddly enough Bruce's subsequent quotation of the original passage
hardly hides the fact from the reader.[86] Acknowledgement of Paez as textual precursor cannot but raise the question of Bruce's claim to priority over Paez as
discoverer of the source of the Nile. But Bruce quickly seeks to dispel such
doubts: 'this relation of Paez's was in my hand the fifth of November, when I
surveyed these fountains, and all the places adjacent. I measured all his distances with a gunter's chain in my own hand, and found every one of them to
be imaginary' (iii. 62). On 5 November—Guy Fawkes' day—the Catholic plot is
unmasked, as Bruce's precision measurements 'negate the negation' of Catholic
priority and Catholic romance.

Bruce's absorption of the antiquarian sublime at the Nile source (his self-
aggrandizing appropriation of the river's fame) can in part be seen as a rhetorical strategy for eliminating the shadow of his precursor, Paez. His narrative then
shifts from an epic into a satirical register, attempting to ironize his excessive
hyperbole. But the really significant element of this passage in the *Travels* is the
tide of depression to which he finally succumbs, representing one further step
from satire into the discursive register of sensibility, doubtless a clumsy and
overcompensatory attempt on Bruce's part to forestall the whole objectivizing
idiom of 'curious' travel. Let us see how this works. After burlesquing his
parodic toast to Maria, Bruce digresses for another forty-odd pages, inserting a
whole chapter on the historical geography of the Nile, triumphantly discre-
diting Pedro Paez's measurements, whilst quoting liberally from the latter's
account. But eventually his narrative returns to the deferred depression, and the
'indifference' which (like a post-coital sadness) follows hard upon his 'complete
enjoyment' of the fountains of the Nile. With nightfall, Bruce succumbs to bitter
homesickness, as his native Scottish rivers seem to reproach him for his inconstancy in preferring the 'coy' Nile:

The marsh, and the fountains, upon comparison with the rise of many of our rivers,
became now a trifling object in my sight. I remembered that magnificent scene in my

---

[84] Chard, p. 5.

[85] Paez had converted the Abyssinian emperor Susenyos to Catholicism, and his travel account was
underwritten by no less an authority than the great Jesuit polymath Athanasius Kircher.

[86] Bruce quotes Paez's account: 'I discovered first two round fountains, each about four palms in
diameter, and saw, with the greatest delight, what neither Cyrus, King of the Persians, nor Cambyses,
nor Alexander the Great, nor the famous Julius Caesar, could ever discover' (iii. 619). The reader can
hardly fail to notice Bruce's debt to his precursor.

own native country, where the Tweed, Clyde, and Annan rise in one hill; three rivers, as I now thought, not inferior to the Nile in beauty, preferable to it in the cultivation of those countries through which they flow; superior, vastly superior to it in the virtues and qualities of the inhabitants . . . I began, in my sorrow, to treat the inquiry about the source of the Nile as a violent effort of a distempered fancy:—'What's Hecuba to him, or he to Hecuba, | That he should weep for her?'   (iii. 640–1)

'Grief or despondency now rolling upon me like a torrent', Bruce shifts from identification with Don Quixote to Hamlet in the grip of his 'antic disposition', staggering out of his tent where the cool of the night, assisted by thoughts of his God and king and the 'honour of my country' help to recompose his troubled mind (iii. 641).[87] Bruce's nostalgia here exemplifies the project of reforming the subjectivity of the 'curious' traveller, commented upon in the previous chapter. In a counter-move to his initial 'antique' temporalization, Bruce puts centripetal in the place of centrifugal desire, as the traveller's 'egotistical sublime', identification with the Nile, is sentimentalized and domesticated by the figure of the feminized Scottish rivers Annan, Tweed, and Clyde.[88]

Felicia Hemans made good use of this episode from the *Travels* in her 1829 poem 'The Traveller at the Source of the Nile'. Whilst remaining quite close to Bruce's account of his sudden collapse from sublime elation into despondency, her quiet elision of the whole 'Quixote at Barataria' passage is revealing,[89] highlighting her preference for representing Bruce's darkling change of mood as a sort of spiritual conversion:

> The rapture of a conqueror's mood
> Rushed burning through his frame,—
> The depths of that green solitude
> Its torrents could not tame;
> Though stillness lay, with eve's last smile—
> Round those far fountains of the Nile.

[87] Bruce attributed this to his anxiety about the perils awaiting him on his return journey. But I suggest that this is only one aspect of the 'centripetal' affect which takes over his discourse at this point.

[88] It is instructive to compare Bruce's nostalgia with the episode in Mungo Park's *Travels*, when the author, lying wounded by robbers and stripped of all his possessions, resolves his deep depression by fixing upon 'the extraordinary beauty of a small moss, in fructification', leading him to the pious and consolatory question 'can that Being . . . who planted, watered, and brought to perfection, in this obscure part of the world, a thing which appears of so small importance, look with unconcern upon the situation and sufferings of creatures formed after his own image?' *Travels in the Interior District of Africa, Performed under the Direction and Patronage of the African Association, in the years 1795, 6, and 7* (London, 1799), p. 244. Park enlists a sentimentalized physico-theology into the service of resolving his gloom, quite distinct from Bruce's histrionic divagation.

[89] By contrast, in her poem 'The Flower in the Desert', based on the analogous episode in Mungo Park's *Travels*, Hemans simply translated Park's pious contemplation of the moss-flower into her characteristic sentimental idiom: 'For the bright flower spoke of one above; | Of the presence felt to brood | With a spirit of pervading love, | O'er the wildest solitude' (Felicia Hemans's *Works*, 7 vols. (Edinburgh, 1839), vi. 279–81). Thanks to Tim Fulford for drawing my attention to this poem.

Night came with stars:—across his soul
There swept a sudden change,
E'en at the pilgrim's glorious goal
A shadow dark and strange
Breath'd from the thought, so swift to fall
O'er triumph's hour—*and is this all?*

No more than this!—what seem'd it *now*
First by that spring to stand?
A thousand streams of lovelier flow
Bathed his own mountain land!
Whence far o'er waste and ocean track,
Their wild, sweet voices called him back[90]

The feminized chorus of Annan, Clyde, and Tweed now drown out the seduction of the 'distant' (replacing Bruce's 'coy') fountains of the Nile. (All the more ironic in this light that Bruce's Scots fiancée Margaret Murray had given up waiting and married a noble Italian bridegroom.) Conquest, discovery, masculine self-aggrandizement give way not to an *askesis* or *contemptus mundi*, as the poem initially seems to suggest, but to the bittersweet melancholy of a feminized, domesticated *amor patriae*. If Wordsworth later reworked Bruce's text by invoking a similar 'mood swing' in the famous Gondo Pass episode of *The Prelude*, Book 6, summoning up the 'fatherless' power of imagination and the rhetoric of apocalypse,[91] Hemans recasts the passage as redolent of a feminized patriotism symbolized by the 'wild, sweet voices' of Scottish womanhood.

Hemans's poem undoubtedly troubles the masculine 'sublime of discovery' (as indeed does Bruce's original passage) but it would be a mistake to read it as a 'domesticated' critique of imperialism in the same light, for example, as Anna Barbauld's poem 'Eighteen Hundred and Eleven'. The brand of nostalgia which Hemans's selective reading rescues from Bruce's text had an important part to play in the construction of a feminized imperial ideal, as we shall see in Chapter 5. (As Letitia Landon wrote in her 1838 elegy 'Felicia Hemans', 'How far thy gentle sway extended!, | The heart's sweet empire over land and sea'.)[92] Notwithstanding his flirtation with a discourse of patriotic sensibility, Bruce's self-promoting temporalization, his bold deferral of affective crisis, and resort

[90] In Andrew Ashfield (ed.), *Romantic Women Poets, 1770–1838. An Anthology* (Manchester and New York: Manchester University Press, 1995), pp. 190–1.

[91] Alan Liu's point in relation to Bruce in *Wordsworth: The Sense of History* (Stanford, Calif.: Stanford University Press, 1989), p. 4. See also John Whale, 'Romantics, Explorers and Picturesque Aesthetics', pp. 180–1, 184–6.

[92] Andrew Ashfield (ed.), *Romantic Women Poets*, p. 220. See Tricia Lootens, 'Hemans and Home: Victorianism, Feminine "Internal Enemies", and the Domestication of National Identity', in Angela Leighton (ed.), *Victorian Women Poets: A Critical Reader* (Oxford: Blackwell, 1996), pp. 1–23.

to Shandeyan self-parody condemned him in the eyes of his critics as an exponent of 'licentious' curiosity. Bruce's unstable version of the traveller's subjectivity (a far cry from Forster's or Humboldt's well-regulated transcendental selfhood) was in dire need of reform and revision, just as his unwieldy and unreliable text would require posthumous redaction by the Revd Alexander Murray, editor of the 1805 second edition, with critical notes.

The Medici Venus and 'Curious' Masculinity

It perhaps comes as a surprise that the most famous contemporary image of James Bruce appears in Zoffany's collective portrait the *Tribuna degli Uffizi* (1772–9), which depicts a group of aristocratic British virtuosi clustered around Lord Cowper and Sir Horace Mann, apparently engaged in the business of viewing (and buying up) the treasures of the Medici collection at Florence (Ill. 3). Bruce, passing through Italy in 1773 on his return journey from Africa, looks just as much at ease in this aristocratic milieu as at the court of Tekle Haimanout at Gonder a year or two earlier: drawn up to his full height, he gazes out of the painting with an air of confident achievement. Zoffany famously described the Abyssinian traveller as 'the wonder of the age, the terror of married men and a constant lover',[93] an allusion to the fact that while in Italy Bruce had challenged the Marquis d'Accoromboni to a dual because he had (unwittingly) married Bruce's fiancée, who had given him up for lost after so many years of waiting without receiving a single letter.

Bruce's positioning in Zoffany's painting is of particular significance because he stands with a proprietorial air in front of the celebrated statue of the Medici Venus, whose figure, as John Barrell has argued in his essay 'The Dangerous Goddess', served to problematize 'the distinction between virtue and *vertu*, between manly politeness and luxurious effeminacy' in eighteenth-century aesthetic discourse.[94] The Venus de Medici, in many ways the icon of the Grand Tour, was commonly compared with the 'Celestial' or Uranian Venus, also in the Uffizi; whilst the latter, also known as 'Venus Pudica', concealed her sexual parts, the Medici Venus seemed rather to draw attention to them. It seems possible that Zoffany here tropes Venus' pudendum as the source of the Nile, her concealing/revealing hand standing for the veil which in conventional Renaissance

---

[93] Cited by Hugh Belsey in his account of Zoffany's 'Tribuna', in *The Grand Tour: The Love of Italy in the 18th century*, ed. by Andrew Wilton and Ilaria Bignamini (London: Tate Gallery Publications, 1996), p. 91.

[94] 'The Dangerous Goddess': Masculinity, Prestige and the Aesthetic in Early 18th-Century Britain', in *The Birth of Pandora and the Division of Knowledge* (London: Macmillan, 1992), pp. 63–87, 75.

3. The '*Tribuna degli Uffizi*' (detail), by Johan Zoffany, 1772–9. James Bruce is the tall figure on
the extreme right. Courtesy of the Royal Collection © 2001, Her Majesty Queen Elizabeth II.

iconography (as in Bernini's fountain in the Piazza Navona in Rome) covered the head of the allegorized figure of the Nile, emblematizing the river's un-discovered source. Bruce's magisterial posture in front of the Medici Venus, strongly contrasted with the prurient virtuosi who peer at her bottom through magnifying-glasses,[95] suggest that Zoffany is paying tribute to Bruce's 'conquest' of the Nile, figured in terms of a post-coital masculinity which confi-dently dispenses with the 'curious itch' and deferred desire of the other tourists.[96]

John Barrell argues that the prestige afforded to the 'dangerous goddess' (the Medici Venus) by mid-century virtuosi reflected a transformation in the eight-eenth-century's understanding of the relationship between masculinity and patrician civic humanist aesthetics. Whilst Shaftesburyan civic humanism had represented sexuality only in terms of stoic abstinence, the emergence of a new aesthetic idealism preferred a notion of masculinity based on sexual enjoyment rather than ascesis, on the condition that such indulgence was limited to a patri-cian private sphere. Barrell's account I think also defines the space of the mid-eighteenth-century *curioso*; patrician, wealthy, freethinking, indiscriminate, and unsystematic in his pursuit of singularities and curiosities, sexually promiscu-ous, and above all élitist, his sociality sealed off from the public domain within the clubbable milieu of the Royal Society, the Society of Antiquaries, or the Dilettante Society. The popular Whig satirist John Wolcot ('Peter Pindar') perfectly expressed this conjunction between curiosity, libertinism, and social privilege when he mockingly lamented (in his 1790 *Complimentary Epistle to James Bruce, Esq.*), 'Lo! moon-ey'd WONDER opes her lap to thee: | How niggardly, alas! to luckless me!'[97]

The Venus of Medici emblematized, then, both the culture of the virtuoso and the exotic allure of Joseph Banks's Tahiti or James Bruce's Abyssinia (remember that observing the Transit of Venus had been a goal of both expe-ditions). Temporalizing links between ethnographic curiosity and aesthetic 'vertu' were common in the period, despite the hierarchy of taste which usually subordinated ethnographic to classical objects of taste. Joseph Banks had waxed eloquent about the classical beauty of the naked Tahitian women, noting in his journal: 'Such the Grecians were from whose model the Venus of Medicis

[95] On the Medici Venus, see Francis Haskell and Nicholas Penny, *Taste and the Antique*, pp. 325–8. On 'curious' looking, see Barbara Benedict, 'The Curious Attitude in 18th Century Britain', particu-larly pp. 86–93.
[96] Implicit here also is a privileging of the achievement of distant travel and exploration over the leisurely amble of the aristocratic Grand Tour. Bruce's attitude as represented by Zoffany is, of course, at variance with his nostalgia at Gish (and Hemans's interpretation of it) as discussed in the previous section.
[97] *The Works of Peter Pindar, Esq., in 2 vols.* (London, 1801), ii. 190. Of course, Bruce was also a Freemason, member of the prestigious Canongate Kilwinning Lodge in Edinburgh (Boswell and Hume were also members), a fact which Miles Bredin makes much of in his speculation that the object of Bruce's quest in Abyssinia was really the lost Ark of the Covenant (*Pale Abyssinian*, ch. 5).

[*sic*] was copied'. The physique of Tahitian women was so striking that they 'might even defy the imitation of the chizzel of a Phidias or the Pencil of an Apelles'.[98] It was only a short step from *vertu* to pornographic voyeurism, evident in the geographical and topographical metaphors which informed much eighteenth-century pornographic literature. In his illuminating essay on Pacific botany and sexual controversy, Alan Bewell quotes a 1773 article in the *Town and Country Magazine* which explicitly linked Banks's ocular exploration of 'unknown geographical "regions"' to his exploration and description of women's bodies': 'That curiosity which leads a voyager to such remote parts of the globe as Mr B—has visited, will stimulate him when at home to penetrate into the most secret recesses of nature . . . we may be suffered to conclude from his amorous descriptions, the females of most countries that he has visited, have undergone every critical inspection by him.'[99]

The erotic charge of Bruce's *Travels* did not go unremarked by his contemporaries. Bruce's friend Hugh Blair, Professor of Rhetoric and Belles-Lettres at Edinburgh University, wrote to him after reading the *Travels*: 'you make me absolutely in love with your Ozoro Esther. Have you never heard a word of what is become of her, and your other old friends there? I should wish much to know.'[100] As in Zoffany's depiction, Bruce the traveller was often represented as Bruce the sexual conqueror. Bruce's proactive masculinity—one aspect of his gigantism—is strongly marked in Fanny Burney's description: 'he is a very manly Character, & looks as [*sic*] dauntless and intrepid, that I believe he could never in his life know what fear meant'.[101] In the Preface to his *Travels* Bruce took pains to link the stylistic plainness of the book (as we have seen, the conventional disclaimer for eighteenth-century travelogues) to his masculinity: 'The language is, like the subject, rude and manly. My paths have not been flowery ones, nor would it have added any credit to the work, or entertainment to the reader, to employ in it a stile [*sic*] proper only to works of imagination and pleasure' (i., p. lxvi). Bruce here draws his masculinity into the construc-

---

[98] Quoted in Bernard Smith, *European Vision*, p. 43. Bougainville also made the connection with 'the dangerous goddess', writing 'Ce peuple ne respire que le repos et les plaisirs des sens. Vénus est la déesse que l'on y sert' (Rennie, *Far-Fetched Facts*, p. 88).

[99] Alan Bewell, 'On the Banks of the South Seas', in *Visions of Empire*, p. 181.

[100] The Revd Alexander Murray, *Account of the Life and Writings of James Bruce* (Edinburgh, 1808), p. 278. At the same time, Blair was shocked by the description of the Polyphemus banquet (discussed in the next section) which he described as 'a very indecent scene, and gives a view of manners carried to a degree of public dissolution, which prevails not in Otaheite, nor in any regular society I ever read of' (ibid., p. 280). Blair did not share the public's scepticism about Bruce's *Travels*, and had no reservations about Bruce being 'so much the hero of your own tale' (ibid., p. 279). Blair's endorsement, in any case, would have done Bruce's credit little good; after all, he was deeply and negatively implicated in the *Ossian* affair, having written a celebrated dissertation in defence of the poem's authenticity.

[101] Fanny Burney, *Early Journals*, p. 45.

tion of personal credit, in opposition to the feminized, flowery paths of the travel romancer.

Bruce's masculinity is nevertheless not to be confused either with Shaftesburyan stoicism or the 'Christian manliness' associated with later explorers, empire-builders, and soldiers. Summing up the personal acquirements which had enabled him to survive countless dangers and adventures, Bruce hinted in the Preface that he owed his survival to his habit of concupiscence, his empathy with, and attraction for, women:

being in the prime of life, of no ungracious figure, having an accidental knack, which is not a trifle, of putting on the dress, and speaking the language easily and gracefully, I cultivated with the utmost assiduity the friendship of the fair sex.   (i., p. lxxii)

Cultural cross-dressing and sexual curiosity are here figured as two sides of the same coin, and there is also a hint of the risk of effeminization, as in the account of Bruce's Abyssinian hairdo mentioned above. Parallels between Banks's courtship of the patronage of 'Queen Obarea' on Tahiti and Bruce's of Ozoro Esther, the Queen of Shendi, or Aiscach of Teawa (beautiful daughter of Sheikh Fidele of Teawa) were not lost on contemporary readers: in both cases, curiosity and sexual desire were seen to be in danger of forfeiting the authority of a stable masculine identity. G. J. Barker-Benfield has discussed the fine line separating civilized manly 'refinement' from over-civilized effeminacy in the writings of David Hume, Adam Smith, and the novelist Henry Mackenzie. The definition of a properly 'manly' sensibility which emerged after the 1770s proscribed both rakish insensitivity and effeminacy, the latter embracing promiscuous heterosexuality as much as 'foppish' homosexuality.[102]

Like Bougainville's and Banks's evocations of the amorous pleasures of Tahiti, Bruce described Abyssinia as a kind of libertine utopia, but one where embraces were exchanged in the spirit of the gift rather than sold for ship's nails. Describing an early encounter with Tigrayan market-women, Bruce handed out beads to the most beautiful

and asked them how many kisses they would give for each? They answered very readily, with one accord, 'Poh! we don't sell kisses in this country: Who would buy them? We will give you as many as you wish for nothing'. And there was no appearance but, in that bargain, they meant to be very fair and liberal dealers.   (iii. 110)

Sexual encounters between eighteenth-century European travellers and African women were not always reported in such utopian language. The allegedly public nature of sexuality in many African societies (as in the 'Polyphemus banquet' discussed below) posed a problem for Europeans even when, like

[102] G. J. Barker-Benfield, *The Culture of Sensibility: Sex and Sensibility in 18th century Britain* (Chicago and London: University of Chicago Press, 1992), p. 145.

Bruce, they claimed sexual interest in, and success with, African women. If nineteenth-century orientalism delighted in a voyeuristic penetration of the Ottoman harem (or its African and Indian equivalents), by contrast pre-colonial travel accounts often represent the harem as a place where the European traveller was himself transformed into a sexual object to be consumed by a public female gaze.[103] Once again we see the early traveller as 'weaker' than the people among whom he travelled, suffering the 'effeminizing' gaze of non-Europeans.

Bruce's self-representation as zealous ladies' man contrasts with Mungo Park's famous account of his subjection to the collective curiosity of a Moorish seraglio at Benowm (the Muslim women wanted ocular proof of the non-circumcision of 'Nazarenes'). Park wrote:

I observed to them, that it was not customary in my country to give ocular demonstrations in such cases, before so many beautiful women; but that if all of them would retire, except the young lady to whom I pointed (selecting the youngest and handsomest), I would satisfy her curiosity. The ladies enjoyed the jest, and went away laughing heartily.[104]

Park's reserved, bourgeois sexuality triumphs by making a joke out of the embarrassing demand, singling one partner out from the collectivity in a synecdoche of European conjugality. Park thus domesticates the 'curiosity' of the Moorish women (his use of the word overdetermined in this context), without losing face.[105]

We might usefully contrast Park's witty probity with Bruce's humiliation in the harem of the Fung King of Sennar, on his return from Abyssinia, in a passage which may well have influenced Park's handling of the episode in his later narrative. Turning his professional gaze upon the queens' naked breasts (Bruce had gained access to the harem in his professional role as 'hakim'), his narrative characteristically slips into the idiom of Swiftian exaggeration: 'I could not but observe that the breasts of each of them reached the length of their knees' (iv. 450). Like Gulliver with the Brobdingnagian women, the women's breasts figure 'a superfluity of nature; [which threaten to] . . . swallow [him] in their immediateness'.[106] But Bruce was disconcerted to find himself instead the object of pruri-

---

[103] Cf. Kate Teltscher's account of a similar inversion in the narrative of Sir Thomas Roe's embassy to the Mogul court in 1615–19, when Roe is observed by Jahangir's wives from the shelter of their harem. 'While Roe can see hardly anything of the women, they can of course see all of him. Normal visual relationships are overturned: the women are in the dominant position, looking at the man; for once the travel writer, more observed than observing, is made aware of his own exoticism' (*India Inscribed*, p. 42). See Chapter 5 below for further discussion of the 'zenana'.

[104] *Travels*, p. 132. See Pratt, *Imperial Eyes*, p. 82 for discussion of this.

[105] Park's response is comparable with George Forster's strong criticism of the sexual commerce of Europeans with Maori women (*Voyage Round the World*, i. 211–13).

[106] Susan Stewart, *On Longing*, p. 88.

ent female eyes, being asked (like Mungo Park) to strip in order to satisfy the
sexual curiosity of 'fifty or sixty [naked] women, all equal in stature and strength
to myself'. Unlike Park, however, Bruce's narrative fails to salvage any sense of
dignity from the situation. If there is an element of racial as well as sexual disgust
in his reaction to the Queens of Sennar, then it is perfectly reciprocated:

Upon seeing the whiteness of my skin, they gave all a loud cry in token of dislike, and
shuddered, seeming to consider it rather the effects of disease than natural. I think in
my life I never felt so disagreeably. I have been in more than one battle, but surely I
would joyfully have taken my chance again in any of them to have been freed from
that examination.   (iv. 450–1)[107]

Bruce's metaphorical 'diminishment' at the periphery here is the reverse image
of his masculine aggrandizement back home, as evoked in Fanny Burney's
description.

Bruce usually assumes a highly self-conscious, 'Shandeyan' literary idiom
when dealing with potentially 'indelicate' matters in his *Travels*:[108] if, to refer
again to Barrell's argument, aristocratic sexual enjoyment was to be introduced
in public discourse, it could only be in (conspicuously) private terms. In one
episode, describing his 'obligation' to accept the customary sexual invitation of
his host Welled Amlac's sister Melectanea, Bruce weighs up his libertine obligations to his Abyssinian host with those owed to his 'proper' English readers
in precisely these terms:

I do not know whether it will not be thought a greater breach of delicacy to have
refused than to have complied:—'But what success Vanessa met | Is to the world a
secret yet; | Can never to mankind be told, | Nor shall the conscious muse unfold.'
Fye upon the conscious muse, says Lord Orrery and fye, too, say I:—a man of honour
and gallantry should not permit himself such a hint as this, though the Red Sea was
between him and his mistress.   (iv. 9)

Despite Bruce's claims in his Preface to have eschewed 'flowery' language for a
masculine plain style, the use of literary allusion (in this case, to Swift and the Earl

---

[107] The episode in the Fung seraglio was excerpted in its entirety in the *Analytical Review*'s serial
review in 1790–1. Bruce's (disputed) claim to have fought in the Battle of Serbraxos at the head of the
emperor's 'Black Horse' might have been intended to save his face after the rebel Fasil had told Bruce
that 'you white people are all effeminate; you are like so many women; you are not fit for going into a
province where all is war, and inhabited by men, warriors from their cradle' (iii. 512). This clearly challenged both Bruce's masculinity and *amor patriae*, prompting him for once to throw diplomacy to the
winds and respond with exemplary John Bullishness: 'there are soldiers, friends and countrymen of
mine . . . who would not think it an action in his life to vaunt of, that with 500 men he had trampled
all yon naked savages into dust' (iii. 513). But unlike his half-brothers, one of whom had died in the
storming of Havana in 1762, another who had led the British assault on the Maratha fortress of Gwalior
in 1780, as a traveller Bruce's belligerence was limited to rhetoric.
[108] Linking his coy 'embarrassment' here to the Shandeyan 'Quixote at Barataria' passage following
his arrival at Gish, as I have argued above, as a form of 'self-protective irony'.

of Orrery) and the coy rhetoric of such passages evoke Sterne's *Sentimental Journey,* that nemesis of 'naïve empiricism' in eighteenth-century travel writing. Bruce here illustrated Vicesimus Knox's complaint that Sterne's 'sentimental and excessive sensibility was found so engaging, that most of the subsequent authors of travels have been induced to interweave into the body of their work an amorous episode', a practice to which, needless to say, he was vehemently opposed.[109]

By the final years of the century, both Bruce's and Banks's sexual transactions with 'nubile savages'[110] were becoming associated, at least in the minds of pious commentators like Vicesimus Knox, with a decadent 'virtuoso' court culture increasingly called to account by the demands of bourgeois moral discipline. Such sexual utopias were beginning to appear as the prurient fictions of an effete masculinity dissipating itself in the senses, 'effeminate' rather than manly, devoid of any moral absolute. In the satirical *Epistle to Mr Banks,* Banks is made to exclaim concerning the Tahitians 'What's vice in us, in you is virtue clear',[111] a failure of ethical universality which matched Edmund Burke's famous denunciation of Warren Hastings's 'geographical morality' in his impeachment oratory.[112] Sexual curiosity was undisciplined, its relation to its object dictated by lascivious desire rather than the quest for rational knowledge. And if the patrician curioso was tarred with the brush of savagery, conversely, it could be argued that, in William Blake's words, 'Savages are Fops & Fribbles more than any other Men'.[113] The nubile savage would thereafter rapidly metamorphose into the ignoble savage as part of the same blanket critique of the 'curious attitude'. The moral distortion wrought by this brand of cultural curiosity which made travellers into virile giants at home and sexually miniaturized them among savages (or vice versa), fed into parallel concerns about gender instability, masculine women, and feminized men. By the late 1790s scientific rationalism, evangelical piety, and imperial expansion, the ideologies of an increasingly militarized, war-based society, demanded the disciplining of sexual ambiguities.[114] The Briton abroad must assume an immutable moral dimension defined over and against the ethical and sexual 'mobility' of his cultural others. The nineteenth-century mythologization of the heroic traveller would make much of the masculinity and sexual probity of its subject: the chaste

---

[109]   Vicesimus Knox, *Essays, Moral and Literary,* i. 115–16.
[110]   I borrow the pun from Neil Rennie, p. 107.
[111]   Bernard Smith, *European Vision,* p. 51.
[112]   Burke used the term on the second day of his opening impeachment speech in February 1788. The whole passage is quoted and commented upon in Conor Cruise O'Brien, *The Great Melody: A Thematic Biography of Edmund Burke* (London: Sinclair Stevenson, 1992), p. 370.
[113]   Annotations to Reynolds's Fifth Discourse, *Blake's Complete Writing,* ed. by Geoffrey Keynes (Oxford University Press, 1966), p. 468.
[114]   See Katherine Binhammer, 'The Sexual Panic of the 1790s', in *Journal of the History of Sexuality,* 6 (1996), 409–35; and Drohr Wahrman, 'Percy's Prologue: From Gender Play to Gender Panic in 18th Century England', *Past and Present,* 159 (May 1998), 113–60.

Mungo Park died heroically in the heart of Africa during his second expedition; promiscuous Bruce, by contrast, was killed falling downstairs at his home at Kinnaird on 26 April 1794, while handing a lady out to her carriage.

The Raw and the Cooked

One of the passages in Bruce's *Travels* which most shocked the contemporary reading public (equivalent to the uproar generated by Hawkesworth's description of the 'Spectacle at Point Venus') was the 'Polyphemus banquet' (iii. 301) described in Volume III, Book V, Chapter xi. This Rabelaisian wedding feast, described by Bruce 'as far as decency will permit me', was elaborated from the *London Magazine*'s 1774 account of the ancient Abyssinian habit of eating raw beef cut from living cows, a habit which Bruce had insisted was a commonplace in Mosaic times. In the face of the universal scepticism which had greeted his original claim, Bruce now protested vehemently that 'people who had never been out of their own country, and others well acquainted with the manners of the world, for they had travelled as far as France, had agreed the thing was impossible, and therefore it was so' (iii. 144). He confessed that he could not but 'admire a dinner so truly soldier-like' (iii. 144) and admitted that he himself had 'for several years, been partaker of that disagreeable and beastly diet' (iii. 145). His own evident ambivalence, and his confession of participation, cast a particularly grotesque light on a custom which, as I argued above, had created such anxiety among the English public in the mid-1770s.

Bruce described how 'a number of people of the best fashion in the villages, of both sexes, courtiers in the palace, or citizens in the town, meet together to dine between twelve and one o'clock' (iii. 301). The undertones of a provincial alderman's dinner-party are soon shattered, however, as his narrative details the brutal carving up of a live cow within the dining hall 'the prodigious noise the animal makes is a signal for the company to sit down to table' (iii. 302). A grotesque parody both of civil decorum and eucharistic ritual ensues as each man, seated between two women, cuts a strip of meat with his knife ('while you see the motion of the fibres yet perfectly distinct, and alive in the flesh') (iii. 303). The women season the palpitating fibres and feed the bloody morsels to their menfolk wrapped in a 'cartridge' of unleavened bread, as 'no man in Abyssinia, of any fashion whatever, feeds himself, or touches his own meat'. With a debt to Hogarth, Bruce evokes the 'idiotic' posture of the male diner, as his mouth is stuffed full by his female companion. Abyssinian table manners invert European, for, 'the more noise he makes in chewing it, the more polite he is thought to be' (iii. 304). Despite the hideous nature of the repast, as the men drink and the ladies eat, toasts are drunk: 'Vive le Joye et la Jeunesse!', and 'a great deal of mirth and joke goes round, very seldom with any mixture of acrimony or ill-humour' (iii. 304). Because in this libertine paradise 'love lights all fires, and everything is permitted with absolute freedom' (iii. 304), the diners, like the Cynics of old, soon turn from the pursuit of alimentary to sexual pleasure, taking it in turn to couple publicly on the floor, for 'there are no rooms but one, in which they sacrifice both to Bacchus and to Venus' (iii. 305). Abyssinian table-manners mirror Abyssinian sexual customs, both equally grotesque and indelicate to the polite European reader: 'if we may judge by sound, they seem to think it as great a shame to make love in silence as to eat' (iii. 305).

Beyond its overt linkage of food and sex (the very reverse of Porphyro's erotic but uneaten banquet in Keats's 'Eve of St Agnes'), the unsettling quality of Bruce's account lies in its confusion of a 'partial' civility with 'savage' eating and public sex. As I suggested above, like 'Christian' Abyssinia itself, the Rabelaisian banquet is neither purely 'civil' nor 'savage', but both at once, thereby disrupting an opposition upon which polite eighteenth-century manners relied for their self-definition. Sceptical responses to Bruce's raw beef story tended to turn it back on itself as a metaphor for the representational practices of the book itself, thereby exemplifying the century's love of gastronomic metaphors, such as Fielding's famous 'bill-of-fare' introduction to *Tom Jones*. Bruce's obsessive claims to representational fidelity, the text as a 'slice of life', raw rather than cooked, its stylistic prolixity and indigestibility, its licentiousness; all seemed perfectly figured in the Polyphemus' banquet, which contemporary readers could read either as an anthropological *lusus naturae* or else qualify as a perverse exercise in literary reflexivity.

The *Analytical Review* was not alone in playing on the gastronomic metaphor when it apologized for the lengthy and numerous quotations which it had 'carved out' of Bruce's narrative in its long serial review of 1791. Whilst some readers may have already gorged themselves on the carcass itself, the conceit continued

there is still a greater number unable or unwilling to help themselves, who like the male guests of an Abyssinian feast, choose to have the viands made up into a spiced cartridge, and without further trouble thrust into their mouths: for these, we must undertake the office of the Ethiopian ladies, and feed them without the trouble of carving or selection.[115]

The *Analytical Review* mediated the crudity of Bruce's narrative by making choice cuts from the 3,000-page carcass and seasoning the morsels, 'undertaking the office of the Ethiopian ladies' in re-presenting Bruce's savage gallantry for the benefit of a polite readership.

[115] *Analytical Review*, IX (March 1791), 248.

The most damaging rebuff to Bruce's claim to represent 'raw' experience (as to all unbelievable travel accounts) was that it was neither raw nor cooked, but rather re-cooked, the left-overs from someone else's banquet. 'Peter Pindar' had aimed his satire at Bruce's fabular dynamics of scale in his *Complimentary Epistle*, from which I have already quoted. Wolcot hailed Bruce as 'Thou dear man-mountain of discovery' . . . 'Whate'er thine action, wonder crowds the tale; | It smells of Brobdingnag—it boasts a scale! | Fond of the lofty, BRUCE no pigmy loves— | Who likes a pigmy, that a giant moves?'[116] But, much more damagingly, Wolcot also accused Bruce of plagiarism, characterizing his prolix narrative as 'A book like Psalmanazar's, form'd to last, | That gives th'historic eye a sweet repast'.[117] Wolcot here alluded to George Psalmanazer's *Historical and Geographical Description of Formosa* (1704), an entirely mendacious travel narrative which provided the eighteenth century with its most extravagant combination of travel-lying, savagery, and raw meat.

Psalmanazar was a French confidence trickster who had claimed to be a native of Formosa, invented a Formosan language, and on the strength of the 'credit' accruing from his *Description*, been awarded a post teaching the 'Formosan' language at Oxford. Among other elaborate claims, he insisted that the Formosans sacrificed 18,000 boys aged under 9 years every New Year to their gods; that they taught Greek in their principal seminaries; and also that 'they commonly eat the Flesh of Venison and of Fowls raw'.[118] To provide an authenticating context for his otherwise unfalsifiable story (given the general ignorance of Formosa in early eighteenth-century England), Psalmanazer was in the habit of eating his meat raw in public. As Susan Stewart has noted in her essay 'Antipodal Expectations', the interplay between Psalmanazar's (bogus) narrative and his contextualizing 'Formosan' behaviour represents an extreme case of the early novelists' paratextual obsession with persuading the public that they were telling factual rather than fictional stories.[119]

Bruce's rage at these sort of accusations is everywhere evident in the defensive/aggressive authorial voice of the *Travels*. It is illustrated by an anecdote about Bruce's behaviour at a dinner party at Kinnaird when one of the guests jokingly remarked on the impossibility of the natives of Abyssinia eating raw meat. The enraged traveller

---

[116] *Works of Peter Pindar*, ii. 197–8.   [117] Ibid., ii, 192.

[118] Percy Adams, *Travels and Travel Liars*, p. 94.

[119] Susan Stewart, 'Antipodal Expectations: Notes on the Formosan "Ethnography" of George Psalmanazar', in *Romantic Motives: Essays on Anthropological Sensibility*, ed. by George W. Stocking, History of Anthropology, Vol. 6 (Madison, Wis.: University of Wisconsin Press, 1989), pp. 44–73. In contrast to early novelists like Defoe, for whom fact and fiction were never explicitly differentiated, Psalmanazer experienced a 'conversion' in later life, exposing his own book as a hoax, and living, until his death in 1763, a pious penitent, a contributor to *bona fide* travel compilations, and a friend of Dr Johnson.

said not a word, but leaving the room, shortly returned from the kitchen with a piece of raw beef-steak, peppered and salted in the Abyssinian fashion. 'You will eat that, Sir, or fight me', he said. When the gentleman had eaten up the raw flesh . . . , Bruce calmly observed, 'Now Sir, you will never again say it is impossible.'[120]

This sort of belligerence contributed to Bruce's reputation as an irascible ogre. The anonymous author of the 1792 *Gulliver Revived: A Sequel to Baron Von Munchausen* incorporated the raw meat-eating Africans into his narrative of the Baron's fantastic adventures, as Munchausen induces the Africans to forgo their savage gastronomy by distributing toffee fudge gratis as a civilizing gift from the British government. Further exploding Bruce's claims to veracity by comparing him to Raspe's fabulous traveller, the *Sequel's* author joked about Bruce's bullying tactics in dedicating his book to the testy Scotsman: 'the Baron conceives that [the account of his adventures] may be of some service to [Mr Bruce], previous to his making another expedition into Abyssinia: but if this advice does not please Mr Bruce, the Baron is willing to fight him on any terms he pleases'.[121]

Bruce's willingness to 'fight for his credit' really only exposed his impotence in the impersonal, increasingly market-driven world of eighteenth-century authorship. Like the spectral, intertextual figure of Psalmanazar (and Bruce, remember, really *had* been to Abyssinia), he could do no more than elaborate his claims in a seemingly endless proliferation of words, a piling up of context upon context which endlessly deferred without being able to ground the veracity of his claims. In this connection Susan Stewart describes 'the historical emergence of a writing so necessarily separated from its referent that a scholarship of documentation and verifiability, a science of universal social laws, and conversely a cult of authorship, originality and genius, were necessary as cures for instability'.[122] This sketches the two principal options for the nineteenth-century travel account as a self-authenticating discourse of 'romantic' genius began to separate from 'scientific' facticity around the decade in which Bruce composed his *Travels,* splitting open the 'curious' travel narrative for once and for all. Although Bruce's *Travels* was recuperated by the romantic generation as a 'work of imagination' (it was a favourite of Coleridge, Wordsworth, and Lamb),[123] its author's rather clumsy attempt to ground readerly credit in licentious egotism was unacceptable to a late-enlightenment readership.

---

[120] Cited in Percy Adams, *Travellers and Travel Liars*, p. 214.

[121] R. E. Raspe et al., *Singular Travels, Campaigns and Adventures of Baron Munchausen*, intro. by John Carswell (New York: Dover Publications, 1960), p. 115.

[122] Susan Stewart, 'Antipodal Expectations', p. 45.

[123] For Lamb see below, and note 133. Coleridge's 'Kubla Khan' seems to engage with Bruce's *Travels* at a number of levels, not least that of the question of narrative credit. Of his vision of the Abyssinian Maid the poet asks '*Could* I revive within me | Her symphony and song . . .' (italics mine). Coleridgean aesthetics shrug off all anxieties of readerly credit (at the cost of isolating the poet in a thrice-woven

Just as misjudged as his recourse to narrative egotism was Bruce's attempt to ground his credit on the sheer physical length of his narrative, in the vain belief that the temporal deferral of disbelief might by some obscure logic shade into conviction: 'I have no doubt, when time shall be given to read this history to an end, there will be few, if they have candour enough to own it, that will not be ashamed of ever having doubted' (iii. 145). He also frequently sought to ground his credit upon an *ad hominem* appeal to the reader as social peer: 'on the word of a gentleman'. For instance, in defending a particularly incredible claim about the sentimentalism of elephants, Bruce insisted that 'I adhere strictly to the truth; and I beg leave to assure those scrupulous readers, that if they knew their author, they would think that his having invented a lie, solely for the pleasure of diverting them, was much more improbable than either of the two foregoing facts' (iv. 303–4). In the impersonal and market-driven world of literary circulation this was indeed pure fantasy: Bruce 'obliged' his reader to take his word as a gentleman, disavowing the possible imaginative licence which might be taken by a professional 'man of letters' or armchair traveller. His pale imitation of Hume's argument from probability in the *Essay on Miracles* is ineffectual, particularly as his own 'curious' claims frequently stick closer to the side of the marvellous than the credible. The tragedy of Bruce as travel writer was that neither the concrete evidence of his mobiles any more than special pleading or textual 'bullying' could make up for the distance that separated the writer from the reality which he sought to represent.

Another rhetorical device frequently employed by Bruce in parrying accusations of plagiarism (touched upon above in relation to Pedro Paez in the Nile source episode) is his 'anti-romance' strategy of rejecting earlier travel accounts as fables.[124] In his *Travels* Bruce turned vindictively upon Dr Johnson's 1735 translation of Jerome Lobo's *A Voyage to Abyssinia* (1728) (the 'Grand Cham' was, of course, no longer alive to defend himself), in particular attacking the claim made in Johnson's Preface that Lobo 'appears, by his modest and disaffected narration, to have described things as he saw them; to have copied nature from life; and to have consulted his senses, not his imagination'.[125] Bruce dismissed Lobo's book (thereby also revenging himself upon the doubting

circle of social isolation) lauding the 'willing suspension of disbelief for the moment, which constitutes poetic faith' [*Biographia* p. 179]. For Coleridge's interest in Bruce, see also Jonathan Livingston Lowes, *The Road to Xanadu: A Study in the Ways of the Imagination* (1927) (London: Pan Books, 1978), pp. 338–46, 363–4, 542.

[124] Michael McKeon notes how, in the discourse of 'naïve empiricism' 'the hope is that anti-romance, the negation of the negation, will thus fulfil itself as the true history of travel narrative. The risk is that for the sceptical reader it will simply seem the "new romance"'. *Origins of the English Novel, 1600–1740* (Baltimore: Johns Hopkins University Press, 1987), p. 113.

[125] Samuel Johnson, *A Voyage to Abyssinia* (trans. from the French), ed. by Joel J. Gold, Vol. XV of *The Yale Edition of the Works of Samuel Johnson* (New Haven and London: Yale University Press, 1985), p. 3.

Johnson) as 'a heap of fables, and full of ignorance and presumption'. Singling out Lobo's claim to have encountered cannibalism among the Abyssinians, he played on the meaning of Lobo's name (Lobo = wolf) by suggesting that 'one would be almost tempted to believe that Jerome Lobo was a man-eater himself, and had taught this custom to these savages. They had it not before his coming; they have never had it since' (iii. 137). Bruce here displaces accusations made against the veracity of his own account of beef-eating Abyssinians, exposed by sceptics as a figment of his farouche imagination, by turning them upon Lobo's account of Abyssinian cannibalism as reflecting the Jesuit's own 'man-eating' proclivities. Ethnocentric disgust characteristic of the later nineteenth-century travelogue is here pitted against the Jesuit missionaries Paez and Lobo rather than the Abyssinians themselves, as part of Bruce's defensive/aggressive textual strategy.

The arrival in Abyssinia of Henry Salt in 1805, travelling on behalf of his aristocratic patron, Lord Valentia,[126] finally allowed for the verification of Bruce's claims. Salt left behind him his English servant 'Mr Pearce' with instructions to check Bruce's ethnographic 'facts', the first foreign visitor to be in a position to do so. Returning a few years later in 1809–10, Salt discovered from Pearce that Bruce's account of Abyssinia, like the curate's egg, was true in parts; for example, the Abyssinians did sometimes feast on raw beef, but normally killed the animal first, thereby somewhat mitigating the savagery of the custom.[127] This typified Salt's scaled-down representation of Bruce's Abyssinia. Among the numerous errors in Bruce's ethnography which he denounced was the description of the 'Polyphemus banquet' and the sexual promiscuity of the Abyssinians:

So far from enjoying a free intercourse with the males, as is asserted by Mr Bruce, it is certain that the married women are watched with some caution by their husbands . . . The gross and disgusting scenes which Mr Bruce describes as following a brinde feast, I firmly believe existed only in his own imagination.[128]

His illustration of the 'Brinde feast' shows nothing untoward, and even includes a priest blessing the decorous diners with a crucifix (Ill. 4). Inverting Zoffany's heroic portrait of Bruce, Salt casts Bruce as a prurient old curioso passing off his distempered sexual fantasies for ethnographic facts. Salt's patron Valentia, whilst accepting that Bruce had visited Gonder, proposed (in an oddly circular argument) that his description of the inaccessibility of the country and his exaggerated account of Abyssinian savagery was a ploy to deter his fellow-

[126] Valentia remained on the Red Sea coast, but included Salt's first account of Abyssinia in his *Voyages and Travels*, 3 vols. (London, 1809), studied in Chapter 4.
[127] Henry Salt, *A Voyage to Abyssinia* (London, 1814), p. 295.
[128] Valentia's *Travels*, iii. 158–9.

countrymen from following in his footsteps, 'conscious, as he must have been, that his own exposure would be the inevitable consequence of an impartial person's comparing his romantic account, with the real habits, manners, and conditions of the Abyssinians'.[129] Bruce is represented as actively sabotaging (for purely egotistical ends) the Latourian 'cycle of accumulation' which justifies travel as a useful as well as a curious pursuit.

The editor of the second (1805) edition of Bruce's *Travels*, the Revd Alexander Murray, diagnosed a kind of 'repetition compulsion' in Valentia's harsh treatment of Bruce. In an 1811 letter to Salt (who was preparing the narrative of his second visit to Abyssinia the previous year) Murray hoped that the cycle of retribution might somehow be broken, comparing Valentia's triumphalism in 'conquering' Bruce to that 'species of glory which the Abyssinian soldiers show when they brandish their spears over the head of the Ras, and throw down the trophies taken from the enemy'. Valentia's treatment of the now defunct Bruce precisely mirrors the

fault which Bruce possessed with respect to Pedro Paez, the Jesuits, etc. Mr Bruce worries his predecessors, Mr Brown, who has many singularities, worries Mr Bruce, and Viscount Valentia joins in the same cry. I foresee with true dissatisfaction the same fate abiding the Viscount. I look with much more pleasure to your own mode of confuting Mr Bruce. You put down hard facts and proclaim no victory.[130]

Significant here is Murray's appeal (as Presbyterian minister and oriental philologist) to Salt as a fellow-professional, disavowing the aristocratic hauteur of intertextual aggression and naïve empiricism which unites the texts of Bruce and Valentia. Murray exposes the complicities between British and Abyssinian court culture, the pride of a neo-feudal nobility with the pride of savages.[131] Rabid disdain for textual authority ('nullius in verba') characteristic of the culture of curiosity is revealed as a form of vanity; in its place is proposed a careful scrutiny of the phenomena of experience, including the philological evidence of previous travel accounts. Anticipating the editorial principles of John Pinkerton's *Voyages and Travels* (discussed in Chapter 1), sober attention to facts, the patient professionalism of the philologist and editor is set up as a model

---

[129]   Ibid., iii. 288.

[130]   Quoted in *Life and Correspondence of Henry Salt*, i. 283–4. For Brown[e] see below.

[131]   Murray had discussed the problem of Bruce's veracity with the historian Malcolm Laing, at the time engaged in judging the authenticity of James Macpherson's *Ossian* [i. 284]. Murray's critical edition of Bruce's *Travels*, seeking to distinguish 'useful' fact from 'curious' fiction, was published around the same time as the Highland Society announced the (sceptical) results of its investigation into what Laing dismissively described as Macpherson's 'savage society of refined atheists' (Malcolm Laing, *The History of Scotland*, 4 vols. (London, 1804), iv. 431). The Murray/Laing collaboration further reveals the links between travel writing and the discourse of antiquarianism in this period. Narrative authority must depend upon careful analysis of the facts, whilst the historical or ethnological object must be separated from 'curious' desire.

4. 'The Brinde Feast', by Henry Salt, from Valentia's *Voyages and Travels* (1809). This represents a 'reformed' version of Bruce's 'Polyphemus' Banquet'. Note for example the priest blessing the diners with a crucifix.

for the travel writer, who, like Salt, will aim to establish systematic certainties rather than scoring points in a relentless and meaningless intertextual warfare. Coleridge, whose oriental idyll 'Kubla Khan' had responded to the more rhapsodic elements of Bruce's *Travels*, in 1807 took pains to recommend Murray's second edition of 1805 to the Wordsworths in the place of the 1790 original.[132] Charles Lamb, by contrast, expressed the charm of the book for the romantic generation (irrespective of its truth or falsehood) in an 1806 letter to Hazlitt:

We just read thro' Bruce's Travels, with infinite delight where all is alive & novel & about kings & Queens & fabulous Heads of Rivers Abyssinian wars & the line of Solomon & he's a fine dashing fellow & intrigues with Empresses & gets into Harems of Black Women & was himself descended from Kings of Scotland: rot farmers & mechanics & industry . . .'[133]

Lamb deserves the last word here.

Coda

Arriving in Egypt in early 1793 with the intention of retracing Bruce's return route via Nubia to Abyssinia (in the end rendered impossible by the outbreak of war between the Mamelukes and the Cashif of Ibrim), the young British traveller William G. Browne met an Armenian merchant who claimed to have known Bruce in Gonder twenty-odd years before. Corroborating the 'raw beef' story and Bruce's claim to have been made governor of Ras-el-fil, the merchant 'narrated of his own accord [Bruce's] story of shooting a wax candle through seven shields; but when I asked him if Bruce had been at the Abyssinian source of the Nile, he affirmed that he never was there'.[134] The Armenian referred to an incident narrated in Bruce's *Travels* which occurred shortly after his arrival at Gonder, when he got involved in a drunken boasting match with Guebra Mascal, one of Ras Mikail's nephews, who fancied himself a crack shot. Bruce challenged him to a contest, boasting that 'every gun of mine, in the hands of my servants, shall kill twice as far as yours . . . When I compare with you, the end of a tallow-candle in my gun shall do more execution than an iron ball in the best of yours' (iii. 234). When Guebra Mascal called him 'A Frank and a liar'

---

[132] Dorothy Wordsworth to Lady Beaumont, 24 January 1807: 'Coleridge says that the *last* edition of Bruce's Travels is a book that you ought by all means to have'. *Letters of William and Dorothy Wordsworth. The Middle Years. Part 1, 1806–1811*, ed. by E. de Selincourt, rev. by Mary Moorman (Oxford: Clarendon Press, 1969), p. 129.

[133] Edwin W. Marrs (ed.), *The Letters of Charles and Mary Lamb* (London, 1976), ii. 199. Thanks to Carl Thompson for this reference. The allusion in the final part of the sentence is to Crevecouer's *Letters of an American Farmer*, which the Lambs had also been reading.

[134] William Browne, *Travels in Africa, Egypt, and Syria* (London, 1799), p. xxi–xxii.

and kicked him, Bruce, 'blind with passion' retaliated and a serious brawl ensued in which both men were slightly injured. This episode of Bruce making a hyperbolic claim, being accused of lying, and fighting to defend his credit seems to allegorize (as it displaces the site of) the anxiety about credit which we have seen permeating the *Travels*. His account of the wounds he inflicted on Mascal the sceptic seem to enact the threat of retaliation levelled at his fellow house-guest in the raw beefsteak anecdote, a threat which Bruce's reader always feels, with a sense of faint disquiet, hanging over his or her own head lest he or she should be tempted to doubt.

Some time after Bruce's brawl with Guebra Mascal, the emperor (Tekle Haimanout II) challenged Bruce to make good his boast. Bruce promised to pierce a three-quarter-inch thick sycamore table with a tallow candle, fired from his rifle. The emperor cautioned him lest his boast be an idle one: 'Ah, Yagoube, Yagoube . . . take care what you say . . . you don't know these people; they will lie themselves all day; nay, their whole life is one lie; but of you they expect better, or would be glad to find worse; take care' (iii. 244). Bruce insisted upon proving himself without further delay (although in the parallel case of his travel credit, it would take him sixteen years to publish the travel narrative which he hoped would vindicate his veracity before the British public): 'I would not wish to remain for a moment longer under so disagreeable an imputation as that of lying, an infamous one in *my* country, whatever it may be in this. Let me send for my gun' (iii. 244). Before an audience of about one thousand people, Bruce promptly fired a farthing candle through three buffalo-hide shields belonging to the emperor's most sceptical young warriors: 'the candle went through the three shields with such violence, that it dashed itself to a thousand pieces against a stone wall behind it' (iii. 245). (Note the *surplus* power with which Bruce's narrative endows the rifle, like the inexorable reach of European expansion pushing its 'soft' representative through a 'hard', hostile, Abyssinia.) The emperor, astonished, cries out 'I did not believe it before I saw it, and I can scarce believe it now I have seen it. Where is Guebra Mascal's confidence now? But what do either he or we know? We know nothing' (iii. 245). Bruce repeated the experiment, this time firing the candle through the king's table, making good his boast before the astonished and admiring Abyssinian crowd. In an anecdote commonplace in the annals of cultural encounter, European technological superiority is transculturated as indigenous 'wonder', thereby giving the traveller a 'supernatural' purchase upon the native's belief. Bruce's fantasy of compelling belief by empirical evidence, the fantasy which underpinned his publication of the *Travels*, is parabolically fulfilled.

Or such at least is the intention. It turns out, however, that credit is just as elusive among the 'refined savages' of Abyssinia as those at home. Some of the priests present at the display though surprised at first, seemed afterward to treat it rather lightly, because they thought it below their dignity to be surprised at anything. They said it was done (mucktoub) by writing, by which they meant magic. Everybody embraced that opinion as an evident and rational one, and so the wonder with them ceased.   (iii. 246)

The conniving priests—so many Dr Johnsons and Horace Walpoles in Abyssinian costume—disenchant Bruce's 'miraculous' action by dismissing it as 'mere' magic; or what they call '*writing*'. (One might also interpret 'mucktoub' here as fate, as in the hyperbolic 'it is written', familiar in the discourse of popular Western orientalism).[135] Because in Abyssinia magic serves to explain out-of-the ordinary phenomena, its agency is to take the threat out of wonder, make it familiar, 'evident and rational'. Just as philosophical scepticism reduces wonder in enlightenment Europe, so, reciprocally, does 'magic' explain the applied power of Western ballistic physics in the mirror image of Bruce's Abyssinia. The apparently miraculous power of European firepower *is* plausibly linked to 'writing' in symbolical terms, for both work by causes which, by means of the accumulation of power and information, can produce extraordinary effects at a distance. But Bruce's solitary bid for self-aggrandizement in the fable of the tallow candle, no less than in the *Travels* as a whole, is in the end an enormous metaphorical failure in its inability to deliver the miraculous promise of *writing* over distance.

Only the young Abyssinian puppet-emperor remains spellbound, and Bruce's feat with the tallow candle ensures thenceforth 'the most implicit belief of every thing I advanced upon any subject from my own knowledge' (iii. 246). The emperor is Bruce's ideal reader, a figure for his book's royal dedicatee George III. The sovereign principle remains the sole symbol of unchallengeable credit in a world of disenchanted, decontextualized, sceptical readership. On the other hand, the dismissive 'writing magic' of the Abyssinian priests mirrors the sceptical argument of those critics at home who have explained away Bruce's conquest of distance as pure 'writing', textuality, or, worse still, *intertextuality*. The credit of Bruce's 'curious' narrative must remain in suspension, until such a time as travel writing could better internalize what Michael Taussig calls 'the colonial mirror of production', 'the mimicry by the coloniser of the savagery imputed to the savage'.[136]

---

[135] See Robert Irwin, *The Arabian Nights: A Companion* (Harmondsworth: Penguin Books, 1994), p. 197.
[136] Taussig, *Mimesis and Alterity*, p. 66. Despite his own cultural permeability with respect to the Abyssinians, this is precisely what Bruce failed to do in his identification with Abyssinia as a 'feudal' rather than a 'savage' world. For an account of later 19th-century travellers in Abyssinia (particularly the 'Brucean' Mansfield Parkyns), see Tim Youngs, *Travellers in Africa*, ch. 1 'Adventures in Abyssinia'.

3

'Young Memnon' and Romantic Egyptomania

Part 1: Shelley's 'Ozymandias' and Napoleon's Savants

I met a Traveller from an antique land,
Who said, 'Two vast and trunkless legs of stone
Stand in the desart. Near them, on the sand,
Half sunk, a shattered visage lies, whose frown,
And wrinkled lip, and sneer of cold command,
Tell that its sculptor well those passions read,
Which yet survive, stamped on these lifeless things,
The hand that mocked them, and the heart that fed:
And on the pedestal these words appear:
'My name is OZYMANDIAS, King of Kings.'
Look on my works ye Mighty, and despair!
No thing beside remains. Round the decay
Of that Colossal Wreck, boundless and bare,
The loose and level sands stretch far away.

'Glirastes'

Between December 1817 and January 1818 two Egyptian statues appeared before the British public. One was a 7-ton antique bust carved out of red and black granite brought from Thebes; the other, miniaturized within the fourteen lines of Shelley's sonnet 'Ozymandias' was first published in *The Examiner*, no. 524 on 11 January 1818.[1] The *Quarterly Review* for that very same month announced

---

[1] The sonnet was written between 26 and 28 December 1817 in friendly competition with Horace Smith, whose own sonnet was published two weeks later in the same journal. The signature 'Glirastes' means 'doormouse lover' ('doormouse' was apparently one of Shelley's pet names for his wife, Mary). Shelley's signature, like his choice of poetic form, juxtaposed 'miniaturized' desire with the colossal ruins of tyranny (*Poems of Shelley*, Vol. 2 1817–19, ed. by Kelvin Everest and Geoffrey Matthews (Harlow, England: Longman, 2000), p. 307. See also Kelvin Everest's ' "Ozymandias": The Text in Time', *Shelley Bicentenary Essays* (Cambridge: The English Association, 1992), p. 34. Despite Everest's strictures on the inadequacies of the *Examiner* text of the poem compared to later versions (ibid., pp. 35–7), I have preferred to retain it both because its publication date nearly coincided with the arrival of the Egyptian bust in London, and because of its odd signature, further illustrating my theme of the 'dynamics of scale' in exotic discourse.

the safe arrival of 'the head of a colossal statue found at Thebes, and brought from that place to Alexandria at the joint expense of [J. L. Burckhardt] and Mr Salt,[2] as a present to the British Museum . . . This extraordinary head is, without doubt, the finest specimen of ancient Egyptian sculpture which has yet been discovered'.[3] Like Shelley's sonnet, the colossal bust—still the pride of the British Museum's Egyptian collection—represents the Egyptian pharaoh Rameses II (1279–1213 BC) often known in the nineteenth century by his Greek name of 'Osymandias'.

The present chapter is concerned with the narratives attached to these two romantic images of Egyptian antiquity, and with the representation of modern and ancient Egypt in contemporary travelogues and museums. With the advent of the global crisis of the Revolutionary and Napoleonic Wars, the European 'cycle of accumulation' changed from incorporating the collections of pre-colonial naturalists and antiquaries like James Bruce to state-sanctioned institutional programmes closely linked to the interests of empire. Antiquarian or naturalistic curiosities were increasingly 'mobilized' for purposes of national prestige as well as for motives of private connoisseurship or the increase of scientific knowledge. The key terms 'utility', 'curiosity', and 'credit' were overladen with new prerogatives of war and empire. Colonization of Europe's 'antique lands' Egypt and India created a new relationship between exotic objects and their contexts, which in turn influenced the 'orientalism' of romantic travel narratives and the fashion for literary exoticism.[4]

In these war years, colonial travellers in 'antique lands' more often wore military uniforms than oriental costume, their itineraries determined by the motives of strategy and intelligence-gathering rather than disinterested 'curiosity'. Transactions between travellers and native peoples began to be increasingly reified in the terms of colonial racial hierarchies and capitalist relations of production. The 'rape of the Nile' (to borrow Brian Fagan's title)[5] passed through two distinct phases in the romantic period as registered in travel accounts, which correspond to the two divisions of the present chapter. The first was the heroic/tragic phase associated with the Napoleonic invasion and occupation, memorialized by the publication of the *Description de l'Égypt* (1809–22). The second phase might be said to replay the first at the level of farce, as pre-archaeological European collectors scrambled to loot Egyptian antiquities to

[2] For Burckhardt, the Swiss explorer, see below. Henry Salt, whom we met in the previous chapter as Lord Valentia's painter and secretary in India and Abyssinia, was now British Consul in Cairo.
[3] 'The Gingo Expedition—African Discoveries', QR, XVIII (Jan. 1818), 368.
[4] On collection and national prestige, see Dolan, *Exploring European Frontiers*, ch. 4; on literary orientalism see my *British Romantic Writers and the East: Anxieties of Empire* (Cambridge University Press, 1992).
[5] Brian Fagan, *The Rape of the Nile: Tomb Robbers, Tourists, and Archaeologists in Egypt* (London: Macdonald and Jane's, 1977).

adorn national museums and private collections. It is epitomized in the present chapter by Giovanni Belzoni's 1820 *Narrative of the Operations and Recent Discoveries within the Pyramids, Temples, Tombs and Excavations*. I shall argue in the first half of the chapter, however, that Shelley's sonnet, whilst contemporaneous with Belzoni's 'operations' and 'discoveries', actually refers back to the earlier, Napoleonic, phase of Egyptomania.

Given the near-contemporaneity of the British Museum's acquisition of the Rameses bust and Shelley's 'Ozymandias', it seems reasonable to suppose that the sonnet was either directly inspired by the bust or else by the wave of popular interest in ancient Egypt stimulated by its arrival. Richard Holmes plausibly supposes that Shelley composed his poem after seeing the statue at the British Museum; given Shelley's frequent visits to the museum, this is certainly a possibility, although unfortunately the dates of his known visits do not in this case tally.[6] There are, however, graver problems with the hypothesis: most obviously, Shelley's description of Ozymandias' 'sneer of cold command' simply does not fit a statue which contemporaries (most famously De Quincey, see below) described as *smiling*. As D. W. Thompson pointed out in 1937, 'the face in the sonnet is not that of an Egyptian king, but that of Shelley's tyrant, a Godwinian monarch'.[7] The fact that the museum's bust was thought in early nineteenth-century Britain to represent the mythological 'Young Memnon' (rather than Rameses II) poses an even greater problem in identifying it with the pharaoh who is the subject of Shelley's sonnet. Shelley's title, as well as the celebrated 'inscription' from the statue's pedestal (quoted from Diodorus Siculus)[8] clearly identifies it with Rameses II and *not* with Memnon.

In fact, 'Young Memnon' was a misnomer, erroneously given to the statue by William Hamilton, FSA, diplomat, antiquary, and secretary to Lord Elgin (of 'Parthenon Marbles' fame).[9] In 1801 a uniformed Hamilton had accompanied a military intelligence expedition led by Major Charles Hayes to survey Upper

---

[6] Richard Holmes, *Shelley: The Pursuit* (Harmondsworth: Penguin, 1974), p. 410. Shelley visited the British Museum, as well as the India Museum, Bullock's Museum, and other 'shows of London'. Mary Shelley's journal records visits on 7 April and 10 May 1815 (with Shelley and Hogg) and then again sometime between 12 and 15 February 1818, dates which do not tally with the period between the arrival of the Rameses bust in December 1817, and the composition of 'Ozymandias' (*Mary Shelley's Journal*, ed. by Frederick L. Jones (Norman: Oklahoma University Press, 1947), pp. 43, 46, 92. For Bullock's Museum, see p. 41.

[7] 'Ozymandias', *Philological Quarterly*, 16 (1937), 59–64, 63.

[8] Diodorus's authority was the Greek traveller Hekataios, who had translated the inscription from the original hieroglyphics. From a literal-minded point of view, Shelley's modern 'traveller in an antique land' (prior to Champollion's breakthrough) would not have been able to read the inscription unless it was written in Greek. See Anne Janowitz, 'Shelley's Monument to Ozymandias', *Philological Quarterly*, 63 (1984), 477–91, 486.

[9] Hamilton is not to be confused with Sir William Hamilton, antiquary and British Consul at Naples. Elgin was British Ambassador to the Ottoman Porte. See William St Clair, *Lord Elgin and the*

Egypt in the wake of Napoleon's invasion; he published his antiquarian researches in the 1809 *Remarks on Several Parts of Turkey. Part I. Aegyptiaca.* Hamilton's work was probably the most influential early nineteenth-century British work on Egyptian antiquity: as the *Quarterly Review* remarked with characteristic Tory panache in 1818: 'there will be found more learning, science, and faithful description in Mr Hamilton's 'Egyptiaca' . . . than the whole corps of [French] savans, engaged in that magnificent and unrivalled monument of literary vanity [the *Description de l'Égypte*], have yet been able to produce'.[10]

Traditionally, the statue of the 'singing' Memnon (classical authors had described it emitting musical notes when struck by the rays of the rising sun) was thought to be one of the two seated colossi, their upper parts and faces heavily disfigured, standing about an eighth of a mile to the south of the Ramesseum on the plain of Thebes, allegedly known by local inhabitants as 'Tommy' and 'Dummy'.[11]

Stumbling upon a smaller, red granite, bust in the second courtyard of the Ramesseum (or 'Memnonium') temple, Hamilton, however, argued that

I am very much inclined to think that there were *two* pretended vocal statues at Thebes; and that the one which Philostratus speaks of, as having, besides its youthful appearance and other circumstances above mentioned, a peculiar intelligence in its eyes, and a mouth as if *on the point of speaking*, was placed within . . . the Memnonion [*sic*]. The head of this statue is still to be seen within this building, and it is certainly the most beautiful and perfect piece of Egyptian sculpture that can be seen

Marbles (Oxford and New York: Oxford University Press, 1998). According to the *Quarterly Review*, XIX (April–Dec. 1818), 194, the French Egyptologist Jomard had accused Giovanni Belzoni of initiating the mistaken appellation 'Young Memnon' in an article in the *Journal des Savants*. But Hamilton's published account was probably the main stimulus for Belzoni's commission, despite the enthusiasm of the French savants. The *Quarterly* was quick to clear Belzoni's name from Jomard's charge, but without pointing the finger of blame at Hamilton, who had in 1809 been made Under-secretary of State for Foreign Affairs (ibid., p. 194). The *Quarterly* remained agnostic about the identity of the bust, but 'Young Memnon' stuck.

[10] Ibid., p. 420.

[11] Belzoni, *Narrative of the Operations and Recent Discoveries, within the Pyramids, Temples, Tombs, and Excavations, in Egypt and Nubia*, 2nd edn. (London, 1821), p. 127. In fact, these statues represent Rameses II and Amenophis III. Vivant Denon, accompanying Napoleon's invasion of Egypt in 1798–1801, identified the 'musical' Memnon with a colossal statue in red granite lying in fragments in the court of the Ramesseum at Thebes (denominated by Denon the 'Memnonion'). Denon's hypothesis concerning the Memnon was attacked by Jomard and other contributors to the first volume of the *Description de l'Égypte* in 1809, who correctly identified the fragmentary colossus with Rameses II ('Ozymandias') and not Memnon. See Johnstone Parr's 'Shelley's "Ozymandias" ', in *Keats–Shelley Journal*, VI (Winter 1957), 31–5, 32. Hamilton's account, in *Aegyptiaca*, of this 'broken colossal statue of red granite . . . the face entirely obliterated' is striking (*Remarks on Several Parts of Turkey. Pt 1 Aegyptiaca, or Some Account of the Antient and Modern State of Egypt, as obtained in the Years 1801, 1802* (London, 1809), p. 167). Hamilton denied Denon's identification of this statue with 'musical' Memnon, however, which he located at the traditional site; graffiti left by early Greek tourists who had come to hear Memnon's miraculous sunrise music seemed conclusive evidence.

throughout the whole country. We were struck with its extraordinary delicacy [and] the very uncommon expression visible in its features. [italics mine][12]

Although Hamilton could not have known it, the bust had recently been admired by the French antiquaries of Napoleon's expedition, although unlike Hamilton they had cautiously refused to identify it with either Memnon or Rameses. The splendid *Antiquités. Planches* (Tome Deuxième) of the *Description de l'Égypte*, praised its execution, high polish, and fine state of preservation, due to the fact that it had been buried face down in the sand: 'Ce morceau de sculpture méritoit d'être apporté en Europe' the *Description* added, 'pour donner une idée du degré de perfection auquelles Égyptiens étoient parvenus dans l'art de tailler et de polis le granit'.[13] (This was rather disingenuous because in fact they had already damaged the heavy bust in a fruitless attempt to remove it, a point to which I return below.) The *Description*'s desideratum was soon to be realized, although the bust would end up not in the Louvre but, thanks to Giovanni Belzoni's logistical and technical skills, in the Egyptian rooms in the Townley Galleries of the British Museum. As a work of art, Hamilton's 'Young Memnon' seemed in every respect superior to the monumental and facially disfigured 'Old' Memnon. Hamilton's was a scaled-down, polished, humanized 'British' equivalent of the faceless Napoleonic colossus, a gentle smile playing on its lips, on the point of speaking.[14]

Although Egyptian art and sculpture were considered inferior to Greek (particularly in the wake of the enthusiasm for the Parthenon Marbles, purchased by the British Museum in 1816), nevertheless an Egyptian aesthetic was emerging into respectability in Regency Britain. This was in part a result of interest stimulated by the researches of eighteenth-century travellers like Pococke, Norden, and Bruce, but it gained new impetus from the intense competition between Napoleonic France and Britain for colonial domination of Egypt and its antiquities after the defeat of the French invasion of 1798–1801.[15] In 1806 the Egyptian antiquities wrested from the French were deposited in the new Townley Galleries, the thirteen rooms of which also displayed Greek and

---

[12] *Aegyptiaca*, pp. 176–7.

[13] *Description de l'Égypte* (*Antiquités, Planches*, Tome Deuxième, Paris, 1812), *planche* 32, np.

[14] Hamilton reminded his readers that Memnon was 'the universal hero of the South, as Hercules was of the West, and Bacchus the hero of the East' (*Aegyptiaca*, p. 176), an appropriate image for the British crusade against Napoleonic depredations and the pompous hauteur symbolized by the imperialistic 'French' Rameses.

[15] Since its inception, the British Museum had possessed Egyptian 'curiosities' donated by the Lethieullier family in 1756, and Edward Wortley Montagu's collection donated by George II in 1766. The floodgates really opened with the Capitulation of Alexandria in 1801, however, when all the antiquities—most famously the Rosetta Stone—collected by the French savants in Egypt became British national property. (The defeated French were allowed to keep their 'natural' curiosities.) Edward Miller, *That Noble Cabinet: A History of the British Museum*, pp. 65, 96.

Roman objects from the Townley and Sloane Collections, as well as Sir William Hamilton's classical vases.[16] Despite the public interest evident in the *Quarterly Review*'s article, the British Museum's reception of the 'Young Memnon' in 1817 was, as Edward Miller writes, 'lukewarm', however much the Trustees were reluctant to look a gift horse in the mouth: 'it was even decided at one time to put the head . . . out in the courtyard of Montagu House, despite the disastrous effects the atmosphere might have on it'.[17] An elderly Sir Joseph Banks, playing down his lifelong interest in Egyptian antiquities,[18] wrote to Henry Salt in February 1819 in his capacity as a Trustee of the Museum:

Though in truth we are here much satisfied with the Memnon, and consider it as a *chef-d'oeuvre* of Egyptian sculpture; yet we have not placed that statue amongst the works of Fine Art. It stands in the Egyptian Rooms. Whether any statue that has been found in Egypt can be brought into competition with the grand works of the Townley Gallery remains to be proved; unless however they really are so, the prices you have set upon your acquisitions are very unlikely to be realised in Europe [Salt was trying to sell his collection to the Museum].[19]

Banks's ambivalence towards Egyptian art was typical of the virtuosi of his generation, who regarded it as 'curious' rather than 'beautiful', 'colossal' rather than 'sublime'.[20] The rise of the nineteenth-century museum order would, however, see Egyptian art beginning to enjoy a secure, if subordinate, place in the historical taxonomy of ethnographic and antiquarian objects.[21] Ian Jenkins points out that as early as 1777 'J. G. Herder had challenged Winckelmann's premiss that Egyptian art should be judged according to the standards of the Greeks. He put forward a relativistic view based upon a plea for recognizing the

[16] Miller, pp. 96–7.   [17] Ibid., p. 200.

[18] See Gascoigne, *Joseph Banks*, pp. 128–30. Despite his reservations, Banks wrote enthusiastically of the 'Young Memnon' that 'it is the very best workmanship of Egypt & has induced Combe [an FRS and antiquary] to think that the Egyptians taught Sculpture to the Greeks' (ibid., p. 129).

[19] Quoted in Stanley Mayes, *The Great Belzoni* (London: Putnam, 1959), p. 266.

[20] The passage from the Greek beau ideal to Egyptian 'curiosity' still underpins the following description in an 1832 guide (published by the Society for the Diffusion of Useful Knowledge) by G. Long, entitled *The British Museum: Egyptian Antiquities*, Vol. I (London, 1832): 'Passing from the contemplation of the almost faultless representations of the human form in marble, the triumph of Grecian art, [the visitor] comes to figures more remarkable . . . for their singular forms and colossal size, than for their beauty. Though the contrast between what he has just left, and the new scene to which he is introduced, creates at first no pleasing impression, feelings of curiosity and admiration soon arise from a more careful examination of what is around him' (p. 4). On the politics of the British Museum guidebooks, see Inderpal Grewal, 'The Guidebook and the Museum', in *Home and Harem: Nation, Gender, Empire, and the Cultures of Travel* (London: Leicester University Press, 1996), pp. 105–20.

[21] Although it should be noted that only by the middle of the 19th century did it 'become the overriding concern of the [British Museum's] Dept of Antiquities to see its sculptures arranged in chronological order . . . grouping of sculpture according to subject had been the traditional method, as exemplified in the Villa Albani, and the Museo Pio Clementino in Rome, and in the Louvre'. Ian Jenkins, *Archaeologists and Aesthetes in the Sculpture Gallery of the British Museum 1800–1839* (London: British Museum Publications, 1992), pp. 56, 58.

functions of Egyptian art as an expression of native religious belief.'[22] Egyptian antiquities were also worthy 'semiophores' (to borrow Pomian's term discussed in Chapter 1) inasmuch as they were linked to the biblical and classical pasts of European civilization: William Hamilton, for example, hailed the ruins of Luxor as 'eternal monuments of the people who first civilised the world, and taught the first truths of science to Greece and Rome'.[23] And, after all, it was Hamilton's account of the 'British' Young Memnon that had proved the primary inspiration for the difficult task of removing the bust from Thebes and 'relocating' it in the British Museum.

Nevertheless, the appeal of Egyptian, like Indian and Mexican, antiquities and the ethnographic 'curiosities' brought back from the South Pacific, was still in the early decades of the nineteenth century largely exotic rather than aesthetic, and as such partook as much of the popular culture of the fairground and the popular exhibition as the museum. In contrast to Greek art like the Parthenon Marbles, Egyptiana was still celebrated for the effect of wonder rather than resonance, singularity rather than typicality, gigantism rather than sublimity. Appropriately enough, one of the major sites of the popular, commercial 'shows of London' in this period was William Bullock's 'Egyptian Hall' at 22 Piccadilly, established in 1812, its architecture loosely inspired by the great temple of Hat-hor at Dendera, fronted by crude statues of Isis and Osiris[24] (Ill. 5). (Bullock will be discussed in the Conclusion as a travel writer in his own right.) Despite the popularity of Bullock's museum with all social classes, it never escaped the stigma which its façade seemed to give away; in the words of Leigh Hunt 'there is no missing its great lumpish face as you go along. It gives a blow to the mind, like a heavy practical joke.'[25] The populism and commercialism of the Egyptian Hall (which underpinned Belzoni's exhibition of the tomb of Seti I in 1821, discussed later in this chapter) were negative blueprints for the 'official' museum as an institution of the modern state. Tony Bennett writes that the political and epistemological regime of the museum depended upon the construction of a space of representation which was 'rational and scientific . . . fully capable of bearing the didactic burden placed upon it, by

[22] Ian Jenkins, ibid., p. 10. See also Martin Bernal, *Black Athena: The Afroasiatic Roots of Classical Civilisation. Vol. 1 The Fabrication of Ancient Greece, 1785–1985* (London: Free Association Books, 1987), pp. 189–280.

[23] *Aegyptiaca*, p. 153.

[24] Richard Altick, *The Shows of London* (Cambridge, Mass., and London: Harvard University Press, 1978), p. 236. Altick describes Bullock's museum in the Egyptian Hall (until its dispersal in 1819, to be replaced by commercial exhibitions dedicated to a single subject) as one of the last 'museums modelled after the miscellaneous cabinets of the old-time virtuosi'. At the same time, the new exhibitions —of which Belzoni's 1821 Egyptian exhibition discussed at the end of this chapter is an example— 'touched on the same fields of interest as their unsystematic predecessors . . . but often went beyond them as they reflected new tendencies in public curiosity' (*The Shows of London*, p. 288). The main point is their common distinction from the official 'museum order' represented by the British Museum.   [25] Ibid., p. 237.

5. The Egyptian Hall, Piccadilly, opened in 1812. It was designed by Peter Robinson, inspired by the temple of Hat-hor at Dendera. The interior was the work of J. B. Papworth.

differentiating it from the disorder that was imputed to competing exhibitionary institutions'.[26] The museum order was dedicated to the moral reform of the 'carnivalesque' world of popular exhibitions.

The next decades saw the increasing consecration of the statue known as the 'Memnon's Head', as historical archaeology began to usurp the place of patrician *vertu*, and the social range of the museum-going public was extended. The 1832 *Guide to the Museum's Egyptian Antiquities*, although it censured the statue's lips as being 'too thick for our notions [of beauty]', endorsed Hamilton's judgement by praising the cast of its face '. . . full of softness, tranquillity and beauty'.[27] Most notably, in 1846 De Quincey remembered 'that object which some four-and-thirty years ago in the British Museum struck me as simply the sublimest sight which in this sight-seeing world I had seen. It was the Memnon's head, then recently brought from Egypt.' For De Quincey the romantic orientalist, the bust was 'symbolic' rather than 'human', betokening sublime peace, eternity, and love, an 'emanation from some mystery of endless dawn. You durst not call it a smile that radiated from the lips; the radiation was too awful to clothe itself in adumbrations or memorials of flesh.'[28]

Shelley and the Savants: Volney, Denon, and the *Description de l'Égypte*

The 'sneer of cold command' sculpted on the visage of Shelley's Ozymandias is a world apart from the 'sublime peace' of De Quincey's 'Young Memnon'. Possibly Shelley took conscious pains to differentiate the expression of his sneering wreck from the museum's smiling bust just as he chose Ozymandias rather than Memnon as a symbol of tyranny. Critics have tended to interpret Shelley's sonnet according to the traditional concern of its genre, the triumph of art over temporality. Anne Janowitz sums this up in her excellent reading:

the rhetorical irony of Shelley's sonnet is made by juxtaposing the heroic inscription of a living tyrant with that same inscription as it becomes a dismal epitaph on the ruler's works, now reduced to dust. But within the sonnet, this passing away of the

---

[26] Tony Bennett, *The Birth of the Museum: History, Theory, Politics* (London: Routledge, 1995), p. 1.

[27] *The British Museum: Egyptian Antiquities*, i. 253. Denon had earlier commented on the 'African' character of the Sphinx: 'the mouth, the lips of which are thick, has a softness and delicacy of execution truly admirable', *Travels in Upper and Lower Egypt* (1803), i. 270. This seems not yet to have presented an obstacle to aesthetic appreciation.

[28] 'The System of the Heavens, as revealed by Lord Rosse's Telescope', *Works of De Quincey*, ed. by David Masson, 14 vols. (Edinburgh, 1890), viii. 17. De Quincey seems to have misremembered the date: in 1812 the bust still lay in the ruins of Thebes. See John Barrell, *The Infection of Thomas de Quincey* (New Haven and London: Yale University Press, 1991), pp. 112–14.

worldly is counter-balanced by the skill of the Egyptian sculptor who is able to make passions permanent and imaginatively realisable.[29]

This should not be taken to imply that Shelley's claim for the power of art to survive the ruins of empire was in any respect an attempt to recuperate a specifically Egyptian aesthetic, on a par with Hamilton's or Denon's revaluation of Egyptian art: after all, Shelley's strong Hellenism is well-attested.[30] Shelley's aestheticism corresponds rather to the transhistorical, Platonic, power of art celebrated in the *Defence of Poetry*, art as at once the harbinger and guarantee of political liberty. Yet in this section I shall sketch a more historically located 'Ozymandias' which responded to the French invasion of Egypt and its 'artistic' expression in the multi-volume *Description de l'Égypte*, the publication of which continued from 1809 right through the period of Shelley's poetic creativity to 1822. To understand the meaning of 'Ozymandias' in context, I believe that we must look to French rather than British concerns with Egypt, and to Shelley's attempt to reconcile revolutionary republicanism, imperial conquest, and the claims of imagination.

Unlike Keats's 'Ode on a Grecian Urn' or 'Elgin Marbles' sonnets, Shelley's 'Ozymandias' is not a museum poem. Whereas Keats views the antique object in the neutral space of the museum (albeit in *imagination* raising unanswerable questions of context and origin), Shelley carefully constructs an Egyptian 'ground' for his sonnet.[31] 'Egypt' is mediated by the 'traveller from an antique land' whose narrative, proffered to the 'persona' of the poet, is presented in quotation marks in the *Examiner* text quoted at the beginning of this chapter.[32] The sonnet's juxtaposition of the pathos of the traveller's account with the Pharaoh's pompous inscription—also represented in quotation marks—adds a second binary configuration to the 'pharaoh/sculptor' contrast which most critics have read as being of focal importance. Shelley's specification of his source as a 'travel account' has prompted literary historians to ransack the copious literature of Egyptian travel in the period in search of a definitive source; as Janowitz rightly indicates, 'in the exchange between travellers' journals and the classical texts which provided the historical map to Egypt, the actual monument of [Shelley's]

[29] Anne Janowitz, 'Shelley's Monument to Ozymandias', p. 478.
[30] See, for example, Michael Rossington, '"The Voice which is Contagion to the World": The Bacchic in Shelley', in *Beyond Romanticism: New Approaches to Texts and Contexts, 1780–32*, and Jennifer Wallace, *Shelley and Greece: Rethinking Romantic Hellenism* (Basingstoke: Macmillan, 1998).
[31] See Grant F. Scott, *The Sculpted Word: Keats, Ekphrasis, and the Visual Arts* (Hanover and London: University Press of New England, 1994), p. 16.
[32] According to Kelvin Everest, rough drafts of the sonnet show that 'Shelley's first attempt at an opening includes no reference to a "traveller"' ('"Ozymandias": The Text in Time', 26). This, of course, merely underscores the importance of Shelley's decision to include the traveller whose 'meeting' with the unnamed deictic 'I' of the first line suggests that he is imagined to be a contemporary, rather than a classical, traveller like Diodorus or Strabo.

Ozymandias recedes further and further into physical obscurity'.[33] In what follows I shall try to combine attention to verbal echoes with plausible contexts in establishing the sonnet's relationship to its sources in order not to lose sight of the poem itself. At the same time I acknowledge, given the overarching concerns of the present book, that my reading serves primarily as a point of entry into selective French and British travel accounts of Egypt, rather than as a new elucidation of the sonnet.

The work which most closely corresponds to the political 'message' of Shelley's sonnet is Constantin Volney's *The Ruins: or a Survey of the Revolutions of Empires*, which we know Shelley drew upon in the composition of *Queen Mab*, *The Revolt of Islam*, and other poems. *The Ruins* opens with a striking account of the author's travels in Egypt and Syria; 'no where perceiving aught but robbery and devastation, tyranny and wretchedness, my heart was oppressed with sorrow and indignation . . . Frequently I met with antique monuments; wrecks of temples, palaces, and fortifications; pillars, aqueducts, sepulchres.' Turning away from the traditional eighteenth-century ruin trope, however, Volney converts despondency into a more affirmative faith in the triumph of reason: 'since the evils of society flow from ignorance and inordinate desire, men will never cease to be tormented till they shall become intelligent and wise'.[34] As Johannes Fabian comments on this passage, Volney's pessimistic 'knowledge of the past is a sort of Archimedean point from which to change the otherwise hopeless present'.[35]

In this respect, Volney seems a promising candidate for Shelley's 'traveller from an antique land', particularly as the French savant was also the author of the influential *Travels Through Syria and Egypt, in the Years 1783, 1784, and 1785*, published in 1787. In so far as it (in some respects) represents an exemplary case of enlightenment 'anti-travel' writing, Volney's book is deeply paradoxical, sceptical of the efficacy or utility of 'personal narrative' as against the purely statistical or topographical account. In contrast to previous travellers like Pococke, Norden, and Bruce, Volney claims to be more interested in the condition of modern Egypt than in its antiquities. There is here absolutely no aesthetic response to Egyptian monuments, the sight of the pyramids simply 'inflam[ing him] with indignation at the tyranny of the despots who enforced these barbarous works, a sentiment which too frequently recurs on viewing the different monuments of Egypt'.[36] (Significant perhaps that Volney, unlike many of his contemporaries, believed the ancient Egyptians to have been 'real

[33] Janowitz, p. 479.

[34] Constantin Volney, *The Ruins, or A Survey of the Revolutions of Empires*, 2nd edn. (London, 1795), pp. 2, 101.

[35] Johannes Fabian, *Time and the Other*, p. 10.

[36] Constantin Volney, *Travels Through Syria and Egypt, in the Years 1783, 1784, and 1785*, 2 vols. (London, 1787), i. 283. (Henceforth V. in text).

negroes' on account of the physiognomy of the Sphinx (i. 81).) Racial attitudes apart, Volney's reading of Eygptian antiquity anticipates the political critique of Shelley's 'Ozymandias', with the proviso that the rationalist ideologue Volney (rather than Shelley's imagined 'sculptor'), unmasks the tyranny of the Egyptian *'ancien régime'* in the name of social progress.

Volney's preface to his *Travels* declares his commitment to objectivity, the suppression of the sensibility paraded in the opening pages of *The Ruins*:

I have rejected, as too prolix, both the order and the details of an itinerary, as well as all personal adventures; I have only exhibited general views, as better calculated to combine facts and ideas, and from a desire of saving the time of the reader, amid the prodigious succession of new publications. (V. I. vii)

One of the last of the major pre-Napoleonic European travellers in Egypt, Volney's polemical target (in addition to his attack on 'decadent' modern Egyptians) is the fetishization of 'wonder' and 'curiosity' by his predecessors. Constantly seeking to 'decompose' his first impressions in conformity with his intellectual training as an 'ideologue' philosopher, his narrative is sustained by critique rather than by nostalgia.[37] For Volney the self-centred impressionism of the curious travel writer entirely misjudges the culture under surveillance. Even the well-informed traveller arriving in Egypt is 'new to all these objects, and dazzled with their variety . . . he remains absorbed in surprise and astonishment' (ibid.). Overwhelmed by the exotic novelty of the streets of Alexandria, he is seduced by the 'dazzle' [V. I. 2] of first contact: 'Amid this crowd of unusual objects, his mind is incapable of reflection; nor is it until he has reached his place of residence . . . that, becoming more calm, he reflects on the narrow, ill-paved streets . . . the meagre and swarthy inhabitants . . . the universal air of misery' (V. I. 4). To 'exchange glances' with modern Egyptians, to aestheticize contact, results in a blindness to the poverty and political oppression which Volney sees as the only realities of modern oriental society. Like his Scots admirer James Mill, Volney as 'anti-traveller' seems to have believed (in the words of Javed Majeed), that 'cultures can actually be understood better in translation and from a distance. Too much sympathy with Indian [or Egyptian] cultures undermines the possibility of a thorough understanding of them. It is only by distancing oneself from [them] that they can be seen in sharp relief and the targets of reform clearly formulated'.[38] As a major practitioner of the 'disenchantment of distance',[39] Volney entitled a whole section in chapter 18 'Of the Exaggerations of Travellers' (V. I. 266).

---

[37] But see Martin Thom's succinct defence of Volney as ideologue and traveller in *Republics, Nations and Tribes* (London and New York: Verso, 1995), pp. 142–9. Thom compares Volney's with Chateaubriand's 'picturesque' travelogue, in some respects similar to Denon's account studied here.

[38] Javed Majeed, *Ungoverned Imaginings: James Mill's History of British India and Orientalism* (Oxford University Press, 1992), p. 139. [39] See Ch. 1, pp. 29–30, 50–1.

In contrast with Bruce, Volney minimizes transactions with Egyptians in his narrative, which is devoid of 'reported dialogues' with indigenous interlocutors. Rather than relying on native informants, Volney prefers to derive his information about Egypt from French merchants resident in Cairo (V. I. 114). Apparently encountering nothing but resistance from native peoples, his movement around the country is severely curtailed:

with us, travels are agreeable excursions; there, they are difficult and dangerous undertakings, especially for Europeans, whom the superstitious natives believe to be sorcerers, come to discover by magic, treasure which the Genii have concealed under the ruins . . . we are confined therefore to the banks of the [Nile], and a route frequented by everyone, which can afford no new information . . . Only by comparing what we have seen ourselves with the observations made by others [can] some general ideas be acquired.   (V. I. 12–13)

Egypt is represented in strictly anti-picturesque terms (V. I. 263), and there is nothing of the erotic charge which we have associated with Banks and Bruce: 'never, except from some extraordinary excitement, will a swarthy Egyptian woman, dripping from these yellow and muddy [Nile] waters, remind him of the bathing Naiads' (V. I. 19). Racial disgust is here entirely unreflexive, studious to reject the 'curious' rhetoric of temporalization.

Anticipating his remarks in *The Ruins*, Volney portrays modern Egyptians as the abject victims of Mameluke tyranny, but nevertheless nurturing 'a latent fire, which waits only for proper agents to put it in motion' (V. I. 204). Liberation, he hints, will only be achieved by French colonial occupation; conquest of Egypt will be no great feat given that the Mameluke troops 'are a mob, their march a riot, their battles duels, and their war a scene of robbery and plunder' (V. I. 178–9). Antiquarianism is employed as a strong argument for colonizing Egypt, rather than as the issue of disinterested aristocratic 'curiosity' (in this respect the modern Egyptians who suspected him of being a grave robber were not far off the mark). Volney could hardly have known how prophetic his words would prove when he wrote

were Egypt possessed by a nation friendly to the fine arts, discoveries might be made there, which would make us better acquainted with antiquity than any thing the rest of the world can afford us . . . we may then be allowed to search every part of the country, the banks of the Nile, and the sands of Lybia . . . It is probable too, that till that period, we must remain ignorant of the signification of the hieroglyphics.   (V. I. 284–6)

The 'antique land' is claimed as the heritage of Europe rather than of its contemporary inhabitants.

How could the radical agenda of Volney's *Ruins* be squared with the imperialistic yearnings of his *Travels in Egypt and Syria*? This problem must have been particularly salient for Shelley, who with historical hindsight could follow the crystallization of Volney's plans in Napoleon's invasion of Egypt in 1798. The transformation of Volney's radical (and for Shelley inspirational) critique of an oriental '*ancien régime*' into full-scale European imperial conquest seemed to represent in miniature the fate of the 'blissful dawn' of the French Revolution itself as seen by many British radicals. Napoleon's invasion was partly an attempt to threaten British imperial interests in the Middle East and India; partly an attempt to secure food supplies for the French Republic, which had been fed with Egyptian grain during the crisis of 1792. The Mameluke rulers of Egypt, Murad and Osman Bey, enforced a strict monopoly on Egyptian resources incompatible with French interests. Because they had failed to modernize their army (as Volney scathingly pointed out), they fell an easy prey to Napoleon at the Battle of the Pyramids. Nevertheless, alongside the Bedouin, they maintained an effective guerrilla war against the French until the final defeat of the latter by British and Ottoman forces in 1801.[40]

Napoleon's invasion was a bizarre mixture of pragmatic modernism and romantic 'temporalization'; in partial emulation of Alexander the Great, he brought along 150 savants (collectively known as the 'Institute de Caire', on the model of the French Academy), with orders to conduct exploration and research into every aspect of Egyptian society, economics, topography, and especially antiquities. Although the French colonization plan was aborted by their expulsion in 1801, the 22-volume *Description de l'Égypte*, published between 1809 and 1822, constituted the sum of the knowledge about Egypt gathered by the savants during their short sojourn, a sort of textual surrogate for France's lost colony. The *Description* is in one sense the apotheosis of eighteenth-century geographical knowledge, aiming to portray the 'totality' of a culture in 10 grand-folio volumes of text, 885 plates (some hand coloured), a 3-sheet geographic map, and a 47-sheet topographic map of Egypt.[41] Nothing as ambitious had yet been attempted for any European country, although the French project was partly inspired by the multi-volume *Asiatic Researches* published by the British Asiatic Society of Calcutta. As we shall see in Chapter 6, the *Description* in turn influenced Alexander von Humboldt's comparatively gargantuan project the *Voyage en Amérique*, published in Paris in thirty-three

[40] C. W. Bayly, *Imperial Meridian*, p. 58. For a critical sketch of the expedition as the foundation-stone of modern orientalism, see Edward Said, *Orientalism*, pp. 79–87.

[41] Anne Godlewska, 'Map, Text and Image: The Mentality of Enlightened Conquerors. A New Look at the *Description de l'Égypte*', *Transactions of the Institute of British Geographers*, ns, 20 (1995), 5–28, 7. For Edward Said the *Description* inaugurated 'a textual attitude to the Orient', *Orientalism*, p. 83. The standard recent account of Napoleon in Egypt is H. Laurens, J.-C. Golvin, and C. Gillespie (eds.), *L'Expédition d'Égypte, 1798–1801* (Paris: Armand Colin, 1989). For an invaluable overview of 18th-century travel literature on Egypt, see Henry Laurens, *Les Origines Intellectuelles de L'Expédition D'Égypte (1698–1798)* (Istanbul and Paris: Editions Isis, 1987). Thanks to Isabelle Vinson for a copy of this book.

volumes between 1807 and 1832 (Humboldt himself had tried to join Napoleon's savants, but ended up crossing the Atlantic instead). Between them these projects illustrate the encyclopaedic ambitions of romantic 'planetary consciousness', and the European fascination with the 'antique lands' of Egypt, India, and tropical America in particular. Unlike the *Asiatic Researches* and Humboldt's *Voyage en Amérique*, however, the *Description* enjoyed state support in both Napoleonic and Restoration Paris.

As historical geographer Anne Godlewska writes in an illuminating essay on the *Description*, the text 'was designed to replace, and indeed, reconstruct Egypt. The *Description*, composed of graphically rendered terrain measurement *and* of the accounts and disputations of all the known or remembered scholars versed on Egypt, was considered better than Egypt itself'.[42] The extent of knowledge about Egypt collected in the *Description* would, of course, not have been possible without Napoleon's colonial army; whereas Volney's movements had been constantly frustrated by Egyptian recalcitrance, travelling savants now wore uniforms and travelled under the aegis of an 'army of modernity'. Conquest and precision went hand in hand: as Fourier wrote in the *Description*'s Preface: 'we were many times obliged to replace our weapons with geometrical instruments and, in a sense, to fight over or to conquer the terrain that we were to measure'.[43] The insecure credit sought by pre-colonial travellers like James Bruce by means of measurement and rhetoric, was now guaranteed by the witness of a whole army and a mobile academic institute 'in the field'.[44]

All the French army's edicts were translated into Arabic by French orientalists; the French claimed to be 'true Muslims' who had come to liberate the Egyptians from the Mameluke yoke, educing their destruction of the Papal See (the previous year) as evidence of the fact. The system of transliterating Arabic place names for the *Description*'s texts and maps was based on Volney's 1794–5 *Simplification des langues orientales*; the French traveller had himself been invited to defend his system before the Dépôt de la Guerre, and had recommended that three mathematicians attended, because in his view transliteration was an 'algebraic operation'. As Jomard, the general editor of the *Description*, put it, the landscape of Egypt was to be changed from a 'chaos of Arabic names' to European order.[45] Although Volney did not himself accompany the expedition to Egypt, in many ways his *Travels* provided the inspiration for its

---

[42] 'Map, Text, and Image', p. 14. Godlewska points out that the 'restructuring' and 'reorientation' of Egypt to conform with the economy, society, and polity of France is a prime example of Latour's theory of the 'combinability' of mobiles at the centre of calculation (p. 26).

[43] Quoted ibid., p. 8.

[44] French cartography restructured indigenous space, employing a 'common prime meridian [which] gave Egypt a location relative to France' (ibid., p. 15).

[45] Ibid., p. 17.

modernizing programme. Like Volney's 'objective' travel account, the topographic maps of the *Description* were 'drawn from a perspective where map maker/reader could see everything and yet not be seen', and like his summary judgements on the country which he had only been able to see with a partial view, the maps 'allowed little in the way of qualified statements'.[46] Appropriately enough, the Cairene *ulema* Al-Jabarti, author of an eloquent and highly critical contemporary account of the French occupation from the Egyptian point of view, found the Arabic grammar of the French edicts to be as inaccurate as their cadastral maps. He denounced their frequent solecisms as 'animal droppings on the road or a boulder in a mountain pass, may God afflict the man who composed it with break-bone fever and may God expose him to all sorts of destruction'.[47]

The modernizing, Volneyan impulse only illuminates one aspect of the *Description de l'Égypte*, however, and needs to be balanced with the strong 'temporalizing' urge whereby the French represented themselves not only as the 'true Musselmans' come to save modern Egyptians from the Mameluke yoke but also the inheritors of the monuments and laws of ancient Egypt.[48] This temporalizing myth permeates Vivant Denon's *Voyage dans la basse et la haute Égypte, pendant les campagns du general Bonaparte* (1801), the first eye-witness account of the French expedition to be published and one which had a wider influence than the expensive and tardy *Description* itself. Denon was a gentleman virtuoso of the old stamp, aged 51 when he accompanied the French army to Egypt; after his return, in 1802, he was appointed Director-General of Museums, restructured the Louvre (swollen with acquisitions from Napoleon's conquests in Italy), and achieved fame as the leading French antiquarian of his generation.[49] In his best-selling *Travels* we find a revival of the principle of 'curiosity' now sanctioned by the author's participation in the French

[46] Ibid., pp. 17, 18. Due to a wrangle between Jomard's Commission de la *Description de l'Égypte* and the Depôt de la Guerre, the topographical maps, in many ways the key to the coherence of the whole project, were not published until 1826.

[47] Al-Jabarti's *Chronicle of the First Seven Months of the French Occupation of Egypt*, ed. and trans. by S. Moreth (Leiden: E. J. Brill, 1975), p. 44. But despite his hatred of the French, Al-Jabarti admired the library and scientific instruments of the Institut du Caire as well as the methodical principles of French administration (ibid., p. 117). Albert Hourani points out that Al-Jabarti's chronicle is redolent of 'the whole ambivalent relationship of modern Egypt and modern Europe', *Arabic Thought in the Liberal Age, 1798–1939* (Oxford University Press, 1970), p. 49. See also Timothy Mitchell, *Colonising Egypt*, p. 133.

[48] As Godlewska points out, 'the monumentality of the *Description* was part of the proof of France's association with the monumentality of Egypt' ('Map, Text, Image', p. 18).

[49] See Judith Nowinski, *Baron Dominque Vivant Denon (1784–1825): Hedonist and Scholar in a Period of Transition* (Rutherford, Madison, Teaneck: Fairleigh Dickinson University Press, 1970). Denon made over 150 sketches during his travels in Egypt: some he included in his own volume of 1802; others he engraved for the *Description*' (p. 83).

expedition, as he followed the campaigns of Bonaparte in Lower and Deltaic Egypt and General Desaix in Upper Egypt. His narrative represents 'curiosity' as manly, muscular, military: 'If a fondness of antiquities has frequently made me a soldier, on the other hand, the kindness of the soldiers, in aiding me in my researches, has often made antiquaries of them.'[50]

Denon's antiquarianism becomes a metonym for uninhibited colonial expropriation, as the necessity for negotiations with Egyptians which had hampered pre-colonial acquisition of antiquities was overridden: 'I took possession of whatever was to be found . . . I extended my conquests as far as Nubia, on the other side of Philoë, that delightful island, where it was necessary to snatch by force from the inhabitants the curiosities with which it abounded' (D. I. xiv–xv). Denon for the first time conceived of transporting whole monuments to Europe as trophies of war—Cleopatra's Needle, or the temple at Philae (D. II. 169): colonial conquest now permitted the mobilization of large-scale objects, not just their paper representations. The scale of Europe's appropriation of ancient Egypt, as well as the sundering of modern Egyptians from their own archaeological heritage is well illustrated by Denon's story of the sheikh who approached him while he was sketching the ruins of Luxor 'and asked me if it was the French or the English who had erected those monuments' (D. III. 187). As Denon reflects upon this example of oriental 'ignorance', he seems totally oblivious of the bitter irony which might well be supposed to have inspired it.

The romantic enthusiasm of Denon's narrative, as well as its temporalizing identification with Egyptian antiquity, is exemplified by his description of the French Army's first sight of the ruins of Thebes during Desaix's pursuit of Murad Bey:

the whole army, suddenly and with one accord, stood in amazement at the sight of its scattered ruins, and clapped their hands with delight, as if the end and object of their glorious toils, and the complete conquest of Egypt, were accomplished . . . by taking possession of the splendid remains of this ancient metropolis.   (D. II. 84)

Here the privatized enthusiasm of the eighteenth-century curioso is redeemed and collectively appropriated by the soldiers of the French army, translated into the rhapsody of a whole nation at war. Denon feels deeply moved by 'the electric emotion of a whole army of soldiers, whose delicate sensibility made me feel proud of being their companion, and glory in calling myself a Frenchman' (D. II. 85). Such sensibility to the antique is not simply the self-indulgence of the 'man of feeling'. In contrast to James Bruce's attack of nostalgia at Gish, the French army here manifests a nostalgia for what it considers to be the origins of civilization itself. Evident here is a phylogenetic rather than an ontogenetic

---

[50] Vivant Denon, *Travels in Upper and Lower Egypt* (1801), trans. by Arthur Aikin, 3 vols. (London, 1803), i. p. xviii. Henceforth D. in text.

homesickness which consolidates the temporalizing myth of French conquest and inscribes the name of Napoleon in the annals of world history.[51]

Dressed in his 'light infantry uniform' (D. III. 127) and thus enjoying an advantage over all previous travellers from 'Herodotus to the present' (D. I. 360–1), Denon summed up his brief as being 'to describe everything' (D. I. ii). He was quick to reject Volney's scepticism about the representational possibilities of travel writing, defending the 'dazzle' (D. I. v) of first impressions from his strictures and insisting that 'to travel, is to enjoy those gifts, which are destroyed by an endeavour to draw a comparison between them' (D. I. 62).[52] Egotism, antiquarianism, and conquest are interwoven in Denon's narrative, which effortlessly combined dialogue, anecdotes, picturesque aesthetics, and Shandeyan-style sentimentalism with antiquarian description and patriotic propaganda. It may not be an overstatement to say that Denon's book rescued the very possibility of travel writing from the sort of problems associated with Bruce's narrative discussed in the previous chapter, as well as warding off epistemological scepticism of the Volneyan kind. Denon's *Travels* in many ways represents the 'personal narrative' omitted from the entirely systematic *Description*, and as such salvages the 'vectoral' travel account from the totalizing objectivity of the *Description*'s programme.[53] The *Edinburgh Review*, true to form, complained about 'the flippant and familiar style' of 'a brisk little old Frenchman, with more vivacity than judgement, and more ease than perspicuity', and the fact that the exorbitantly expensive French text (in Grand Folio) was 'as large as a panel [*sic*] charged with hieroglyphics, proving that Denon's 'taste has been formed perhaps upon the gigantic monuments of the Thebaid'. Nevertheless, it conceded that 'few publications, we believe, have ever obtained so extensive a circulation in the same space of time as these travels.'[54]

One important aspect of the Napoleonic temporalization of Egypt was its bid

[51] Participation in a Hegelian world-historical event here becomes the locus of memory, rather than the private associations of childhood which nostalgia draws upon, and which we shall see informing much British colonial discourse in India.

[52] Ironizing Volney's account of the dangers of misinterpretation attendant upon first impressions in his account of Alexandria (quoted above), Denon wrote, capriciously: 'everything . . . is represented by [Volney] with such a degree of truth, that, on looking over his work some months after, I fancied that I was entering Alexandria once more' (D. I, 88). Volney had succeeded as a travel writer better than he himself thought possible.

[53] Denon seemed unperturbed by the forthcoming publication of the Institute's researches, declaring that, in deference to the larger work, he had 'struck out from my journal all that I had there hazarded of critical research' (D. III, 127). His *Travels,* he argued (in an appropriately military metaphor) would serve as the 'advance guard' for the *Description* (ibid.). In one respect at least, however, Denon anticipated the monumental scale of the *Description*: the sheer physical size of his two grand folio volumes, with their lavish plates and detailed explanatory notes.

[54] ER 1 (Jan. 1803), 345, 330, 344–5, 330. In the three-volume 1803 English translation by Arthur Aikin, the bookseller reduced the lavish and expensive French original to more manageable proportions, left out some of the plates, and 'incorporated with the text such parts of the notes as appear to have been thrown to the end of the original work' (translator's advertisement, p. viii).

to consecrate Egyptian art, sculpture, and architecture to rival the hegemony of the Graeco-Roman beau ideal. The ideology of this 'Egyptian aesthetic' reflected the new French state's combination of monumentality and rationalism. In Denon's text there appears an attempt to resolve the tension between the 'Greek' taste of the eighteenth-century virtuoso and the aesthetics of the French Directory. Although Denon shared Volney's deprecation of the pyramids, he discovered in the Sphinx a successful combination of colossal scale with 'mild, gracious and tranquil' expression (compare with Pococke's 'pedantry' discussed in Chapter 1) (D. I. 270). Denon judged the artistic qualities of the Sphinx as inferior to the Greek, but felt that 'sufficient justice has been rendered to the fine simplicity and character of nature which is displayed in the figure' (D. I. 270). (In contrast to Volney, he seems to have believed that only the earliest Egyptians had been negroes, but that the later monuments were the work of 'a copper coloured' nation.[55]) He was on easier ground in comparing Egyptian architecture with Hindu; without borrowing anything from the latter, Egyptian architecture had 'become the basis of all that is the subject of admiration in modern art, and of which we have considered as exclusively belonging to architecture, the three Greek orders, the doric, ionian and corinthian' (D. II. 70). He thus aimed a blow at British orientalism with its high claims for the priority of Hindu over Egyptian style.[56]

The aesthetic climax of Denon's book is surely his visit to Dendera. When he has recovered from his sublime astonishment (D. II. 71), he set about interpreting the ruins in terms of the new aesthetic of rationality and colossal scale: 'With these people, the idea of the immortality of the Deity is presented by the eternity of his temple: these ornaments, which are always rational, always consistent, always significant, demonstrate a steadiness of principle, a taste founded upon truth, and a deep train of reasoning' (D. II. 66). 'In the ruins of [Dendera] the Egyptians appeared to me giants' (D. II. 68) (compare Benjamin Haydon's account of Fuseli's famous pronouncement upon first seeing the Elgin Marbles: 'De Greeks were Godes! de Greeks were godes!')[57] For Denon Dendera

---

[55] As reported by Benjamin Haydon in conversation with Denon, *Autobiography of B. R. Haydon* (Oxford University Press, 1927), p. 265.

[56] The British soon countered with the claims of Indian antiquity. In the first part of his *Travels, Russia, Tartary and Turkey*, 6 vols. (Cambridge and London, 1810), E. D. Clarke recounted the 'extraordinary testimony' of some Brahmins who accompanied General Baird's East India Company army from the Red Sea coast across Egypt to join General Abercrombie in 1801 (the first time that the two armies had fought together outside India). The Brahmins 'saw at Denderah the representation of their God *Vishnu* among the ancient sculptures of the place; and were with difficulty restrained by their officers from assaulting the Arabs, on account of the neglected state in which *his* temple, as *they* supposed, was suffered to remain' (III, 58). Whether this anecdote belongs in the archives of colonial history or colonial fantasy, it exemplifies the ideological importance of antiquarianism in the early colonial period. British India represented the source of ancient civilization preserved *in the present*.

[57] Haydon, *Autobiography*, p. 87.

told of the 'progressive lapse of ages' marking the rise of the arts to 'perfection and sublimity', but also of the cultural decline which had returned modern Egypt to a 'state of nature' (D. II. 67). His bid to draw the ruined monuments is plagued by anxiety that he lacks the 'eyes, hands and intelligence vast enough to see, copy, and reduce to some order, the multitude of striking images' (D. II. 77) before him. Like the chaos of Arabic place-names, the ruins of Egyptian antiquity needed to be restructured, measured, drawn, perfectly 'mobilized' so that, in the words of Fourier in the *Description*, 'one could use them to construct edifices identical to those that we have described' in Europe.[58] What a contrast to the more familiar romantic aesthetic of ruins—captured especially in the second and fourth cantos of Byron's *Childe Harold*—which reads them as irrecoverable, the objective correlative of Harold's *weltschmerz*.

In contrast to Denon's rational sublime at Dendera, his account of Karnak shows the strain of consecrating Egyptian gigantism. Karnak proves an overwhelming disappointment, the remnants of primitive and purely material sublimity: 'mountains are piled together, and hewn out into massive proportions' (D. II. 259). The problem here is that 'it was not yet known, that a perfection in the arts bestows on their productions a grandeur which is independent of their magnitudes (D. II. 259). With great resourcefulness, however, Denon prevents the 'melancholy wisdom' of Karnak from becoming a stumbling-block to the French Directory's 'mythic identification' with Egyptian antiquity. Karnak becomes a symbolical representation of the Directory's liberation of France from the austere rigour of the despotism of the General Will. Ancient Egyptian politics of the sort memorialized here are characterized by the gigantic Hobbesian image of the stern Egyptian priest, a hook in one hand and a flail in the other: 'the former, no doubt, to restrain, and the latter to punish: everything is measured by the law, and enchained by it' (D. II. 288). Under this 'monastic' severity, the fine arts are 'bent under the weight of fetters, and their soaring genius . . . pinioned to the earth' (ibid.). Even the sacred phallus frequently represented here in the *relievos* (Denon alludes to his own earlier *Oeuvres Priapiques*, as well as to the work of De Hancarville and Dupuis) destroys sexual pleasure by 'converting it into a duty'. 'Not a single circus, not a single theatre, not a single edifice for public recreation' relieves the gloomy theocracy of ancient Egypt. 'Surely', Denon comments, 'in the evil hour of France, some demon evoked the gloomy ferocious soul of an Egyptian priest to animate the monster, who imagined, by making us sullen, to render us happy' (D. II. 289). The grim monumentality of Karnak here becomes an image of Robespierre's Reign of Terror, ideologically proscribed under the Directory and Napoleonic Empire.

[58] 'Map, Text, Image', p. 9.

In one of the most extraordinary moments of synthesis between modern pre-cision and temporalization in the French campaign, the savants carefully mea-sured the Memphis pyramid and supposed it (in the words of Jomard) to have been 'a metric monument . . . designed to serve as the national repository of the unity of measures'.[59] Metrication, the rationalization of the measurement of space espoused by the French Assembly in 1798, was a major preoccupation of the First French Republic; the *Description* is accordingly one of the first publi-cations to introduce precise metric scales beneath its plates and maps. French modernity represented itself as simply returning to an ancient order of nature, enshrined in the ancient Egyptian metre. Denon attempts an analogous defence of Egyptian aesthetics, which he supposed provided 'a canon of proportions' for artists based on the 'constant equality observable in their works' (D. III. 5). He nevertheless betrays an ambivalence about a practice which, whilst it leads to 'the perfection of uniformity, convert[ing] drawing into a mechanical art', was 'detri-mental to the sallies of genius and the expression of delicate sentiment' (ibid.). Taking issue with the Hellenic beau ideal associated with Wincklemann and Lessing, Denon's special pleading for the public monumentality of Egyptian art here nevertheless appears forced. 'If the group of the Laocoon' he writes,

which speaks to the soul as well as to the eyes, were executed in a proportion of 60 feet, it would lose all its beauty, and would not present so striking a mass of work-manship as this; in short, if these statues were more agreeable, they would be less beautiful, as they would then cease to be . . . eminently *monumental.* (D. III. 80)

The cult of monumentality associated with Napoleonic art (one thinks of J.-L. David's vast contemporary history paintings) and consolidated by identifica-tion with the sublime scale of ancient Egyptian building was vulnerable to charges of gross gigantism. As the *Edinburgh Review* complained, it also appeared incongruous in combination with Denon's sentimental egotism.

If Dendera represented the climax and Karnak the nadir of Denon's anti-quarian enthusiasm for Egypt, his account of Thebes seems to contain a trou-bled element of reflexivity. Of particular interest for my present argument is the fact that Denon's ambivalence is focused upon his location of the colossal statue of Ozymandias, as described by Diodorus Siculus, Herodotus, and Strabo, therefore linking his travel account to Shelley's sonnet. Denon places Ozy-mandias not in or near the Ramesseum temple but rather in the open desert near where most travellers chose to place the 'singing' Memnon (Denon iden-tified the 'Memnon' with a gigantic shattered colossus lying inside the funereal temple, see note 11).[60] Ozymandias, the largest of the three sitting colossi, had

---

[59] 'Map, Text, Image', p. 12.
[60] This already suggests Denon as a more plausible source for Shelley than Pococke's *Description of the East,* whether in the original 1743 edition or as included in Vol. 15 of Pinkerton's *General Col-*

towered between the other two statues ('Tommy' and 'Dummy') whose eroded figures remain. 'Ozymandias', Denon argued,

had prided himself so much on the execution of this bold design [the seated colossus] that he had caused an inscription to be engraven on the pedestal of the statue, in which he defied the power of man to destroy this monument, as well as that of his tomb, the pompous description of which now appears only a fantastic dream. The two statues still left standing are doubtless those of the mother and the son of this prince, mentioned by Herodotus; that of the king himself has disappeared, the hand of time and the teeth of envy appear to have united zealously in its destruction, and *nothing of it remains* but a shapeless rock of granite. (D. II. 92–3) (italics mine)

Although Denon does not quote the 'Look on my works, ye Mighty' inscription from Diodorus, this passage seems a highly plausible source for Shelley's 'Ozymandias', and indeed the phrase I have italicized in Arthur Aikin's translation verbally resonates with the twelfth line of the sonnet 'No thing beside remains'. (Of course, Shelley knew Diodorus Siculus independently of his reading in contemporary travel literature, and in any case, as Johnstone Parr points out, 'the arrogant epitaph of Ozymandias had become virtually a commonplace' in the romantic period.[61]) Denon describes how he set about drawing 'these colossal figures' (including the 'shapeless rock of granite' which is all that remains of Ozymandias) 'when I found that I was left alone with the stupendous originals. Being alarmed at my unprotected situation, I hastened to rejoin my comrades . . .' (D. II. 96). His sense of loneliness and vulnerability here—he fears being shot in the back by marauding Bedouin—perhaps resonates in the final couplet of Shelley's sonnet, as the 'traveller' evokes the exposure of the statue's placement out in the open desert: 'Round the decay | Of that Colossal Wreck, boundless and bare | The loose and level sands stretch far away'.[62]

lection . . . of Voyages and Travels (London, 1814). Pococke located the 'Osymanduas' statue by the gate of the Temple of Luxor rather than in the open desert. His relaying of Diodorus' account, whilst mentioning a giant foot and citing the inscription adapted by Shelley, makes no reference to the statue's visage or expression. *Description of the East*, 2 vols. (London, 1743), i. 106. Pococke's plate showing an imagined reconstruction of the statue (ibid., i. 107) was not included in Pinkerton's 1814 text, which would have been most easily accessible to Shelley.

[61] Parr correctly infers from this fact that Denon is a major source for Shelley's poem, although misunderstanding the significance of Denon's location of the Ozymandias statue, 'Shelley's Ozymandias', p. 34.

[62] An article entitled 'A Brief View of the Fine Arts among Various Nations of Antiquity', published in the *Annals of the Fine Arts, for 1819* (the same issue which contains the first text of Keats's 'Ode to a Nightingale') concurred with Denon's judgement: 'According to Herodotus and Strabo, the statue of Osimandias was placed between these two colossi, which are the largest in Egypt. Several artists, who accompanied the French Expedition to Egypt, speak with enthusiasm of an immense fragment of a statue of basalt, which they discovered near this spot, with its face turned to the ground'. Uncovering the statue, the French 'found it as perfect, and in as fine preservation, from this circumstance, as if it had but just come from the sculptor's chisel'. A footnote to this sentence reads 'This we believe is

Verbal source-hunting must remain at the level of speculation unless it can be reinforced by a convincing general context. According to my reading, Denon's account of the fate of the Ozymandias colossus is highly reflexive inasmuch as it foreshadows the fate of French conquest in Egypt (his book was, of course, published after the Capitulation of Alexandria in 1801). Like the colossal statue of the all-conquering Rameses, French power in Egypt has vanished, driven out by 'the hand of time and the teeth of envy'. Except, of course, for the 'pompous inscription' of a monumental publication to be entitled the *Description de l'Égypte*, like the colonial project itself a 'fantastic dream'. French power over Egypt, a country which Fourier described as 'the richest museum in the world',[63] remains purely textual and graphic, a surrogate for Egypt itself. Denon's account of the statue of Ozymandias, close as it is to the theme of Shelley's sonnet, of course contains no equivalent of the Shelleyan sculptor whose representations of tyranny 'yet survive, stamped on these lifeless things', and it is the burden of Shelley's sonnet that art survives while tyranny is overthrown by 'time and envy'.

Nevertheless, as I have argued, Denon (unlike Shelley) *was* preoccupied with consecrating Egyptian sublimity over and against the prevailing Hellenism. Both Denon's Grand Folio *Travels* and the *Description* embody the survival of imperial art after the political collapse of empire.[64] The monumental scale and ambition of the French works—dedicated to Napoleon—tempt the reader to reiterate 'Look on my works ye Mighty, and despair!' with the ironic inflection of Shelley's sonnet. In an example of 'reverse temporalization' the sonnet maps the project of Napoleonic antiquarianism onto its object, the ruins of Egyptian empire, but with one important difference: whereas Denon's book (not to mention the *Description* itself) resounds with a fading echo of imperial vainglory, the chisel of Shelley's 'imperial' sculptor *ironizes* the pretensions of political tyranny.[65] Performing a manœuvre similar to Hegel's

the colossal head now in our [i.e. the British] Museum', *Annals of the Fine Arts*, iv., xiii (London, 1820), 191–2. This is the only contemporary source which I have found which identifies the statue of Ozymandias with the 'Young Memnon' bust in the British Museum, but unfortunately it is too late to provide a source for Shelley's poem. In any case, it is based on a garbled conflation of the account of the discovery of the 'fragment d'un colosse Égyptien' (i.e. the British Museum's head) *inside the Rameseum temple* in the *Description* (*Antiquités, Planches*, Tome Deuxième, *planche* 32) and Denon's description of the 'lost' Ozymandias statue out in the plain of Thebes beside the two colossi.

[63] *Description de l'Égypte* (Paris, 1809), Preface, p. vi.

[64] This pathos is particularly striking in the *Description*'s fourth volume of *planches* (1814), where the place of publication changes from 'L'Imprimerie Imperiale' to 'L'Imprimerie *Royale*', as well as in the ideological changes made to the work's second, 'restoration', edition.

[65] Horace Smith's 'Ozymandias' is more concerned with reading the ruined statue as an emblem of the future fate of British civilization than with meditating on the politico-aesthetic pathos of recent revolutionary history. Anticipating Shelley's Preface to *Peter Bell the Third*, Smith contemplates the 'gigantic Leg' in the desert: 'We wonder,—and some Hunter may express | Wonder like ours, when thro' the wilderness | Where London stood, holding the Wolf in chase, | He meets some fragment huge, and stops to guess | What powerful but unrecorded race | Once dwelt in that annihilated place' (*Poems of Shelley*, vol. 2, p. 307).

dialectical 'sublation', Shelley at once preserves Denon's romantic and antiquarian evocation of empire whilst cancelling it according to Volneyan critique, in conformity with his own sceptical and republican view of Napoleonic
power.

One other distinction remains between Denon's Ozymandias and Shelley's,
a difference of countenance. All that remains of Denon's statue is 'a shapeless
rock of granite', whereas the fragmented visage of Shelley's statue still bears a
'sneer of cold command'. Shelley's 'Ozymandias' thus embodies *prosopopoeia*,
a refigurement rather than a disfigurement.[66] None of the 'actual' statues discussed here answers to Shelley's description: the faces of the two colossi out
on the plain of Thebes are eaten away by time and envy, as are the features of
the gigantic fragment lying inside the Ramesseum. Only the British Museum's
'Young Memnon' retains its countenance intact, but, as we saw above, it smiles
rather than sneers. The most likely candidate for influencing Shelley's
prosopopoeia therefore seems to be the lavish antiquarian engravings of the
Description, which, in addition to depicting with minute accuracy the ruins of
Egyptian sites, also imaginatively reconstructed monuments as they might have
looked in their classical heyday.[67]

D. W. Thompson many years ago scotched speculation about the possible
influence of the *Description* on Shelley on the grounds that 'the French work
was rare and expensive and evidently unknown to the poet'.[68] He was perhaps
too hasty in making this claim: Shelley might have seen the all-important second
volume of the *planches* of Egyptian antiquities—published in 1812—in the book-
shops during his week's sojourn in Paris in the summer of 1814,[69] or else during
one of his several visits to the British Museum when he was supposed to have
seen the bust of 'Young Memnon'.[70] (His friend T. L. Peacock had a reader's
ticket to the British Library.) Although I do not think that one can point to
any single *planche* and recognize a source for 'Ozymandias' (as if in any case
Shelley's imagination worked by transcribing a single image or textual allusion),
the fact that many of the *Description*'s images work hard to refigure the ruined
monuments which it depicts approximates to the verbal art of the sonnet. If we
look at the *Description*'s plates of the ruins of the two seated colossi between
which, according to Denon, the Ozymandias statue stood, we see that whereas

[66] See Paul de Man, 'Shelley Disfigured', in *The Rhetoric of Romanticism* (New York: Columbia
University Press, 1984).

[67] As Godlewska writes, 'The reader, imagining him or herself to be gazing upon the ruins of ancient
Egypt, is suddenly catapulted back in time . . . to gaze upon ancient scholars . . . as they wander about
contemplating and discussing higher matters of state and philosophy' ('Map, Text, Image', p. 22).

[68] 'Ozymandias', *Philological Quarterly*, 16 (1937), 60.

[69] See Richard Holmes, *Shelley: The Pursuit*, pp. 234–7.

[70] Shelley's sonnet, with its deictic opening line, also resembles the visual idiom of many of the antiquarian *planches* of the *Description*, with their representations of the French savants in the act of
drawing or measuring monuments and sites. As Godlewska notes, this tendency is completely absent
in the plates depicting contemporary Egypt ('Map, Text, Image', p. 21).

planche 20 shows the statues in ruins with a group of uniformed French savants clustered at the feet of the nearest colossus, *planche* 22 attempts a striking reconstruction of one of the colossi (Ill. 6). (Note the Greek inscription on the pedestal.) Its face, as refigured by the artists of the *Description*, seem as close as one can imagine to the 'wrinkled lip' and 'sneer of cold command' of Shelley's 'Ozymandias'.

Despite its status as a monument to a failed enterprise, the *Description* as a 'totalizing' text, more truthful to Egypt than Egypt itself, established a paradigm for nineteenth-century colonial representation as well as functioning as a kind of surrogate for France's lost colony. After its publication, as Godlewska writes, Egypt could be 'rigorously interpreted in the silence of French laboratories and museums without the difficult complications associated with colonialism, subject peoples and the bizarreries of other cultures'.[71] But the complex relationship between mobile and centre, 'Egyptian' context and European museum-recontext, is exposed in the *Description*'s bizarre treatment of the 'Young Memnon' itself. When in 1813 the Swiss explorer J. L. Burckhardt stumbled upon the 'Young Memnon' bust during a visit to Thebes, he noted that the French savants had drilled a large hole in the right breast of the statue and turned it face up. The savants had meant to blow the head from the trunk by means of gunpowder introduced into the hole which they had drilled for that purpose, as the 7-ton bust was otherwise too heavy to be transported. Burckhardt wrote that he was 'ignorant for what reason they relinquished that scheme, but it is somewhat curious to find that in the drawing which they have given of that head, in their great work (the *Description de l'Égypte, planche* 32) they have represented it as it would probably have been, after the lower parts should have been destroyed'[72] (Ill. 7).

This anecdote exposes the constitutive role of the *Description* in the construction of the nineteenth-century European museum order (for all its claims to contextualize Egyptian antiquities), as the destructive traces of extraction and expropriation are simply effaced from objects in order to ensure their auratic value. In a telling prolepsis, the *Description* envisages Egyptian antiquity *after* it has already been incorporated into the order of the colonial museum, magically transported from its point of origin to the museum without bearing the

[71] 'Map, Text, Image', p. 24.
[72] *Travels in Nubia, by the Late John Lewis Burckhardt, Published by the Association for Promoting the Discovery of the Interior Parts of Africa*, 2nd edn. (London: John Murray, 1822), p. lxxxii. Although Burckhardt's *Travels* were not published until 1820, the *Quarterly* in Jan. 1818 reported Burckhardt's 'find' in detail in its article on 'African Discoveries' (QR, XVIII (Jan. 1818), 362–70). Hamilton, who had visited the bust after the depredations of the savants, would not have noticed the damage because, unlike Burckhardt, he could not see how the statue was represented in the *Description*'s *planche*. The story of the French 'hole' rapidly became current as nationalist propaganda: see G. Long's 1832 guide, *The British Museum*, p. 47.

6. 'Statue Colossale de Memnon', *Description de l'Égypte*, II (1812), pl. 22. The inscription on the pedestal is in Greek.

7. 'Tête de l'une des statues du tombeau d'Osymandyas' ('Memnon's Head'), *Description*, II, pl. 32.

violent traces of historical mediation. It is ironic in this light that the present custodians of the bust of Rameses II (the Trustees of the British Museum) have recently seen fit to complete the process of decontextualization begun by Napoleon's savants, removing the names of its donors, Henry Salt and J. L. Burckhardt, previously inscribed on its base.

Part 2: Belzoni, Burckhardt, and the 'Rape of the Nile'

In this part of the chapter, still taking the 'Memnon's Head' statue as my focus, I turn to the second, post-Napoleonic, wave of romantic Egyptomania, which I shall discuss in relation to Giovanni Battista Belzoni's *Narrative of the Operations and Recent Discoveries within the Pyramids . . .* (1820). I have mentioned Belzoni's role in removing the 'Memnon's Head' from Thebes and transporting it down the Nile to Alexandria, under the auspices of the British consul, Henry Salt. The fact that his name did not appear alongside Salt's and Buckhardt's on the statue exhibited in the British Museum is symptomatic of Belzoni's ambivalent relationship to respectable antiquarianism. It certainly qualified for inclusion: in the course of his four-year career in Egypt, in addition to the 'Memnon's Head', he had removed and sent back to England a splendid statue of Amenhophis III from Thebes, the sarcophagus of Seti I from his tomb in the Valley of the Kings (which Belzoni discovered in 1817), the obelisk of Philae, as well as scores of mummies and papyri from nearby Qurna. Belzoni also opened up the second pyramid at Gizah and excavated the Temple of Abu Simbel in Nubia, 'discovered' a few years earlier by Burckhardt.

Unlike Vivant Denon and William Hamilton, post-Napoleonic travellers and antiquarians like Salt, Burckhardt, or Belzoni could no longer depend on the backing of a colonial army. With the seizure of power in Egypt by Muhammad Ali Pasha, however, at least they could rely on political stability. The new Pasha, a young Albanian officer formerly in the Ottoman service, had benefited from the power-vacuum left by the defeat of the Mamelukes and the expulsion of Napoleon's army in order to impose a new political order in Egypt. After defeating the British at Rosetta in 1807, the new Pasha (born in 1769, the same year as Napoleon, and taking the latter's dictatorial style as his political model) set about modernizing Egypt where Napoleon had failed. The political and economic success of 'para-colonial' Egypt[73] in part depended upon trade with the European powers, but also upon Egypt's fortuitous role in the lucrative internal 'haj' commerce, 'stand[ing] comparison with contemporary British trade with Bengal'.[74] With the profits accruing from his state monopolies, particularly the Egyptian cotton industry, Muhammad Ali established huge irrigation projects, hired foreign advisers to build modern factories, schools, and prisons, and rationalized and equipped his army along the latest European lines. He soon began to develop an expansionist foreign policy which resembled a scaled-down version of French and British imperialism: annexing many of the Ottoman territories in Western Arabia, Syria, and Greece, in 1822 his generals conquered Sudan, quelling opposition with extreme brutality. Further campaigns in Greece and Turkey followed, and Ali's meteoric rise to imperial domination of the Eastern Mediterranean was only blocked by European intervention at the Battle of Navarino in 1826, and again in the wake of the successful Egyptian invasion of Turkey in 1839. Britain would only finally succeed in colonizing Egypt in 1880, after the terms of the 1839 settlement had severely weakened Egyptian economic and military power.

Although Egypt's new status as a regional super-power temporarily blocked French and British political ambitions in the region, the scramble for Egyptian

---

[73] Bayly, *Imperial Meridian*, p. 231. As Bayly points out, in assessing the new imperial dispensation of the early 19th century it would be a mistake to overlook regional states and élites which had emerged from the decline of earlier Asiatic empires to form 'para-colonial' powers, such as Muhammad Ali's Egypt, the Qajar regime in Iran, the Emirs of Sindh, and the partially independent states of Awadh and Hyderabad, Ranjit Singh's Punjab, Rama I's Thailand, Tokugawa Japan (ibid., pp. 228–9).

[74] Ibid., p. 232.

antiquities continued, resembling (as I have suggested) a farcical reprise of the military campaigns of the previous decades. With the cessation of internal conflict in Egypt and Napoleon's defeat at Waterloo, a flood of European travellers arrived on the Nile, following in the footsteps of Lady Hester Stanhope, who had visited briefly in 1812, or Mr Legh and the Revd Smelt, who got as far as Upper Egypt in 1813, harbingers of the leisurely tourists who would sail up the Nile in the custody of Thomas Cook later in the century. The new travellers were aristocrats like Lord Belmore, Lt.-Col. Fitzclarence, William John Bankes, and Sir Archibald Edmonstone, eager to add to their collections or fill in some blanks in the maps of the region; or more adventurous explorers like George Waddington and Barnard Hanbury, who followed Ibrahim Pasha's army into the Sudan as far as Merow in 1820. The French were also there in force, notably the intrepid Frédéric Cailliaud (described by Alan Moorehead as a 'one-man' Institut de France),[75] and the egregious French (ex) Vice-Consul Bernardo Drovetti, a veteran of Napoleon's 1798 campaign.[76] As Richard Burton later expressed it in *The Cornhill Magazine*: 'Nile-land was then, as now, a field of plunder; fortunes were made by digging, not gold, but antiques; and the archaeological field became a battle-plan for two armies of Dragomans and Fellah-navvies. One was headed by the redoubtable Salt; and the other owned the command of Drovetti.'[77] Salt and Drovetti had reached an agreement dividing up the Nile Valley into French and British spheres of influence where they controlled firmans and the deployment of the native work-force.[78]

Belzoni's removal of the 'Young Memnon' from Thebes aptly illustrates the new style of antiquarianism in Muhammad Ali's Egypt (it is still premature to use the term 'archaeology', given the emphasis on discovering 'singular' objects rather than the holistic recovery of the total environment of a site). Whereas the eighteenth-century traveller, and even to some extent the savants of the French occupation, had been content with drawing and describing 'mobiles', purchasing or looting only smaller pieces, now larger monuments were within reach of European collectors. In the wake of Napoleon, Egypt could be removed wholesale to the European museum. Muhammad Ali, on the other hand (in a sort

---

[75] Alan Moorehead, *The Blue Nile* (London: Hamish Hamilton, 1962), p. 175.

[76] Ronald Ridley, *Napoleon's Proconsul in Egypt: The Life and Times of Bernardino Drovetti* (London: Rubicon Press, n.d.). See also Paul and Janet Starkey (eds.), *Travellers in Egypt* (London: I. B. Tauris, 1998), pp. 41–50.

[77] Quoted by Stanley Mayes, *The Great Belzoni*, p. 225.

[78] The competition between Drovetti and Salt echoed that between Elgin's agent Lusieri and the French antiquary Fauvel in Athens in the previous decade. See William St Clair, *Lord Elgin and the Marbles* (p. 206). Italians, who had traditionally played a prominent part in promoting European interests within the Ottoman Empire, were well represented: Bruce's assistant Luigi Balugani, Lusieri, Drovetti (of Piedmontese extraction), and, of course, Belzoni. An Italian dialect was the traditional lingua franca in the Eastern Mediterranean.

of inversion of European antiquarian greed) was concerned with importing European modernity on an unprecedented scale, and had no compunction in trading antiquities for diplomatic or economic advantage, thereby playing his part in the 'temporal exchange' of romanticism formulated in Chapter 1. Ali Pasha controlled excavations along the Nile by means of firmans or permits; the British and French agents could obtain as many as they wanted. He seemed unaware of the mounting market value of Egyptian antiquities in Europe; as Burckhardt noted: 'the Pasha of Egypt is luckily not yet aware of the value of these statues; if he was, he would probably imitate Wely Pasha of the Morea, and ask for passage money.'[79] (This is not to say, however, that antiquities did not already have a 'semiophoric' value for Egyptians, despite constant attempts by Europeans to argue the contrary, as I argue below.)

The association of the names of Burckhardt and Belzoni in the acquisition of the 'Memnon's Head' is a particularly rich conjuncture, in terms of the similarities and differences between the two men as travellers and travel writers. Both were foreign anglophiles (and francophobes) working for the British interest, their travel accounts—particularly Belzoni's—published in unidiomatic English. Both were also culture chameleons able to construct identities for themselves as the occasion required, and both died in Africa as explorers in the service of their adopted country. Yet, despite these similarities, they were distinguished by the fact that Burckhardt enjoyed fame as a scientific traveller and explorer in the heroic mould of Mungo Park, Friedrich Hornemann, or William Browne, whilst Belzoni never cast off the stigma associated with his former career as a pantomime actor and circus strong-man. If the Göttingen- and Cambridge-educated Burckhardt belonged securely in the gentlemanly circles of Banks's African Association or the British Museum, Belzoni's world (even after he had turned to antiquarianism) was that of the popular exhibition order. In John Whale's words: 'Belzoni's story switches dramatically from popular to polite culture, from freak show to gentleman traveller, from Sadler's Wells to the British Museum, from geek to artist manqué.'[80] If Burckhardt's posthumous *Travels in Nubia* (1820) is the heroic epic of European attempts to open up the Nile region, Belzoni's *Narrative of the Operations*, published in the same year, is in many ways its 'pantomimic' double.

Burckhardt's expeditions on behalf of the African Association (his principal patrons were—formidably—Professor Blumenbach at Göttingen and Sir Joseph Banks in London) to discover the supposed confluence of the Nile and Niger rivers represented a new form of geographical and anthropological

---

[79] J. L. Burckhardt, *Travels in Nubia*, p. lxxxv. Henceforth B. in text.
[80] John Whale, 'Sacred Objects and the Sublime Ruins of Art', in *Beyond Romanticism: New Approaches to Text and Contexts 1780–1833*, ed. by Stephen Copley and John Whale (London: Routledge, 1992), p. 228.

professionalism quite distinct from the 'curious' antiquarian tradition of Bruce or Denon.[81] While preparing himself for his expedition at Cambridge, Burckhardt 'allowed his beard to grow and assumed the Oriental dress: he attended lectures on chemistry, astronomy, mineralogy, medicine and surgery, and in the intervals of his studies, he exercised himself by long journeys on foot, bareheaded, in the heat of the sun, sleeping upon the ground, and living upon vegetables and water' (B. p. v).[82] While in Aleppo in 1810 improving his language skills, Burckhardt had attempted 'the metamorphosis of the well-known novel of Robinson Crusoe into an Arabian tale: adapted to the Eastern tastes and manners'. He gave it the title 'Dur-el-Bahur, the Pearl of the Seas' (B. p. xxxi). This perhaps symptomizes Burckhardt's orientalism: in many respects he represents Defoe's castaway in oriental costume, thrown entirely upon his own resources and the use-value of his few possessions, so that at the end of his 'captivity' he can emerge to benefit the expansion of enlightened colonialism and European capitalist entrepreneurship.

Burckhardt's total absorption in Arabic culture appears superficially like Bruce's, but actually 'Hakim Yagoube' and 'Sheik Ibrahim ibn Abdullah' (the Arabic name assumed by Burckhardt) are quite different personalities. The latter's 'total' cultural disguise (he prided himself on having been one of the first Europeans to enter the Kaaba at Mecca) prohibited the use of scientific instruments, and his 'equipment' was a function of the scientific and philological education branded on his memory alone, and the information recorded 'to the moment' in his field journals. Both his training and his sponsorship by the African Association rendered his credit unimpeachable, in contrast to Bruce. Beneath his oriental disguise, Burckhardt was a highly trained intelligence gatherer, whose ascetic professionalism was pledged to the scientific institutions of the nation in whose service he was employed.[83] In 1813 he had 'discovered' the

---

[81]   Scion of an eminent Bâlois family, he was related to the famous 19th-century historian Jacob Burckhardt, a connection explored by Lionel Gossman in an unpublished essay entitled 'La Suisse Nomade: Trois Voyageurs Bâlois'. Thanks to Martin Ruehl for making this available to me. See also Katherine Sims, *Desert Traveller: The Life of John Lewis Burckhardt* (London: Gollancz, 1969).

[82]   Burckhardt was thus better prepared than many 'official' African explorers in the period, however. For a highly readable account of Hugh Clapperton, George Lyon, and Gordon Laing's disastrous expeditions to discover the course of the Niger, or the site of Timbuktu, organized by John Barrow at the African Association, see Fergus Fleming, *Barrow's Boys* (London: Granta Books, 1998).

[83]   In an 1820 review of Burckhardt's *Travels in Nubia*, the *Quarterly* favourably compared Burckhardt with Bruce, whose narrative, it argued 'is in general substantially true, but often circumstantially false'. It also compared the Swiss traveller with Humboldt: 'Mr Burckhardt was not unacquainted with the systematic nomenclature of objects of natural history, but he deemed it more useful to insert the native names than to encumber his journal with technical terms, or to load it with scientific descriptions or philosophical discussions . . . In this respect no two travellers, each excellent in his own way, could differ more widely than Humboldt and Burckhardt. Of the former, science and philosophy were the leading objects; while the chief concern of the latter was men and manners . . . and the means resorted to for supplying their wants or increasing their comforts through the instrumentality of commerce' (QR, xxii (Jan. 1820), 438).

Abu Simbel temple and reported enthusiastically the 'Grecian model of beauty' of the statues half buried in the sand (B. p. 84). But Burckhardt was an explorer before he was an antiquary, and, despite his constant illness, he was more concerned with penetrating Sudan as far as Dongola and studying this virtually unknown tract of the Nile than pursuing his archaeological discoveries, a task which he would leave to Belzoni and Salt.

Burckhardt died of dysentery in Egypt in 1817 before he had achieved his goal of reaching the alleged confluence of the Nile and the Niger. Nevertheless, his premature death made the three 'preparatory' expeditions which he had undertaken since 1813 appear all the more sensational when his account of them was published in 1820, in the form of his journals edited by the African Association. Fully in character with its ascetic Swiss author, his narrative is spare, objective, precise. Like Mungo Park, Burckhardt was quickly lionized by the British public as a romantic hero who had made the ultimate sacrifice for his adopted country (B. p. xcvi). Belzoni, who had become acquainted with Burckhardt in 1816–17, transformed the Swiss into an idol:

the most candid, disinterested, and sincere being I have ever met with: totally free from that invidious and selfish disposition, which is so often to be found in travellers, who wish to be alone in one quarter of the world, to relate their story agreeably to the suggestions of their imagination to the people of another.[84]

This was a 'sublimity' of character and achievement to which Belzoni could only aspire.

Belzoni's background and training could not have been more different from Burckhardt's. A barber's son from Padua, born in 1778, Belzoni arrived in England in 1803 as a refugee from the Napoleonic occupation of Italy. The gigantic 6-foot 6-inch bearded Paduan soon caused a sensation in his role as the 'Patagonian Sampson' at Sadler's Wells theatre. Strolling around the stage with a 127-pound weight harness of his own design on his chest, he carried ten to twelve members of the company on his shoulders. In his stage career as a pantomime actor, Belzoni specialized in the exotic and the awe-inspiring, on account of his thick black beard and gigantic statue. In the role of Pero in *Goody Two-Shoes* and the giant in *Jack the Giant Killer* he played to an audience which included Charles and Mary Lamb and Robert Southey (Lamb loved it; Southey slept), and, judging from his lines in Book 8 of the *Prelude*, Wordsworth was present at another performance.[85] Wordsworth later declared that 'willingly he

---

[84] Belzoni, *Narrative of the Operations and Recent Discoveries within the Pyramids, Temples, Tombs and Excavations, in Egypt and Nubia; and of a Journey to the coast of the Red Sea, in search of the Ancient Berenice; and another to the Oasis of Jupiter Ammon* (1820), 2nd edn. (London: John Murray, 1821), p. 134. Henceforth Narr. in text.

[85] Mayes, *The Great Belzoni*, pp. 38–9. In May 1803, Belzoni starred in another pantomime called *Philip Quarll*, based on a captivity narrative which took *Robinson Crusoe* as its model; Belzoni, of

would go three days' journey through a wilderness to see Belzoni', although presumably not on account of his pantomimic talents.[86]

Although in later life Belzoni was deeply ashamed of his pantomime career, which threatened to jeopardize his desire for social acceptability as a 'gentleman traveller', it provides the key to understanding his contradictory and liminal status between cultures and social classes, posing as a polite antiquary while acting the role of capitalist entrepreneur and severe foreman to his Egyptian work-force. Although there is no mention of the pantomime years in the *Narrative*, Belzoni's acquaintances commented on his striking, 'stagy', presence: Lt.-Col. Fitzclarence described him in early 1818, as

the handsomest man I ever saw . . . about six foot six inches high, and his commanding figure set off by a long beard . . . [his] amazing strength and height, which ever have in barbarous countries a great effect, as we learn from the travels of Bruce, aid him much in his enterprises[87]

Unlike the gentlemanly Bruce (I allude to Fanny Burney's comment quoted in Chapter 2), Belzoni was a giant whom one *did* pay to see. Nevertheless, in contrast to Bruce, Belzoni's travel narrative was legitimized by the exhibitionism which it promoted, the antiquities whose acquisition it related. As his French translator put it: 'in France people are ready to forgive a traveller for tampering with the truth a little, so long as his story grips. With Belzoni the interest lies in facts or ultimately in things; form is almost ignored.'[88]

If Burckhardt endeavoured to merge indistinguishably with the modern Arabs whom he studied with ethnographic professionalism, Belzoni's trick of identification was rather with the ancient Egyptian 'colossi' which he prised from their centuries-old resting ground in the temples and ruined cities of the Nile. Acting as a kind of parodic impersonator of Napoleonic temporalization, Belzoni seemed to mimic the colossal scale of the Egyptian aesthetic, dwarfing the 'ideal' proportions of Hellenic beauty. In Belzoni's *Narrative of the Operations*, the personified fragments of gigantic antiquity spring to life whilst, in exchange, the living beings who labour to release them from their ancient settings mummify and crumble into dust. Like Marx's critique of the fetishized commodity, Belzoni's *Narrative*, however unintentionally, reveals that the 'fan-

course, did not play the English hero, but rather the 'Black Chief' or 'Cannibal king' who threatens Quarll's life but is dispatched before he can make off with the heroine (ibid., pp. 42–3).

[86] *De Quincey's Works*, ed. by Masson, 14 vols. (Edinburgh, 1890), v. 325. De Quincey was scornful of Wordsworth's admiration, attributing it (by a characteristic exaggeration) merely to the fact that Belzoni was 'nearly seven feet tall'!

[87] Lt.-Col. Fitzclarence (Earl of Munster), *Journal of a Route across India, through Egypt, to England, in the latter end of 1817 and the beginning of 1818* (London: John Murray, 1819), pp. 433, 466. See also Burckhardt's description in B. p. lxxxiv.

[88] Quoted in Mayes, p. 252. See also Peter A. Clayton, 'A Pioneer Egyptologist: G. B. Belzoni, 1778–1823', in Starkey and Starkey (eds.), *Travellers in Egypt*, pp. 41–50.

tastic form of a relation between things' embodied in the consecrated romantic artwork, is in fact a 'definite social relation between men'. As such its amateurish and unidiomatic text reveals many truths occulted in half-a-century of European travel writing about the Nile.

Belzoni's 'Broken English': The Narrative of the Operations

Belzoni's description of his first encounter with 'Memnon's Head' in the Ramesseum temple at Thebes sums up the timbre of his whole book. Entering the temple, he described how 'I found [the bust] near the remains of its body and chair, with its face upwards, and apparently smiling on me, at the thought of being taken to England. I must say, that my expectations were exceeded by its beauty, but not by its size' (Narr. p. 39). Belzoni's account animates the Memnon's stony countenance in anticipation of what Walter Benjamin calls the 'aura' of the artwork ('the expectation that what you look at looks back at you provides the aura').[89] The personified statue looks forward to its rescue and recontextualization in the British 'museum order'. Like Bruce at the Nile source, Belzoni's own gigantism implicitly dwindles the scale of the statue, although in no way detracting from its beauty or desirability.

The statue is content with the idea of 'going home' to London, where it clearly belongs; in the course of his own peripatetic life, the exiled Paduan, by contrast, finds it hard to name a home for himself. Near the end of his *Narrative* he writes of Thebes: 'I felt no small degree of sorrow to quit a place which was become so familiar to me . . . I must say, that I felt more in leaving Thebes, than any other place in my life' (Narr. pp. 372–3). Belzoni *changes places* with the gigantic granite statue which he caused to be dispatched to London, 'establishing' himself in a hut amongst the ruins of pharaonic antiquity; even his long-suffering wife, Sarah, domesticates at Thebes 'equally indifferent with myself

---

[89] As reported by a sceptical Berthold Brecht, who continued 'it is all mysticism, in a posture opposed to mysticism, it is in such a form that the materialistic concept of history is adopted! it is rather ghastly' (quoted by Susan Buck-Morss, *The Dialectics of Seeing: Walter Benjamin and the Arcades Project* (Cambridge, Mass., and London: MIT Press, p. 246). The extreme dislocation of the 'Memnon's Head' as it is recontextualized from Thebes to the British Museum, whilst conforming to Benjamin's account of the artwork's transition from 'cultic' to 'exhibition' value, seems to question his association of the 'aura' with 'all that is transmissible from its beginning, ranging from its substantive duration to its testimony to the history which it has experienced'. However much the 'museum order' sought to construct an illusion of seamless tradition, the mobilization of antique objects and their 'combinability at the centre' in the romantic period already anticipated the 'detachment of the reproduced object from tradition', which Benjamin attributes to 'mechanical reproduction'. We might say that the aura was itself a romantic invention, only comprehensible as such in the romantic artwork after the 'ungrounding' or decontextualization of objects had already been effected. See 'The Work of Art in the Age of Mechanical Reproduction', *Illuminations*, ed. with intro. by Hannah Arendt, (London: Fontana Collins, 1973), p. 223; and Daniel J. Sherman, 'Quatremère/Benjamin/Marx: Art Museums, Aura, and Commodity Fetishism', in *Museum Culture*, ed. by Sherman and Rogoff, pp. 135–9.

about accommodation' (Narr. p. 40). (Unlike the gallant Bruce trying to barter beads for kisses with Abyssinian market women, Belzoni's mobile artisanal domesticity is guaranteed by Sarah's presence, as she handles negotiations with Egyptian women, while caring for the childless couple's pet chameleon as if it were a cherished offspring.) Undeterred by the attempts of Drovetti and his henchman to obstruct his project, Belzoni assumes a gigantic 'Egyptian' impassivity, 'determined to stand, like a pyramid defying the wind, against all their numerous attacks, which poured on me like a torrent' (Narr. p. 113). There is after all perhaps an appropriateness to the omission of Belzoni's name from the British Museum's bust. For, in contrast to Salt or Burkhardt, the gigantic Belzoni 'remained behind' in Egypt, haunting the empty places along the Nile ruins left vacant by what the *Times* called 'his mechanical ingenuity and indefatigable diligence'.[90] Moreover, the suppression of Belzoni's name masks another silence, that of the Egyptian work-force which had actually performed the physical labour of removing the bust (as well as other objects), 'explaining' their organized labour as the work of the devil. I argue below that the active agency of both foreman and work-force is troublingly reinscribed in the *Narrative*.

Belzoni's *Narrative of the Operations* was an instant popular success when it was published in quarto by John Murray in late 1820, selling for the price of 2 guineas, quickly going into a second edition and being translated into French, German, and Italian. It had been written in several months at great speed after Belzoni's return to England in March 1820, and was published with an essay by his wife Sarah entitled 'A Short Account of the Women of Egypt, Nubia and Syria',[91] as well as an appendix describing Dr Thomas Young's progress in deciphering hieroglyphics, extracted from the *Encyclopaedia Britannica*. The *Narrative* was accompanied by a companion volume of plates of Egyptian wall-paintings and topographical views by Giovanni and Sarah Belzoni, and the Italian artist Alessandro Ricci.[92] A juvenile version of Belzoni's book appeared

[90] May 1821, quoted by Mayes, p. 260.

[91] Sarah Belzoni's 'Short Account' as it were miniaturizes her husband's adventures among the tombs and pyramids of Egypt. (Mayes cites it as her 'Trifling Account', and it was indeed omitted from the French translation on grounds of 'triviality', (Mayes, 255).) But Sarah, about whom little is known except that she was born Sarah Banne, and was of Irish extraction, had little formal education but strong religious leanings, was no mere cipher to her husband. When she got bored at Thebes, she went off to Jerusalem on a pilgrimage disguised as a boy. Whilst camping out among the ruins, or whiling away the time at Cairo struggling with terrible opthalmia, she entertained herself with the chameleons, perfect emblems in the animal kingdom of Belzoni's world of shifting colours and identities: 'when in a house, if it is watched, it will change every ten minutes: some moments a plain green, at others all its beautiful colours will come out, and when in a passion it becomes of a deep black, and will swell itself up like a balloon, and from being one of the most beautiful animals, it becomes one of the most ugly', p. 478.

[92] Compared to the standard of illustration set by the *Description de L'Égypte,* it is a curiously naïve and homespun production, an appropriate visual companion for the *Narrative*.

almost instantaneously in 1820 from the hand of children's author Sarah Atkins, entitled *Fruits of Enterprise Exhibited in the Travels of Belzoni in Egypt and Nubia; Interspersed with the Observations of a Mother to her Children.*[93] Belzoni may have been a giant but, unlike Bruce, he was constructed as a gentle, domesticated giant who could be set up as a paradigm of steadfastness, social advancement, and patriotic moral purpose. He may never have achieved the 'cultural capital' for which he yearned from the gentlemanly world of the African Association, the British Museum, or the Society of Antiquaries, but, as Richard Altick points out, he did succeed in becoming a popular legend in the Samuel Smiles tradition.[94]

The *Narrative* is written in the rather solemn, first-person style of an *apologia pro vita sua*, replete with the uneven discursive energy of the auto-didact (Belzoni persistently confuses Herodotus and Diodorus, for instance). In his Introduction he insists that he has written without assistance, a fact for which the modern reader must be grateful. 'Belzoni *is* a grand traveller, and his English is very prettily broken', wrote Lord Byron after their mutual publisher John Murray had sent him a copy of the *Narrative*.[95] The subordination of style to matter may well have helped the book on its way, and in contrast to Bruce's 'overwritten' *Travels*, Belzoni seems to have had no trouble with readerly credit.[96] As the *Quarterly Review* put it in an appreciative review of the *Narrative*:

> it is not to him . . . that we are to look for erudite historical disquisitions, or antiquarian elucidations; but, what is probably of more real value and importance, we may implicitly trust his pen and his pencil in what he has described and delineated . . . he points out the road and makes it easy for others to travel over.[97]

The main distinction claimed by Belzoni's book, setting it apart from numerous contemporary travelogues, was its account of the author's transactions with modern Egyptians, in particular the work-force which he mobilized to excavate and remove seemingly intractable antique objects. 'A traveller who has all the accommodation possible', Belzoni insisted, 'and nothing to do with these people but in passing, can never judge of their ideas, their system of conduct, and their rapacious manners; for in the little interval, and the limited business he has to transact with them, they do not appear to be the people they really are . . . But let a traveller deal with them in any transaction, where their

---

[93] Mayes, p. 294.   [94] Altick, *Shows of London*, p. 243.
[95] *Letters and Journals of Lord Byron*, ed. by Leslie Marchand 12 vols. (London: John Murray, 1978), viii. 79.
[96] Nevertheless, like Bruce's *Travels* (which Belzoni cites admiringly) (Narr. p. 325), the *Narrative* is rich in dialogue, perhaps the most 'transactive' Egyptian travel account written in the period, however unreliable its antiquarian information and however lacking in evocative picturesque description.
[97] QR, XXIV (Oct. 1820), 140.

interest in concerned, and where their execution of any undertaking is required, he will soon find, that in every point they are the most cheating people on earth' (Narr. p. 108).

Belzoni here claims privileged knowledge of modern Egyptians, because he has organized their labour and bartered for their antiquities. The racialist disdain which frequently marks his description of Egyptians, although by no means uncharacteristic in travel accounts of the period, in part betrays an anxiety about his own unstable social and cultural identity.[98] Belzoni's 'trans-active' dealings with Egyptians set him apart (he might claim) not only from 'galloping philosophers' like Volney and Denon but even from heroes like Bruce or Burckhardt, who have only really skimmed over the surface of the Arab world. In Belzoni's world (anticipating Marx) social reality is primarily a function of labour relations rather than a romantic phenomenology of spirit. But the fact that Belzoni worked in the 'para-colonial' space of Muhammad Ali's Egypt, rather than in a formal colonial situation in which capital and labour would have been institutionalized, exacerbated his problems. Not only his transactions with indigenous Egyptians but also those with his British employers and his French/Italian rivals provided a constant source of conflict which constitute one of the *Narrative*'s main points of interest.

Belzoni's claim to know the 'reality' of the modern Egyptian as *homo economicus* of course jeopardized his desperate desire to transcend his status as a kind of capitalist entrepreneur with a pantomime background. As Lt.-Col. Fitzclarence noted with the patronizing perspicuity of his rank: 'Fame appears to be the object for which [Belzoni] is most anxious, though he has nothing to live on but the produce of a few statues sold to the Count de Forbin'.[99] Desperate to achieve 'disinterested' status, Belzoni offered to remove the 'Memnon's Head' 'without the smallest view of interest, as it was to go to the British Museum' (Narr. p. 22), although Salt did pay him 50 pounds in addition to the advance of 25 pounds which had been provided by Burckhardt and himself when the project was first mooted.[100] Belzoni constantly distinguished his own 'curiosity' and 'enthusiasm for antiquities' (Narr. p. 25) from the selfish commercialism of his 'French' (although really fellow-Italian) rival, Drovetti, 'who did not search antiquity for the love of these relics, but merely from interest' (Narr. p. 436).

Although the Italian found himself mired in circuits of complicated exchange, his financial negotiations with his 'employer' Salt (although he energetically

---

[98] Ironically, Belzoni's drawings of ancient Egyptian types confirmed the Victorian racialist Robert Knox's thesis of the 'unalterable character of races' during his visit to Belzoni's exhibition in the Egyptian Hall. This is discussed by Robert Young in *Colonial Desire: Hybridity in Theory, Culture and Race* (London and New York: Routledge, 1995), p. 78.

[99] *Journal of a Route . . .* , p. 433.   [100] Fagan, *Rape of the Nile*, p. 155.

denied that the relationship had ever been one of agent/client) were complicated by his attempt to trade antiquities not for hard cash but rather for gentlemanly kudos. Belzoni proposed to Salt that he would open up the temples of Abu Simbel ('discovered' by Burckhardt) if 'he should give me an official letter of introduction to the Society of Antiquaries, when I should return to England' (Narr. p. 135). Belzoni was so sensitive on this issue (and Salt so moodily unpredictable) that Burckhardt needed to intervene on more than one occasion, slipping money to Belzoni in the guise of 'gifts' rather than as a fixed stipend. As a result of Belzoni's status-sensitivity and Salt's obduracy, Belzoni received the sum of only 600 pounds in repayment for his enormous labour in collecting an unprecedented quantity of antiquities over the course of three years. Paradoxically, the same man who actively introduced wage-capitalism to an Egyptian peasant work-force, would only himself accept payment in the form of 'gifts'.[101]

Whilst in one sense the *Narrative* is only a textual 'supplement' to the Egyptian antiquities displayed in the British Museum and (more ephemerally) Bullock's Egyptian Hall, its narrative of acquisition nevertheless disturbs and disrupts the auratic composure of the material objects themselves. The categories which demarcate Belzoni's own agency in Egypt, negotiating between British collectors and Egyptian tomb-robbers, keep blurring as he identifies with one side or the other, or both at the same time (in one episode, mentioned below, his *doppelganger* appears among the ruins of Luxor). Belzoni is a permeable medium in which discrete cultural and social identities dissolve, a constant mimic who constantly distorts the dynamics of scale and the hierarchies of race and social status. His own multiple identities—product of his chameleon-like mimetic drive—fissure his text's desire for stability and eminence, as the narrative itself becomes the locus of a struggle for value.

Belzoni's Antiquarian Sublime

Belzoni works hard throughout the *Narrative* to remind his readers that his 'mechanical' success in expropriating antiquities and his entrepreneurial skills with his Egyptian workers are motivated by aesthetic appreciation rather than pecuniary self-interest. Given his evident ignorance of polite aesthetics, the *Narrative* is clumsily dependent upon textual precursors, although even so his

---

[101] Marcel Mauss, *The Gift: The Form and Reason for Exchange in Archaic Societies*, trans. by W. D. Halls, foreword by Mary Douglas (New York and London: Norton, 1990). Mauss's 'archaic' spirit of the gift survives in Belzoni's world of expansionist capitalism in the form of status acquisition or gentlemanly 'curiosity', just as a pragmatic modern understanding of commodity-exchange and 'commodity-fetishism' flourished among the pre-capitalist Egyptian peasants with whom Belzoni had to deal. See Nicholas Thomas, *Entangled Objects: Exchange, Material Culture, and Colonialism in the Pacific* (Cambridge, Mass., London: Harvard University Press, 1991), p. 18, for a sympathetic critique of Mauss.

essays in aesthetic judgement often seem to hover on the verge of self-parody. Visiting the ruins of Luxor on his first journey to Upper Egypt to stake out the 'Young Memnon', in July 1816, Belzoni recalled reverently that 'it was here that Denon thought himself in the sanctuary of the arts and sciences' (Narr. p. 37). His account of Luxor is largely a paraphrase of Denon, down to the conventional trope of sublime inarticulacy and his perception of the incommensurability of ancient and modern Egypt. Belzoni adds a homespun touch in evoking Luxor as 'a city of giants, who, after a long conflict, were all destroyed, leaving the ruins of their various temples as the only proofs of their former existence' (Narr. pp. 37–8).[102] With Belzoni the delicate membrane established by Denon and Hamilton, dividing the aesthetics of the Egyptian sublime from mere gigantism, is ruptured.

Visiting Karnak *en route* to Abu Simbel in 1817, on his second journey, Belzoni's prose once again struggles hard for aesthetic 'possession' of the mighty ruins, coming under even greater strain than it had done at Luxor: 'I was lost in contemplation of so many objects; and being alone in such a place, my mind was impressed with ideas of such solemnity, that for some time I was unconscious whether I were on terrestrial ground or in some other planet' (Narr. pp. 152–3). An elephantine, seventeen-line sentence of description then follows, concluding with a botched attempt at sublime discourse which sounds more like a fantasy of status, rather than of aesthetic, elevation: 'I seemed alone in the midst of all that is most sacred in the world . . . separat[ing] me in imagination from the rest of mortals, exalt[ing] me on high over all, and caus[ing] me to forget entirely the trifles and follies of life' (Narr. p. 153). Mobilizing the trope of 'self-protective irony'[103] against the dangers of hyperbole (like Bruce at Gish) Belzoni promptly humiliates himself for his pretensions: 'I was happy for a whole day . . . but the obscurity of the night caused me to stumble over one large block of stone, and to break my nose against another, which, dissolving the enchantment, brought me to my senses again' (Narr. p. 153). Just like Belzoni's 'broken English', his accident in the ruins of Karnak once again serves to identify him—in the most literal way—with the sublime fragments of

---

[102] When the American traveller John Lloyd Stephens visited Thebes twenty years later he cited Belzoni's whimsical 'city of giants' (*Incidents of Travel in Egypt, Arabia Petraea, and the Holy Land* (1837) ed. with Intro. by Victor Von Hagen (San Francisco: Chronicle Books, 1991), p. 107); Belzoni now represented a threshold of authenticity for Stephens, just as Denon had done for Belzoni, as the ruins of Thebes were reappropriated by a new generation of tourists. Belzoni's shade had remained to haunt the ruins as that of an authentic 'explorer'. Stephens described how 'an old Arab who accompanied us remembered Belzoni, and pointed out a chamber where *the fortunate explorer* entertained a party of European travellers . . . making the tomb of Pharaoh ring with shouts and songs of merriment' (ibid., p. 112, italics mine). By 1836, however, the Nile seemed to have become a tourist playground, which disappointed the future explorer of the Mayan cities of Central America: 'A woman and child might go safely from Cairo to the Cataracts; and my blood began to run sluggishly in my veins' (ibid., p. 113).   [103] Chloe Chard, *Pleasure and Guilt . . .* , p. 6.

antiquity. And like a sphinx his nose is broken[104] as the materiality of the ruins interposes a stumbling-block to sublime reverie. What a contrast to the 'heroic' Denon, whose sublime transport soared beyond the reach of materiality, and for whom 'real' danger in the form of enemy marauders was never far behind.

The antithesis of Belzoni's descriptions of Luxor and Karnak is his rather gothic account of his visit to the labyrinths of Qurna in search of papyri, a 'counter-sublime' which in the nineteenth century became one of the best-known passages in the *Narrative*. Belzoni represents his purpose quite candidly as a physical intrusion upon the dead: 'to rob the Egyptians of their papyri; of which I found a few hidden in their breasts, under their arms, in the space above the knees, or on the legs, and covered by the numerous folds of cloth that envelop the mummy' (Narr. pp. 157–8). In contrast to antique statuary (the 'Young Memnon', for example), history brought to life by the sculptor's art, the mummy represents the living human body itself as an antique, transmuted into permanence by evisceration and embalmment. As Susan Stewart writes: 'Physical relics [mark] the horrible transformation of meaning into materiality more than they mark, as other souvenirs do, the transformation of materiality into meaning . . . souvenirs of the mortal body are not so much a nostalgic celebration of the past as they are an erasure of the significance of history'.[105] Like the prurient eighteenth-century 'curioso', Belzoni 'researches' the private places of mummified bodies in search of ancient hieroglyphic letters. These are, of course, still illegible signifiers, although the *Narrative* appeared on the eve of Champollian's famous breakthrough.

At Qurna sublime distance is replaced by an engorgement of pure materiality as Belzoni 'tastefully' registers the dust of ancient Egyptians:

though, fortunately, I am destitute of the sense of smelling, I could taste that the mummies were rather unpleasant to swallow . . . I sought a resting place, found one, and contrived to sit; but when my weight bore on the body of an Egyptian, it crushed it like a band-box . . . I sunk altogether among the broken mummies, with a crash of bones, rags, and wooden cases, which raised such a dust as kept me motionless for a quarter of an hour . . . I could not pass without putting my face in contact with that of some decayed Egyptian . . . I could not avoid being covered with bones, legs, arms, and heads rolling from above.   (Narr. p. 157)

The 'presentism' and proximity of popular curiosity is grotesquely literalized in this description, making an implicit contrast with the temporalized distance of polite antiquarianism. The mummy-pits at Qurna struck a chord in the nineteenth-century literary imagination, compromising the 'Samuel Smiles' legend attached to Belzoni's name. De Quincey's paranoiac dream of

---

[104] One of Belzoni's many oddities was his total lack of any sense of smell.
[105] Susan Stewart, *On Longing*, p. 140.

immolation in a hallucinogenic Orient in the *Confessions of an English Opium Eater* translates Belzoni into the idiom of visionary Gothic; whilst Rosa Budd, in Dickens's *Edwin Drood* (1870) brings the episode to mind whilst parrying her egregious lover's enthusiasm to 'do some good in Egypt'; 'then there was that Belzoni or somebody, dragged out by the legs, half choked with bats and dust. All the girls say serves him right, and hope it hurt him, and wish he had been quite choked.'[106]

In these passages the circus returns to haunt the museum; if colossal Egyptian busts evoke Belzoni's showbusiness past in his role as the 'Patagonian Sampson', the mummy episode casts him as the 'cannibal king', mired in dismembered bodies, choking on mortal dust in prurient quest of illegible letters. The depiction of his Arab guides 'naked and covered with dust, themselves resembling living mummies, absolutely formed a scene that cannot be described' (Narr. p. 157) represents the final twist of Denon-style temporalization, although it is a temporalization in which Belzoni is himself absorbed.[107] The fearsome Qurna troglodytes, with whom Belzoni enjoys cordial relations, having abandoned wholesome labour in their fields in order to profit from the material remains of their ancestors, seem to satirize and materialize the pretensions of European antiquarians like Belzoni and Drovetti who also need to 'live off the past'. 'They always killed a couple of fowls for me', Belzoni noted, 'which were baked in a small oven heated with pieces of mummy cases, and sometimes with the bones and rags of the mummies themselves . . . I also became indifferent about them at last, and would have slept in a mummy pit as readily as out of it' (Narr. pp. 181–2).

Although Belzoni blames the troglodytes' dereliction of their fields upon European travellers who have created a lucrative market economy in mummies, he is envious of their happiness as they live off the profitable dust of their ancestors, about whose civilization they neither know nor care. The troglodytes are supported by their grisly environment with little effort or labour. However, never one to miss the main chance, Belzoni organized their haphazard labour by establishing a cottage industry at Qurna, paying them a regular weekly wage enhanced by bonuses for intact specimens. By this method he succeeded in extracting unprecedented numbers of mummies in a contracted time-span, the

[106] For De Quincey see my *British Romantic Writers and the East*, pp. 224–8; *The Mystery of Edwin Drood*, ed. with Intro. by Margaret Cardwell (Oxford University Press, 1972), p. 20. Thanks to Chuck Rzepka for this reference.

[107] John Whale comments that 'the collapsing of historical difference turns contemporary Arabs into ancient Egyptians . . . there is no dream of difference, only the nightmare of an invasion of the body' ('Sacred Objects', p. 232). Whale's argument that Belzoni's contact with antiquarian objects is cleared and purified from actual human interaction (ibid., p. 229) does not quite do justice to the *Narrative*'s description of his cordial relationship with the fearsome tomb-robbing troglodytes who inhabit the mummy labyrinths of Qurna, or indeed to Belzoni's understanding of cultural encounter in terms of labour relations.

perfect capitalist : labour equation. The Qurna espisode of Belzoni's career, although (at least in comparison with labour relations at Abu Simbel) in some ways the utopian moment of his transactions with Egyptian labour, also represents the very antithesis of the 'antiquarian sublime' and the Denon/Hamilton heroic narrative of archaeological discovery.

Modern Egyptians

Belzoni's original reason for visiting Egypt had been a commission to design an improved water-wheel for Muhammad Ali Pasha. Like the many European soldiers, capitalists, and technicians who were being drawn into the construction of Ali's new Egypt, Belzoni arrived as a harbinger of modernity rather than an exporter of antiquity.[108] Belzoni's water-mill was designed to abridge labour: powered by a single ox, it would do the same amount of work as four sakiehs, the traditional water-wheels of the Nile. Unfortunately, when demonstrated in the Pasha's presence, an accident occurred and the pump was rejected; the Pasha's advisers, according to Belzoni, 'supposed that the introduction of such machines into the country would throw many of them out of work; consequently I was not welcome amongst them' (Narr. p. 12).[109] Although the accident compelled Belzoni to exchange the role of inventor for that of antiquarian, he nevertheless continued to participate in the socio-economic modernization of 'para-colonial' Egypt.

One of the unusual features of the *Narrative* is its fascination with Egyptian popular culture and pantomime, and especially its mimicry of European manners. For Belzoni, in contrast to Burckhardt, mimicry as a form of cultural understanding works in both directions; after all, one might expect Belzoni as a former professional mimic to be sensitive to his own mimicry by others.[110] Mimicry becomes a kind of stock-in-trade when it becomes a precondition for doing business in antique 'stones'; for this reason, despite a frequent note of racism, Egyptians are given a considerable voice and agency in Belzoni's amorphous, polyphonic text. Most of his anecdotes about Egyptian mimicry are concerned with the problem of wealth, about avoiding conflict in the negotiation of a commensurable scale of value. As Nicholas Thomas writes: 'in cross-

[108] In his account of his training as a hydraulics engineer, Belzoni assiduously avoids mentioning the fact that his technical skills had been acquired while preparing a spectacular 'Exhibition of Hydraulics' called *Fire and Water* for Charles Dibdin, manager of Sadler's Wells theatre (Mayes, p. 44).

[109] Belzoni also describes his demonstration of an electrical machine to the Pasha; like Bruce's rifle anecdote, Muhammad Ali was apparently impressed by the machine's 'power at a distance' (Narr. p. 15).

[110] Michael Taussig notes 'there is a way in which imitating and trading, as much as imitating and stealing, amount to the same system of gift exchange . . . there is indeed an intimate bond between the spirit of the gift and the spirit of the mime' (*Mimesis and Alterity*, p. 93).

cultural exchange on colonial peripheries . . . the discrepancies between esti-
mations of value are one of the crucial sources of conflict'.[111] Evident in
Belzoni's account is an Egyptian anxiety about the presence of Europeans in
their culture (hardly surprising in the light of the French invasion of 1798 and
the antiquarian 'rape of the Nile' after 1815) and the perception that Europeans
are fantastically wealthy, extremely rapacious, but easily duped.

In one practical joke described in the *Narrative*, Muhammad Ali sends his
buffoon disguised in European costume with a money draft for a huge sum of
money on the Egyptian treasury. Nervous laughter greets the revelation of his
true identity (Narr. p. 14). In another pantomime piece, performed at the Soubra
festival, a traveller dressed in 'Frankish' costume arrives at the house of an Arab,
who, despite his poverty, wishes the European to think him rich. He orders his
wife to slaughter a sheep, but she declines, claiming (mendaciously) that the
flock has strayed; when he repeats the order with fowls and pigeons, she
employs the same excuse: 'At last the traveller is treated only with sour milk and
dhourra bread, the only provisions in the house' (Narr. p. 20). Rather like
Volney's description of the European traveller's false impression of Alexandria,
the play captures the unstable relationship between a shared fantasy of oriental
opulence and the reality of poverty. The European traveller-clown is offered
fantastical banquets but in the end has to make do with the plainest fare.
However, the pantomime is also subject to an interpretation more favourable to
the Egyptian audience; after all, the Arab is none the poorer thanks to his wife's
cunning. In the end the European clown is tricked whilst the Arab has saved
his pride.[112] Belzoni doubtless reported this fable as a strategy of appropriation
in order to demonstrate his own superior cunning. Just as the Arab's mutton
becomes dhourra bread for the European, so in Belzoni's *Narrative* objects
which to Egyptians are mere 'stones' are revealed as priceless artworks, by the
transmutative magic of romantic aesthetics. Belzoni inoculates himself with the
Arab wife's cunning in order to wrest wealth from poverty.[113]

Whatever the Egyptians' initial evaluation of antique 'stones', they were
quick to cotton on to the deflationary tendencies of Europeans: as Belzoni
writes, 'it is a fixed point in their minds, that the Franks would not be so liberal,

[111] *Entangled Objects*, p. 31.
[112] Compare with Banks's and Solander's account of a drama enacted on the Pacific island of
Raiatea in which questions of barter and 'traffic' with Europeans were very much at the forefront
(Hawkesworth, *Account of the Voyages*, ii. 269). C. A. Bayly mentions that in this period in 'both Java
and south India, puppet shows played a part in mobilising popular resistance to British and Dutch
conquests' (*Imperial Meridian*, p. 173).
[113] Ironically, in the end the Egyptians might have the last laugh, as the traveller returns home to
find his precious antiquities marked down as classy bric-à-brac in the Hellenistic 'museum order'. One
might also recall Edward Clarke's comparison of Lord Elgin to a nobleman who, 'delighted at a puppet
show, bought Punch and was chagrined to find when he carried him home, that the figure had lost all
its humour' (quoted in St Clair, *Lord Elgin and the Marbles*, p. 190).

unless the articles were worth ten times as much as they pay for them' (Narr. p. 159).[114] On the evidence of Belzoni's and other travel narratives about Egypt in this period it would seem that Egyptians frequently represented the 'surplus value' of European aesthetics in terms of 'treasure' concealed inside antiquities. The resourcefulness with which this 'metaphor' (if it is indeed a metaphor) is deployed leaves the modern reader marvelling at the fluent cross-cultural negotiation which it permitted, however much the story itself is educed by travel writers as evidence of indigenous indifference to, and ignorance of, their own cultural heritage. In one typical incident, Belzoni described how Calil Bey, Muhammad Ali's brother-in-law, asks him 'have you a scarcity of stones also in Europe, that you come here to fetch them away? I answered, that we had plenty of stones, but we thought those of Egypt were of a better sort'. 'O ho!' replied he, 'it is because you find some gold in them perhaps, thank God!' (Narr. p. 119).[115]

Whatever the inspiration of Calil Bey's argument, it is certainly effective; if the Europeans do not pay enough for the 'stones', the Egyptians will demand a half-share of their 'internal' treasure, the value of which they are free to set at any price they desire. In a similar incident at Abu Simbel, Hussein Kachif, the ruler of nearby Ashkit, demanded of Belzoni a share of the treasure to be extracted (by native labour) from the temple. When Belzoni remonstrated that he would find only 'stones', his labourers rejoined 'that if I took away the stones, the treasure was in them; and if I could make a drawing or likeness of them, I could extract the treasure from them also, without their perceiving it. Some proposed, that, if there were any figure discovered, it should be broken before I carried it away, to see the inside of it' (Narr. p. 99). Once again this shows a pragmatic understanding of European aesthetics: if negotiations prove futile, the Nubians can threaten to break the 'stones' in order to establish their exchange value, thereby entirely destroying their *aesthetic* value as integral artworks.

Negotiations with indigenous rulers over the value of antiquities became even more complex when they involved rivalry between French and British agents. On a trip to the island of Philae, Belzoni had noticed and laid claim to a beautiful obelisk, which he later promised to procure for the collection of the English antiquarian, Byron's friend, William J. Bankes. Drovetti reacted to the news of his plan by dispatching one of his more unscrupulous agents, Lebolo, up the

[114] Robert Irwin comments that 'in the Arab lands . . . treasure hunting was both a sophisticated occult science and a popular obsession. The number of tales on the subject in the [Arabian] Nights bear witness to this' (see 'The Universe of Marvels', in *The Arabian Nights: A Companion* (Harmondsworth: Penguin, 1994), p. 185).

[115] For an identical anecdote from Ottoman Greece, see John Cam Hobhouse, *A Journey through Albania, and other Provinces of Turkey in Europe and Asia, to Constantinople, during the years 1809–10*, 2 vols., 2nd edn. (London, 1813), i. 383.

Nile to Philae. Lebolo promptly tricked the local people who had already offered the obelisk to Belzoni by 'pretend[ing] he could read the hieroglyphics on the obelisk, and said it was written, that the obelisk belonged to Mr Drovetti's ancestors; consequently, he had a right to it. The people believed him, and he gave them some trifling presents' (Narr. p. 354). The 'genealogical' European claim to possess Egyptian antiquities is reminiscent of the sheikh's question to Denon cited above, as to whether the temples of Luxor had been built by the British or the French.

Lebolo's claim to be able to 'read' the inscriptions was an underhand one, and Belzoni presents it as such. Nevertheless, he had himself earlier employed a very similar argument in bargaining down the value of objects extracted from the temple with Daud Kachif at Abu Simbel:

> what had I to do with stones, [he asked] if it were not that I was able to procure gold from them? I answered, the stones I wished to take away were broken pieces belonging to the old Pharaoh people; and that by these pieces we were in hopes of learning, whether our ancestors came from that country; which was the reason of my coming in search of ancient stones.   (Narr. p. 82)

Belzoni's argument (itself a 'transculturated' version of contemporary antiquarian research into the origins of European civilization) is certainly more tentative than Lebolo's bald and coercive claim, but both rehearse the well-known colonialist 'myth of return' which is still found circulating on European colonial peripheries in the romantic period from Mexico to India. In this sense, these objects are rightfully 'our' patrimony, not 'yours'; they have no real market value in indigenous terms as they contain no 'treasure', but may be exchanged for some 'trifling gifts'. Their aesthetic aura is explained away as a 'family matter': it is a family to which modern Egyptians definitively do not belong.

The Devil in the Stones

Belzoni's successful 'mobilization' of antiquities depended as much on his negotiations with local labour power as with local rulers. In his study of the removal of the Parthenon Marbles from Ottoman Greece in the previous decade, William St Clair writes of the absence of any formal identification on the part of modern Greeks with the classical heritage embodied by the Marbles, and their corresponding lack of concern for the expropriation of Greek antiquity.[116] His citation of John Cam Hobhouse's account of the popular local belief that purloined classical statues contained spirits called 'Arabim', which

---

[116] William St Clair, *Lord Elgin and the Marbles*, p. 208. See also Reinhold Schiffer, *Oriental Panorama: British Travellers in 19th Century Turkey* (Amsterdam and Atlanta, Ga.: Rodopi, 1999), pp. 101–10 for indigenous attitudes to antiquities in Ottoman Turkey.

frequently 'cried out and moaned [their] condition' suggests that this was not always the case, however, at least among the 'subaltern' peasant class. Hobhouse's journal entry for 6 January 1810 recorded a story about Greek workers refusing to load Marbles bound for England on the grounds that they 'heard an Arabim groan and scream most piteously within them. Some of these statues, they say, have been heard to bewail their friends and fellow marbles in the Acropolis.'[117] Subaltern Greek recalcitrance may have been expressed in the language of magic rather than of national heritage, but could nevertheless sometimes serve as an effective obstacle to expropriation. We find a very similar situation in Belzoni's Egypt (also within the Ottoman zone) which suggests that antiquities did after all have a traditional 'semiophoric' value for local peoples beyond their potential exchange value. Significantly, as in the Greek example, local Egyptian resistance seems to have been principally aimed at the formation of a capitalist work-force necessary to extract and transport heavy antiquities.

Having failed in the water-wheel venture, Belzoni set about realizing Salt and Burckhardt's scheme to remove the 'Memnon's Head' from the ruins of Thebes. Having located the bust, his first task was to organize a work-force and extract permission from the local governor at Acmin to remove the head. The *Narrative* records the latter's reluctance to allow the sculptures to go, notwithstanding Salt's firman from Muhammad Ali: 'Oh! but you cannot have them', he replied, 'they are all enchanted by the devil; and no one can take them from where they are!' (Narr. p. 32). Belzoni is often scathing about the 'Arabian nights' quality of local tradition concerning antiquities, but in this case he does seem to have been impressed by the notion of diabolical ownership. After being marshalled into heaving the huge bust down to the Nile bank using only fourteen poles, four ropes of palm leaves, and four rollers without tackle, the fellahin labourers appeared suddenly to recognize the manner in which their labour was being 'alienated', in Marx's term. (Ill. 8) 'Though it was the effect of our own efforts, it was the devil, they said, that did it; and, as they saw me taking notes, they concluded that it was done by means of a charm' (Narr. p. 43). European writing—in this case doubtless Belzoni's haulage calculations—is connected with diabolical power. Moreover, 'when the Arabs found that they received money for the removal of a stone, they entertained the opinion, that it was filled with gold in the inside, and that a thing of such value should not be permitted to be taken away' (Narr. p. 44).

Although it might seem strange that the devil should both safeguard

[117] St Clair, p. 209. In the published version of this story (*A Journey through Albania*, i. 348), Hobhouse changed the ideological function of the 'Arabim' to read: '. . . they heard the Arabim crying out, and groaning for his fellow-spirits detained in bondage in the Acropolis. The Athenians suppose that the condition of these enchanted marbles will be bettered by a removal from the country of the tyrant Turks' (St Clair, ibid.). The indigenous complaint is now made to support both philhellenism and the British expropriation of the Elgin Marbles.

8. Belzoni's 'Transportation of "Young Memnon"', *Plates Illustrative of the Researches and Operations of Giovanni Belzoni* (1821), pl. 46.

antiquities, and preside over their removal, his appearance in this context is telling. In his book *The Devil and Commodity Fetishism in South America*, Michael Taussig describes 'certain fantastic and magical reactions to our non-fantastic reality as part of a critique of the modern mode of production'.[118] In the very different context of twentieth-century Bolivia and Colombia, Taussig describes the rise of a practice of 'devil contracts' among recently proletarianized peasants working in sugar plantations and silver mines; the devil, it seems, never appearing as an icon among non-proletarianized peasants in these same areas. As with Taussig's proletarianized peasants, so with Belzoni's Theban fellahin: both protest in their different ways against the wage incentive, the production of surplus value, and the fetishization of the commodity. The removal of 'Memnon's Head' is on a different scale from transactions with small-scale vase dealers at Sakkereh or the troglodyte tomb-robbers of Qurna, as Belzoni literally coaxes surplus value out of his work-force. 'In point of skill, [they] are no better than beasts' (Narr. p. 45), he thunders, as his labourers unwittingly participate in the construction of the 'museum order' and romantic aesthetics. The 'Young Memnon' assumes an autonomy and a vitality (figured in its smile at being transported to England) at the same time as the labour of Egyptian peasants is reified as the effect of diabolical intervention. Belzoni brutalizes his workers, who in turn find a magical description for their alienated labour and its instrumentality in expropriating ancient statues. As yet unversed in ideologies of proletarian solidarity or national heritage, the labourers 'anthropomorphise their subjugation in the figure of the devil, redolent of the power of evil'.[119]

Belzoni's voyage to Nubia and his attempts to excavate Abu Simbel represent the most ambitious transaction in the whole *Narrative*; namely the creation of a money economy *ex nihilo* and the establishment of a wage incentive in this remote reach of the Upper Nile, where barter still prevailed. Napoleon's savants had never penetrated so far up the river, so the ground had not been 'prepared' for archaeological excavations, not to mention any vestige of a modern economy based on organized labour. Upon arrival, Belzoni discovered that Drovetti had beaten him to it, and had already offered Daud Kachif, the local headman, 300 piastres to open the temple. The offer, however, had fallen flat because money here has literally no value. To outstrip Drovetti, Belzoni was obliged single-handedly to create a system of financial credit, in order to establish a work-force to clear the tons of sand from the face of the temple. Because the Nubian inhabitants of Abu Simbel were only accustomed to a barter economy, they were 'not easily led by promises, for there is so little faith among them, that what is

---

[118] Michael Taussig, *The Devil and Commodity Fetishism in South America* (Chapel Hill: University of North Carolina Press, 1980), p. 10.
[119] Ibid., p. 36.

not obtained is considered as imaginary. It was with such a race of people I had to deal' (Narr. p. 81).

In a paradigm of the interventionist practices of European capitalism, Belzoni sets about challenging the 'oriental despotism' of Daud Kachif, who 'is absolute master to do what he pleases: there is no law to restrain him' (Narr. p. 81). Having come to a prior agreement with his servants on board his boat moored on the Nile, Belzoni gives a piastre to one of the natives, telling him that if he goes to the boat, he will be able to exchange it for a measure of dhourra (grain), an experiment which he found 'had a good effect not only on the minds of the people, but also on that of the Cacheff' (Narr. p. 84). The unearned piastre and its magical purchasing power was a gift, not a wage, so the inhabitants speedily encountered money in its most agreeable aspect. Belzoni established a salary scale of 2 piastres per man per day, whilst harbouring no illusions concerning the devastating effect which the establishment of a money economy would have upon the agricultural society of Abu Simbel.[120] Unfortunately for Belzoni's plans, the next day, none of the ' "wild men", for such I must call them,' turned up for work (Narr. p. 94). Drawing a logical conclusion from the 'free' measure of dhourra, the Nubians failed to make the connection between the spending power of money and the toils of labour.

Returning to Abu Simbel in July 1817 with two British officers called Irby and Mangles, Belzoni showered gifts upon Daud Kachif and his retinue, and urged his workers back to the task of clearing sand. Work proceeded slowly, because 'they spent much of their time singing a Nubian song which proclaimed that they were going to get as much Christian money as they could. "This song, though cheering to them," remarked Mangles, "was not much so to us." '[121] With the onset of Ramadan, work ceased, and among food shortages and demands for wage increases Belzoni's work-force drifted away. The Europeans (co-opting their Egyptian crew) were forced to finish the clearing themselves, and after seemingly endless setbacks they finally entered the portico of Abu Simbel, marvelling at its imposing hall flanked by eight huge Osiris-like figures of Rameses II. Few of the monuments were movable, so the officers mapped out the temple and Belzoni sought to draw the statues in the steam-bath atmosphere of the interior. Otherwise, the party left the site practically empty-handed, in the course of their 'researches' having introduced a money-economy to the

[120] As the kachif warns Belzoni, the whole community would simply desert their fields and flocks and head for Egypt to spend their wages, given that the money could not be spent at home, similar to what had already happened among the troglodytes of Qurna. Belzoni later failed to single out some of the workers who had robbed his boat because the Nubians 'were all like so many lumps of chocolate seated on the sand . . . and not to be distinguished the one from the other' (Narr. p. 100). Belzoni's racist simile here reflects both the reification of labour involved in proletarianizing Nubian peasants, and a tone of pantomimic puerility which frequently obtrudes into his *Narrative*.

[121] Quoted in Fagan, *Rape of the Nile*, p. 172.

'wild men' of Nubia, while signally failing to bind them to the yoke of organized labour.

The Sham Belzoni

At least Belzoni's transactions at Abu Simbel did not involve much competition with European rivals. Arriving back at Philae from Abu Simbel he discovered that a set of reliefs representing Osiris in judgement, which Belzoni had cut from the walls of the Temple of Isis at Philae the previous year and which lay awaiting shipment to Alexandria, had been deliberately smashed, and the words *operation manqué* charcoaled over the fragments. Drovetti's agents had been at work. Not native recalcitrance so much as French rivalry finally limited Belzoni's spectacular success in extracting an unprecedented quantity of antiquities from the loot-quarries of the Nile valley. By the end of his stay in Egypt he was in litigation with Drovetti's agents over an unsavoury incident which had happened at Thebes at the end of 1819.

Matters had started badly when Belzoni and Salt met up with Drovetti at Thebes in order to settle their respective 'spheres of influence'. Visiting Karnak together, Drovetti informed Belzoni that his 'double' had been seen walking among the ruined temples, clearly a veiled threat on Drovetti's part. Like so many apparently 'factual' episodes in the *Narrative*, this seems almost to allegorize the author's legendary 'double' persona as gentlemanly antiquarian and colonial grave-robber, patriot, and sensationalist showman. The 'magical' form of the story seems to identify it as a product of the colonial rumour-machine, where stories circulated from Europeans to Egyptians and back again, metamorphozed by the distorting mirror of linguistic and cultural incomprehension. Belzoni could only attempt gentlemanly composure in the face of the duplication of his identity: 'I informed Mr Drovetti that I hoped he would tell his European people to inquire before they should fire at the supposed person representing me, whether it was the real or sham Belzoni, as it would not be quite so pleasant or satisfactory to me if the mistake had been found out after' (Narr. p. 349).

The rivalry really came to a head when Belzoni was assaulted on Boxing Day 1819 in the ruins of Luxor by Antonio Lebolo and another of Drovetti's agents (Narr. p. 366). Although the incident blew over without anyone being killed or wounded, he had finally had enough, returning to Cairo where he begun an unsuccessful litigation against Drovetti's party.[122] The bitter closing words of the *Narrative* denounced the spirit of jealous rivalry which had forced his precipitate departure from Egypt:

[122] The case collapsed because, as Piedmontese citizens, Lebolo and his henchmen could only have been prosecuted in Turin.

not that I disliked the country I was in, for, on the contrary, I have reason to be grateful; nor do I complain of the Turks or Arabs in general, but of some Europeans who are in that country, whose conduct and mode of thinking are a disgrace to human nature.   (Narr. p. 437)

The British Museum and the Egyptian Hall

During his short sojourn in Egypt, Belzoni's most spectacular achievements had been the removal of 'Young Memnon's Head', the opening of Abu Simbel, and the discovery of the virtually intact tomb of Seti I in the Valley of the Kings. But none of these ventures had left him any better off financially, although he managed to sell off two pieces (from the pitiful handful of objects which Henry Salt had permitted him to keep) to the Count de Forbin, director of the French Royal Collection, for 7,000 piastres. Belzoni also came to an agreement with Salt for 500 pounds and half the price of the beautiful alabaster sarcophagus of Sethi I when it was eventually sold.[123] When Salt offered his Egyptian collection (much of it procured by Belzoni) to the British Museum in 1819 for the sum of 8,000 pounds the offer was rejected by the Trustees (see Sir Joseph Banks's letter quoted at p. 107). Salt was in the end forced to sell for only 2,000 pounds, making another 2,000 pounds from the sale of the sarcophagus to Sir John Soane (it can still be seen in the basement of the Soane Museum in Lincoln's Inn Fields). The fact that the Trustees had in 1805 paid 20,000 pounds for the Townley Collection of classical Marbles and terra-cotta vases, and a further 8,200 pounds for assorted bronzes and gems in 1814; and that, albeit reluctantly, they had paid out 35,000 pounds for Lord Elgin's Parthenon Marbles in 1816, demonstrates the relatively low market value for Egyptian, compared to Greek, antiquities in the romantic period. Salt had fallen victim to the strong Hellenism of the British establishment, but at least he achieved some remuneration, going on to sell his next collection to the king of France for 10,000 pounds, in all netting the respectable sum of 20,000 pounds from the sale of Egyptian antiquities before his death in 1827, 'still a lonely consul without the pension and scholarly recognition he had craved all his diplomatic life'.[124]

Belzoni, on the other hand, received not a penny from the sale of these collections, nor did his widow, Sarah, benefit financially from the 2,000 pounds

---

[123]   Fagan, *Rape of the Nile*, p. 198.

[124]   Fagan, p. 247. There is a considerable irony in the fact that Salt, the British Consul, ended up enriching the Egyptian collection in the Louvre, the French Consul Drovetti founded the collection of Turin, and the Paduan Belzoni contributed the lion's share of Egyptian artworks to the British Museum (Mayes, p. 292). The logic of the commodity rather than national affiliation clearly determined the acquisition of 'semiophores'. For an account of Salt's melancholy state of mind in 1824, see his 'Egypt, a Descriptive Poem, with Notes', published in the *Life and Correspondence of Henry Salt*, Esq, FRS, 2 vols. (London, 1834), i. 387–420.

netted from the sale of Seti I's sarcophagus to Soane. Yet the real triumph of Belzoni's public career was not financial success so much as the exhibition which opened on 1 May 1821, in Bullock's Egyptian Hall in Piccadilly, a more appropriate venue for Belzoni the showman than the haughty British Museum. (As Richard Altick writes: 'it was as if the Egyptian Hall had been built expressly for Belzoni'[125]). Although Benjamin Robert Haydon had recently exhibited his vast painting 'Christ's Entry into Jerusalem' in one of its upstairs rooms, the Hall more often played host to the populist and commercially oriented 'shows of London' described so vividly by Altick.[126] As the published guide makes clear, Belzoni's exhibition was centred upon a life-size plaster-of-Paris facsimile of two chambers of Seti I's tomb, the decorations of which he and Ricci had laboriously moulded in wax, a process which had taken nearly a year's work in the sweltering heat of Thebes. Added to this, he had devised a scaled-down 50 foot model of the tomb in its entirety, as well as miniature wax models of Philae, the second Pyramid, and Abu Simbel at a scale of one to thirty; miscellaneous mummies, vases, papyri, and fragments; 'a multitude of collateral curiosities', were displayed inside glass cases.[127] Influenced by Bullock's 'habitat' museology, Belzoni succeeded in creating an atmosphere more 'authentic' than that conveyed by the stilted prose style and broken English of his travel account: 'deep ochrous reds and royal blues lapped the beholder in a warm tide, bright yellows and greens flamed exotically about him. The low roof and lamp-light sought to recreate Belzoni's first impressions as he entered the tomb.'[128] This was the romantic answer to the British Museum's austere display of decontextualized objects, a more successful and sensationalist equivalent of Belzoni's colourful travelogue.

Despite the shortage of 'authentic' antiquities (Belzoni was particularly galled at being denied permission to exhibit Seti I's sarcophagus when it arrived in London in 1821), the exhibition attracted over 1,900 visitors on the first day alone, each of whom paid half a crown for admission to see 'Belzoni's Tomb' and admire his miniaturized habitat recreation of Egyptian antiquity.[129] The *Times* was of the opinion that

[125] Altick, *The Shows of London*, p. 244.

[126] As Stanley Mayes writes, 'the Siamese Twins and "General" Tom Thumb, a Murillo and more Haydons, a fake Japanese mermaid and a machine for composing Latin hexameters all drew their sadly discrepant followings' in Bullock's 'Egyptian Hall' (*The Great Belzoni*, p. 258). In my conclusion I shall have more to say about the hall in connection with Bullock's 'Ancient and Modern Mexico' exhibition in 1824.

[127] *Description of the Egyptian Tomb, Discovered by G. Belzoni* (London: John Murray, 1821). The guide advertises the second edition of Belzoni's *Narrative* and its accompanying 44-plate *Atlas*. See Susan M. Pearce, 'G. B. Belzoni's Exhibition of the Reconstructed Tomb of Seti I in 1821', in *Journal of the History of Collections*, 12: 1 (2000), 109–25 for a full list of contents.

[128] Altick, p. 245.   [129] Mayes, pp. 258–63.

the mechanical ingenuity and indefatigable diligence by which Mr Belzoni has been enabled thus to transport to the arena of European controversy the otherwise immovable excavations of Egypt reflect no less credit upon him as an artist than his sagacity and success in discovering the subject matter of this extraordinary exhibition has distinguished him above all European travellers in modern times.[130]

This was high praise, although tortuous prose, illustrating how the concept of traveller's 'credit' had been transformed since the days of Bruce. The Piccadilly exhibition, together with the success of his *Narrative*, had brought Belzoni to the peak of his popular fame, although the financial rewards were still slow in coming. Yet the *Times*'s remark about his distinction over all other modern European travellers clearly rang hollow in his ears.

Belzoni basked in celebrity as a sort of five-day wonder, but he evidently failed to convince himself that he was safely extricated from the world of Sadler's Wells and Bartholomew's Fair. The auctioning of the contents of the Piccadilly exhibition in 1822 reads like a scaled-down parody of Salt's negotiations to sell his 'authentic' collection to the British Museum. The plaster-of-Paris bas-reliefs which made up the facsimile of Seti's tomb, (according to the sales catalogue 'highly coloured in Imitation of the Original') were knocked down at 490 pounds, two authentic statues of Sekhmet went for 380 pounds, and even the wax model of the Second Pyramid made 34 guineas. Unfortunately for Belzoni, the romantic cult of 'authenticity' embodied in the Elgin Marbles and enshrined in the 'museum order' which had failed to accredit his name, made plaster-cast copies and scale-models look shoddy and second-rate. When Henry Bankes aroused Belzoni's ire during his wrangles with Salt and the Trustees of the British Museum over the ownership of the Seti Sarcophagus,[131] a choleric Belzoni wrote from Paris: 'I hope Mr Bankes will reflect that the low in Ingland is administrated for a Stranger on the sam scole with an Inglishman, though he may be related to poiple of influence, as he, Mr B—, boast to be'.[132] Belzoni had not succeeded in leaving intrigue behind in Egypt, and perhaps he had overestimated the quality of the accolades showered upon him by his adopted countrymen.

In many ways, Belzoni's *Narrative* and exhibition set the tone for subsequent exotic exhibitions of a commercial stamp aimed at a wider nineteenth-century public. In a study of A. H. Layard's *Ninevah and its Remains* (1849), Frederick N. Bohrer has compared the British Museum's display of Layard's Assyrian antiquities with their popular 'appropriation' in the pages of the *Illustrated London News* and in Layard's own account. In contrast to the 'categorical' orga-

[130] Mayes, p. 260.
[131] Father of the William John Bankes for whom Belzoni had risked his neck procuring the Philae obelisk, eventually erected in the park of the Bankes' home of Kingston Lacy in Dorset.
[132] Quoted Mayes, p. 277.

nization of antiquities in the British Museum, which increasingly 'distanced' the viewer and organized objects in chronological sequence,[133] the Victorian culture of popular curiosity relied on a 'presentist' and personalized mediation of exotic objects. The fact that Layard had Belzoni in mind in preparing his enormously popular travel account is suggested by the frontispiece to his second volume ('Procession of the Bull Beneath the Mound at Nimroud'), with its allusion to Belzoni's image of the removal of 'Memnon's Head'. However, in conformity with the general tone of Layard's work, the Nimroud excavation is represented as a large-scale, disciplined affair in which armed and apparently uniformed archaeologists supervise their Arab work-force from horseback. Layard's abridgement, the *Popular Account of the Discoveries at Ninevah* (published in John Murray's 'Railway Reading' Series in 1853) took the reader, Belzoni-style, on a guided tour of the excavations for all the world as if the text were an exhibition-guide rather than a travel account ('Let us imagine ourselves issuing from my tent near the village . . . I have already described my feelings when gazing for the first time on these majestic figures. Those of the reader would probably be the same . . .').[134] In Layard's narrative (compared to Belzoni's) the authority of the traveller/archaeologist is unimpeachable, his ego stabilized in relation to distant places and peoples, whilst excavating the past is confidently represented as part of imperial Britain's 'civilizing mission'.

The closing episode in Belzoni's career takes a tragic turn, revealing the status anxiety which still dogged archaeological excavation in the 1810s compared to the 1840s. In disgust at the exhibition world in which he found himself once more immured (every bit as cloying as the mummy labyrinths of Qurna), Belzoni suddenly resolved to have one last bid at the status of gentleman traveller. His two expeditions in search of the site of the ancient city of Berenice and the Oasis of Jupiter Ammon had represented an earlier bid for status, both proudly paraded in the full title of his *Narrative*.[135] Now, in 1823, at the height of his fame but haunted by the memory of his 'polite' *alter ego*, J. L. Burckhardt, Belzoni determined to return to Africa, this time to Benin, in search of the source of the Niger and the city of Timbuktu. Financed by the small capital raised from his publishing and exhibiting exploits (as well as by a Cambridge University subscription to defray the costs of his voyage as far as Fez), Belzoni

[133] 'The Times and Spaces of History: Representation, Assyria, and the British Museum', in *Museum Culture*, ed. by Sherman and Rogoff, pp. 197–222.

[134] *A Popular Account of Discoveries at Ninevah Arranged from his Larger Work* (London: J. Murray, 1854), p. 307. The abridgement left out the scholarly 'Enquiry into the Manners and Arts of the Ancient Assyrians', which took up most of the second volume of the original work. This example confirms Timothy Mitchell's argument about the importance of exotic exhibitions in organizing European perceptions of the orient in *Colonising Egypt* (Cambridge University Press, 1988).

[135] As Fagan writes of the latter expedition, 'Belzoni's primary interest seems to have been to discover and examine the great temple [of Jupiter Ammon] rather than to bring home another load of antiquities' (*Rape of Nile*, p. 228).

turned his back on the trials and tribulations of making a business out of the past to seek fame as an explorer. In her last letter written to him, Sarah warned her husband 'do not be too ventursome recollect poor Mungo Park if you find too many difficulties turn before it is too late write by all Caravans . . . May God Bless and Protect you trust in him my dear jovanni and happy return to England'.[136] But is was too late. The 'Patagonian Sampson' died of dysentery on 3 December 1823 at Gwato in Benin, West Africa, before his epic journey ever got off the ground. Richard Burton, visiting Gwato forty years later, could find no trace of his grave. Belzoni's ruling passion for mimicry, to be someone else, had finally got the better of him.

[136] Mayes, p. 284.

4

Indian Travel Writing and the Imperial Picturesque

> The spirit of enterprize seemed to have disappeared; the means which a long and quiet residence in [India] afforded of obtaining more accurate knowledge concerning [the natives of India] than could possibly be acquired by mere travellers however diligently inquisitive, served rather to destroy curiosity than to quicken it. Men lived so long among the Hindoos that they became accustomed to their manners; they appeared to think that what they had acquired so imperceptibly could not be worth imparting, and to imagine that the public could not be curious about things with which they themselves had so long been familiar.
>
> Robert Southey, Review of Lord Valentia's 'Voyages and Travels to India', *Quarterly Review*.[1]

Southey's review of Valentia's *Travels* provided him with the opportunity to lament the poverty of modern Indian travelogues compared with the rich seventeenth-century legacy of Thomas Coryat, François Bernier, and Sir Thomas Roe. Although Southey's criticism of colonial 'incuriosity' was somewhat mitigated by his acknowledgement of the contribution to British knowledge about India made by *Asiatic Researches* and the 'very valuable, though unarranged diary of Dr [Francis] Buchanan' (to which I return below), he reserved for Lord Valentia, who had toured India between 1802 and 1805, the accolade of being 'the only English traveller who for more than a hundred years has visited India for the purpose of gratifying his own curiosity and imparting his observations to the public'.[2] In the wake of the romantic enthusiasm for India stimulated by Sir William Jones, and the flood of publications on India which issued from the European press, Southey's might seem an ill-judged claim. Closer examination reveals, however, that it was by no means an isolated one.

The publication of Valentia's *Travels* and metropolitan interest in the India Act of 1813 improved matters to the extent that the *Monthly Magazine* could write in the same year that 'that meagreness of information relative to the con-

---

[1] QR, 2 (Aug. 1809), 88–126, 89. [2] Ibid.

quered, which, until lately, disgraced the modern conquerors of Hindostan, is, by the labours of Mr Forbes, Dr Buchanan, Messrs Daniell, Mrs Graham, Captain Williamson, and Lord Valentia, no longer a subject of just reproach'.[3] Nevertheless, in his remarks on Bishop Reginald Heber's *Narrative of a Journey through the Upper Provinces . . .* (1828) fifteen years later, John Gibson Lockhart could still combine praise for Heber with condemnation of Anglo-Indian[4] incuriosity; 'ere [British residents] begin to think of describing India, they have lost the European eyes on which its picturesque features stamp the most vivid impressions'.[5] Implicit in Lockhart's view (and I return in the next section to the all-important question of the picturesque) is the venerable notion that good travel writing was the fruit of first impressions invariably dulled by familiarity. Colonial overfamiliarity bred incuriosity, if not contempt. The arousal of curiosity is now, significantly for my argument in the second half of this book, equated with a *picturesque* response to distant lands.

That Lockhart's view was not simply Tory *parti-pris* (Heber had after all been a frequent contributor to the *Quarterly Review* before his departure for India) is evident from Francis Jeffrey's contemporaneous review of Heber in the Whig *Edinburgh Review*. Although the *Edinburgh Review* had not seen fit to review (the Tory) Valentia's *Travels* in 1809, it showered praise on Heber's book, which it hailed as 'the most instructive and important publication that has ever been given to the world, on the actual state and condition of our Indian Empire'. Heber's view of India had been written while the author's first impressions were still fresh in his mind, and 'the fairness of the first judgement unperverted by the gradual accumulation of interests, prejudices, and deference to partial authorities'.[6] Once again a review of a recent travel account of India provided an opportunity for denouncing the military and civilian employees of the East India Company who had failed to meet the criteria of curious enquiry or disinterested observation.[7] In the hands of Company commentators, the project of 'representing India', Jeffrey argued, had been mired in a host of inconsequential local details obsessed with military expeditions, topographical surveys, or commercial transactions, any objectivity of tone marred by the factional infighting which had characterized the Company regime since the days of Warren Hastings. Evidently only the magisterial overview of the polite metropolitan traveller in India, a peer like Valentia, or a clergyman of Heber's

[3] MM, 36 (1813–14), 577.
[4] I use the term in its 19th-century sense of a British resident in India (i.e. in comparison with metropolitan travellers like Valentia, Graham, and Heber) rather than a person of mixed racial descent, although the first sense does not necessarily exclude the second.
[5] QR, 37 (Jan. 1828), 101.   [6] ER, 48 (Dec. 1828), 314–15.
[7] Jeffrey exempted Sir John Malcolm and Mountstuart Elphinstone. This may not have been unconnected to the fact that, in addition to being distinguished as historians and orientalists, both were Scotsmen of Whig leanings.

intellectual calibre[8] was capable of redressing the self-interested partiality of the colonial perspective.

But things looked different to the much-maligned colonialists themselves. In its 1809 review of Valentia's *Travels*, the *Asiatic Register* had fought back, defending the Anglo-Indians against such attacks from the metropolis. The reviewer unfavourably compared Valentia's superficial knowledge of India with that of Sir William Jones, complaining that the travel journal format was 'less accommodated to research, and too rapid and extemporaneous for philosophical arrangements'.[9] What might be novel and exotic to British readers was old hat to Anglo-Indians: 'we may yawn over verandahs, and palanquins and bearers, and musnuds, if seen too often, as much as over balconies, and close carriages, sofas, sedan chairs, and running footmen. Elephants will be no more, if appearing too often, than mountain mules.'[10] The *Asiatic Register* greatly preferred James Bruce's *Travels* to Valentia's (this should be put in the context of Valentia's cavalier treatment of Bruce, discussed in Chapter 2) on the grounds that, unlike Abyssinia, 'the peninsula of Hindostan has been explored in every direction, and by people of every description'.[11] The disagreement about Valentia's *Travels* suggests the problematic nature of travel writing in the discourse of early nineteenth-century British India. Rather than confirming a more or less simple binary opposition between colonizers and colonized, it further suggests that colonialism was riven by its own internal contradictions as well as being actively contested by its colonized subjects.[12]

Underlying these debates about the epistemological value of 'first impressions'—style travelogues can be discerned an anxiety concerning Anglo-Indian identity. Unlike British settler colonists in the Caribbean, South Africa, or Australasia, Anglo-Indians were not allowed to settle permanently or to buy land in Company territory, and were expected to retire from service back to Britain. As G. W. F. Hegel noted in his *Lectures on World History* (one of his very few shrewd observations on India) 'the English have . . . adopted the policy in India of preventing the rise of a native Creole population, i.e. a people of mixed European and native blood'.[13] Neverthless, P. J. Marshall has described how, by the early nineteenth century, a small but independent body of Anglo-Indian opinion had emerged with some links to metropolitan radicalism. For a brief period until the collapse of 'white' liberalism in the 1850s, this

[8] As we shall see, the *Edinburgh Review* often ignored earlier Indian travel accounts, as opposed to history, politics, regional topography, linguistics, and anthropology. The publications of Lord Valentia, James Forbes, and Maria Graham, for example, were all passed over.

[9] AR, 11 (1809), 491.   [10] Ibid., p. 491.   [11] Ibid., p. 493.

[12] See Nicholas Thomas, *Colonialism's Culture: Anthropology, Travel, and Government* (Princeton, NJ: Princeton University Press, 1994), p. 51.

[13] Hegel, *Lectures on the Philosophy of World History: Introduction*, trans. by H. B. Nisbet, intro. by Duncan Forbes (Cambridge University Press, 1975), p. 164.

body of opinion found some common ground with emergent Indian élites. One thing that both communities had in common was the fact that both groups were ruled autocratically by the 'Honourable Company', so that even 'whites had little part in the administration of the towns in which they lived'.[14] Needless to say, imperial policy studiously resisted the formation of any such Indian 'public sphere' which might have seen the emergence of a creolized 'colonial society' something along the lines of Iberian America.

In the eighteenth century, hyphenated colonial Britons (or 'nabobs') had been tarred with a reputation for vulgarity and ostentatious new wealth, to which were added corruption and peculation in the wake of the impeachment of Warren Hastings.[15] The different perspective of Anglo-Indians is illustrated by Sir William Jones's comment (in a letter of 1787) that 'in Europe you see India through a glass darkly: here, we are in a strong light; and a thousand little *nuances* are perceptible to us, which are not visible through your best tele-scopes, and which could not be explained without writing volumes'.[16] Jones's strong deixis (here/there), his espousal of a 'tropical aesthetic' ('a strong light'), and the sense of the myriad details of cultural difference vie with his critique of the obscurity plaguing British perceptions of its South Asian colonies. As we have seen, the eighteenth-century aesthetics of travel writing demanded the 'dazzle' and freshness of first impressions, the sort of 'intimate distance' derived from a fast, fleeting survey of a foreign country. How could Anglo-Indians, many of them resident in India for twenty or thirty years, and all to some extent pro-fessionally employed in the colonial project of 'knowing the country', be expected to share in such an aesthetic?[17] Many recent studies of travel writing and colonialism have omitted any consideration of India in the early period,[18]

[14] P. J. Marshall, 'The Whites of British India, 1780–1830: A Failed Colonial Society?', in *Trade and Conquest: Studies on the Rise of British Dominance in India* (Aldershot and Brookfield, Vt.: Ashgate, 1993), pp. 33, 36.

[15] Cf. Philip Lawson and Jim Phillips, '"Our Execrable Banditti": Perceptions of Nabobs in Mid-18th Century Britain', *Albion*, XVI (1984), 225–41; and Percival Spear, *The Nabobs: A Study of the Social Life of the English in 18th-century India* (New Delhi: Oxford University Press, 1932).

[16] To the Second Earl Spencer, 4–30 August 1787, no. 764, *Letters of Sir W. Jones*, ed. by Garland Cannon, 2 vols. (Oxford: Clarendon Press, 1970), ii. 743. For an account of Jones's career, see Garland Cannon, *The Life and Mind of Oriental Jones* (Cambridge University Press, 1990).

[17] Perhaps the most striking instance of this 'dual perspective' is Mountstuart Elphinstone's descrip-tion of the Afghanis in his *Account of the Kingdom of Caubul, and its Dependencies in Persia, Tartary, and India* (London, 1815). Whereas a British traveller might start at 'their sun-burned countenances, their long beards, their loose garments, their shaggy mantles of skin' and wonder 'how a nation could subsist in such disorder', the 'English traveller from India' would 'admire their strong and active forms, their fair complexions and European features', as well as the 'independence and energy of their char-acter', compared to the natives of 'effeminate' Bengal (pp. 149–50).

[18] The standard study is still Ketaki Kushari Dyson's 1978 *A Various Universe: A Study of the Jour-nals and Memoirs of British Men and Women in the Indian Subcontinent, 1765–1856* (Delhi: Oxford University Press, 1978), which makes a case for the literary value of the texts which she studies in the tradition of the English diary and autobiography, thus avoiding specific problems associated with 'travel' literature as such.

riage, or a train. They were uncomfortable in the narrow confines of a city street, a bazaar, a *mela*—anywhere they were surrounded by their Indian subjects.[34] In fact, Buchanan had not wanted to publish his book in the form of a 'Journey' at all, having intended to rework it into an 'analytical and organised regional description'. He had sent his manuscript to the Company's librarian in London, and to his chagrin the latter had passed it straight to the printer without consulting the author. Buchanan's Preface hoped that the book's comprehensive index would make up for its immethodical (by which he meant 'personal narrative') structure (*Journey*, i., p. vii). In the event, some reviewers dealt harshly with his lack of method, to the point when, as we saw above, Southey could refer in 1809 to Buchanan's 'valuable, but unarranged diary'.[35] (Others, like Reginald Heber, writing in the same review the month after Southey, were of the opinion that 'of statistical [travel] writers, there are indeed enough, and to spare . . . it is a defect inherent in their system, to want the power of delineating with force and expression the temper and character of a country'. This, Heber felt, constituted 'the essential difference between the travels of Bruce, and the dull common-place book of Dr Shaw'.[36]) Partly on account of the problems associated with his *Journey Through Mysore*, Buchanan's subsequent report on Bengal remained in manuscript until after his death, whilst his account of Nepal was published in 1819 in highly systematic, impersonal form.[37]

In striking contrast to the work of the French Institute of Cairo, administrative inertia on the part of the East India Company seems to have deadened the impetus of the 'survey modality' of the early 1800s. At least Buchanan managed to make the results of some of his work publicly available; by contrast Colin Mackenzie's enormous compendium of information on southern India was never even published. In 1808, following Buchanan's example, Mackenzie sent a seven-volume manuscript descriptive of his survey of Mysore to London, but by 1827 it became clear that the Company had lost it.[38] To a greater extent than Buchanan, Mackenzie was possessed of an antiquarian sensibility and an orientalist respect for Hindu culture; when he died in 1821, he left an enormous collection of 3,000 stone and copperplate inscriptions, 1,568 literary manuscripts, 2,070 local tracts, and large portfolios and collections of drawings,

[34] Cohn, p. 10.

[35] As a member of Wellesley's inner circle, Buchanan's career suffered from the political changes in British India after the replacement of his patron by Lord Minto, who blocked his ambitions as a naturalist, despite his appointment as director of the Bengal survey in 1807 (Vicziany, p. 638). Despite its 'non-literary' form, Buchanan's *Journey* was the inspiration for James Lawrence's orientalist and anti-matrimonialist novel *The Empire of the Nairs* (1811), which in turn influenced Shelley. See Walter Graham, 'Shelley and the Empire of the Nairs', PMLA, XL (1925), 881–91.

[36] 'On Robert Ker Porter's *Travels*', QR, 2 (Nov. 1809), 288–9.

[37] My remarks here are indebted to Edney's excellent account of Buchanan as an instance of 'geographical narrative', pp. 77–81.

[38] Cohn, p. 85.

plans, images, and antiquities today known as 'the Mackenzie Collection'.[39] In his essay 'The Transformation of Objects' Bernard Cohn tells the story of Mackenzie's excavation of the Amaravati tope in the Guntur district of the Madras Presidency, and the fate of the beautiful Buddhist sculptures which were eventually shipped to London. The low ranking of Indian sculpture on the aesthetic hierarchy ensured a repeat of official indifference to the Egyptian collection of Henry Salt discussed in the previous chapter, one of the pieces being cemented to an outer wall of the India Museum at Fife House on White-hall. In 1866 James Fergusson located the other Amaravati Marbles under piles of rubbish in the coach house of Fife House.[40]

The Picturesque Modality

Coeval with the development of the 'survey modality' in British India was the antithetical visual discourse of the picturesque, which (despite its European provenance), would exercise a profound effect on Indian travel writing in the romantic period and thereafter. In contemporary eighteenth-century British painting from Richard Wilson to Gainsborough, the picturesque aesthetic combined the atmospheric Italianate landscapes of Claude Lorraine, Gaspar Poussin, and Salvatore Rosa with the more particularized Dutch style of Ruys-dael and Hobbema; its theorists in the 1780s and 1790s (when the phenome-non peaked in Britain) included the Revd William Gilpin, Sir Uvedale Price, and Richard Payne Knight. Given that the picturesque already represented the British landscape in an exotic, Italianate idiom, it was particularly suitable for blending the aesthetic qualities of tropical with temperate landscapes in the Indian context. The first professional landscape painter to tour India (in

[39] Nicholas Dirks, 'Guiltless Spoliations', p. 214. His work was never published; as Dirks comments: 'we know Mackenzie principally through the sedimented remains of his archive; otherwise his autho-rial voice is largely buried, or at least hidden in pencilled marginalia and modest footnotes' (p. 214).

[40] Cohn, p. 91. On the India Museum of the East India Company in London, founded in 1798, see Ray Desmond, *The India Museum 1801-79* (London: H. M. Stationery Office, 1982). This museum seems to have been one of the last bastions of officially sanctioned 'curiosity': ill-arranged, cluttered with miscellaneous objects on high shelves, as Desmond writes 'a bewildering confusion of curious and colourful objects' (p. 1). Nevertheless, it seems to have been extremely popular with the public (probably because of the lack of any rival), to the extent that in 1817 access had to be limited by an advance booking system. For a discussion of the related issue of colonial museums in 19th-century India, see Gyan Prakash, *Another Reason: Science and the Imagination of Modern India* (Princeton, NJ: Princeton University Press, 1999), ch. 2, 'Staging Science'. Although the colonial museum had 'reformed' itself by the period covered by Prakash's book, Prakash argues that even the rationalized exhibitory order was subject to subaltern misappropriation: rather than 'dazzling superstition into science' (p. 31) the museum could be understood as pure entertainment, a *jadu ghar* [wonder house]' (p. 47), like the Lahore Museum in Kipling's novel *Kim*.

1780–3) was William Hodges, whose spectacular aquatints were published in 1786 as *Select Views in India* (initiating the fashion for 'picturesque views' imitated by the Daniells, Fraser, White, and many others) followed in 1793 by his narrative account *Travels in India*.[41] Hodges was succeeded in 1788 by Thomas and William Daniell, who developed Hodges' aquatint technique (as Partha Mitter notes 'admirably suited [to] the transfer to print of their delicate water colour renderings of Indian monuments'),[42] publishing the highly successful *Picturesque Voyage to India* in 1810 and *Oriental Scenery* from 1795 to 1808. As well as their successful landscape views, the Daniells succeeded in creating a taste for Indian architecture, monuments, and 'costume' in Britain which contrasted with the sort of official recalcitrance concerning Colin Mackenzie's antiquarian collection noted above. Other notable picturesque artists (both amateur and professional) working in India in this period were James Wales, George Chinnery, Henry Salt (travelling with Valentia), and James Baillie Fraser. The apogee of the Indian picturesque would seem to have been in the 1830s, when expensively produced publications such as *The Oriental Annual*, with steel engravings or lithographs of Indian monuments, landscapes, and peoples, were in great popular demand.[43]

Recent work on the picturesque in eighteenth- and nineteenth-century Britain by John Barrell, Anne Bermingham, Stephen Copley, and Elizabeth Bohls has tended to focus on the links between aesthetics and social changes in the ownership of property, urbanization, and the gendering of domestic tourism.[44] Clearly, analysis of the equivalent aesthetic in British India must look elsewhere for the social and ideological forces underpinning the picturesque movement, considering that Anglo-Indians in this period were forbidden from owning land, that tourism in the domestic 'leisurely' sense did not yet exist, and that urbanization was hardly an issue in the overwhelmingly rural and pre-industrial society of South Asia. Moreover, the Indian picturesque needs to be

---

[41] See Harriet Guest, 'The Great Distinction: Figures of the Exotic in the Work of William Hodges', in *New Feminist Discourse*, ed. by Isobel Armstrong (London and New York: Routledge, 1991).

[42] Partha Mitter, *Much Maligned Monsters: History of European Reactions to Indian Art* (Oxford: Clarendon Press, 1977), p. 126.

[43] The best overview is Mildred Archer and Ronald Lightbown's *India Observed: India as Viewed by British Artists, 1760–1860* (London: Trefoil Books, V&A Museum, 1982); see also G. H. R. Tillotson, 'The Indian Picturesque: Images of India in British Landscape Painting, 1780–1880', in *The Raj: India and the British, 1600–1947*, ed. by C. A. Bayly, (London: NPG Publications, 1990), pp. 141–250. For the Daniells, see Mildred Archer, *Early Views of India: The Picturesque Journeys of Thomas and William Daniell, 1786–1794* (London: Thames and Hudson, 1980).

[44] John Barrell, *The Dark Side of the Landscape: The Rural Poor in English Painting, 1730–1840* (Cambridge University Press, 1980); Ann Bermingham, *Landscape and Ideology: The English Rural Tradition, 1740–1860* (Berkeley, Calif. and Los Angeles: University of California Press, 1986); Stephen Copley and Peter Garside (eds.), *The Politics of the Picturesque: Literature, Landscape and Aesthetics since 1770* (Cambridge University Press, 1994); Elizabeth Bohls, *Women Travel Writers and the Language of Aesthetics 1716–1818* (Cambridge University Press, 1995).

distinguished from the representational practices marking early nineteenth-century 'settler colonialism' in South Africa, Australasia, or North America.[45]

I shall consider this complex phenomenon under three headings: anti-utilitarianism; curiosity; and associationist aesthetics; although I am aware that my present remarks can only sketch the outlines of what might be a much fuller theory of the Indian picturesque. Firstly, then, in relation to the 'survey modality' discussed above, the Indian picturesque represented itself as anti-utilitarian and anti-georgic, even while it engaged in the appropriation and commodification of Indian landscape.[46] As such, it initiated the claim made by later travel writers and critics to a disinterested overview of colonial India. Gilpin had insisted in his seminal *Three Essays on Picturesque Beauty* (1794), that 'the province of the picturesque eye is to *survey nature*: not to *anatomize matter*. It throws its glances around in the broad-cast stile. It comprehends an extensive tract at each sweep. It examines *parts*, but never descends to *particles*.'[47] Motivated by the 'broad-cast style' of viewing the land, the picturesque eye (quite distinct from Buchanan's mode of viewing Mysore) could skim over any features which disturbed the composure of aesthetic form, as well as utilitarian traces of industry, improvement, or modernity. Ostensibly the British picturesque rejected georgic conventions of prosperous husbandry and smiling cornfields for wild, uncultivated 'shaggy' terrain marked by 'intricacy' and 'variety',[48] neat rural dwelling places for the 'roughness' of rundown cottages, ruined castles, and abbeys, industrious rustic labourers for socially marginalized banditti and gypsies. In this respect it differed from the georgic aesthetic of 'beauty' which one would expect to find privileged in the colonial discourse of 'agrarian patriotism'.[49] In contrast to the busy georgic landscape, the formal

[45] See David Bunn, '"Our Wattled Cot": Mercantile and Domestic Spaces in Thomas Pringle's African Landscapes', in W. J. T. Mitchell (ed.), *Landscape and Power* (Chicago and London: University of Chicago Press, 1994). Mitchell's essay 'Imperial Landscapes' in the same volume is also useful for thinking about the Indian picturesque.

[46] This is not to say that British travellers did not often resort to georgic descriptions of Indian landscape, normally reserved for comparison between territory under the Company sway and territory controlled by native rulers. See William Hodges' description of Bengal in the early 1780s: 'flourishing in tillage of every kind, and abounding in cattle. The villages are neat and clean and filled with swarms of people' (*Travels in India During the Year 1780-3*, 2nd edn, (London, 1794), p. 17). Mughal Agra, by comparison, although a 'fine country', 'exhibits, in its present state, a melancholy proof of the consequence of a bad govenment . . . now all is desolation and silence' (ibid., p. 121). See also Teltscher, *India Inscribed*, p. 128. Valentia employs an identical comparison in describing Awadh in *Voyages and Travels in India . . .* 3 vols. (London, 1809), i. 128.

[47] William Gilpin, *Three Essays on the Picturesque*, 'Essay 1 on Picturesque Beauty', in Malcolm Andrews (ed.), *The Picturesque: Literary Sources and Documents*, 3 vols. (East Sussex: Helm Information, 1994), ii. 15.

[48] Ibid., ii. 14.

[49] In Gilpin's formulation the picturesque might be achieved by vandalizing formal beauty, as in his famous account of 'improving' a Palladian building with a mallet (ibid., p. 8). On 'agrarian patriotism' in Britain and in British India, see C. A. Bayly, *Imperial Meridian*, pp. 121-6, 155-60.

composure of the picturesque provided a forced repose, the sense of arrest in experience, in history, in narrative.

As Richard Payne Knight argued in his *Analytical Inquiry* (1805), the painterly eye had the power of separating the pleasing visual qualities of picturesque objects from other sensory effects: bad smells, excessive heat or cold, sympathy for the poor or socially marginalized, dangers anticipated from roving bandits, and so on.[50] This painterly 'screening effect' worked as an existential formula for viewing territory where unseen horrors might lurk, the poverty, famine, and squalor which often met the eyes of Europeans travelling in colonial India. The picturesque eye could thus imagine the scene as a *representation*, and by identifying with the rules of painterly composition put the copy in the place of the unsightly original. Sara Suleri eloquently evokes the colonial picturesque as 'a desire to transfix a dynamic cultural confrontation into a still life, converting a pictorial imperative into a gesture of self-protection that allows the colonial gaze a licence to convert its ability not to see into studiously visual representations'.[51]

What, then, is the relationship of the picturesque to the colonial survey modality? Raymond Williams, comparing the 'irregularity' of the picturesque vista with the mathematical grid of contemporary land enclosures in eighteenth-century England, writes that '[both] are related parts of the same process—superficially opposed in taste but only because in the one case [i.e. enclosures] the land is being organised for production . . . in the other . . . it is being organised for consumption—the view, the ordered proprietary repose, the prospect'.[52] Whereas the colonial surveys of Buchanan and Mackenzie organized Mysore for the institution of private property in the form of the *ryotwari* system—the creation of a class of yeoman farmers whose productivity might guarantee the Company a fixed income from land rents—the picturesque aesthetic set about 'organizing' British India for consumption in the imperial metropolis. As we shall see, picturesque viewing represents another manner of enclosing and framing Indian land.[53]

[50] Richard Payne Knight, *An Analytical Inquiry into the Principles of Taste*, 4th edn. (London, 1808), p. 71.

[51] *The Rhetoric of English India* (Chicago and London: University of Chicago Press, 1992), p. 76. As will be obvious below, however, Suleri's attempt to read this as contributing to what Francis Hutchins calls the 'illusion of permanence' (p. 76) seems problematic. Whatever its claims about the durability of Britain's imperial presence in India, at the level of the viewer's consciousness the picturesque largely depended upon associative nostalgia for home.

[52] Raymond Williams, *The Country and the City* (London: Hogarth Press, 1985), p. 124.

[53] The ideological underpinning of the exotic picturesque has been the subject of some debate. Although Barbara Stafford argued for a complete break between associationist picturesque viewing and the empirically based 'voyage into substance' characteristic of the enlightenment travel account (e.g. *Voyage into Substance*, p. 4), recent studies such as those of Matthew Edney and Nicholas Dirks have argued instead for a continuity between the aesthetic and surveillance modalities. As Edney indicates, Stafford's privileging of the scientific aesthetic 'actively denies the ideology that permeates

The importance of the picturesque's claim to disinterestedness lay in the fact that it grounded the claims of the imperial metropolis to a stake in representing its Indian colonies, for the benefit of an inexpert British public as well as an 'interested' Anglo-Indian one. For this reason, the picturesque came to dominate the visual and literary descriptions of colonial travel texts (as well, of course, as non-colonial writing) in the romantic period as it subsumed the eighteenth-century insistence on the 'dazzle' of first impressions. For example, William Hodges insisted that only a passing traveller from Britain (like himself) could adequately evoke 'the face of the country' in India, for 'gentlemen who have resided long in India lose the idea of the first impression which that very curious country makes upon an entire stranger . . . reasoning assumes the place of observation, and the traveller is lost in the philosopher'.[54] This is reiterated by the Daniells in their celebrated introduction to *A Picturesque Voyage to India*, although now combined with criticism of the Hastings regime which had sponsored Hodges. Acknowledging the achievements of European 'curiosity' in 'penetrating the veil of mystery' which had long hidden India from outside eyes, they wrote that 'it remains for the artist to claim his part in these guiltless spoliations, and to transport to Europe the picturesque beauties of those favoured regions'.[55] If the metaphorical identification/disavowal in the oxymoronic term 'guiltless spoliations' parades the painter's stake in the colonizing project, the last part of this statement tellingly identifies the picturesque view with the Latourian 'immutable mobile' exported back to the centre and exposed to the tastes and judgement of an imperial public sphere. The picturesque thus commodifies British India for a metropolitan public, but without partaking in the 'guilty' private interest of the nabobs of Hastings's generation. Under the aegis of the picturesque, Anglo-Indians would have to see 'their' India with the same eyes as their relatives at home in Britain, thereby strengthening the bonds of imperial solidarity.

I turn now to the relationship between the picturesque and the themes of antiquarian curiosity and 'temporalization' formulated in Chapter 1. If we take two representative views such as the Daniells' 'Cape Comorin' or 'Entrance of an Excavated Hindoo Temple at Mauveleporam' (Ills. 9 and 10), we find that the focal object of interest in each case is an ancient Indian building or ruin with markedly 'curious' features, but that the focalizing 'curiosity' of the singular object is now distributed into the 'intricate variety' of its 'typical' landscape

topographical views' (*Mapping*, p. 55). Edney notes the picturesque descriptions which occasionally punctuate the 'geographical narratives' of Lambton and Buchanan (p. 63).

[54] Hodges, *Travels in India*, p. iv. For the importance of Hodges' Indian travelogue, see Archer and Lightbown, *India Observed*, pp. 74–80.

[55] Thomas Daniell RA and William Daniell RA, *A Picturesque Voyage to India, by the Way of China* (London, 1810), p. ii.

Cape Comorin, near Calcut.

9. Thomas and William Daniell, 'Cape Comorin', *Oriental Scenery* (1812–16), part 4, no. 1.

The entrance of an excavated Hindoo Temple at Mauveleporam.

10. Thomas and William Daniell, 'Entrance of an Excavated Hindoo Temple at Mauveleporam', *Oriental Scenery* (1812–16), part 5, no. 2.

setting.[56] I have discussed the passionate investment of the curious gaze in the 'novel' or 'singular' object which engaged vision close up. Unlike the topographical painting or the panorama, the picturesque view still concentrated upon a single central feature, albeit distanced by perspectival layering and chiaroscuro effects (in this respect many of the Daniells' aquatints, particularly those representing architectural features, are closer to the topographical tradition than the more 'imaginative' work of Hodges or Salt).[57] Contemporary attempts to theorize the role of curiosity in picturesque viewing oscillated between positive and negative attitudes to the phenomenon. I have already commented (in the Chapter 1) on Uvedale Price's attempt to enlist curiosity in the service of the picturesque in his 1794 *Essay on the Picturesque*: 'the effect of the picturesque is curiosity; an effect which, though less splendid and powerful [than the sublime], has more general influence; it neither relaxes nor violently stretches the fibres, but by its active agency keeps them in full tone . . . correct[ing] the languour of beauty, or the horror of sublimity'.[58] (Price's aesthetic is still anchored in Burke's physiological idiom rather than the associative psychology of Payne Knight or Archibald Alison). But in his *Essay on Picturesque Travel* of the same year, Gilpin approved of curiosity when elicited by ancient ruins, but not by nature on the grounds that 'the *lusus naturae* is the naturalist's province, not the painter's'.[59] Whilst the picturesque is by definition deeply invested in a chiastic relationship between art and nature, it rejected the superficial visual puns of baroque curiosity. Interest is shifted to the normative threshold between the beautiful and the sublime—Uvedale Price's placement of the picturesque—from the 'curious' threshold of the sublime and the grotesque.

The picturesque's reformation of curious vision is intimately linked to temporalization, for, as noted above, the picturesque landscape is also a *past* landscape which manifests the ruinous agency of time. Unlike the antiquarian

[56] Charlotte Klonk cites Robert Thornton's (exactly contemporaneous) collection of botanical paintings, *The Temple of Flora*: 'the images . . . will not only express the different gradations of the flowers, but will generally have . . . Back-Grounds expressive of the situation to which each naturally belongs'. (Although Thornton's backgrounds, any more than the paintings of Hodges or the Daniells, did not represent a 'straightforward depiction of the plant's actual environment'.) *Science and the Perception of Nature: British Landscape Art in the late 18th and early 19th Centuries* (New Haven and London: Yale, 1996), p. 37. According to Mildred Archer, the temple featured in 'Cape Comorin' was invented by the artist in order to provide an architectural 'reflection' of the mountain. See *Early Views of India: The Picturesque Journeys of Thomas and William Daniell 1786–94* (London: Thames and Hudson, 1980), plate 123.

[57] Cf. Klonk (p. 99) who suggests that this picturesque concentration gave way later in the period to a decentralized study of objects in their environments, which she terms 'phenomenalism'. (Something similar to this will be evident in my discussion of Humboldt in Chapter 6.) See Stafford, *Voyage into Substance*, pp. 401–2, for a different view of the relationship between picturesque 'reverie' and 'the apprehension of a striking detail in nature'.

[58] *Essay on the Picturesque*, 2nd edn. (London, 1796), pp. 195–6.

[59] Andrews, II. 20.

attitude which often reconstructed the ruin in terms of its former splendour, picturesque stasis has arrested the turmoil of history and contemplates its passing in the spirit of nostalgic detachment. Ruined castles and abbeys in Britain often betokened the triumphant banishment of feudal oppression and popish superstition, providing a kind of historical negative of the post-1688 Whig regime of liberty and property. Transculturated to the landscape of colonial India, the melancholy contemplation of Mughal or Hindu ruins, one of the most persistent tropes of Indian landscape description, signals the 'ruins of empire', the triumph of British liberty over oriental despotism, and the erasure of colonial conquest past or future. In contrast to the suppression of indigenous history in Thomas Pringle's South African picturesque,[60] in the eyes of early nineteenth-century British travellers and artists, Indian ruins figured the historical triumph of liberty over tyranny, rather than the guilt of colonial dispossession.

Whilst the taste for ruins depended upon the trope of *sic transit gloria mundi* (in India equally as in Greece and Rome), the 'ethnographical picturesque' represented modern Indians—the Company's colonial subjects—in a temporalized framework which emphasized living continuity rather than the absence of the past. In an example of the temporalizing trope, William Hodges cast Indians as antique Greeks or Romans, mingling classical decorum with the sort of erotic voyeurism which we have observed in the writings of Banks and Bruce: 'To a painter's mind, the fine antique figures never fail to present themselves, when he observes a beautiful female form ascending these steps from the river, with wet drapery, which perfectly displays the whole person'.[61] The Daniells, in *A Picturesque Voyage*, found that, 'happily for curiosity, [Indian monuments] are often elucidated by the manners of the present inhabitants, who with unexampled fidelity have preserved their primitive customs unimpaired by time or conquest; and in their domestic institutions still present the image of a remote and almost obsolete antiquity.'[62] In contrast to the belittlement of modern Egyptians under the eyes of Napoleon's savants, the British observers' temporalized, picturesque view of modern Hindus imbued them with a sense of classical grandeur, however much their current subjugation might also render them objects of pathos. At the same time, the 'temporal exchange' implicit in the picturesque paradoxically played an important role in colonial modernization.[63]

[60] See Bunn, 'Our Wattled Cot'; 'The settler landscape cannot afford the Romantic luxury of bathing in the past, in deep history, because the past is the domain of the Other, and history is the history of dispossession' (p. 143).

[61] Hodges, *Travels in India*, p. 33. Compare with Volney's anti-picturesque account of Egyptian women in *Travels through Syria and Egypt*, i. 19. Hodges' trope became standard for eroticizing Indian women; cf. Capt. John Seely, *The Wonders of Elora* (1824), p. 50.

[62] *A Picturesque Voyage to India*, p. ii.

[63] The 'ethnographic picturesque', whether those carefully grouped figures appearing in the picturesque paintings of Hodges or the Daniells, or the more descriptive typifications of Baltazard Solvyns (*Les Hindous*, 4 vols. Paris, 1808–12), would play a significant role in the development of colonial eth-

Victor Jacquemont noted in the early 1830s that the 'British have destroyed in their possessions the originality of Asiatic manners, beyond the domestic circle of each individual. They have no longer any picturesque feature, but are very convenient for use.'[64]

In this way, the picturesque commodified Indian landscape for sentimental consumption in the metropolis, explicit in the Daniells' statement that

there are . . . associations of sentiment, which in this country [i.e. Britain] must lend to oriental scenery peculiar attractions: a large part of Hindustan is now annexed to the British empire; and it cannot but afford gratification to our public feelings to become familiar with a country to which we are now attached by the ties of consanguinity and affection.[65]

The picturesque's associative power over distance could also work in the other direction, from colony to metropolis. By mediating exotic subject-matter with perspectival layering and chiaroscuro lighting effects it 'translated' the brilliant light of the tropics into the sombre sepia tints of an Italianate landscape. Shrouding India in the melancholy, static idiom of the eighteenth-century culture of sensibility, it thereby privileged the associative subjectivity of the (European) viewer over his or her (Indian) object. At the very moment at which it split the British eye from the Indian landscape, the picturesque sutured together colonial and metropolitan vision, eliciting a lachrymose nostalgia as the present landscape dissolved in sentimental memories of home and childhood, in many cases evoking the rugged 'fringe' landscapes of Scotland, Ireland, or Wales.

The picturesque thus marks the *stabilization* of bourgeois European subjectivity in the discourse of travel, as it represented (in Price's formulation) a *via media* between the lassitude of the beautiful and the violence of the sublime. If the picturesque frames 'unimproved' and 'shaggy' terrain it is filtered, according to Payne Knight, through an 'improved medium' of association and memory.[66] The picturesque reformed the subjectivity of the European in India just as the 'agrarian patriotism' of the new conquistador regime claimed to reform territory which it had wrested from oriental tyranny. As the violent history of colonial conquest was screened out of the picturesque vista, so the intrusive curiosity or unregulated egotism of promiscuous subjectivity (associated with 'pre-picturesque' travel writers such as James Bruce) was regulated and disciplined. Unlike the settler colonies, where sites of domesticity were encoded in the 'transitional' picturesque landscape,[67] the Indian picturesque

nology in later 19th-century works such as *The People of India*, 1868–75. (See Suleri, pp. 103–10; and Chris Pinney, 'Colonial Anthropology in the "Laboratory of Mankind"', in *The Raj: India and the British 1600–1947*, ed. by C. A. Bayly, pp. 252–63.)

[64] Victor Jacquemont, *Letters from India*, 2 vols. (London, 1834), ii. 219.
[65] *A Picturesque Voyage*, p. ii.   [66] *Analytical Inquiry*, p. 152.
[67] See Bunn, pp. 142, 143.

translated sensibility into the personal nostalgia of the imperial viewer. As I commented in my discussion of Felicia Hemans' poem 'The Traveller at the Source of the Nile' in Chapter 2, the centrifugal object-orientation of 'curiosity' was reformed by means of an associative ligature which mapped the exotic scene onto a nostalgic landscape of childhood and of home (the patriotic 'scene of infancy'), rendering it an especially approved idiom for women writers and artists.[68]

With its preference for the glowering mountainscapes of the Celtic fringes, the metropolitan picturesque also played its part in composing the irregular variety of Scots, Welsh, Irish, and English identities into the *concordia discors* of the imperial British state. Envisioned in this way as the visual setting for 'imagined community', it struck a compromise between the smiling beauty of English tillage and pasturage and the sublime 'terror' of Scottish or Welsh mountain landscapes. In India the catchment of the picturesque was extended from Celtic periphery to distant colony, particularly apt in a period when India (in the words of Walter Scott) was 'the Corn Chest for Scotland, where we poor gentry must send our younger sons as we send our black cattle to the south'.[69] Scott's protégé, for example, the Borderer Dr John Leyden, typically found that in Coorg, the 'grotesque and savage scenery, the sudden peeps of romantic ridges of mountains bursting through the bamboo bushes, all contributed strongly to recall to memory some very romantic scenes in the Scottish High-lands'.[70] Several decades later, Fanny Parks found her English background and ignorance of Highland landscape an initial disadvantage for an appreciation of the Indian picturesque when travelling to the Himalayas. As a patriotic Briton and reader of Scott's novels, it was a disqualification which she swiftly sur-mounted, however: 'when we arrive at the hills, I hear we are to be carried back, in imagination, to the highlands of Scotland. I have never been there; *n'importe*, I can fancy as well as others.'[71]

---

[68] In 1822 a School of Art was opened for aspiring European women picturesque painters in Bombay (Indira Ghose, *The Power of the Female Gaze: Women Travellers in Colonial India* (New Delhi: Oxford University Press, 1998), p. 44). I return to this topic in the next chapter.

[69] To Lord Montagu, 1 July 1821. Quoted by Iain Gordon Brown, in 'Griffins, Nabobs and a Sea-soning of Curry Powder: Walter Scott and the Indian Theme in Life and Literature', *The Tiger and the Thistle: Tipu Sultan and the Scots in India, 1760–1800* (Edinburgh: National Gallery of Scotland, 1999), p. 71.

[70] *Poetical Remains of Dr John Leyden*, ed. by the Revd James Morton (London, 1819), p. xli.

[71] Fanny Parks, *Wanderings of a Pilgrim in Search of the Picturesque*, 2 vols. (London, 1850), i. 63. The 'Celtic' referent in picturesque aesthetics also functioned in the ethnographical field; the most pic-turesque natives were often located on the militaristic tribal or ethnic margins of British India, like the rugged inhabitants of Britain's Celtic fringes compared to bland urban southerners. This aestheticiza-tion of 'feudal', peripheral populations was commonplace, exemplified in Mountstuart Elphinstone's privileging of the 'independence and energy' of Afghans over the 'indolence and timidity' of Hindus; James Tod's championship of 'feudal' Rajputs over despotic Marathas or Mughals; and James Bailly Fraser's more qualified comparison of Gurkhas to his native Highlanders (to provide three more Scot-tish examples).

As we saw above, one of the major anxieties of the post-1800 regime in British India, and one amply discussed by Lord Valentia in his 1809 travelogue, was the fear of European creolization, the formation of a 'country-born' class, product of colonial miscegenation with native Indians. In his *Voyages and Travels*, Valentia regretted the 'increase in half-caste children [in Calcutta]. They are forming the first step to colonization, by creating a link of union between the English and the natives. In every country where this intermediate caste has been permitted to rise, it has ultimately tended to the ruin of the country. Spanish America and Santo Domingo are examples of this fact.'[72] What seems to disturb Valentia's imperialist vision here is not so much a racist aversion to miscegenation in itself as a political distrust for what he calls 'colonization', namely the creation of a creole caste of hyphenated Europeans. Like the rebellious subjects of the French Caribbean or Spanish America, or (even more problematically) of Britain's own former American colonies, creoles had a tendency to demand republican independence from their colonial mother countries, thereby bursting the 'ties of consanguinity' in a political as well as an ethnic sense. Valentia was full of praise for the East India Company's policy of preventing European 'colonization' in India, which he dignified as 'the grand object of the judicious policy of England'.[73] Wellesley's Fort William College (and later the Company's college at Haileybury) were 'designed to release the oriental Briton' from the dangers of corruption by 'the depravity of the peoples of India'.[74]

Another means of preventing creolization was to cement affective links with home, thereby disenchanting distance between colony and metropolis. Sounding like a contemporary philosopher of association such as Archibald Alison, Payne Knight, or Dugald Stewart, Valentia explicitly embraced sentimental association as a means of preventing creolization: 'nothing could have a stronger tendency to hinder the Europeans from establishing themselves in India, than the prospect . . . of a speedy return to their native climates, while the scenes of youthful days were fresh in their remembrance, and the ties of friendship, and

---

[72] George Annesley, Viscount Valentia, *Voyages and Travels to India, Ceylon, the Red Sea, Abyssinia, and Egypt, in 1802, 3, 4, 5, and 6*, 3 vols. (London, 1809), i. 241. Henceforth Valentia in text. Robert Southey disagreed, as is evident in his advocacy of miscegenation in his 1804 epic, *Madoc*. In his otherwise positive review of Valentia's *Travels* in the *Quarterly Review*, he took issue with Valentia on this point, praising the *mestizaje* of Spanish and Portuguese colonialism and describing British rule as being precarious like a coco tree: 'it lifts a beautiful head to heaven; it renders an abundant harvest, but it spreads its roots along the surface of the soil, and is therefore at the mercy of the winds; the first hurricane lays it prostrate, and not a sucker springs up to mark the place where it flourished' (QR, 2 (1809), 99).

[73] Valentia, I. 257.

[74] The college inculcated 'Christian sobriety and Indian languages . . . the latter . . . obviat[ing] dependence on native informants and factotums' (Bayly, *Imperial Meridian*, p. 142), one powerful means of enforcing the cultural barrier.

of kindred, neither broken nor forgotten'.[75] In the most literal sense, Valentia's 'prospect' evoked the sentimental ligatures of the picturesque. Francis Hutchins comments on the fact that the Anglo-Indian of the Victorian era 'never became Indianised . . . the British kept themselves apart with all the exclusiveness of an Indian caste'.[76] Hutchins fails to mention that the self-isolation of the later nineteenth-century sahib—which, by a sort of cunning of historical reason he discovers fanning the flames of incipient Indian nationalism—was at least in part the result of an earlier policy of anti-creolization in which the aesthetics of the picturesque had a significant, although unacknowledged, role to play. What P. J. Marshall calls the 'failure' of Anglo-India as a colonial (as opposed to an imperial) society may well been at least in part prompted by the 'approved' medium of the picturesque, working out on an aesthetic level the dissolution of a 'mixed' colonial public sphere, and implementing an associative linkage of white colonial and metropolitan societies.[77]

The Peer and the 'Bishop Sahib': The Indian Travel Narratives of Lord Valentia and Reginald Heber

The Indian travel accounts of George Annesley, Viscount Valentia, and of Bishop Reginald Heber helped to establish, in Cohn's words, 'a repertoire of images and typifications that determined what was significant to the European eye . . . places could be made to seem familiar by following predetermined itineraries and seeing the sights in a predictable way'.[78] Just as both travellers depended on the routes and sights of picturesque painters like Hodges and the Daniells, and the compendia of information contained in *Asiatic Researches*, so their texts in turn became reference points for subsequent nineteenth-century travelogues. Proceeding from Calcutta to Delhi via the Ganges, the nineteenth-century traveller typically headed northwards to the Himalayas or the Punjab, or else south-west through Rajasthan and Gujarat to Bombay, then down to Malabar, Ceylon, and up the east coast to Madras. Certain sights were obliga-

---

[75] Valentia, I. 257.

[76] *The Illusion of Permanence: British Imperialism in India* (Princeton, NJ: Princeton University Press, 1967), p. 118.

[77] See P. J. Marshall, 'The Whites of British India, 1780–1830: A Failed Colonial Society?'

[78] Cohn, p. 6. This approximated to the well-established 'beaten track' of the Grand Tour itinerary in Europe. In this respect, another contemporary account, James Forbes' retrospective *Oriental Memoirs* (1813) belongs to a different genre, albeit representing the first substantial account of the Bombay Presidency. Forbes had been Company Collector in Bombay, Gujarat, and Malabar in the years between 1765 and 1783: his conversion to the cause of Indian evangelization provided a lens through which the 'second empire' could contemplate the strengths and weaknesses of the first (cf. K. K. Dyson, p. 181). Whilst it represents a compendium of current discourses on India, *Oriental Memoirs* cannot be said to be a travel narrative in the strict sense.

tory: 'the river front in Benares, the fort at Allahabad, a visit with the Nawab of Oudh, sightseeing in Agra and Delhi'[79] whilst others, less desirable, were erased by the screening framework of the picturesque.

Although Valentia was widely praised for his 'curiosity' in extending the conventional aristocratic Grand Tour to India, in the event he spent much of his time fulfilling the diplomatic duties of a titled emissary of the East India Company. The flunky who announced Valentia in the court of the Nawab of Awadh as 'the Lords (Wellesley's) sister's son, and the grandson of Mrs Company' (the author explains that 'these titles originated from a belief of the natives that the East India Company is an old woman, and that the Governors General are her children') (Valentia I. 137)[80] was perhaps not far off the mark. Valentia exchanged expensive gifts, the cost of which were met from the Company's coffers, and the customary 'pan and attar' with a variety of Indian nobles and princes. These included the Rajah of Benares, the Nawab of Awadh (he stopped in Lucknow for four months), the impoverished Nawab of Furruckabad, the Rajah of Tanjore, and, most sensitive from a diplomatic point of view, the Paishwa of Pune, recently re-established by the British on his dewan at Pune after being ousted by the Maratha ruler Holkar. Valentia's gifts to the Paishwa, provided by the Company, were worth 20,000 rupees (Valentia II. 129).

Valentia participated in all the pomp and circumstance of the Indian native courts, in line with his view of the princely obligations of Wellesley's new 'proconsular' regime in British India.[81] Neither Anglo-Indian[82] nor British reviewers found much to praise in this aspect of Valentia's travel journal; as the liberal *Monthly Review* opined disapprovingly, 'the man of rank is more prominent than the man of science' and 'the public are no further interested in such pageantry than as it indicates the manners and character of the people'.[83] Unfortunately, in contrast to less-affluent travellers, princes and servants seem to be the only South Asians whom Valentia *did* meet; the unreality of his sense of native courts is evident in his constant tendency to compare them to fashionable English 'masquerades', which they 'excelled in one respect: the characters were well supported, and the costume violated by no one' (Valentia. I. 62).[84] At times the tricks of Indian jugglers and the exotic dancing of Nautch-girls conspired to render India one huge exhibition: Valentia 'fully expect[ed] to be

---

[79] Cohn, p. 6.
[80] The book was fulsomely dedicated to Richard Wellesley, former Governor-General of India, and, like Valentia, an Anglo-Irish aristocrat, under whose patronage he had travelled.
[81] Cf. Bayly, *Imperial Meridian*, pp. 193–216.   [82] Cf. *Asiatic Register*, 11 (1809), 483–96.
[83] MR, LXII (June, 1810), 114, 117.
[84] Cf. Terry Castle's *Masquerade and Civilisation: The Carnivalesque and Civilization in 18th-century English Culture and Fiction* (London: Methuen, 1986), for the morally ambivalent connotations of masquerades.

entertained with a panorama at Benares, and a phantasmagoria in the caves of Elephanta' (Valentia I. 202). Despite his claims to have achieved an unprecedented 'overview' of India, Valentia frequently seems to have confused realities with spectacular European orientalist representations.

Nevertheless, there is no doubt that Valentia had also internalized the discourses of both 'survey' and 'picturesque' modalities in his Indian travel narrative. He met Major Lambton at Bangalore, and busily collected minerals, insects, and ethnographical curiosities, thus participating in his patron Wellesley's project of 'knowing the country' (Valentia I. 411). In the eighteenth-century tradition of the patrician Grand Tourist, Valentia's 'secretary' was the landscape painter and antiquarian discussed in Chapter 3, Henry Salt, and there is considerable seepage of Salt's picturesque aesthetics into Valentia's journal narrative. Salt's role was to 'take picturesque views' and visit (with or without his patron) notable beauty spots such as the falls of the Kaveri, his account of which is inserted wholesale into Valentia's narrative (Valentia I. 443). Although Valentia generally leaves picturesque representation to Salt's visual medium (the handsome engravings of Salt's landscape views were one of the book's major selling-points), he is evidently alert to the associative and screening imperatives of the aesthetic. Touring the recently conquered state of Mysore in early 1804, Valentia and his party stopped at the mountainous view-point of 'Ooscottah' 'to refresh our bearers, who were exhausted with the heat, and to give Mr Salt an opportunity to take a sketch of the scenery, which was finer than anything I had yet beheld in India. Herefordshire, with the distant view of the Welsh mountains, may be honoured by being in some degree compared to it' (Valentia I. 450). Valentia's curiosity was not long satisfied by picturesque viewing, with its nostalgic frisson, however; his gaze quickly focused upon

the branches of the loftiest trees [which] were covered by the parasitical tribe; the Epidendrons and Filices were various and beautiful; but the most conspicuous was the Dracontium pertusum, which perfectly covered the gigantic stem of the Ficus bengalensis with its leaves . . . I frequently stopped to wander a little from the road to collect seeds, in which I was very successful.   (Valentia I. 451)

Botanical particularism and a Linnaean nomenclature typical of the eighteenth-century 'integrated' travel account here take over from aestheticized landscape description.

A little later on his tour, making his way from Bombay to Pune, Valentia was horrified by the ravages of famine, devastated villages, and the stench of decaying bodies, which he quickly attributed to the recent depredations of the Maratha leader, Holkar, thereby absolving the British from any responsibility. His appetite for breakfast ruined, he 'hasten[ed] from this scene of horror', and shortly afterwards his party had 'the good fortune to [establish camp] . . . at a distance from any village, and its melancholy accompaniments; a mango tope formed a screen to the south, and a pellucid tank was in our front' (Valentia II. 112). Choosing a camping ground out of sight of famine-struck villages, he employs picturesque terms of art to describe the mango clump which 'screens' the unpalatable signs of human misery behind it: a 'pellucid tank' in the middle distance draws the eye towards a more attractively 'curious' vision of harmonious Indian village life, thereby, in Suleri's words, 'converting a pictorial imperative into a gesture of self-protection'.[85]

At the same time, Valentia's particularist eye and botanical interests (not to mention the evangelical leanings which he takes care to emphasize throughout his rather dry narrative) render him impatient with sentimental generalizations or picturesque impressionism. Notably, he criticizes both William Hodges (Valentia I. 85) and the Daniells (Valentia I. 356) for topographical inaccuracy and embellishment, notwithstanding the representational licence which Gilpin and other theorists had permitted the picturesque artist. Like other 'integrated' travel accounts of the period, Valentia's book combined the apparently antithetical modalities of the survey and the picturesque, a combination which (together with his supposedly 'disinterested' motives for undertaking the Indian tour) earned him Southey's plaudits. On the other hand, the eighteenth-century division of labour between 'precision' and 'curiosity' is marked in his account of employing his assistants Salt, Capt. Young, and 'Messrs Frissel and Murray' to draw, measure, and copy inscriptions in Karle cave temples (Valentia II. 164). Valentia travelled as an enlightenment aristocratic patron rather than a romantic traveller in the Burckhardt or Humboldt mould, lacking, in the words of the *Monthly Review*, 'that comprehensive knowledge which teaches us to form general conclusions from the particular objects that are offered to our observation'. One should not expect such authority from 'fashionable life', the reviewer continued; it is rather 'the province . . . of the philosopher, who unites the habit of contemplation to a familiarity with active life'.[86]

Valentia's reticence may equally well be seen as the result of a skeleton concealed in his cupboard. Unusually for a travel account of this period, *Voyages and Travels* lacks any 'methodological' Preface, and its curt, patrician tone delegates emotional or aesthetic affect to Salt's picturesque plates. This eccentricity was noted by reviewers who expected a more developed idiom of subjectivity, for, as the *Monthly Review* commented, 'the paucity of reflections is the great deficiency of the book'.[87] Fortunately for Valentia, contemporary reviewers were apparently ignorant of the underlying motive for his Indian 'Grand Tour'; the fact that, despite his evangelical airs, he was a reformed rake on the run from a damaging personal scandal. In 1796 he had been awarded

[85] Suleri, p. 76.   [86] MR, LXII (June, 1810), 239.   [87] Ibid., p. 120.

considerable financial damages from his former friend, John Gawler (who later changed his surname to Bellenden Ker), on the grounds of the latter's 'criminal conversation' with Valentia's wife, Anne, despite the suggestion that he had himself encouraged the liaison for the sake of providing him with an heir. The judge of the case, Lord Kenyon, had reproved Valentia for having used language disgracing one 'whose conduct ought to be marked out in such a way as not to corrupt the lower orders'.[88] In 1811 the young Lord Byron 'saw nothing very 'cat[t]tivo' in Valentia, a fellow associate of 'Alfred's Club' in London, and confessed with uncharacteristic embarrassment that 'as every body speaks to him, one can't very well avoid it'.[89] Despite Byron's willingness to accept Valentia, this throwaway remark nevertheless reveals the extent to which Valentia had been ostracized in Regency high society, a secret carefully safeguarded in the *Travels* and apparently honoured by those reviewers who were privy to it. If Valentia's terse, objective style of travel writing presents a strong contrast to James Bruce's sentimental promiscuity, the reason lies not only in his participation in a colonial 'disciplining' of the Indian landscape; British patrician masculinity is also being reformed in line with the requirements of imperial rule.

Although botany is Valentia's favoured discourse for 'disciplining' the Indian landscape (an interest he may have picked up from Gawler, future editor of the *Botanical Register*), he also collected antiquarian specimens and visited, surveyed, and described sites of historical or archaeological interest such as the 'Seven Pagodas' at Mahabalipuram and the ancient cave temples of Karle, Kanheri, and Elephanta.[90] When Valentia discusses the celebrated *Maheshamurti* (which he mistakenly called the 'triune deity') in Elephanta Cave, Bombay, he referred to Carsten Niebuhr's 'accurate description' (Valentia II.

[88]   *Trial for Adultery. The Whole Proceedings in the Trial of J. B. Gawler, Esq., for Criminal Conversation with Lady Valentia, in the Court of the King's Bench, before Lord Kenyon* (London, 1799), p. 131. The adultery scandal may explain the surpassing omission of Valentia from the *Dictionary of National Biography*. George Annesley, Viscount Valentia (1770–1843) succeeded to the title of the Earl of Mountnorris in 1816 upon his father's death. Educated at Rugby and Oxford, he was MP for Yarmouth, 1808–10. His adulterous wife, Anne, was the eighth daughter of William Courtenay, 2nd Viscount Courtenay of Powderham, and the sister of William Courteney with whom William Beckford had been accused of having a homosexual affair. Lady Valentia had two illegitimate sons by Gawler (a notable regency rake and—shades of Banks—a distinguished botanist), one of whom became a cadet in the Bengal Army in 1823. *The Complete Peerage* (London: St Catherine's Press, 1959), XII. ii. p. 210. Byron had a notorious flirtation with Valentia's sister, Lady Francis Wedderburn Webster, in 1813.

[89]   17 November 1811, to John Cam Hobhouse, *Byron's Letters and Journals, Volume Two: 1810–1812*, ed. by Leslie Marchand (London: John Murray, 1973), p. 131. According to Hobhouse's *Journals*, it was widely rumoured in Malta that Valentia had contracted 'shittenpox' while in Egypt on his return journey, a sexually transmitted disease picked up from prostitutes. Thanks to Peter Cochran for this information.

[90]   Valentia's account of Karle was published separately in the *Transactions of the Bombay Philosophical Society* (V. ii. 163). Antiquarian interest in the monuments of India was relatively recent, prompted by the researches of Alexander Dalrymple, William Hunter, and Richard Gough in the 1780s. See Archer and Lightbown, *India Observed*, pp. 22–4.

199) and proceeded instead to evoke the statue's iconography: 'Bramah's countenance admirably expresses the undisturbed composure of the creator of the
world; Vishnou's, on the left, has every feature of benevolence, while the lotus
which he holds in his hand seems to be expanding under the genial ray of his
eye' (Valentia II. 199). Behind his carefully researched Hindu iconography,
Valentia's remarks read more like an allegory of British colonial rule in an era
of 'agrarian patriotism'. Brahma's 'undisturbed composure' seems to evoke the
new self-assurance of Wellesley's imperial regime for which Valentia's book is
an enthusiastic apologia: Vishnu's countenance represents the benevolence of
Anglican evangelicalism; and the expanding lotus represents the agricultural
prosperity soon to be expected from the Company's reform of Indian land
tenure and husbandry. Like Sir William Jones's exercise in cultural appropriation in the *Hindu Hymns*, Valentia's iconography evokes Hindu deities as
muses for British rule in India.[91] It is instructive to compare this with the reactions of Lt.-Col. Fitzclarence (future Earl of Munster), to the Hindu antiquarian sublime on a visit to the caves of Ellora a decade later. Struck by the
rock-hewn Kailasha Temple, Fitzclarence wondered 'whether the object of
amazement, next to this in the history of India, was not that of the inhabitants
of an island in the outskirts of Europe . . . who, during little more than half a
century, had by a gradual extension of military operations . . . established over
the country an influence or dominion, which may now be said to be universal'.
Fitzclarence then dined on 'some slices of a round of beef' inside the temple,
which 'relished uncommonly well, and suffered nothing from the idea of feast-
ing on the flesh of the most sacred and venerated animal of the Hindoos, in their
most singular temple'.[92]

Reginald Heber's *Narrative of a Journey Through the Upper Provinces of India*

Whereas historians have been attentive to the influence of 'advanced' Anglican
or dissenting evangelicals on the British Empire in the early nineteenth century,
as C. A. Bayly has indicated, less has been said about the influence of 'establishment evangelicals' such as Bishop Reginald Heber.[93] Valentia had been
horrified to discover that Calcutta only contained one Anglican church and no
episcopal see, and warmly supported the ideas of Dr Claudius Buchanan, East
India Company chaplain, who proposed the establishment of an Anglican
episcopacy in India to cement links between Anglo-Indians and their native

[91] For Jones, see Teltscher, p. 208.
[92] *Journal of a Route across India* . . . (London, 1819), pp. 194, 208.
[93] *Imperial Meridian*, p. 143.

land. Both men, however, stopped short of proposing the full evangelization of the Company's Hindu and Muslim subjects. Apart from the fact that Reginald Heber's very presence in India as second bishop of Calcutta (appointed 1823) realized Valentia's earlier wish for an Anglican see in India,[94] there are striking differences of tone, style, and ideology between the narratives of Valentia the Wellesleyan imperialist and Heber the liberal 'broad church' Anglican. In many ways Reginald Heber embodies the spirit of the Lake School poets, Coleridge, Wordsworth, and Southey at large in British India. As J. G. Lockhart wrote, Heber was no ordinary bishop, but possessed 'the eye of a painter and the pen of a poet . . . [his] mind stored with the literature of Europe, both ancient and modern'. He prophesied that Heber's *Narrative of a Journey Through the Upper Provinces of India* (published posthumously by Heber's widow, Amelia), 'one of the most delightful books in the language', would 'command popularity, as extensive and as lasting as any book of travels that has been printed in our time'.[95] Lockhart was right: two further editions of Heber's book were published in 1828, a fourth in 1829, and a fifth in 1844. Despite his fifteen years as a country vicar at Hodnet in Shropshire, Heber was experienced in the practices and discourses of contemporary travel: he had toured Scandinavia, Russia, and the Habsburg Empire in 1805–6, and (alongside John Barrow) was a frequent reviewer of new travel books in the *Quarterly Review*, including works by Abu Taleb Khan, Robert Ker Porter, and E. D. Clarke.[96]

Like Valentia, Heber was critical of earlier Company misrule,[97] strongly opposed to the creolization of Anglo-Indians, and sceptical about the chances of a successful mass conversion of Indian non-Christians, despite his respect for Baptist missionaries such as Carey and Marshman (H. I. 57). Also like Valentia, Heber toured his enormous Indian diocese in an official role (under the patronage of the Governor-General Lord Amherst), his ecclesiastical duties within the Anglo-Indian community combined with 'state' visits to Indian princes. In some respects his itinerary followed that of Valentia twenty-odd years earlier, although the wider loops east, north, and westwards reflect the

---

[94]   Coleridge's old Christ's Hospital schoolmate Dr Thomas Middleton had been by all accounts, a remarkably inefficacious first Bishop of Calcutta.

[95]   QR, 37 (Jan. 1828), 102, 104. It is interesting to compare this with Southey's 1821 description of Alexander von Humboldt: 'He is among travellers what Wordsworth is among poets. The extent of his knowledge and the perfect command which he has of it are truly surprising; and with this he unites a painter's eye and a poet's feeling' (*New Letters*, ed. by K. Curry, 2 vols. (New York and London, 1965), ii. 231). See Derrick Hughes, *Bishop Sahib: A Life of Reginald Heber* (Worthing: Churchman, 1986).

[96]   See QR, 4 (Aug. 1810) (Abu Talib); 2 (Nov. 1809) (Ker Porter); and 9 (March 1813) (Clarke). For attributions, see the *Quarterly Review Project*, http://www.dreamwater.com/edu/earlyqr/index.htm. Thanks to Isamu Takahashi for this information.

[97]   The Late Right Revd. Reginald Heber, DD, Lord Bishop of Calcutta, *Narrative of a Journey through the Upper Provinces of India, from Calcutta to Bombay, 1824–1825 (with Notes upon Ceylon), An Account of a Journey to Madras, and the Southern Provinces, 1826, and Letters written in India*, ed. by Amelia Heber, 2 vols. (London: John Murray, 1828), i. 426–7. Henceforth H. in text.

Company's enormous territorial gains in the interim years. In addition to the customary account of his 'voyage out' and domestic life in Calcutta with his wife, Amelia, and his two daughters, Heber's narrative describes two long pastoral tours, the first of which took him, in 1824–5, to Dacca in eastern Bengal, through the Upper Provinces, to the fringes of the Himalayas at Almor, back to Delhi and Agra, then southwards via Rajasthan and Gujarat to Bombay, where he was joined by his wife. After a brief visit to Ceylon (Sri Lanka), the second tour traces his journey to Madras and Southern India in 1826. Heber never made it back to Calcutta: he died suddenly while bathing in Trichinopoly (Tiruchchirappali) on 3 April 1826 at the age of 43, worn out by the gruelling round of his episcopal duties in the tropical heat of southern India.

Heber's *Narrative* represents the softer side of British power in India at a historical moment when the 'proconsular' despotism of Cornwallis, Wellesley, and Hastings was giving way to the liberal era of William Bentinck. Heber is perhaps now best known for his strident missionary hymn 'From Greenland's icy mountains, | From India's coral strand', with its ringing denunciation of 'The savage in his blindness | Bow[ing] down to wood and stone'. His contemporary biographer is surely correct to doubt whether he 'would have written such a hymn . . . after his arrival in India'.[98] In striking contrast to the narratives of 'advanced' evangelicals like Henry Martyn and Mary Sherwood, who saw Satan's work all around them in heathen India,[99] Heber shows a remarkable capacity for tolerating Hindu and Muslim religion. In accord with the programme of 'establishment evangelicalism' Heber's main concern was with the proselytization of the Anglo-Indian community and its Asian dependants, as well as with bringing the Indian Christian churches into line with Anglican orthodoxy. Although possessed by a mission to bring about the abolition of sati (H. I. 56) and critical of Company sponsorship of Hindu educational establishments such as the Vidyalaya or Hindu College at Benares (H. I. 295), he admitted that he had met hardly any converts from the Hindu or Muslim communities (apart from soldiers' wives) and was depressed by the strength of Hindu faith (H. I. 85).

Heber's accounts of Hindu temples and religious rituals are remarkably free from the sort of negative value-judgements which permeate many contemporary Indian travelogues. Visiting a small Shaiva temple at Chittoor, for example, he described a 'frightful figure of the blood-drinking goddess, with her lion, her many hands full of weapons, and her chaplet of skulls . . . the pavement was stained with the blood of sacrifices from one end to the other' (H. II. 60). Nevertheless, he gave alms to the blind Brahmin presiding over the temple, and

---

[98] Hughes, p. 73. Apparently Heber quickly changed 'savage' to 'heathen' in the quoted couplet (ibid.).

[99] See Dyson, p. 172.

admired the 'solemn effect produced by their style of architecture . . . a Gothic or Grecian building of the same size would merely have been beautiful, but these, small as they are, are aweful' on account of their thick pillars, cornices, and domes, and the repetition of simple motifs (H. II. 61). Heber clearly felt that only an objective understanding of the phenomena of Hindu religion would enable Christianity ever to make any inroads in India; moreover, Anglican ritual and church architecture could even learn from the encounter with Hindu sublimity.

Although well-versed in orientalist scholarship, Heber was sceptical of 'temporalizing' claims respecting the antiquity of cave temples at Elephanta, Salsette, and Kanheri, which he visited in 1825, arguing that 'we multiply, as it were, the geographical and moral distance into the chronological' (H. II. 390). Informed by the recent scholarship of William Erskine, he was able to correct Valentia's mistaken identification of the *Maheshamurti* with the 'triune god' of the Christian trinity (H. II. 181).[100] In his miscellaneous correspondence published at the end of the second volume (often more overtly critical of India than the familial letters which make up the text), Heber remarked conventionally enough 'how little can these trifling relics [Ellora and Elephanta] bear comparison with the works of Greece and Egypt' (H. II. 392). None the less, his romantic imagination was impressed by the functional sublimity of the cave temples, writing of the Buddhist Temple of Kanheri that 'even in its present state [it] would make a very stately and convenient place of Christian worship' (H. II. 189).

Like many of his contemporaries, Heber has a lot to say about race, but unlike the majority view believed that 'the deep bronze tint [of Indians] is more naturally agreeable to the human eye than the fair skins of Europe' or the dark skin of negroes (H. I. 3). Following the theories of the abolitionist Thomas Clarkson, he argued that both white and black skins represented a modification of the primal 'dark olive', the 'primitive complexion' of Noah and his sons, the originals of all the modern races.[101] Heber believed that skin colour was largely a result of climate and custom, rather than an essential quality of human ethnic groups, an argument which had been commonly deployed among his fellow-

---

[100]   Mitter, *Much-Maligned Monsters*, p. 157.

[101]   See Peter Kitson, 'Races, Places, Peoples, 1785–1800', in *Romanticism and Colonialism*, ed. by Tim Fulford and Peter Kitson (Cambridge University Press, 1998), pp. 21–5 on Clarkson's ideas and their influence on Coleridge and Southey. Heber's attempt at a 'dispassionate' theory of skin colour is, however, betrayed by his comment that hardship and exposure to the sun 'may have *deteriorated* the Hindoo into a Negro, [whilst] opposite causes may have changed him into the *progressively* lighter tints of the Chinese, the Persian, the Turk, the Russian, and the Englishman' (i. 55, italics mine). This may have been influenced by Blumenbach's notion of racial 'degeneration', although unlike Heber the latter believed white to be the 'primitive colour of mankind' (Kitson, p. 19).

abolitionists in Europe and the United States (H. I. 54).[102] Commenting at one point, for example, upon the difference of skin colour manifest in a crowd of Indians 'by whom we were surrounded', he felt that it was merely 'an accidental difference, like that of the light and dark complexions in Europe' (H. I. 8). Refusing alteritist stereotypes, Heber elsewhere described the 'inhabitants of the Deccan, and of the Presidencies of Madras and Bombay' as being 'as different from those which I have seen . . . as the French and Portuguese from the Greeks, Germans or Poles' (H. II. 380). His resistance to the simplistic temporalization of India also led him to question the common aestheticization and typification of its inhabitants.[103] Although he felt that the British in India were now innocent of 'injustice, or wilful oppression', he criticized the fact that 'we shut out the natives from our society, and a bullying, insolent manner is continually assumed in speaking to them . . . the English, wherever they go, [are] a caste by themselves, disliking and disliked by all their neighbours' (H. I. 591). As these remarks show, Heber's is clearly the voice of hegemonic liberalism, for all his criticism of British cultural attitudes, incapable and unwilling to criticize the fundamental facts of imperialism, which in any case he believed justifiable in providential and ethical terms. Nevertheless, it is refreshing to encounter a voice which targets British arrogance rather than the usual list of orientalist defects attributed to its Indian subjects.

In contrast to the 'official' journal form of Valentia's *Travels*, Heber's narrative is presented as a series of edited letters to his wife, Amelia, and his older daughter, Emily, supplemented by (mainly footnoted) passages from his wife's own journal. The fact that Heber's discourse largely takes the form of domestic correspondence gives an intimacy to many of his observations which seemed to contemporaries to contrast strikingly with his 'heroic' death in the pursuance of his ecclesiastical mission. Robert Southey's 1830 'Ode on the Portrait of Bishop Heber', for example, opens with a apostrophe to his late friend's genial countenance ('His comprehensive eye, | His open brow serene'), before delivering a panegyric upon his role as a hero of Christian imperialism: 'A messenger of love he went, | A true Evangelist', to pay off England's 'debt to Heathenism'.[104] The metaphor of the 'portrait' seems to derive from the

---

[102] Cf. Nicholas Thomas, *Colonialism's Culture*, pp. 89–90.

[103] In political terms, Heber was critical of many aspects of Company rule, identifying with the 'wise and liberal' policies of Mountstuart Elphinstone, Governor of the Bombay Presidency, with whom he stayed in 1825 near the end of his first tour (H. II. 219), supporting light taxation, *ryotwari* land tenure, the practice of indigenous legal systems, and the employment of Indians in an official capacity. He regretted the Company's current policies towards the Nawab of Awadh and the Mughal emperor, which, he felt, encouraged Indo-Muslim hatred of the British (which, like Valentia, he openly acknowledged) (H. I. 298).

[104] Southey's 'Ode to Bishop Heber', *Southey's Poetical Works, Complete in One Volume* (London: Longman, 1876), pp. 207–8.

personal form in which contemporary readers were familiarized with Heber's Indian mission, also evident in Lockhart's comment that 'in his description of India, one of the most *loveable* of men has unconsciously given us also a full-length portrait of himself'.[105] This approved 'self-portrait' of the romantic travelogue—in stark contrast to the objectivity of the 'survey modality'—embodies a vision of public virtue erected firmly on the foundation of private faith and the domestic affections.

Although his accounts of Calcutta and Bombay represent Heber in the bosom of his family, the major part of his long (1,100-around) page narrative is concerned with his pastoral tours, which he described as a 'dreary banishment' from his wife and daughters (H. I. 83). Heber constantly registers his double homesickness—first from England, secondly from his family back in Calcutta. Absence from family exacerbated his homesickness for England, for 'in my wife and children I still carried with me an atmosphere of home' (H. I. 104). After the death of his curate, Martin Stowe, on the river journey to Dacca in 1824, he indulged in the melancholy and romantic thought that he 'was indeed a lonely wanderer!' (H. I. 172). Rebuking himself, he asserts his faith in Providence and 'the power of constant correspondence with my beloved wife'. On this trip Heber composed a nostalgic love lyric to Amelia as well as his best-known poem 'An Evening Walk in Bengal', both of which were interpolated into his narrative (H. I. 185). Anglican faith, familial affections, and national identity are closely intertwined, furthering Heber's ideological goal of fostering associative ties between Britons in India and the imperial homeland. Exacerbating the itch of nostalgia occludes the possibilities of achieving sentimental satisfaction in the here and now.

Heber's narrative is frequently picturesque in the 'associative' manner discussed above: a ruined pagoda at Sibnibashi 'reminds me of some parts of the Roman wall at Silchester' (H. I. 92); the battlements and round towers of Fatehpur-Sikri evoke the 'remaining part of the city walls at Oxford' (H. I. 595); and the Himalayan landscape constantly brings him memories of Wales (H. I. 451, 475, 476). (In his 1809 review of Abu Talib's *Travels*, he had commented on the Indian traveller's reverse associationism: 'he noticed, on his road from Holyhead, Conway [Castle], with its ancient walls resembling Allahabad; and Chester, with the *verandahs* which line the principle streets'[106]). But Heber's writing also partakes of a particular form of referentiality which might be called the 'literary picturesque', replacing historical and painterly by literary associations which provide the scene with an incremental interest.[107] This illustrates

---

[105]   QR, 37 (Jan. 1828), 104.   [106]   QR, 4 (Aug. 1810), 87.

[107]   I borrow the term from Susan Manning, who employs it to describe the American Washington Irving's frequent allusions to the British literary canon in his English travelogue *The Sketchbook of Geoffrey Crayon (1820–1)*, ed. by Susan Manning (Oxford University Press, 1996), pp. xvii–xxiii. Heber's equivalent was the 'new' canon of English romantic orientalism.

the gradual permeation of the 'integrated' travelogue by a more 'aesthetic' literary style in the decade of the 1820s, to be further discussed in the next chapter. Never before had a British travelogue paraded so many allusions to contemporary fiction and poetry; in which sense K. K. Dyson accurately comments that 'with Bishop Heber's report on India we move into a period when Romanticism becomes a prominent feature of the Indian journal'.[108] As a prolific member of the *Quarterly Review* coterie, Heber had reviewed a wide range of contemporary poetry and fiction (as well as travel writing), evident in the literary allusions scattered through the *Journal*. On a loose count I have noted eleven major allusions to, and citations of, the poetry of Heber's acquaintance Robert Southey, six to the novels of Sir Walter Scott (a friend of his half-brother, Richard Heber, the celebrated bibliophile), two to Coleridge, as well as references to other contemporary writers such as Thomas Moore and Anne Radcliffe.[109]

The Daniells had argued that 'the pencil is narrative to the eye'[110] (p. ii), but in the literary travelogue it was unclear how picturesque description might be translated from visual synchronicity into sustained narrative. Picturesque description worked best as vignette, but (as readers of the Gothic novelist Ann Radcliffe rapidly discovered) repetition could easily tire the reader.[111] Heber discovered in the oriental 'quest romances' of his romantic contemporaries the means of adding progressive moral interest to picturesque stasis. Southey's oriental romances, *Thalaba the Destroyer* (1801) and *The Curse of Kehama* (1810), seem to have provided Heber with literary models for shaping his apostolic mission in India into a moral unity. (In his review of Southey's *History of Brazil*, Heber suggested that 'his name [as a poet] has not yet arrived at the reputation which it is hereafter destined to attain'.[112]) One of the major differences between Valentia's and Heber's narratives is the Bishop's personal calling, compared to Valentia's dry, impersonal sense of participation in the plot of empire. Heber's first resolution upon arriving in India was 'that I might in some degree, however small, be enabled to conduce to the spiritual advantage of creatures so goodly, so gentle, and now so misled and blinded' (H. I. 13), a commitment which he

---

[108] Dyson, p. 22.

[109] For attribution of Heber's reviews, see note 96 above. Some of the many allusions to Southey are at i. 6, 66, 76, 88, 94, 130, 287, 630; ii. 280, 286, 446 (*Kehama, Thalaba, Madoc, Oliver Newman*). Allusions to Scott's novels are i. p. xvi, 97, 189, 263, 376; ii. 85 (*Quentin Durward, Bride of Lammermoor, Heart of Midlothian, Waverley, Fortunes of Nigel, Rob Roy*) and to Coleridge, i. 481; ii. 286 (*Ancient Mariner, Kubla Khan*). Byron is noticeably absent, not surprisingly given that Heber had contributed to the *Quarterly*'s campaign against the 'Satanic School' of poetry.

[110] *A Picturesque Tour*, p. ii.

[111] As the Indian picturesque's most scathing critic, Victor Jacquemont, pointed out, a single page of Tom Moore's orientalist picturesque in *Lalla Rookh* might please, 'but thirty (and his tales are longer) makes one sick' (*Letters*, ii. 72).

[112] QR, 4 (Nov. 1810), 454.

sustained throughout his Indian mission. Heber lacked the 'geographical' preparation to appropriate the country in objective terms; instead he wielded a discourse of the 'literary picturesque' which reformed colonial subjectivity and its relationship with the colonized.

Although Heber read some of the 'Marcumdeya Purana' (which he thought resembled the work of Moses) with his pandit, he dismissed it as a 'strange rhapsody' without 'moral lesson' or 'practical wisdom' (H. I. 74).[113] In general, Sanskrit literature made little impact on his sensibility, and despite the 'very great antiquity' of Hindu civilization, he agreed with James Mill that the Hindus 'had made no great progress in the arts, and took all their notions of magnificence from . . . their Mahommedan conquerors' (H. II. 392). Unlike Greece or Italy, the Indian landscape itself had few literary connotations for picturesque travellers, at least until the advent of eighteenth-century orientalism; for which reason it was not Sanskrit literature but rather the 'picturesque' transformation of the Indian tradition in Southey's Hindu *Curse of Kehama* which fed Heber's romantic imagining of South Asia.[114] In a revealing entry in his *Commonplace Book*, written while Southey was working on *Kehama*, the poet had written 'the Hindoo is a vile mythology . . . There is no mapping out the country, no reducing to shape the chaotic mass. It is fitter for the dotage dreams of Sir William Jones, than the visions of a poet.'[115] This reveals the more-than-metaphorical links between Southey's poetic project and the cartographic surveys of Rennell, Buchanan, Mackenzie, and Lambton. Despite Southey's difficulties in translating Sanskrit translations and Indian travel accounts into poetry which appealed to European taste, appropriately enough *Kehama* was now transcribed back into the idiom of travel writing by Southey's acquaintance Heber, as a picturesque template for figuring subcontinental realities.[116]

When Heber cites a descriptive passage from *Kehama* (or any of Southey's other poems) in his text, the moral context of his allusion in the poem's narrative has the effect of tacitly framing his present 'picturesque' experience. For example, in an otherwise remarkably 'value-free' description of a Hindu

---

[113] Heber read the Saptasátí or Devīmāhātma, a thirteen-chapter interruption of the *Markandeya* which has been called 'the principle text of the worshippers of Dūrga in N. India'. Thanks to Dr Eivind Kahrs for this information.

[114] In *Kehama*'s 1810 Preface Southey complained that 'no figures can be imagined more anti-picturesque and less poetical, then the mythological personages of the Bramins' (*Poetical Works*, p. 548). Nevertheless the poem represented an attempt to square the circle by translating Hindu culture into pictureque quest romance. Many of the poem's critics acknowledged its failure in this respect. See my 'Wandering through Eblis: Absorption and Containment in Romantic Exoticism', in Fulford and Kitson (eds.), *Romanticism and Colonialism* (Cambridge University Press, 1999), pp. 183–8.

[115] *Southey's Commonplace Book*, 4th series, ed. by J. Warter (London, 1851), p. 11.

[116] I have commented elsewhere on the ideological valences of *Kehama*'s plot which allegorizes the nascent civic virtue and domestic affections of a putative Indian 'yeoman' class, patronized by British rule and Christian values, bringing down the whole tottering edifice of oriental despotism and Brahminical superstition. See *British Romantic Writers and the East*, pp. 95–7.

festival in Calcutta, the 'Churruck Poojah', which included hook-swinging and tongue- and arm-piercing by devotees, the text quotes from *Kehama*, Book 14: 'The double peal of the drum was there, | And the startling sound of the trumpet's blare' (H. I. 76). Out of context this merely seems to add to what Amelia's note calls the picturesque *coup d'oeil*; considered in context, however, it refers to a moment in the narrative when Southey's heroine, Kailyal, has been kidnapped by a band of wandering Yogis and brought to Jaggarnaut, where she is carried on the 'ponderous car' to be sacrificed to the huge seven-headed idol. The lines immediately following those quoted in the *Narrative* continue: 'To astound the living, and waken the dead. | The ear-strings throb as if they were rent, | And the eyelids drop as stunned and spent'.[117] The literary allusion adds the moral nuance of narrative to the picturesque image.

Near the end of his second, fatal, tour of southern India, Heber visited the coastal 'Seven Pagodas' at Mahabalipuram (Māmallapuram), which had provided Southey with the setting for an important episode in Book 15 of *Kehama*. The heroine Kailyal waits for seven days and nights in the ruined city while her father, Ladurlad, descends to the submarine Baly to fight the guardian sea monster and free her lover, the imprisoned Glendoveer. The scene resonates in Heber's imagination as he describes the site:

the noise of the surf, the dark shadow of the remaining building, the narrow slip of dark smooth sand, the sky just reddening into dawn and lending its tints to the sea, together with the remarkable desolation of the surrounding scenery, were well calculated to make one remember with interest the description in Kehama, and to fancy that one saw the beautiful form of Kailyal in her white mantle pacing sadly along the shore, and watching until her father and lover should emerge from the breakers. (H. II. 280)

Heber's 'literary picturesque' evocation of Mahabalipuram again breaks out of the static visual frame into narrative temporality as he identifies with the domestic afflictions sustaining Kailyal's heroic endurance. In this respect, Jeffrey's comments on Heber's faithful rendering of 'first impressions'[118] seem less accurate than Lockhart's praise for Heber possessing 'the eye of a painter and the pen of a poet'.[119] Picturesque associationism and the 'esemplastic' romantic imagination here replace the empirical obsession of eighteenth-century travel writing. Kailyal's sorely tried patience as she awaits the outcome of her father's battle against evil, tyranny, and superstition provide a potent metaphor for Heber's own uncertain mission in India, dedicated to proselytization but despairing of success.[120]

---

[117] *Southey's Poetical Works*, p. 598.   [118] ER, 48 (1828), 315.   [119] QR, 37 (1828), 102.

[120] The allusive field of Heber's 'literary picturesque' is far from being limited to Southey's poetry. Scott's novels also provided him with an important paradigm for his mission in India. Heber, alone and homesick after Stowe's death in the flat country *en route* to Bhaugalpoor, cited Jeanie Deans's

The Radical Anti-Picturesque: James Mill and Victor Jacquemont

In the January 1810 issue of the *Edinburgh Review*, James Mill took time off from his *History of British India* to review an Italian missionary narrative about India, providing him with a stalking-horse for questioning the value of autoptic travel narrative:[121] 'If the country which is the object of curiosity has, by any cause . . . been for a long time regarded as containing wonderful things, and more particularly if . . . the country be very distant, *ex longinquo reverentia*, the passion for the wonderful may then be expected to be seen at its height.'[122] In the sceptical 'anti-travel' tradition of Volney and Cuvier, Mill insisted (against the traveller's plea that only first-hand experience can provide reliable knowledge of a distant country), that 'the vivid impressions of the senses are a cause of darkness, as well as of light. They are the cause of partial, and of confused apprehensions.' By contrast, 'the man who can combine and compare, with the soundest judgement, all those varying testimonies, is the man who will have the most complete and valuable knowledge of the subject to which the testimonies refer'.[123] Disenchanting the aesthetics of distance (as we saw him, in Chapter 1, disenchanting the rhetoric of temporalization), at one blow Mill writes off the 'curious' travel narrative, as well as, by implication, the picturesque idiom favoured by much romantic-period travel writing. His comments strongly favour the form of the 'geographical narrative' inspired by Francis Buchanan, whose antipathy to Brahmanism would strongly influence Mill's own *History*.[124] Javed Majeed comments on Mill's development of this argument in

complaint in *The Heart of Midlothian*, as she travels alone and on foot to London to plead a pardon for her sister, Effie, about the flatness of the English landscape compared to her native Scotland (H. I. 189). Again Heber implicitly identifies with Jeanie Deans's unswervable moral rectitude, Christian piety, and exemplary familial affections in risking all to save her condemned sister; like Southey's Kailyal, she provides a useful moral paradigm for his own evangelical mission in India. For a more ambivalent allusion, in which he identified with the usurper Sir William Ashton in *The Bride of Lammermoor*, see H. I. 97. Heber noted approvingly that Scott's novels were supplied by the Company to libraries in remote stations such as Kairah, Gujarat, the only literary fare alongside Paley's *Natural Theology*, Pinkerton's *Geography*, and the Indian histories of Orme and Wilks (H. II. 155).

[121] For an account of Mill's intellectual milieu and 'Scottish Orientalism', see Javed Majeed, *Ungoverned Imaginings*, pp. 123–95; and Jane Rendall, 'Scottish Orientalism: From Robertson to James Mill', *Historical Journal*, 25, 1 (1982), 60.

[122] 'Voyage aux Indes Orientales, par P. de S. Barthelemy', ER, 15 (Jan. 1810), 368.

[123] Ibid., p. 367.

[124] Cf. William Hazlitt's attack on Bentham's and Mill's prejudice against autoptic travel as representative of the abstracting 'spirit of the age': 'I humbly conceive that the seeing half a dozen wandering Lascars in the streets of London gives one a better idea of the soul of India . . . than all the charts, records, and statistical reports that can be sent over . . . By a very few specimens you fix the great leading differences, which are nearly the same throughout' (*Works*, xii. p. 50). Yet, as John Whale points out in his commentary on this passage, Hazlitt's argument invokes 'an unwelcome taxonomy of natural history: a potentially dehumanising discourse of "specimens" and "kind" . . . [he] seems to endorse rather than to oppose a perversely myopic vision of India from "home"'. 'Indian Jugglers: Hazlitt, Romantic Orientalism and the Difference of View', in *Romanticism and Colonialism*, ed. by Tim Fulford and Peter Kitson (Cambridge University Press, 1998), pp. 218–19.

his *History of British India* that it is 'based on the Benthamite notion of the universal legislator, who from his superior position could take a more comprehensive view of cultures and their differences, and so achieve command of a set of laws which could be universally applicable'.[125]

The political effect of Mill's disenchantment of distance (in many ways the culmination of the Scottish enlightenment's critique of wonder studied in Chapter 1) was the establishment in 1833 of a commission to frame a body of codified laws for the whole of British India.[126] By a paradox Mill would also inspire one of the most widely read Indian travel narratives of the 1830s, Victor Jacquemont's *Letters from India*. Jacquemont was a young French naturalist who mounted a series of scientific expeditions into Kashmir and the Himalayan region in the years between 1828 and his death in western India in 1831. A pupil of the comparative anatomist Georges Cuvier (whose attacks on Humboldt's travel writing in many ways parallel Mill's, and will be discussed in Chapter 6), Jacquemont was financed on a shoestring by the Jardin des Plantes in Paris, at least until after the 1831 republican coup, when his stipend was raised and he took to proudly sporting a tricolour cockade. The son of a prominent ideologue philosopher who had been close to the circle of Condillac, Destutt de Tracy, and Cabanis, like his father Victor was a staunch republican, atheist, and utopian socialist. In June 1830 he wrote to his father recommending Mill's *History of British India* as 'beyond all comparison the best work on that country. Perhaps [he added as an afterthought] the two quarto volumes of Dr Heber, the late Bishop of Calcutta, might amuse you more, but they would give you very little information; *it is regular milk and water*.'[127] Despite this perfunctory dismissal, there are some fortuitous parallels between Jacquemont and the late Bishop of Calcutta. Both described India with the eyes of outsiders rather than Anglo-Indians; both died in the pursuit of their professional duties; and both were constructed as colonial martyrs of European civility in their respective homelands, a civility defined as evangelical Christianity in Heber's case, science in Jacquemont's. Both also planned extensive and carefully methodized travel narratives, but in the event, due to their premature deaths, their most influential published works on India took the form of edited

---

[125] Majeed, p. 136.

[126] Majeed explains that the act embodied the principle of centralized authority and uniformity expressed by James Mill in his evidence before the Parliamentary Committee in 1832, although it did not follow the recommendations exactly (Majeed, p. 192). As Eric Stokes points out, despite the currency of Mill's *History* and the influence of Bentham's ideas at the East India Company's college at Haileybury, the 'specific influence of Utilitarianism . . . was surprisingly distinct and isolated from the broad body of liberal opinion' (*The English Utilitarians and India* (Oxford: Clarendon Press, 1959), p. 52).

[127] Victor Jacquemont, *Letters from India; Describing a Journey in the British Dominions of India, Tibet, Lahore, and Cashmere, during the years 1828, 9, 30, 31. Undertaken by Order of the French Government*. 2 vols. (trans. anon.) (London, 1834), i. 234. Hereafter Letters in text.

correspondence written to family and friends. But there the resemblances end.

Despite his scepticism about the genre, Jacquemont aspired (like his mentor and correspondent Humboldt in his *Personal Narrative*) to write a travelogue which would intermix with entertaining narrative 'general physics and the higher branches of natural history, with pictures of political history, and sketches of Indian manners'. At the same time he feared that the combination raised nearly insurmountable problems of style and address: 'could I do this without imparting to the [personal narrative] a disagreeable dryness and harshness, and without forgetting the simple severity of language in which matters of science ought to be expressed?' he asked. 'Could I master this concord, nothing more would remain for me than a series of special, and absolutely technical memoirs' (Letters II. 20). As a scientific traveller, Jacquemont was engaged in the Humboldtian project of comparing the vegetation and fauna of the Himalayas with the Alps, Rockies, and Cordilleras (Letters I. 331–2). Among his most controversial claims (at least in British geological circles) was the theory—against Humboldt—that the Himalayas were of comparatively recent formation (Letters I. 332).[128] Like the controversies surrounding the dating of Hindu cave temples at Elephanta or Ellora to which Heber contributed, this seemed to impugn cherished orientalist notions about the antiquity of everything Indian. In the event Jacquemont's 5,800-page manuscript journal and a description of his scientific collection were published posthumously in six volumes between 1835 and 1844 under the auspices of Guizot, entitled *Voyage dans l'Inde pendant les années 1828–1832*.[129] His more popular and widely read *Letters from India* (to which I limit my discussion here) were edited by Prospere Merimée and published posthumously in 1833 'by order of the French Government' and quickly translated into English.[130]

---

[128] In his 1824 *Wonders of Elora*, the eccentric Capt. John Seely (about as unHumboldtian a figure as one can imagine) had called for a 'Humboldtian'-style study of the Western Ghats: 'Such men as Humboldt and Bonpland, would, in these mountainous and unknown regions, find a rich harvest . . . a scientific exploration of these mountains is . . . a great desideratum. I do not mean the thing called in India surveying; the mere taking of bearings and distances, placing spots for mountains, and little blue serpentine lines for rivers, and the whole pretty looking map illustrated with neat penmanship! Something more is wanting; the botanical, geological, and mineralogical data, with other scientific matter, are required' (pp. 65–6). For the failure of Humboldt's plan to mount an expedition in India, see Chapter 6 below.

[129] The first three volumes contain Jacquemont's travel journal, accompanied by a thorough analytical index of his itinerary; the fourth is a description of his zoological and botanical specimens destined for the Muséum d'historie naturelle, and the final two are atlases containing (respectively) topographical and picturesque views of India and the Himalayas taken by Jacquemont and ethnographical drawings of Indian 'types', and his natural history specimens (many represented in full colour). In general Jacquemont's journal represents India in less negative terms than his letters, written to amuse his friends at home at the expense of 'the orient' and 'orientals'.

[130] There is also a more recent edition, *Jacquemont's Letters from India*, trans. and intro. by Catherine Phillips (London: Macmillan, 1936). Although undoubtedly a better translation than the 1834 English text, it is an abridgement, and I have therefore opted for the first, unexpurgated, trans-

Although containing little in the way of scientific information, Jacquemont's *Letters* were promoted by their anonymous British translator/editor as a propaganda coup for the liberal administration of Lord William Bentinck. On account of his French nationality, Jacquemont had been able to penetrate areas of the subcontinent (such as the court of Ranjit Singh, the powerful ruler of the Punjab) from which Englishmen were barred. Jacquemont's first-hand knowledge of Kashmir and the Himalayan region was also important from a strategic point of view given growing fears of Russian designs on the region, the beginning of the 'great game' immortalized in Kipling's *Kim*. Although Jacquemont mapped Kashmir for Ranjit Singh, the latter rightly suspected him of spying for the British, a charge which the Frenchman openly admitted in his correspondence: 'A secret agent! It is perfectly well understood by all my English friends that I shall gather other information from my travels than what may relate to natural history, when I have emptied my collection of stones, and analysed my trusses of plants' (Letters II. 235). Jacquemont's intimate liaison with William Fraser, British resident and spymaster at Delhi, seems in this case to support his characteristically self-advertising claim.

Despite official reluctance to allow Jacquemont entry into British India on account of traditional Anglo-French jealousy, his request was eventually approved by the Company and the London Royal Asiatic Society in 1828. Privy Councillor Sir Alexander Johnston interceded on Jacquemont's behalf with Lord William Bentinck, liberal governor-general from 1828 to 1836.[131] Despite his criticism of the philistinism of British society in Calcutta ('people do not come here to live, and enjoy life; they come . . . in order to gain something to enjoy life elsewhere') (Letters I. 84), Jacquemont was full of praise for his patron the new governor-general, with whom he stayed upon arrival in India; sitting 'on the throne of the Great Moghul, [he] thinks and acts like a Pennsylvanian Quaker' (Letters I. 86–7). In India, national differences between French and British now seemed to dissolve into a common, and superior, European identity. In the tradition of Hodges and Valentia, Jacquemont compared the 'oriental tyranny' of Ranjit Singh's Punjab to the Company's Indian dominions, hyperbolically proclaiming that 'European civilization *deserves* to invade the universe' (Letters II. 52).

His extreme personal vanity aside, the high-minded and extremely short-sighted young French naturalist was horrified by the dissipation and heavy

---

lation, from which Croker quoted in the *Quarterly Review*. The only extended account of Jacquemont's travels in English is David Stacton's *A Ride on a Tiger: The Curious Travels of Victor Jacquemont* (London: Museum Press, 1954).

[131] The political leanings of Jacquemont's British editor are evident from his remark that the Frenchman obtained his credentials from 'the Board of Merchant Kings, in Leadenhall St, who there govern a vast empire 10,000 miles off, and a hundred million subjects whom they have never seen' (I. xiii). In the Cambridge University Library copy, an outraged Tory reader has pencilled in the margin here 'far better than a set of ungodly Radicals could do'!!

drinking which he encountered among Anglo-Indians. Ironically, he believed that abstinence from alcohol and the daily practice of rectal irrigation would ensure his own survival, for, as well as the heavy drinking, 'it is for want of *lave-mens*, that the English for the most part die' (Letters I. 122). As Croker observed with a certain justice in his acerbic 1835 review of Jacquemont's *Letters*: 'all the numerous friends to whom he had predicted early death—the Bentincks, Wades, Kennedies, Halls, etc—were—every man of them—alive to lament his loss, and what they may probably consider a not much lighter misfortune—the publication of his letters'.[132] Jacquemont seems to have regarded his silver rectal syringe as of more value than any of his scientific instruments during his various expeditions to north-western India, a perfect symbol of his 'anal' disdain for Indian culture. When the silver syringe was stolen from his tent in Patiala, messengers and hircarrahs were dispatched to retrieve it, whilst Jacquemont boasted that 'the news is in the Akbars [manuscript gazettes]' of the court of Delhi . . . 'one would say that it was a barometer or pneumatic machine' (Letters I. 254–5).[133] The case of the rectal syringe indicates that for Jacquemont the *homus clausus* (shades of Humboldt) the traveller's bodily regime was part of his scientific inquiry into the natural and human environment of the tropics. Overridingly concerned with purging his own system of faecal residues, he also fulfilled the time-honoured role of European travellers in Asia by distributing aphrodisiac 'cantharades' pills made of crushed dried beetles to Sikhs, Kashmiris, and others, 'stimulants of that description being the most necessary to the Orientals, whom debauchery very often reduces to premature debility' (Letters I. 357).

Jacquemont's account of India in his *Letters* embodies many of the contradictions of the 'Age of Reform' of the late 1820s and 1830s. On the one hand, the expansionist 'proconsular' despotism of the first decades of the century has been replaced by an economizing, modernizing regime influenced by many of the advanced utilitarian ideas of Bentham and Mill.[134] The rejection of 'orientalist' empathy with Hindu tradition seems to have led to a hardening of racial attitudes, evident in Jacquemont's sustained racialist disdain for the native peoples with whom he interacted. Like Volney in Egypt, Jacquemont distrusted information deriving from indigenous sources, to the point of avoiding contact

---

[132]   QR, 53 (1835), 31.

[133]   Jacquemont seemed mercifully ignorant of the fact that (according to Emma Roberts), the Akbars often ruthlessly satirized Europeans without scrupling to name names, and that moreover 'it [was] not very easy for a European to procure a sight of the animadversions passed upon the conduct of himself or his friends' (*Scenes and Characteristics in Hindostan*, iii. 187–8). One can imagine what they made of Jacquemont's stolen syringe.

[134]   Jobs at the lower end of the judiciary and revenue service were opened to lowly paid Indian professionals, and military aggression against neighbouring states was reduced, although one should not overlook the fact, in Bayly's words, that 'the conditions for the annexation of Sindh and the Punjab were already in gestation' (*Imperial Meridian*, p. 239).

with Indians whenever possible: 'I gain a great deal of information in my sojourning in *Europeanised* places' he wrote to Victor de Tracy in 1830, 'if I meet with a good Persian scholar . . . I seek to rectify, from his knowledge, the little I have drawn from suspicious native sources' (Letters I. 181). He had little time for oriental languages, writing off Sanskrit as 'triple nonsense for the makers and consumers' (Letters I. 235) and mocking the German romantic enthusiasm for Indian philology.

During his stay in Calcutta Jacquemont complained of his Indian servants that 'a man is degraded, and brutalised, by living amongst such debased beings. I can now understand and excuse Frederick's harshness [his brother, a plantation owner in the French Caribbean colony of St Domingue]—I was going to say violence, and his great readiness in planting a kick on the hinder part of one of God's images' (Letters I. 133). Jacquemont's Saint-Simonian faith in revolutionary progress seems to have been inapplicable to more practical humanitarianism (Letters I. 304) and even his republican principles seemed to be forgotten in colonial space (he approved Simón Bolívar's plan to crown himself king of the newly independent Colombia on the grounds that 'liberty is a superfluity for nations in want of food and laws') (Letters I. 31).

Jacquemont's megalomania is best illustrated by the account of his exploits during his expedition to the little-known eastern Himalayas and the borders of Chinese Tartary in the spring of 1830. Dressed in a white bearskin with long mustachios (no Asiatic disguises for him), he boasted that he had thrashed his Gurkha escort and thirty-six bearers when they refused to climb higher into the snowfields, and one man in particular for failing to address him as 'your highness' (Letters I. 213). Whilst critical of the English explorer William Moorcroft who had died (or been killed) on his return from Bokhara in 1825 for allowing curiosity to lead him too far, so that he 'soon perished the victim of his own impudence' (Letters I. 307),[135] Jacquemont nevertheless boasted that he had assaulted a Chinese guard who had stopped him on the Himalayan border. He excused himself for this act of international aggression on the grounds that after 'living a year in India a man thinks himself very sincerely insulted by every act which is not servile' (Letters I. 267). Sounding like Kurtz in Conrad's *The Heart of Darkness*, he insisted that he 'could have performed the double of Dr Francia [notorious dictator of Paraguay]. I would willingly undertake the conquest of central Asia with a hundred Gurkhas' (Letters I. 308).

[135]   For Moorcroft, a traveller very much in the Bruce/Mungo Park/Burckhardt mould, see G. Alder, *Beyond Bokhara. The Life of William Moorcroft, Asian Explorer and Pioneer Vetinerary Surgeon 1767–1825* (London: Century Publishing, 1985). (Thanks to Jenny Robertson for this reference.) Jacquemont claimed to be the first European since Bernier to visit Kashmir without disguise, although in this respect he was wrong about Moorcroft. See John Keay, *Where Men and Mountains Meet: The Explorers of the Western Himalayas 1820–75* (London: John Murray, 1977), pp. 58–9.

In his devastating but hilarious review of Jacquemont's book, Croker rightly criticized this incident as an 'abuse of the confidence which the British authorities had placed in him' which might have caused retaliatory raids against Company territory. The Tory Croker hoped that the Company, now under the control of the liberal Bentinck, 'had not been put to any expense in furthering the mission of a *toad-eater*'.[136] However, Croker was sceptical of Jacquemont's lofty claims; echoing earlier doubts about James Bruce's swashbuckling in Abyssinia, he damagingly suggested that '*Le vrai n'est pas toujours vraisemblable.* His statements *may* be true, but they look to us very improbable; and we suspect the whole journey may be a fable—or at least an exaggeration.'[137] Even more insultingly, Croker suggested that some of the adventures recorded in Jacquemont's correspondence had been plagiarized from the Himalayan adventures of Captain Mundy, a touring British officer whose 'purely entertaining' *Pen and Pencil Sketches* had been published in 1832.

Jacquemont praised Humboldt for his poetic description of the 'first impression made by scenes near the equator: a natural philosopher ought to be more sensible when the study of nature's details does not close his eyes to the whole' (Letters I. 165). The sort of aesthetic sensibility which we have studied in this chapter in relation to the picturesque in Hodges, Valentia, and Heber (as we shall see in Chapter 6, refined and methodized by Humboldt) is, however, entirely absent from Jacquemont's account. Judging from his accounts of his own inner life, he seems to have suffered from pathological depression and troubling psychic disturbances. During the rigorous period of study in Calcutta in preparation for his first expedition (following the example of J. L. Burckhardt) he wrote: 'I doubt my identity', suspecting in a country of metempsychosis that 'some one else's has turned mine out of doors'. He contemplated the world 'not as an actor, but as a critical and disinterested spectator of its different scenes' (Letters I. 164). Jacquemont internalizes the fissure of the Indian picturesque, in seeming to differ from himself. One is reminded of Wordsworth's crisis of rationalism (attributed to an excess of Godwinian or *ideologue* analysis) in Books 9 and 10 of *The Prelude*. There was, however, nothing sublime about Jacquemont's egotism: as Croker noted perspicuously, amidst all his Tory bluster about atheism and republicanism, 'there was no *dip* in *his* magnetism . . . Jacquemont's work is a real curiosity . . . the most marvellous portrait of personal vanity which has ever been produced to our eyes'.[138]

Croker blamed the absence of picturesque description in Jacquemont's narrative upon his chronic short-sightedness.[139] This, however, overlooks the fact that the anti-picturesque appears to be a major theme, rather than a merely acci-

---

[136] QR, 53 (1835), 33   [137] Ibid., p. 38.   [138] Ibid., p. 26.   [139] Ibid., p. 41.

dental presence, in his writing, particularly in those letters written to his young 'romantic' cousin, Zoe Noizet de St Paul-Arras, in Paris. Jacquemont denies that his viewing practices as a scientific traveller had anything to do with his failure to register the supposedly picturesque beauty of India: 'it is not that the minute and critical examination of the productions and phaenomena of nature closes my eyes against their collective pictorial effect; but the source of the charm, and of the rapture, which I heretofore experienced on beholding their beauties, is dried up' (Letters I. 177). Coleridgean dejection is blamed instead (Jacquemont was not devoid of a taste for romanticism, as an admirer of Byron and a friend of Stendhal) but he hoped that his journey to the Himalayas in the coming spring would revive his aesthetic sense. Increasingly, however, Jacquemont's imaginative incapacity seems to come under the sway of a James Mill-style scepticism about the country in which he travels. Purging his mind of the habit of picturesque curiosity, he blames India itself: if India is 'very poorly gifted' in the picturesque, 'the evil is not in me; the fault is in the objects in the country' (Letters I. 238). In an aggressively masculinist metaphor, he wrote in 1829 to his father that 'the admiration of the beauties of nature has its virginity; but it will soon be sullied by enjoyment'. The French colony of St Domingue, home to Frederick Jacquemont, which he had earlier visited in a spirit of Humboldtian enthusiasm for the tropics, remained his 'beau ideal of equinoctial nature' (Letters I. 164).[140] In comparison, 'the magnificence of nature in Bengal possesses a fatiguing monotony' (Letters I. 182): Jacquemont's progressivist predilection for the New over the Old World was matched by aesthetic denigration of the latter.

The links between Jacquemont's anti-picturesque and his ideological critique of orientalism is particularly evident in his accounts of his trips to the Himalayan sources of the Yamuna and Ganges rivers, and to Kashmir in 1831, described in his second volume. The Himalayan fringes had been opened up to Europeans after the Gurkha War of 1815, and their status as the world's highest mountains established by the trigonometric surveys of Everest and his team, although the Western Himalayas were still largely unexplored. The Calcutta businessman and amateur artist James Baillie Fraser, travelling with his brother William (Jacquemont's friend mentioned above) in the last stages of the war in 1815, had published a lavish volume of aquatint *Views of the Himala Mountains* (1820) accompanied, in the Hodges tradition, by a narrative *Journal*

---

[140] In his journal, Jacquemont quoted Humboldt's first impressions of tropical nature at Cumana from the *Personal Narrative*, comparing it with his disappointed reaction to Bengal 'Je vois partout la main de l'homme qui a modifié la nature suivant le gout de l'Europe . . . Peut être que loin des établissments européens, les paysages de l'Inde me feront éprouver des sensations inconnues'. *Voyage dans l'Inde . . . pendant les années 1828–1832*, 6 vols. (Paris: Firmin Didot Frères, 1841), i. 180–1.

of a Tour through Part of the Snowy Range of the Himala Mountains, and to the Sources of the Jumna and Ganges.[141] Claiming, Bruce-like, to be the first European to reach the source of the Ganges at Gangotri, Fraser indulged in a rhetorical bravura evoking the sublime of discovery, representing the dramatic mountainscapes of the Himalayas in a highly romantic idiom.[142] Fraser's book inspired a torrent of travel accounts of the regions, peaking in the 1830s, by touring Indian army officers such as Skinner, Mundy, Archer, Bacon, and White; the latter's splendid *Views in India, chiefly among the Himalayan Mountains* (1838), for example, sought to combine Fraser's picturesque, rendered in the more sophisticated medium of steel engravings, with geologically informed detail.[143]

Jacquemont's account of the 'youthful' mountain range in the *Letters* broke with this recently established tradition. Unlike the sketching Fraser, Jacquemont occupied his time performing scientific experiments, examining and collecting specimens of Himalayan flora, fauna, minerals etc., at least when not beating his servants or assaulting Chinese border guards. Like the ideologue Volney systematizing the chaos of Egyptian place-names, Jacquemont wrote of his endeavour 'to unravel the confusion in the rocks of the Himalaya, and to separate the truth from their ambiguous testimony concerning the revolutions of this part of the globe' (Letters II. 131). Nature and culture alike seemed to suffer from oriental disorder awaiting only the taxonomic gaze of Western reason to be methodized. The Himalayas possessed a 'purely scientific interest: the landscape is poor and monotonous. In the highest mountains in the world there is necessarily grandeur; but it is grandeur without beauty' (Letters I. 241–2). Later, travelling into the Punjab and Kashmir (piqued by Ranjit Singh's refusal to permit his friend William Fraser to accompany him), his complaints rose to a crescendo. Picturesque associationism, with its linkage of sublime Indian scenery to cherished European landscapes, is converted into a rhetoric of bathetic comparison: the lake at Kashmir, for example, is 'poor in comparison with those of the Alps . . . how many towns on the banks of Lago Maggiore surpass Shalimar in beauty!' (Letters II. 86). Kashmir's mountains, like the Himalayas, are 'grand rather than beautiful . . . magnificent outlines, and no more. Nature has done nothing to adorn the interior—it is an immense

[141] Although, like Buchanan or Mackenzie, Fraser participated in the military surveillance of recently conquered territory, scientific ignorance rather than choice seems to have limited him to the picturesque idiom, as he admitted with a note of apology: 'I could only admire the beauty and variety so strikingly visible, without being able to ascertain with accuracy the place those subjects would occupy in a scientific arrangement' (p. 65).

[142] James Baillie Fraser, *Journal of a Tour through Part of the Snowy Range of the Himala Mountains, and to the Sources of the Rivers Jumna and Ganges* (London, 1820), p. 469.

[143] Lt. George Francis White's *Views in India, chiefly among the Himalaya Mountains* (London and Paris, 1838) was edited, and evidently 'ghost-written', by Emma Roberts, who will be studied in the next chapter.

border, inclosing nothing. There are none of those picturesque details which make the Alps so attractive' (Letter II. 86). Asian landscape, like Asian populations, are ripe for scientific classification, but barren of aesthetic or affective content.

Jacquemont's assault on the picturesque representation of Asian landscape is closely linked with his contemptuous attack on European orientalism: 'The tales of the west about the east are truly absurd'! (Letters I. 344), Tom Moore (author of the 'Kashmiri' *Lalla Rookh*) is 'not only a perfumer but a liar to boot' (Letters I. 368). Even the traveller George Forster, who can hardly be accused of having idealized Kashmir, 'must have embellished the truth furiously, which ought to be allowed to poets only' (Letters II. 87). Jacquemont's racism often combines with sexual disgust, turning Hodges-style erotic idealization on its head. Of the 'witchlike' Kashmiri women, for instance, he writes knowingly, 'I should like to see a chorus of Cashmerian country-women make their entrance on the stage of one of our theatres, before the lovers of the Exotic' (Letters II. 157). The only female faces which he admits to admiring are 'white, gentle, delicate, and noble', and he is unconvinced by Byron's 'brown or gloomy beauties' (Letters II. 86–7).

Following Mill's advice but 'in the field', Jacquemont evidently chose not to get close enough to India to see for himself, content simply to trade denigration for orientalist idealization. Absent from his *Letters* is any sense of how he himself figured in the Indian context; how he might have been viewed by the people he met or upon whose labour or authority he depended. Apart from Ranjit Singh, Indian servants and Anglo-Indian friends seem to represent the sum of his meaningful human contacts, at least as registered in his *Letters*.[144] Jacquemont's account of India, unlike that of a Bruce, a Belzoni, or even a Heber, is utterly monologic and intransitive, even as it exposes many of the illusions of romantic travel writing. In some respects Jacquemont appears to reveal the underlying truth about European orientalism in Said's sense by skimming off the picturesque veneer and exposing the deep-set cultural aggression towards Asian culture and peoples underlying the surface. Moreover, as a Frenchman in a British colony, he could afford to dispense with the hegemonic idiom of the picturesque, which, I have argued above, was more an expression of British imperial 'associationism' than an attempt at objective description of Indian landscape or peoples. It is important in studying a text such as Jacquemont's not to end up simply defending those 'susceptible imaginations' of a

---

[144] John Keay underlines Jacquemont's proactive heterosexuality in noting the venereal infection which he picked up from 'the dancing girls of Ludhiana'; but Jacquemont's self-description as 'the Socrates and Plato of his age', the attentions lavished upon him by the homosexual Ranjit Singh, and his passionate attachment to William Fraser suggest that at least some of his considerable libidinal energy was dedicated to members of his own sex. Keay, *Where Men and Mountains Meet*, p. 52.

romantic India which Jacquemont set out to demolish. But, at the same time, it would be a mistake to read Jacquemont's style of denigration as entirely representative of nineteenth-century Indian travel accounts.

We have seen Jacquemont accusing India of anti-picturesque 'monotony', but in the end there is nothing more monotonous than his relentless denunciation of everything which comes within range of his consumptive egotism. Volney's sceptical critique of the world's religions in *The Ruins* still had a lot going for it in the revolutionary moment of bourgeois rationality. Jacquemont, inheritor of Volney's intellectual tradition, applies the same criteria in the changed context of European imperialism; as a result, his judgement embodies the values of what Gellner calls the 'world-levelling, unificatory epistemologies'[145] in a state of pathological mortification. Writing from Ellora (he passes through Ajanta without even mentioning the recently discovered Buddhist cave temples) (Letters II. 314), he likens the Buddhist and Brahminical periods of Indian history—like most of his contemporaries he confused the sequence—to the plague and the cholera morbus which had ravaged Europe (Letters II. 322). Ellora is the 'head-quarters of the madmen, fools, and scoundrels, who lived upon the stupid credulity of the nations of Southern Asia' (Letters II. 322). Enough of a romantic to admit that the temples in places sometimes display 'exquisite workmanship' and that the 'effect is most extraordinary', he gives himself away by confessing that 'the idols always put me a little out of temper; they give the idea of bad reasoning, and the caves of Ellora are peopled with them' (Letters II. 323). Seven months later he was dead, victim of an agonizing inflammation of the liver which had been exacerbated by the 'pestilential miasma' of—of all places—Salsette, with its famous cave temples. The young Jacquemont—obsessed by his own health—had died as a result of the irrationality which he metaphorized as the disease of Hindu culture.

---

[145] In *Relativism and the Social Sciences* (Cambridge University Press, 1985).

5

Domesticating Distance: Three Women Travel Writers in British India

'There are peculiar powers inherent in ladies' eyes', wrote Lady Elizabeth Eastlake in an 1845 review of twelve recently published travel books by women, a belated acknowledgement of the importance of women travel writers by mid-century. Because women were accustomed to 'count canvass stitches by the fire-side', she continued, they could see perspicuously where men remained content with 'sweeping generalities'.[1] Woman's domestic confinement and the assumption that she possesses a particularized, unsystematic world-view are here converted into a narrative strength, supported by what we have seen to be the strongly empirical tradition of travel writing: 'a man either starts on his travels with a particular object in view, or, failing that, drives a hobby of his own the whole way before him . . . [the woman traveller, in contrast] is less troubled with preconceived ideas as to what is most important to observe, goes picking up material much more indiscriminately.'[2] For Eastlake, in contrast to an earlier woman traveller such as Mary Wollstonecraft, there is no chance of the 'woman of observation' being characterized by her tendency to 'ask *men's questions*'.[3]

Evidently the 'superiority' of woman travel writers proposed here is contingent upon an ideology of separate spheres for men and women. Whilst men describe public life, British women (and the reviewer is nationally specific) excel at observing the private, female spaces in the lands they visit because of their innate domesticity 'wherever [she] goes, a little fertile patch of household comfort grows beneath [her] feet'.[4] This notion of separate spheres is governed by the unity-in-diversity of the marriage contract. Because every country has a private as well as a public life, 'every country, therefore, to be fairly understood,

[1] QR, 76 (June–Sept. 1845), 98–9; Eastlake (1809–93) was the author of *Letters from the Baltic* (1841) and wife of the painter Sir Charles Eastlake, elected president of the Royal Academy in 1850.

[2] Ibid., p. 100.

[3] Wollstonecraft, *Letters Written During a Short Residence in Sweden, Norway and Denmark* (1796), Letter 1, in Mary Wollstonecraft and William Godwin, *A Short Residence in Sweden and Memoirs of the Author of 'The Rights of Woman'*, ed. by Richard Holmes (Harmondsworth, Middlesex: Penguin, 1987), p. 68.   [4] Ibid., p. 105.

requires reporters from both sexes . . . [a] kind of partnership should be formed between books of travel [to form a kind of] matrimony'.[5] Judging from the reviewer's strictures on some of the twelve 'lady travellers' which follow, these general remarks were designed to sketch the beau ideal (rather than the actual state) of nineteenth-century woman's travel writing. Travel—by definition the negation of domesticity—is converted by a rhetorical sleight of hand into an apologia for the domesticity of British women: distance itself is not so much disenchanted as domesticated. In part Eastlake's essay is a response to changing facts on the ground, the large number of women travel writers now contending for positions in the literary field. The increasing absorption of travel writing into the literary sphere from the 1820s (illustrated by Heber's writing, and to which I return later in this chapter) rendered specialist scientific knowledge less necessary for travel writers in general, a fact which empowered many women authors. The consolidation of colonial societies in 'exotic' India, Africa, and the Caribbean had meant an increasing flow of British women visiting and residing in these countries. Middle- and upper-class women published their experiences of colonial life, complimenting the 'survey modality' of male empire-builders with the 'female picturesque', or else the more mundane chronicle of colonial domesticity.[6]

In this chapter (itself a 'belated acknowledgement' in my book of the new importance of women travel writers, marked by their relative scarcity in Europe, and virtual absence from Egypt, if not India, in the eighteenth century),[7] I examine the Indian travel accounts of three upper-middle class British women, all of them military or naval daughters, against the gendered parameters established by Eastlake's article. This, of course, involves addressing the contentious question of European woman's collusion with imperialism, inasmuch as they occupied the amphibious subject position (in Indira Ghose's words) of being 'colonised by gender, but colonisers by race'.[8] A number of issues are raised in

[5] Wollstonecraft, p. 99. Unsurprisingly, Eastlake lambasted *Jane Eyre* in the *Quarterly Review* in 1848, regretting its 'anti-Christian tendency' and reading it as the work of a male author (*DNB Supplement*).

[6] For a historical overview, see Kenneth Balhatchet, *Race, Sex and Class under the Raj: Imperial Attitudes and Policies and their Critics, 1793–1905* (London: Weidenfeld & Nicolson, 1980); and Ronald Hyam, *Empire and Sexuality: The British Experience* (Manchester University Press, 1990).

[7] For early women travellers in Egypt, see Deborah Manley, 'Two Brides: Baroness Menu von Minutoli and Mrs Colonel Elwood', in *Travellers in Egypt*, ed. by Starkey and Starkey, pp. 97–107. According to Katherine Turner: 'fewer than twenty British women published travel narratives during the 18th century', 'From Classical to Imperial: Changing Visions of Turkey in the 18th Century', in *Travel Writing and Empire: Postcolonial Theory in Transit*, ed. by Steve Clark (London and New York: Zed Books, 1999), p. 113. This situation had, of course, changed dramatically by the date of Eastlake's review in the *Quarterly Review*.

[8] Indira Ghose, *The Power of the Female Gaze: Women Travellers in Colonial India* (Delhi: Oxford University Press, 1998), p. 5. One might, however, consider the exceptional case of the English travel writer Mrs Mir Hasan Ali, author of *Observations on the Mussulmauns of India* (1832). Little is known of her except that she married her Indo-Muslim husband while he was teacher of Hindustani at the

relation to my preceding argument. We saw in the previous chapter that the picturesque was far from being a specifically female discourse in British India, although it was deemed particularly appropriate for women. In the pages that follow I seek to test Sara Suleri's contention that the 'feminine picturesque' enclosed the peoples of India within an aesthetic stasis, thereby 'transfixing a dynamic cultural confrontation into a still life', while at the same time, inadvertently mapping out the European woman's enclosure within the picturesque idiom.[9] Moreover, the 'broadcast style' of viewing prescribed for the picturesque appears to contradict Eastlake's advocacy of the 'seamstress's vision', which gave women the edge over men as travel writers. If Eastlake's essay represents a prescriptive rather than a descriptive account of woman's travel writing, we must ask to what extent a gendered ideology of separate spheres actually shaped woman's experiences and texts, rather than merely providing a regulative ideal. The case of Fanny Parks in particular suggests that there was a female version of male 'curiosity' which refused picturesque distance and sought the collector's proximity to exotic objects and peoples as an antidote to colonial domesticity. The relationship of the private, female collection of curiosities to élite and popular collections raises important questions about the role of women in creating a popular taste for the exotic in nineteenth-century Britain.

Maria Graham: The Oriental Traveller as Female Moralist

One of the 'older' books discussed by Eastlake in the *Quarterly Review's* article was Lady Callcott's *Residence in the Brazils*.[10] In an earlier incarnation, bearing the surname of her first husband, the Scottish-born Maria Graham (1785–1842) had published two books based on her three-year stay in India in 1809–11, entitled *Journal of a Residence in India* (1812) and *Letters from India* (1814). The first of these (the second is not a travelogue proper but rather an account of

Military College, Addiscombe, and lived with him in India between 1816 and 1828. She returned to England for the sake of her health and wrote the account of her former life in India under the sponsorship of Queen Adelaide and Princess Augusta, to whose household she seems to have been attached. See William Crook's Introduction and notes to the 1917 edition of *Observations* (reprinted Karachi: Oxford University Press, 1974), pp. x–xv.

[9] Suleri, *The Rhetoric of English India*, pp. 76, 78.

[10] This was a sequel to Lady Callcott's *Journal of a Residence in Chile during the Year 1822* (1824), which narrated the Scots-born traveller's experiences in Chile during the wars of independence against Spain, studied by Mary Louise Pratt in *Imperial Eyes*, pp. 157–71. Another of the books reviewed by Eastlake was Fanny Calderón de la Barca's *Life in Mexico* (1843). See my essay 'The Ghost in Chapultepec: Fanny Calderón de la Barca, William Prescott and 19th Century Mexican Travel Accounts', in *Voyages and Visions*, ed. by Jas Elsner and Joan-Pau Rubiés, p. 187, for an account of Eastlake's negative review of Calderón.

Indian society, history, and mythology aimed at the general reader) described her voyage to Bombay in 1809 with her father, Rear-Admiral George Dundas, and their life in Bombay and Pune, as well as expeditions to visit the ancient cave temples of Elephanta, Salsette, and Karle. Following her marriage in India to a naval officer, Thomas Graham, she narrates her trip to Ceylon and Madras, and a brief solo visit to Calcutta, culminating with her return journey to England in 1811 via the Coromandel coast and the Cape of Good Hope. *Journal of a Residence* is the work of a dedicated 'exploratrice sociale',[11] as well as of an accomplished scholar and orientalist, and although more limited in terms of the range of places visited, deserves to rank with the travel books of Lord Valentia and Reginald Heber as a pioneering Indian travelogue of the romantic period. As a woman, Graham obviously did not qualify for the rank of 'disinterested' British traveller of the sort commended by Francis Jeffrey and J. G. Lockhart. Although the *Monthly Magazine* had high praise for Graham's *Journal of a Residence*, comparing it to Lady Mary Wortley Montagu's *Letters from Constantinople*,[12] the *Edinburgh Review* completely ignored it, and the *Quarterly Review* (already harping on the matrimonial theme) patronizingly suggested that, as the casual offshoot of a young woman's trip to India in search of a husband, it was 'a literary curiosity which we are not disposed to overlook'.[13] (In fact, Graham makes no reference to her marriage and hardly mentions her husband anywhere in the book.)

Maria Graham's Preface to *Journal of a Residence* repeats many of the familiar strictures on Anglo-Indian 'incuriosity' discussed at the beginning of Chapter 4, and the absence, at the time of writing, of any 'popular and comprehensive view of [Indian] scenery and monuments, and of the manners and habits of its natives and resident colonists', such as existed in abundance concerning countries 'incomparably less deserving of notice'.[14] Once again we encounter the complex, non-causal relationship between colonization and travel writing, and we shall have occasion to note the 'reformist' role of Graham's book in establishing imperial ligatures between Britain and colonial India. Like Valentia's and Heber's narratives, Graham's differentiated its object

---

[11] I borrow the term from Pratt's account of Maria Graham's Chilean travelogue. Pratt has adapted it from the German critic Marie-Claire Hoock-Demarle, who defines the discourse of the *exploratrice sociale* as avoiding specialized technical language, producing 'a subtle fusion of the literary and the social carried out at the level of style' (*Imperial Eyes*, pp. 160–1). This is perhaps difficult to sustain in relation to Graham's scholarly orientalism in her two books on India.

[12] MM, 34 (1812), 632.

[13] Graham had travelled out with her father, and married in December 1809. In the second, 1813 edition of her *Journal of a Residence* she angrily rebutted the *Quarterly Review*'s patronizing suggestion that she 'went thither, like most young ladies, to procure a husband instead of information' (QR, 8 (Dec. 1812), 406).

[14] Maria Graham, *Journal of a Residence in India*, 2nd edn. (Edinburgh, 1813), p. v. Henceforth G. in text.

from the numerous contemporary specialist publications on Indian military
affairs, politics, commerce, or antiquities, seeking rather to present the 'new
impressions' of an 'observant' stranger, targeting the British rather than the
Anglo-Indian reader (G. p. vi). This, however, did not prevent her (any more
than Valentia or Heber) from informed commentary on *all* these specialist
topics.

In a startling rebuttal of the sort of 'separate sphere' limitations laid down for
woman travel writers in the 1845 *Quarterly Review* article, Maria Graham's
Preface makes no attempt to disavow the scope of her narrative in terms of a
gendered division of intellectual labour. If anything, her 'observer position' as
a woman seems to have enhanced rather than limited her 'disinterestedness',[15]
and there is little sense of the claustrophobia of female confinement which
occurs in many later women's accounts of India. Graham apologizes for the fact
that as a sailor's wife she has been unable to penetrate the interior of the subcontinent, and that her 'coastal view' has resulted in the fact that 'her character
of the natives [is] more unfavourable than that of some other writers' (G. p. viii).
Alluding to a well-known passage in Mary Wollstonecraft's 1796 *Short Residence
in Sweden*, she adds that 'she did not go far enough to meet with any of those
remnants of the age of gold; any of those combinations of innocence, benevolence, and voluptuous simplicity, with which the imaginations of some ingenious authors have peopled the cottages of the Hindoos' (G. p. viii).[16] (The
latter is an allusion to Bernardin St Pierre's primitivist novella *La Chaumière
Indienne*, mentioned later in the *Journal* (G. p. 15).)

Graham's veiled allusion to Wollstonecraft, and her critique of sentimental
orientalism, links her travelogue to an important contemporary strain of
British woman's writing studied by Marilyn Butler, Janet Todd, and Gary
Kelly. In common with Mary Wollstonecraft, Eliza Hamilton, and Maria
Edgeworth, Graham sought both to criticize the excessive sensibility of late
eighteenth-century woman's writing whilst at the same time developing a 'post-
revolutionary' and reformist idiom to empower the female author as a rational
agent rather than a passive vehicle of passion and prejudice. As Gary Kelly has
indicated, travel writing was particularly serviceable for these women writers,
not only because it was 'the most important and widely read form of non-fiction
prose' of the period but also because it 'conventionally allowed for a degree of
apparent immediacy, desultoriness, and spontaneity' whilst giving women
writers access to 'discourses from which [they] would normally be excluded by
convention and education'.[17] Although Maria Graham's *Journal* is by no means

---

[15] I use this term in scarequotes, for reasons which will, I hope, be obvious in what follows.
[16] See Wollstonecraft, Letter 14, p. 149.
[17] Gary Kelly, *Women, Writing and Revolution, 1790–1827* (Oxford: Clarendon Press, 1993), pp. 69,
208.

the first Indian travelogue written by a woman, its authority and scope is under-written by the 'rational-reformist' literary background of the female moralist.[18] Like her eighteenth-century predecessors Eliza Fay and Jemima Kindersley,[19] she adopts the familiar epistolary style of writing, specifying her correspondent as a witty, intellectual Edinburgh woman who can share her amused frustration at the philistinism of Anglo-Indian life: 'to you, in the midst of the wits of our Scottish Athens, jokes from the Mahratta country must be dull indeed!' (G. p. 119).

Whilst preferring narrative and description to sentimental reflection, Graham's gendered subjectivity is conveyed in terms both of pleasure and critique, often by means of a picturesque description of Indian peoples and places which transforms, as she achieves a closer view, into pejorative moral judgement. As the skilfully executed views which make up the plates to *Journal of a Residence* remind her readers (as well as contributing to its high price, as reviewers complained), Graham's claims to skill as a picturesque artist balance her claims to be a semi-professional writer (Ill. 11). (She proudly mentions having dined with 'Mr Daniell [*sic*] the painter' at Negumbo in Ceylon (G. p. 101).[20]) Her 'Indian picturesque' embodies all three traits discussed in the previous chapter: anti-utilitarianism; the 'framing' of indigenous curiosities; and associative ligatures with home, exemplified in her account of the view from Malabar Point near Bombay:

The whole island lay to the north and east, beautifully grown with the young rice, varied with hills and woods, and only separated from Salsette and the Mahratta shore by narrow arms of the sea, while the bay and harbour to the south, scattered with beautiful woody islands, reflected the grand monsoon clouds, which, as they rolled along, now hid and now discovered the majestic forms of the ghauts on the mainland. Within a few yards of the bungalo is a ruined temple; from what remains, it must have been a fine specimen of Hindoo architecture: almost every stone is curiously carved with groupes of figures, animals, and other ornaments.   (G. p. 10)

Picturesque variety, the serpentine line of the 'narrow arms of the sea' separating middle-ground from background, the chiaroscuro effect of the clouds,

---

[18] Despite ideological differences between the Whiggish Graham and the evangelical Eliza Hamilton, the latter's anti-Jacobin novel of 1796 entitled *Translation of the Letters of a Hindoo Rajah . . . during . . . his residence in England*, a fictionalized travelogue in the tradition of Montesquieu's *Lettres Persanes* (1721), seems an unacknowledged influence on Graham's *Journal*. See Teltscher, pp. 138–42. The generic links between Hamilton's novel and Mirza Abu Talib Khan's (factual) *Travels in Europe* (1810) are fascinating and demand further study.

[19] Eliza Fay, *Original Letters from India (1779–1815), Containing a Narrative of a Journey through Egypt, and the Author's Imprisonment at Calicut by Hyder Ali* (1817), new edn., with intro. and notes by E. M. Forster (London: Hogarth Press, 1925). Jemima Kindersley, *Letters from the Island of Teneriffe, Brazil, The Cape of Good Hope, and the East Indies* (London, 1777). Fay's brief account of Egypt is one of the few by a woman in the 18th century.

[20] Graham married the celebrated landscape painter A. W. Callcott in 1827.

11. Maria Graham, 'Banyan Tree', *Journal of a Residence in India* (1812).

the distant mountains, and the 'curious' ruined temple in the foreground (balanced by the domestic reassurance of the 'bungalo') here exemplify Graham's Indian picturesque. Elsewhere (although not in this example) picturesque contemplation of Indian landscape connects her with her native land: during her expedition to Karle caves in December 1809, the wild landscape reminds her of 'Scottish Highland scenery' (G. p. 62) and the 'scenery of Trincomale [Ceylon] is the most beautiful I ever saw; I can compare it to nothing but Loch Catrine on a gigantic scale' (G. p. 120).[21]

As remarked in the previous chapter, the static repose of picturesque scenery raised a problem for the sequential narrative of the travel account; as Suleri notes 'the picturesque constructs a metonymic chain which, confounding all notions of narrative coherence, bespeaks its own distraction: with the impulse of a collector, it barely finishes one of India's charms when its attention is displaced onto another.'[22] Like Heber's, Graham's narrative resists the dissipation of 'distracted' aestheticism in favour of its moralizing mission, however, in the awareness that 'the scenes of nature, however charming to the eye, must tire in description, for want of a sufficient variety and precision in the language we must use' (G. p. 78). Not the craftsmanlike problem of language but rather the moral imperative of Graham's social vision motivates her rupture with the aesthetic distance and stasis of the picturesque.

This is particularly evident in Graham's essays in the 'ethnographical picturesque', for instance her description of coolies washing clothes observed at Bombay near the beginning of her Indian sojourn. Parading the compositional skills of the painter, she notes that 'groupes of men and women are continually employed in beating the linen, while the better sort of native women, in their graceful costume, reminding one of antique sculpture, are employed in drawing, filling, or carrying water from the neighbouring well' (G. p. 2). This account of pre-capitalist labour employs the temporalizing trope common in Indian travel writing noted in the previous chapter. Familiarity seems to have bred contempt, however, and in a later description, this time of a Hindu religious procession, the familiar aesthetic idiom is converted into an opportunity for critical moralizing. 'The picturesque dresses of the natives, and their graceful attitudes, the torches carried by children, and the little double pipe blown by boys, whose wildness might make them pass for satyrs . . . puts one strongly in mind of the ancient Bacchanals' (G. p. 35). As in James Mill's critique of the 'distant view' of orientalist curiosity, the temporalizing image is punctured by proximity: 'All

---

[21] Nostalgia is indicated here without being strongly marked, compared, say, to Sara Mills's account of a later text like Nina Mazuchelli's *The Indian Alps and how we Crossed them* (1876): 'the stress on nostalgia for Britain and home ratifies the narrator within feminine discourse . . . at the same time as inscribing her within colonial discourses whereby the other nation is seen as a poor substitute for the British landscape', *Discourses of Difference: An Analysis of Woman's Travel Writing and Colonialism* (London and New York: Routledge, 1991), pp. 182–3. [22] Suleri, p. 88.

this looks very well at a distance, but, on coming near, one is shocked at the meanness and inelegance of the god, and at the filth and wretchedness of his votaries' (G. p. 35). Manifest here is a contradiction between the sort of 'picturesque distance' considered appropriate to European women travellers in India whereby 'all subcontinental threats could be converted . . . into water-colours'[23] and the 'peculiar powers inherent in a lady's eyes'—the power of proximate vision—commended by the *Quarterly Review* article, which is not without its physical dangers.[24] Colonial filth is no longer picturesque, but rather stinks.

Commenting on a Hindu wedding procession which reminds her of 'the groupes we see on antique bas-reliefs', Graham again qualifies her exotic, temporalizing metaphor:

I every day find some tracers of the manners and simplicity of the antique ages; but the arts and the virtues that adorned them are sunk in the years of slavery under which the devoted Hindoos have bent. Those people, if they have the virtues of slaves, patience, meekness, forbearance, and gentleness, have their vices also. They are cunning, and incapable of truth; they disregard the imputations of lying and perjury, and would consider it folly not to practice them for their own interest.   (G. p. 27)

Graham's critique here partakes of a common colonial complaint about the Indian's lack of civic virtue. The percieved degree of civic virtue, a progressive 'British' value, enabled the moral calibration of other peoples. It also, of course, justified the colonial rule and reform of those who (like the Hindus) were thought to have fallen from a state of former grace into their present condition.[25]

To Graham the domestic and plebeian manifestations of civic virtue are independence, frugality, and industry. Later in her narrative, on the banks of the Hooghly, she is reminded of the scenery of the Thames valley, with one difference: 'the village and the cottage are wanting, whose inhabitants cannot suffer oppression unredressed, and to whom every employment is open of which their minds are capable, or their hearts ambitious enough to undertake' (G. p. 144). Graham explicitly misses the presence of St Pierre's sentimentalized 'Indian Cottage', along with 'the village', both icons of bourgeois female philanthropy and reform which mark out the utopia of a pious, independent, and rationally motivated labouring class in the writings of Wollstonecraft, Hannah More, Elizabeth Hamilton, and Maria Edgeworth. The complete absence of a

---

[23] Ibid., p. 75.

[24] The 'exquisite beauty of the landscape' through which Graham passes *en route* to the Great Cave at Karle seduces the traveller into forgetting that 'the tiger prowls through the overhanging forest, and that the serpent lurks beneath the many-coloured bower' (G. p. 63). Graham's tropical aesthetic, it seems, in contrast to Bernardin St Pierre's, is haunted by a sense of lurking danger.

[25] As Nicholas Thomas points out, such confident and sweeping assertions about the nature of whole populations 'are taken as emanations of the native's essential characters, rather than facts arising from the circumstances of contact' (*Colonialism's Culture*, p. 87).

bourgeois notion of upward mobility among the 'lower Hindoos' distinguishes them from this idealized version of a reformed British labouring class. Although Graham hints (beyond her acknowledgement of the social determinism of caste) that the predicament of the Indian poor is partly the result of colonial misrule as well as of oriental despotism, she takes refuge in the familiar trope of 'Hindu resignation'.[26] Scenery and moral critique are thus closely imbricated.

Like Wollstonecraft and Edgeworth, then, Graham's 'viewing position' as a woman is empowered not only by picturesque pleasure in landscapes but also by her discourse of moral improvement. Endorsing Elizabeth Eastlake's claim for women travellers, Graham's social curiosity was powerfully drawn to the private spaces of both plebeian and patrician Indian women. No less than Mary Wollstonecraft inspecting the cottages of Norwegian peasants, or Eliza Hamilton criticizing the vices of the cottagers of Glenburnie, Graham is fascinated by the domestic arrangements of the Indian lower castes, traditionally difficult of access for Europeans.[27] She nevertheless managed to visit rural dwellings in the environs of Bombay, noting that 'the inside of the huts was beautifully neat' and detailing the preparation of food (G. p. 20). On another occasion she entered a 'toddy hut' and engaged its female occupant in conversation (one wonders in what language?) (G. p. 26).

Sara Suleri describes the desire of women travellers to penetrate the zenana as a 'repetition in miniature [of] the entire structure of the colonial project'— the diminutive female equivalent of 'the male sublime'.[28] But Maria Graham's encounter with patrician Indian women in a Bombay zenana is narrated without any of the breathless exoticism which we shall see informing Fanny Parks's later account, maybe due to the fact that Parks had had to wait for four years without meeting any upper-class Indian women at all [*Wanderings of a Pilgrim*, I. 59]. Although Graham acknowledges the curious scrutiny of herself and her sister by the zenana women, it only served to give her an excuse for openly indulging

[26] This attitude lives on in Claude Lévi-Strauss's now embarrassing account of the resignation of the Indian poor in ch. 15 of *Tristes Tropiques* (1955): 'Here again it is the [beggar's] attitude which compels you to deny him those human qualities you would so much like to acknowledge in him . . . It never occurs to them . . . to set themselves up as equals. But, even from human beings, it is impossible to tolerate such constant pressure, and the unflagging ingenuity with which they try to deceive you . . . win something from you by guile, lies or theft', *Tristes Tropiques* (trans. by John Weightman and Doreen Weightman (New York: The Modern Library, 1977), p. 149.
[27] Reginald Heber, for example, complained that Bengali villagers prevented him and his wife from looking into their cottages, despite his wife Amelia's intense curiosity (*Narrative of a Tour*, I. 14).
[28] Suleri, p. 93. There is now a substantial literature on colonialism and the harem/zenana. See, for example, Alloula Malek, *The Colonial Harem* (Minneapolis: University of Minnesota Press, 1986); Billie Melman, *Women's Orients: English Women in the Middle East, 1718–1918* (Basingstoke: Macmillan, 1992); Lisa Lowe, *Critical Terrains: French and British Orientalisms* (Ithaca: Cornell University Press, 1991); Janaki Nair, 'Uncovering the Zenana: Visions of Indian Womanhood in Englishwoman's Writings, 1813–1940', *Journal of Woman's History*, 2:1 (1990), 8–34; Kate Teltscher, *India Inscribed*, pp. 37–51; Indira Ghose, *Woman Travellers in Colonial India*, pp. 52–68.

her own curiosity (G. p. 17). If Maria and her sister are under-ornamented, Fatima (the wife of Graham's Indo-Muslim friend) spoils her natural beauty by excessive nose and ear-piercing (G. p. 18). Once again the point of reference for this passage is not so much Lady Mary Wortley Montagu's famous description of the Turkish harem, but rather Mary Wollstonecraft's critique of the enervated upper class female character in *A Vindication of the Rights of Woman*. Fatima is 'modest, gentle, and indolent' but 'can hardly move without permission from the elder ladies of the harem'. Zenana women, Graham concludes with disgust, are 'totally void of cultivation . . . still fewer can read their own language . . . and the only work they do is a little embroidery' (G. p. 18).[29] If Suleri is right, then Graham's version of the colonial sublime (miniatured in her visit to the zenana) is devoid of either excitement or disappointment. Critique of class privilege here takes priority over race or ethnicity, echoing the metropolitan bourgeois feminist's critique of court culture, and the imprisonment of upper class women within an irrational and merely fashionable idiom of sensibility.

Graham's social critique is in fact just as marked in her accounts of the domestic manners of Anglo-Indians, where she is often as biting as Fanny Trollope on the North Americans.[30] Maria Graham's role as a reform-minded 'exploratrice sociale' motivates her surveillance of all the sites of social and cultural life in India, including visits to the female orphanage at Madras, the botanical gardens in Madras and Calcutta, and the orientalist collections of Col. Colin Mackenzie, Dr John Leyden, and Sir James Mackintosh (whose hospitality she and her father had enjoyed upon arrival at Bombay). As in the case of Wollstonecraft, travel is itself an expression of her personal cultivation, differentiating her from the philistinism and vanity of 'static' Anglo-Indians in general (whom she refers to as 'our colonists') (G. p. 27), and women in particular. Graham implicitly highlights her own cosmopolitanism in her account of Anglo-Indian female society at Bombay: 'I found our fair companions, like the ladies of all the country towns I know, under-bred and over-dressed, and, with the exception of one or two, very ignorant and very grossière' (G. p. 28). Like Wollstonecraft on provincial life in the Norwegian town of Risor,[31] this is not so much social as intellectual snobbery, as is clear from Graham's lament that 'the small number of rational companions, make a deplorable prospect to one who anticipates a long residence here' (G. p. 28). She has nothing more positive to say about Madras or Calcutta, despite the greater proportion

---

[29] Compare this with Mrs Mir Hasan Ali's account in *Observations of the Mussulmauns of India*: 'the ladies' society is by no means insipid or without interest; they are naturally gifted with good sense and politeness, fond of conversation, shrewd in their remarks, and their language is both correct and refined' (p. 64), and her positive description of zenana life in ch. 12.

[30] Trollope's *Domestic Manners of the Americans* (1832) became paradigmatic of this kind of social satire in 19th-century travel writing.

[31] Wollstonecraft, Letter 11 (pp. 130–4).

of intellectual refinement in the latter city (G. p. 136). Whilst Bombay preserved a certain openness towards Indians, she complained that in Calcutta she was unable to 'get acquainted with any native families' on account of the national prejudice of the English (G. p. 136).[32]

If Graham is guilty of an alteritist stereotyping of Indian society (which, selectively, she certainly is) then the fault line of 'otherness' divides her own subject-position as an 'imperial' British traveller from the whole conglomerate of colonial society, whether represented by the 'degrading superstitions of the Hindoos', the more 'active fanaticism of the Musselmans', or the 'avarice, the prodigality, the ignorance, and the vulgarity of most of the white people . . . our colonists' (G. p. 134). Consistent with her climactic rather than racialist explanation of cultural difference, it seems hard to imagine how civic or domestic virtue could ever have flourished, or might yet be made to flourish, in the tropics (G. p. 93). Yet Graham is not content to leave India without at least establishing a model of Anglo-Indian female philanthropy, the foundation-stone of benign colonialism, in the persona of 'Mrs A', the wife of the Grahams' host at Salsette:

I have followed her in admiration through a village where her appearance made every face to smile. She is blessed alike by the old and the young; she knows all their wants, and listens to all their complaints . . . The work of charity over, she enjoys a walk amidst those beautiful scenes with all the gaiety natural to her age . . . Would that there were a few more such European women in the East, to redeem the character of our country-women, and to shew the Hindoos what English Christian women are. (G. p. 115)

The power of female exemplarity underlines Grahams' boldest statement in favour of British imperialism.

Like contemporary novelists Eliza Hamilton and Lady Morgan in their Indian novels *Letters of a Hindoo Rajah* (1796) and *The Missionary* (1811), Graham parades a confident knowledge of orientalist scholarship as well as the 'scientific' discourses of exotic botany and natural history.[33] (It is noteworthy that, in contrast to Valentia or Buchanan, she often gives vernacular as well as

---

[32] John Leyden's translation of the Malay Munshi Ibraham's account of a visit to Government House in Calcutta which appears as Appendix 2 to Graham's *Journal*, although on one level satirizing 'oriental' travel writing, is really a tilt at 'glistening' Anglo-Indian society women whom Ibraham likens to 'fish fresh caught', adding, poetically, 'These pretty fish, so blithe and brave, | To see them fishing on the wave! | Were I an angler in the sea, | These fishes were the fish for me!!' (p. 206). This is (ironically) not far from the *Quarterly Review*'s slight about Graham coming to India with the 'fishing fleet' in search of a husband.

[33] Graham's ideological position is, however, distinct from both Hamilton's Tory evangelism and Morgan's sentimental nationalism; like Edgeworth and to some extent the English dissenter Wollstonecraft, her intellectual background represents a feminized version of Scottish enlightenment civic humanism and 'improvement'. See Anne Elwood's *Narrative of a Journey Overland from England . . . to India* (1830), for another work of female orientalism, and Ghose, pp. 19–37.

Linnaean names for plants, as in her account of the 'pitcher-plant, Nepenthes distillatoria, or as it is here called, the monkey cap', the horn of which contains two gills of fresh water. (G. p. 105).) Her account of her visit to the Elephanta Caves is prefaced by an essay on the Hindu pantheon (mandatory in the Indian travelogues of male orientalists), expanded in her subsequent *Letters from India*,[34] and her learned comparison between the ancient sculpture of the Hindus and the Egyptians cites Denon's *Travels* as well as the writings of Anquetil du Perron, D'Ohsson, and Colebrooke (G. pp. 36–48). She also claims the first account of the history and manners of the Guebres (or Parsis); as Ghose notes, 'no feminine disavowal is to be found [here] . . . the narrator informs us that her informant is none other that the chief priest of the community, Moola Firoze'.[35] She included a history of the Maratha hero Shivaji (G. p. 80), of the Jain religion (G. p. 66), and an appendix on the Persian poet Firdousi's *Shah Nameh*, based on D'Ohsson (G. pp. 191–200). Despite her reluctance to support the full-scale conversion of Hindus, her attitude to Hinduism is nevertheless marked by a disdain for superstition, priestcraft, and idolatry associated with her Protestant and rationalist background.

It is instructive to compare Graham's remarks on the cave temples of Western India with those of the Anglo-Indian Capt. John Seely, who visited Ellora in 1810, the same year as Graham's visits to Elephanta, Karle, and Kanheri.[36] Seely's 1824 *The Wonders of Elora* is marked by a Belzoni-style amateurism which indulges a homespun discourse of the sublime punctuated by moments of (welcome) self-parody. If Graham's problem of narrative progress adheres to the aggregative, non-sequential nature of picturesque description, Seely's lack of headway is a result of constant blundering authorial interjection and digression ('Now, kind reader, lest I, a poor half-pay captain . . .').[37] Seely's egotism appears crude in relation to Graham's tight command of narrative pace, aesthetic affect, and moralizing judgement. The difference between the 'curious' colonial and the semi-professional metropolitan travel writer is nowhere more clearly highlighted than by a comparison of *Journal of a Residence* with *The Wonders of Elora*. Appropriately enough, Seely's template for his sense of the wonders of Ellora is James Bruce's 'vivid or tumultuous emotions on first beholding the springs of the Nile'; Belzoni-like, grammar and syntax

[34] Here Graham repeats the well-worn anecdote of Hindu sepoys worshipping their gods in the ruins of the Egyptian temple of Dendera during the British expedition against the French in 1801 as evidence of the antiquity of Indian religions (p. 53). The earliest provenance of this story is in E. D. Clarke's *Travels* (see Ch. 3), although it resurfaces in travel writing by Seely, Fitzclarence, and Thomas Medwin.   [35] Ghose, p. 28.

[36] Capt. John Seely, *The Wonders of Elora: or, The Narrative of a Journey to the Temples and Dwellings excavated out of a Mountain of Granite* (London, 1824). Seely visited Ellora with a military escort, as in 1810 it was still in the dominions of the Maratha leader Holkar. He pointed out that the dangers of the road had prevented Valentia, Edward Moor, and Maria Graham from visiting Ellora, although Sir James Mackintosh had gone with an escort (pp. 97–8).   [37] Ibid., p. 45.

break down as he is overwhelmed by 'a painful' degree of 'awe, wonder, and delight'.[38] His attempt to spend the night in the Kailasha Temple is thwarted by its 'gloomy solemn silence' and thoughts of the 'mighty race who formed [the cave]', robbing him of sleep.[39] As his title proclaims, Seely's 'wonder' knows no bounds.

Although Graham's first reaction to Elephanta is one of sublime 'astonishment', rational judgement quickly overcomes aesthetic transport. Commenting on the *Maheshamurti* statue, for example (like Valentia's, Graham's visit preceded Erskine's scholarly account of the statue's iconography which informed Reginald Heber's remarks),[40] she identifies Brahma as 'placid', Vishnu as 'beautiful', and Siva as 'frowning', attributes which seem to register her own progressive reactions to India as a picturesque and antique land calling for moral reform. With a Radcliffean note of Gothic intrigue, she observes that 'concealed steps behind Siva's head lead to a convenient ledge or bench behind the cap of the bust, where a Bramin might have hidden himself for any purpose of priestly imposition' (G. p. 55). Admitting that the temples display the skills 'of a people far advanced in the arts of civilised life', she indicates that they were maintained 'in the hands of a crafty priesthood, who kept science, affluence, and honour for their own fraternity, and, possessed of better ideas, preached a miserable and degrading superstition to the multitude' (G. p. 58). Like her 'proximate' debunking of the Indian picturesque, Graham translates sublime affect into sceptical critique of Brahminical 'double doctrine'. In contrast to Elephanta, she passes a more positive judgement on the Jain cave temple of Karle, 'one of the most magnificent chambers I ever saw, both as to proportion and workmanship' (G. p. 64). Here there are 'no personifications of the deity, no separate cells for secret rites' (G. p. 65); the altars are dedicated to an invisible and omniscient God who bears a striking resemblance to Graham's own deistic Supreme Being. She does not, however, miss the chance of adding a domestic touch; the small adjacent caves 'are occupied by the wives and children of the priests, who live in a little modern building close to them' (G. p. 68).

Later in the *Journal*, following in Valentia's footsteps from Bombay to Pune, Graham stops to visit an 'alive god', the Deo of Chimchore, an avatar of Ganesha incarnated in the body of a 12-year-old boy (G. p. 70). Characteristically, Graham remarks the dirtiness of the Deo's palace, and the wild, opium-soaked stare of the young Deo himself; describing the bustle of activity as priests poured libations over the figures of gods, and pilgrims performed puja, she writes that 'all go[es] on in a manner which might beseem the inhabitants of the Castle of Indolence' (G. p. 72). Frustrated by being forbidden entry as a woman

---

[38] Capt. John Seely, p. 106. Despite his disdain for the 'monstrous lies and fabled impostures' of Hinduism, at least Seely (unlike Lt. Col. Fitzclarence) kept his beef sandwiches hidden (p. 137).

[39] Ibid., p. 139.   [40] See Partha Mitter, *Much-Maligned Monsters*, p. 157.

to the 'palladium of Chinchore' with its lingam shrine, she tacitly identifies with James Thomson's 'Knight of Arts and Industry', who breaks the spell of the Wizard and sets the drone-like inhabitants of the *Castle of Indolence* to useful and rational employment. In the face of this 'degrading instance of superstitious folly' (G. p. 72), she writes, 'if I could be assured that the communication with Europe would in ever so remote a period free the natives of India from their moral and religious degradation, I could even be almost reconciled to the methods by which the Europeans have acquired possession of the country' (G. p. 72). Noteworthy here is the conditional mood of the sentence: although Britain's moral claim on India is untenable, it might just be redeemed by the moral agenda of 'reformed' imperialism. Graham's active and interventionist overview of India (the textual equivalent of 'Mrs A's' practical philanthropy) issues a challenge both to Anglo-Indian complacency and the apparent intractability of traditional Indian society.

Emma Roberts, Oriental Tourism, and the 'Moonlight Picturesque'

If there are strong stylistic and thematic continuities between the Indian travel narratives of Lord Valentia, Reginald Heber, and Maria Graham, Emma Roberts's acclaimed *Scenes and Characteristics of Hindostan, with Sketches of Anglo-Indian Society* (1835) marks a rupture with the 'integrated' travel text and the transformation of the genre into 'light literature'.[41] Greater correspondence between metropolitan and colonial societies in the 'reformist' Bentinck regime, plus the increasing volume of British men and women travelling to India in the 1820s and 1830s, created a new demand for Indian material on the part of the British reading public. Emma Roberts, aware of the tremendous proliferation of tourist literature in Europe (John Murray's famous *Handbooks* were initiated in 1836),[42] conceived of her own book as a kind of picturesque guidebook to India, filling the yawning space previously occupied by such practical works as Capt. Thomas Williamson's *The East India Vade-Mecum*.[43] 'In this age of tourists', she wrote, 'it is rather extraordinary that the travelling mania should not extend to the possessions of the British

---

[41] This is captured in the *Calcutta Literary Gazette*'s praise for the original *Scenes*, published as separate articles in the *Asiatic Journal*, as 'light, animated and graphic, they describe manners and people with spirit, and scenery with a tone of poetical feeling which alone can do justice to the magnificence of the Eastern World'. Quoted in Introduction to Emma Roberts, *Scenes and Characteristics of Hindostan, with Sketches of Anglo-Indian Society*, 3 vols. (London: William Allen, 1835). Henceforth R. in text.

[42] James Buzard, *The Beaten Track*, pp. 65–7.

[43] *The East India Vade-Mecum; or, Complete Guide to Gentlemen intended for the Civil, Military, or Naval Services of the Hon. East India Company* (1808).

Government in India, and that so few persons are induced to visit scenes and countries in the East, embellished with the most gorgeous productions of nature and art' (R. II. 289). Those weary of 'Cheltenham, Baden, Spa, and other springs of fashionable resort' might spice up their lives, she urged, by taking a trip to the Himalayas or a cruise on the Ganges (R. II. 291). Roberts recommends the cooler months of October to January and even proposed a rough itinerary for the aspiring tourist.

Roberts's remarks do, however, indicate that it is still too early to talk about 'tourism' in India of the kind discussed in relation to Europe by James Buzard in *The Beaten Track*. Still, the travel accounts of Valentia, Graham, and Heber had paved the way for a new breed of Indian travel writers, mainly military men on leave, who explored, hunted, and sketched in their leisure time rather than on official commission. As George Francis White put it disparagingly in 1838, 'hosts of idlers from the plains are continually ranging through the most accessible places, or extending their wanderings to others less known'.[44] A spate of travel books describing such leisurely tours (which we might dub 'military tourism') appeared around the early and mid-1830s: Capt. Godfrey Mundy's *Pen and Pencil Sketches of India* (1832), with its conviction that 'egotism is the very essence of a journal',[45] Capt. Thomas Skinner's *Excursions in India* (1832); Major Edward Caulfield Archer's *Tours in Upper India* (1833); Lt. Thomas Bacon's *First Impressions and Studies from Nature in Hindostan 1831–1834* (1837); and Capt. Thomas Medwin's romantic redaction of his Indian journal in (the misleadingly titled) *Angler in Wales* (1834).[46]

Chloe Chard defines tourism (which, in its modern sense, she dates to the decade of the 1820s) as 'a system for managing pleasure and keeping danger and destabilisation at bay', whilst acknowledging that 'in propounding the view of travel as an incipiently dangerous adventure of the self, [the romantic, destabilized] approach provides tourism with its crucial starting point'.[47] Both pleasure and danger were intensified in the exotic setting of British India even if distance still prohibited the development of bourgeois tourism as understood in Europe (a situation which would change with steam and, later, air transport). Nevertheless, changing expectations about the literary representation as well as the practices of travel are signalled by Frances Jeffrey in his review of one of the

<hr />

[44] Lt. George Francis White, *Views in India, Chiefly amongst the Himalayan Mountains*, ed. by Emma Roberts (London and Paris, 1838), p. vii.

[45] K. K. Dyson, *A Various Universe*, p. 247.

[46] See my *British Romantic Writers and the East*, pp. 154–69; and Tilar Mazzeo, 'A mixture of all the styles: Colonialism, Nationalism, and Plagiarism in Shelley's Indian Circle', *European Romantic Review*, 8:2 (Spring, 1997), 155–68 for an account of the Indian writings of Shelley's cousin Medwin.

[47] Chloe Chard, *Pleasure and Guilt on the Grand Tour*, p. 215. Buzard's point about the discrimination of social class needs to be reiterated here: 'tourist' belatedness also contains a sense of social subordination to those aristocratic (especially 'Byronic') travellers who purported to be 'first on the scene' (*The Beaten Track*, p. 6).

'new' military travelogues (*Sketches of India* by 'An Officer') in the *Edinburgh Review* for October 1824. In striking contrast to James Mill's disparaging remarks on Indian travel writing in the same organ fourteen years earlier, Jeffrey distinguished the purely pleasurable from the 'integrated' travel account, but now to the detriment of the latter, which he dismissed on the grounds that they were not properly 'books of travels . . . but works of science and philosophy'. He continued:

As the principal delight in travelling consists in the impressions which we receive, almost passively, from the presentment of new objects, and the reflections to which they spontaneously give rise, so the most delightful books of travels should be those that give us back these impressions in their first freshness and simplicity . . . by aiming too ambitiously at instruction and research, this charm is lost.[48]

The enormous success of Byron's 'poetical travelogues' *Childe Harold* and *Don Juan*, as well as the challenge (notwithstanding, as I argue in the next chapter, the discursive failure) of Humboldt's *Personal Narrative*, both contributed their share to the emergence of a new style of literary travel writing which appeared in the 1820's and 1830s. Of course, Jeffrey's emphasis on 'first impressions' was nothing new in the aesthetics of travel writing; what *was* novel was the abandonment of epistemological inclusiveness, and the aggressive anti-antiquarianism and anti-scientism of 'touristic' travel narratives of the 1830s. Lt. Thomas Bacon, in his belle-lettristic *First Impressions in Hindostan* (1838) urged that 'If the reader be not a natural historian, or pretender of the same, he will yawn at the very sight of class; order; genus, etc; so I will leave the learned one to go on with his technical discourse in soliloquy'.[49] A. W. Kinglake's *Eothen, or, Traces of Travel Brought House from the East* (1844) (one of the most popular English travel books of all time) announced in its Preface that

it is right to forewarn people . . . that the book is quite superficial in its character . . . I believe I may truly acknowledge, that from all details of geographical discovery, or antiquarian research—from all display of 'sound learning, and religious knowledge'—from all historical and scientific illustrations—from all useful statistics—from all political disquisition's—[*sic*] and from all good moral reflections, the volume is thoroughly free.[50]

---

[48] ER, 41 (Oct. 1824), 31. Jeffrey's review seems to have influenced the *Edinburgh Review* in favour of the 'agreeable and instructive tourists' Skinner, Mundy, and Archer in 1833; the reviewer approved the 'lively representations of all that strikes the eye as new, beautiful, or strange' in these authors, despite the fact that they were men of no deep learning (ER, 57 (July 1833), 359).

[49] Lt. Thomas Bacon, *First Impressions and Studies from Nature in Hindostan . . . from 1831–34*, 2 vols. illus. with lithographic plates (London: William Allen, 1837), i. 305.

[50] *Eothen, or, Traces of Travel Brought Home from the East* (London: John Ollivier, 1844), p. v. Buzard points out that Murray published a pocket-size edition of Byron's poetry to be carried alongside his tourist 'Handbooks' (p. 119).

This new attitude in exotic travel writing is partly traceable to a corrosive anxiety about belatedness which had earlier been a familiar feature of Grand Tour narratives,[51] and which Byron's *Childe Harold* (not to mention the facetiousness of *Don Juan*) had addressed with considerable success. As Kinglake put it: 'where the countries which one visits have been thoroughly, and ably described . . . one is fully at liberty to say as little (though not quite so much) as one chooses'.[52] But in the Indian case there seems to have been a sudden leap from a prevalent notion that the Indian travelogue did not yet exist (as we saw in contemporary responses to Valentia's book) to a sense that the genre was *already* exhausted.

The rise of the 'purely picturesque' literary and touristic travelogue in the 1820s clearly empowered women writers unwilling to 'ask men's questions', although women travellers like Mary Wollstonecraft, H. M. Williams, or Maria Graham had, of course, done just that, sometimes under the pretext of acceptable female pedagogy. An equivalent to European female domestic tourism needed to be constructed by women writers in India because it did not yet exist. On the other hand, the rise of the 'separate spheres' ideology which increasingly confined bourgeois women to the domestic sphere in the 1820s and 1830s—especially in the anxious colonial climate of India—raised the problem of what exactly women were to write *about*.[53] The freedom to tour and tiger-hunt in 'picturesque' India, particularly in the exotic peripheries, enjoyed by the Skinners, Mundys, and Archers, was not an option for most women; as Fanny Parks complained in her journal in 1833, 'I am reading Capt. Mundy's "Sketches in India", a much more amusing journal than I can write. I have no tigers to kill, no hurdwar to visit; nor have I even seen the taj.'[54] Emma Roberts's solution, in her romantic scenes of an abject Mughal India, was to assume the role of the picturesque tourist, thus discovering a rationale for movement and agency which might distinguish her own predicament from the 'imprisonment' of Asiatic women.

Emma Roberts (1793–1840) initially came to India as a companion to her sister, wife of an officer in the Bengal Army, in 1827; after her sister's death, in 1831, she lived in Calcutta for a year, where she worked as editor of the *Oriental Observer*, before returning to England, exhausted by overwork. In 1839 she returned to Bombay to pursue her journalistic career, but died, unmarried, in Pune the following year, aged 47.[55] Roberts launched her literary career as a

[51]   See Chard's discussion of Lady Morgan on Naples, p. 99.   [52]   *Eothen*, p. viii.

[53]   As Indira Ghose notes in her critique of the essentialist notion of the 'female gaze', 'what it was possible to *see* as a woman was determined by the discourses of femininity in circulation at a specific moment in history' (p. 10), or rather what it was *permissible* to see as a woman.

[54]   Fanny Parks, *Wanderings of a Pilgrim in Search of the Picturesque*, 2 vols. (London, 1850), i. 268.

[55]   Dyson, p. 255. Roberts's *Notes of an Overland Journey to Bombay* was published posthumously in 1841, prefaced by a memoir of her life.

poet with *Oriental Scenes, Sketches and Tales*, published in Calcutta in 1830 (it was seen through the press by the progressive Eurasian intellectual Henry Derozio) and again in London two years later. The volume is a medley of oriental historical romances influenced by Byron's *Turkish Tales* and Moore's *Lalla Rookh* ('The Sacrifice: A Tale of Hindoostan', 'The Dying Hindu', 'Noor Jaffeir Khan'), combined with shorter poems descriptive of picturesque scenes like 'The Taje Mahal', 'An Evening Scene in Hindoostan', or 'Stanzas, Written on the Banks of the Ganges'. Roberts dedicated the volume to her close friend Laetitia Landon ('L.E.L.'), and she contributed a biographical memoir of Landon to the posthumous publication of *The Zenana, and Minor Poems of L.E.L* after the latter's death in mysterious circumstances in Africa.[56] Both Roberts's and L.E.L.'s poems are marked by a strain of female exoticism—in part inspired by Felicia Hemans's tales of female heroism in distant lands—which enjoyed great currency in the lavishly illustrated *Keepsakes* and *Annuals* of the 1830s and 1840s.[57]

Emma Roberts's major contribution to Indian travel writing is unquestionably *Scenes and Characteristics of Hindustan*, a long, three-volume series of 'desultory' essays which combined critical sketches of Anglo-Indian society and manners with 'picturesque' descriptions of particular Indian sites and cities. In keeping with the 'letterpress' text of many picturesque travels, and the 'impersonal' literary formula of many of the *Annuals* and *Keepsakes*, Roberts drops 'personal narrative' and in general adopts a diffident, third-person, descriptive style quite distinct from the self-assertive and moralizing narrative persona of Maria Graham. In striking contrast also to the colourful egotism of male colonial adventurers such as Capt. Mundy and Thomas Medwin, Roberts's literary professionalism is marked by her self-absorption in a nuanced descriptive style, with only occasional intrusions by 'the humble writer of this paper' (R. II. 300). The *Quarterly Review* thoroughly approved this authorial decision in its glowing review of Roberts's book, on the ground that 'we are conducted through no attenuated details, serving only to unite, by the slender thread of the author's personal identity, parts which have no necessary connection, but

---

[56] *The Zenana, and Minor Poems of L.E.L., With a Memoir by Emma Roberts* (London and Paris, nd).

[57] See my discussion of Hemans's 'Traveller at the Source of the Nile' in Ch. 2. During her sojourn in England, Roberts pursued an active literary career catering for the public demand for picturesque and exotic representations of India. She wrote the text for Commander Robert Elliott's *Views in India, China, and the Shores of the Red Sea* (London, 1835) and Lt. George White's expensive and lavish *Views in India*, published in 1838 by the London and Paris-based firm of Fisher & Sons, who specialized in illustrated travelogues such as Fraser's *Oriental Keepsake* (Archer and Lightbown, pp. 119–21). On the short-lived phenomenon of *Annuals* and *Keepsakes* (starting with the *Forget Me Not* in 1823 and rising to 63 rival titles by 1832), see Sonia Hofkosh, 'Disfiguring Economics: Mary Shelley's Short Stories' in Audrey Fisch, Anne Mellor, and Esther Schor (eds.), *The Other Mary Shelley* (Oxford and New York: Oxford University Press, 1993), 204–19.

are presented with a succession of vivid pictures, each of which is attractive throughout'.[58] The *Quarterly Review's* enthusiasm for Roberts's self-effacement (so differently motivated from Humboldt's 'transcendental self' discussed in Chapter 6) overlooks the fact that it may have been dictated by a crippling sense of incongruity between the 'proper lady' and the professional female author.

Reading between the lines, Roberts's suppression of her 'personal identity' barely succeeds in disguising an obsessive theme of female imprisonment. Unlike Maria Graham, Roberts was a resident Anglo-Indian rather than a travelling European, although her critique of Anglo-Indian society, and particularly its treatment of women, was every bit as damning as her precursor's. All Anglo-Indian women are prisoners of home and hearth, she proclaimed, whilst those who reside in 'Mofussil' (up-country stations remote from Calcutta) are 'condemned to a long melancholy sojourn . . . offering little society, and none to her taste' (R. I. 35). Those who do enjoy company relieve their 'nearly unmitigated ennui' by gossip and slander which outmatches the most provincial English town or village (R. I. 73–6). Even gardening ('that truly feminine employment') is impossible except before sunrise, and 'even then, the frame is too completely enervated by the climate to admit of those little pleasing labours, which render the green-house and the parterre so interesting' (R. I. 34). Anglo-Indian family life offers little solace; only in marriage can woman hope to find any happiness, for the relationship between parent and child is 'subject to many shocks' (R. I. 36–7).

Whilst generally steering clear of the sort of moral and political issues which interested Maria Graham,[59] Roberts is driven by the same anxiety about creolization as Valentia and Heber. She is particularly damning about 'country-born' creole girls of mixed race, in whose mouths the English language is in a state of 'degeneration' due to mispronunciation and wrongly accented syllables (R. I. 43). (A common double standard is evident in her fascination with the 'picturesque' Col. Gardiner and the Begum Sumroo, both of whom had married across the cultural divide. Miscegenation in the upper classes was clearly acceptable, whilst it was frowned upon in the middle and lower classes (R. III. 141–6).) The dangers of cultural hybridization are even more alarming in the case of children. Whilst English children (the 'Baba Logues' of her chapter 4) are rendered exceedingly attractive by the manner in which their 'exceeding fairness' contrasts with the 'Asiatic swarthiness around them' (R. II. 109), their upbringing in the hands of native *ayahs* results in a clumsiness with their mother-tongue, preventing fluent communication with monolingual parents (R. II. 117). To avoid the 'creolization' of British children, Roberts recommends that

---

[58]   QR, 55 (Dec. 1835), 176.
[59]   Although she does advocate the British annexation of Awadh (R. II. 130), and complains of the 'niggard parsimony' of Bentinck's regime in neglecting Barrackpur Park Zoo (R. I. 129).

they should be sent back to Europe to be educated, however much this 'occasions early separation, which, in too many instances, proves fatal to the enjoyment of a re-union' (R. I. 37).

If life is difficult for married women, it is much worse for the colonial spinster. In a strikingly autobiographical passage, Roberts evokes her fear of entrapment within the Anglo-Indian household: the single woman 'must remain a prisoner. She cannot walk out beyond the garden or the verandah, and all the out-of-door recreations, in which she may have been accustomed to indulge in at home, are denied her' (R. I. 34).[60] This, in fact, constitutes a double imprisonment; not only is she confined within the British domestic circle, she is also confined in colonial India itself, trapped within an imperial plot in which she feels that she has neither agency nor instrumentality: 'few young women, who have accompanied their married sisters to India, possess the means of returning home; however strong their dislike may be to the country, their lot is cast in it, and they must remain in a state of miserable dependence . . . until they shall be rescued from this distressing situation by an offer of marriage' (R. I. 36). If, as we have seen, all the associative ligatures of the Indian picturesque point back home, in Roberts's case the nostalgic impulse is blocked by her social disability as an unmarried and sickly woman. (All reference to her career as a professional 'woman of letters' in India is carefully suppressed.)

This claustrophobic realization runs like a theme through her writing, as in her conventionally anti-exotic 'Stanzas, Written on the Banks of the Ganges' published in *Oriental Scenes*:

> The mighty Ganges' regal streams,
> Through the wide landscape flow,
> And gorgeously the noon-tide beams
> Upon its bosom glow;
> But in a small sequestered nook,
> Beyond the western sea,
> There rippling glides a narrow brook,
> That's dearer far to me.[61]

More interesting than the poem itself, with its familiar preference for domestic brooks over exotic rivers, is the footnote in which Roberts writes 'to do justice to the sunny land of India, its visitors should have the power to leave it for Europe at pleasure; when the lot seems finally cast, the spirit becomes too

---

[60] Confirmed by Mrs Mir Hasan Ali's comments on her greater freedom as wife of an Indo-Muslim to 'indulge in long walks at Kannoge, which would be prohibited to "European Ladies". Should any English woman venture to walk abroad in the city of Lucknow, for instance . . . she would be judged by the Natives as a person careless of the world's opinion' (*Observations*, pp. 287–8).

[61] *Oriental Scenes, Sketches, and Tales* (London, 1832), p. 130.

much depressed to enjoy the dazzling novelties which give but too forceful an assurance that we are far from home'.[62] The ultimate nightmare hinted at here for the constitutionally delicate woman (one sadly realized in Roberts's own case) was to die in India, thereby enforcing physical incarceration in perpetuity. One of the most disturbing passages in Roberts's book is her description of unkempt and chaotic Anglo-Indian cemeteries:

all are over-crowded, and many exhibit the most frightful features of a charnel house, dilapidated tombs, rank vegetation, and unburied bones whitening in the wind. The trees are infected with vultures and other hideous carrion-birds; huge vampire-bats nestle in the walls . . . wolves and jackalls [*sic*] . . . tear up the bodies interred without the expensive precautions necessary to secure them from such frightful desecration. (R. II. 34–5)

The uncharacteristic excess of her ghoulish description portrays the nightmare of the final dismemberment of Anglo-Indian bodily relics in the jaws of tropical carrion; significantly, it verbally echoes an earlier description of the urban squalor of the native 'Black Town' in Calcutta, 'dirty, crowded, ill-built' (R. I. 13). Death in India for those who are caught short by fatal disease represents the irreversible nemesis of creolization, mingling one's remains with the Indian dust, or (even worse) symbolical identification with the 'living dead' of India's urban poor.

Half-way through the first volume of *Scenes and Characteristics* the tone lightens as Roberts narrates a 'cross-country trip to a large station' made with a friend. Picturesque tourism empowers the Anglo-Indian spinster, providing an escape route from the stultifying enclosure of Anglo-Indian domesticity. Because of her dread of domestic interiority, Roberts's narrative studiously avoids the sort of detailed observation extolled by the *Quarterly Review*, taking refuge in a picturesque idiom which 'converts its ability not to see into studiously visual representations'.[63] Whereas Graham's narrative deconstructs picturesque distance in 'taking a closer look', Roberts's rather enhances it. Like the heroines of Anne Radcliffe's gothic novels *The Mysteries of Udolpho* (1794) or *The Italian* (1797), the picturesque alleviates the sufferings of the imprisoned heroine in affording her aesthetic agency and moral composure.[64] Roberts's 'literary picturesque' of India evokes the literary world of childhood and fairytale rather than historical orientalism informing Graham's narrative, alluding to Byron's reminiscences of 'Othello, Shylock and Pierre' as he stood on the Bridge of Sighs in Venice (R. II. 300). Roberts's romantic evocation of India is based on a myth of unconstrained movement symbolized, in one key passage, by the sylvan exile of the melancholy Jacques in Shakespeare's *As You Like It*. In some respects this is Roberts's feminized version of the male Anglo-Indian

[62] *Oriental Scenes*, p. 130.   [63] Suleri, p. 76.   [64] Bohls, *Women Travel Writers*, pp. 224–9.

obsession with hunting as a means of eking out the boredom of colonial leisure. Undomesticated India is refigured in her imagination as the Forest of Arden, albeit with a climactic qualifier: 'If the heat of the day could be born with impunity, this kind of sylvan life, realising the romantic notions of early youth, the forest wanderings so often indulged in fancy, would be very delightful' (R. I. 279).[65]

But blazing tropical heat is as much of a problem as colonial dirt and poverty, both of which Roberts surmounts by an aesthetic of the moonlight picturesque:

It is only when night spreads its mysterious spell over the scene, that an Indian land-scape, during the dry weather, can captivate the eye . . . however romantic the temples, more than half their charm is lost when they spring from an arid soil; but starlight or moonlight can invest them with a divine aspect; the barren sands become soft and silvery. . . .   (R. I. 219)[66]

Crepuscular, moonlit landscape symptomize the abject feminine aesthetic which dominates Roberts's writing, as well as the fey romanticism which describes the Taj Mahal as 'constructed of gathered moonbeams' (R. II. 297). At the same time it performs (almost too blatantly) the social 'filtering' of vision embodied in the 'daytime' picturesque: 'beneath the midnight planetary beam, the most simple and unpretending building is decked with beauty; the mud hut of some poor native, with its course drapery of climbing gourds, shews like a fairy bower' (R. I. 220).[67] Imagination, rather than unifying mind and object as in the formulations of Coleridge and Wordsworth, here offers instead a phan-tasmagorical escape route from the colonial quotidien, evading all responsibil-ity for the poverty which it conceals in crepuscular moonlight.

Throughout *Scenes and Characteristics* Roberts repudiates the proximate vision which shows only dirt and squalor, the Black Town, or the Anglo-Indian graveyard. The 'gorgeousness of the picture' of Lucknow, for example, 'when visited in detail . . . is obscured by . . . dirt, filth, and squalid poverty' (R. II. 135). The achievement of picturesque distance from India and Indians (as opposed to the uncomfortable circumscription of Anglo-Indians) is illustrated

---

[65] Compare this with a remarkably similar passage on 'landscape ecstasy' in Lt. George Francis White's *Views in India*, betraying Emma Roberts's hand at work: 'It is even more than realising the early dreams of youth, inspired by the perusal of Shakespeare's beautiful description of the forest of the Ardennes, while thus living under the greenwood tree—thus enjoying the contemplation of nature in her wildest and most magnificent solitudes' (pp. 65–6).

[66] See also L.E.L's exercise in the genre in 'The Zenana': 'A tremulous and silvery beam | Melts over palace, garden, stream; | Each flower beneath the tranquil ray, | Wears other beauty than by day | All pale as if with love, and lose | Their rich variety of hues— | But ah, that languid loveliness | Hath magic, to the noon unknown, | A deep and pensive tenderness, | The heart at once feels is its own' (*The Zenana, and Minor Poems*, p. 26).

[67] The moonlight picturesque was not, of course, peculiar to India. See Chard, p. 228: 'a moonlight setting . . . is . . . often described as imposing visual unity upon a scene into which other distracting elements might otherwise intrude' in Grand Tour literature.

in her 'birds-eye view' of Benares: looking down at the bustling city from a minaret, 'the hum of the busy multitude below is scarcely heard'. Unlike Maria Graham, Fanny Parks, and a host of other nineteenth-century women travellers in India, Graham seems content with a distant view of the zenana, maybe in part because of the uncomfortable self-recognition involved in such 'ethnographic' description of female confinement.

Gothic towers open upon luxuriant parterres, affording a more pleasing idea of the seclusion to which the ladies of the city are doomed, than those high, narrow houses, wedged closely against each other, where from the roof alone glimpses may be caught of living trees, where flowers withering in pots convey the only notion which the imprisoned females can obtain of the beauties of nature.   (R. I. 239)

The fate of Indian women seems to mirror that of their Anglo-Indian sisters, ignorant, pampered, and imprisoned in a 'dull monotony enlivened only by the gossip of some privileged old woman' (ibid.). The forceful symbolism of zenana women as withering flowers conjures up by an undesirable parallelism the dusty, sun-baked Anglo-Indian gardens described in an earlier chapter. Roberts perhaps also alludes to a major romantic text of female abjection, John Keats's *Isabella, or, the Pot of Basil*, with its narrative of proscribed female sexual desire metamorphosed into melancholy. The mobility of Roberts's own vocation as tourist and travel writer nevertheless provides an ethnological marker which distinguishes her from incarcerated native women, at the same time as picturesque associationism allows for the articulation of a manageable degree of colonial melancholy.

This combination underpins Roberts's most celebrated picturesque set piece, her 'moving panorama' of the Ganges (K. K. Dyson's 'Ganges-scape')[68] seen from a boat. The river-view at once enforced distance between the observer and the observed, whilst forcefully distinguishing mobile Europeans from immobile Indians.[69] The static repose of the Daniells' Indian picturesque is here replaced by an 'animated' scene prompted (as the title suggests) by the visual technology of Louis Daguerre's diorama, which became popular in Paris and London in the 1820s and 1830s.[70] As if by the play of moving dioramic mirrors, one scene imperceptibly takes the place of another; the bustling river-side ghat, with its Hodgesian 'graceful female forms' carrying waterpots is transformed

[68] Dyson, *A Various Universe*, p. 123.

[69] See Inderpal Grewal, *Home and Harem*, p. 101.

[70] Cf. Fanny Parks's explanatory text for one such Indian diorama, *Asiatic Gallery, Baker Street Bazar, Portman Square. Grand moving diorama of Hindostan, displaying the scenery of the Hooghly, the Bhagirathi, and the Ganges, from Fort William, Bengal, to Gangoutri, in the Himalaya* (London, 1851). Before the introduction of the railway, of course, river travel, and to a lesser extent elephant riding, were the only resources for 'mobile' viewing of Indian landscape. See Archer and Lightbown, p. 154 for a description of Dibdin's and Buss's *Diorama of the Ganges* (1850).

into a 'lofty overhanging cliff' crowned with oriental ruins. Next, a pastoral scene with 'glimpses of rustic villages' raises the illusion that 'these sequestered lanes lead to the cottage-homes of England' (a nostalgia-soaked reference to Felicia Hemans's patriotic lyric 'The Homes of England') until it is dissipated by a herd of buffaloes. Deep forest with elephants is replaced by European stately dwellings, then the 'wild barbaric pomp' of a native city, followed by a 'beautiful pagoda' inhabited by a solitary brahmin (R. I. 272–4).

And so on. More important here than the stereotypical scenes themselves (which could simply describe the experience of flicking through a volume of Hodges or the Daniells' picturesque views) is the kinetic narrative effect, an agency which, without constructing an authorial persona, permits discrete movement from one scene to another.[71] We are now within the realm of Timothy Mitchell's 'exhibitory order' as texts like Roberts's *Scenes and Characteristics* employ a sophisticated 'kinetic' rhetoric to provide the European reader with a 'touristic' substitute for India itself, like other oriental sites increasingly confused with its own representation in the nineteenth-century imperialist imagination.[72]

'A Pencil instead of a Gun': Fanny Parks and Curiosity

At a first glance the title of Fanny Parks's *Wanderings of a Pilgrim in Search of the Picturesque, during four-and-twenty years residence in the East; with Revelations of Life in the Zenana* (1850) seems to conform to the *Quarterly Review*'s desiderata for woman's travel writing. At once collusive with, and yet marginal to, British rule in India, Parks's book proclaims its distance from the masculine project of 'knowing the country' (it is based on letters written home to her mother), focusing instead on the purposeless wanderings of the female picturesque traveller. At the same time as it represents its distance from masculine public life by a studious anonymity (Parks's name only ever appears in the text in Persian letters), it panders to readerly prurience by pledging 'revelations'

---

[71] As Stephen Bann points out, the 'continuous and repetitive process of temporal disclosure' effected by the diorama 'should not be confused with a structured articulation in time . . . it required the specific situation of the museum . . . to convert a mere accumulation of distinct historical elements into an orderly representation of past epochs', *The Clothing of Clio*, p. 62. The transcendental equivalent in travel writing would be 'geographical narrative'. See also Inderpal Grewal, *Home and Harem*, pp. 85–130.

[72] Timothy Mitchell, 'Orientalism and the Exhibitory Order', in *Colonialism and Culture*, ed. by Nicholas Dirks (Ann Arbor: University of Michigan Press, 1992), pp. 289–318. In his *First Impressions* (1837), Thomas Bacon imitates Roberts's 'moving panorama' of the Ganges, asserting that the varied scenes 'will scarcely afford the artist an opportunity of exhibiting his skill in composition, being already as tastefully disposed as if they had been arranged by the design of a painter' (I. 239). So, in a sense, they had.

concerning the zenana, that inner sanctum of Indian female domesticity. Even Parks's title is 'picturesque' to the extent to which it glosses over the sublunary realities of a long Anglo-Indian residence; colonial India is generalized into a vaguely evocative 'East' and romantic high-colouring rescues the book from the tedium conjured up by those 'twenty-four years'.

Closer consideration of the title, however, suggests a satirical sub-text, the Byronic fustian of which (so different from the matter-of-fact titles of most travel narratives) connotes the mock-Spenserian style of *Childe Harold's Pilgrimage* grafted rather elegantly onto the title of William Combe's satirical poem 'Dr Syntax in Search of the Picturesque' (1811). The title's hint that Parks's Indian picturesque (in contrast to the moonlit intensities of *Scenes and Characteristics*) is to be taken with a pinch of salt is supported by her comment: 'I have a great sympathy for Dr Syntax, and perfectly comprehend the delight he took even in a picturesque horsepond. India would have driven him wild;—it is the country of the picturesque.'[73] Although, as we saw in the last chapter, theorists like Payne Knight argued that the picturesque could filter out the bad smells of rural poverty from the painterly scene, in Parks's text aesthetic composure is frequently subverted by her overriding fascination for the grotesque, macabre, and distasteful. Early in the narrative, for example, her curiosity is aroused by the sight of a mendicant who has sat for years with his arms in the air so that 'the nails of the clenched fist had penetrated through the back of the hands, and came out on the other side like the claws of a bird' (P. I. 27). This disturbingly grotesque, metamorphic figure aptly emblematizes her own narrative, a 'curious' disturbance of picturesque stasis which disrupts the taxonomic order of bourgeois Victorian travel writing, while at the same time participating in the colonial 'mobilization' of the distant world.

At the start of *Wanderings*, the 'Pilgrim' invokes Ganesha, the elephant-headed Hindu deity associated with writing, a god whom Sara Suleri reads perspicaciously as 'surrogate for [Parks's] own cultural amalgamation'.[74] But, rather than the Hindu god himself, Parks's invocation is actually addressed to a *statue* of Ganesha which formed part of her extensive collection of 'Hindoo idols' and which sits before her in her English study, 'made of solid white marble, and weigh[ing] 300 weight and a quarter. It is painted and gilt, as in the Frontispiece [where it is illustrated in a coloured plate, see Ill. 12]. It was brought down from Jeypur to the sacred junction of the triple rivers at

---

[73] [Fanny Parks], *Wanderings of a Pilgrim in Search of the Picturesque, during four and twenty years residence in the East; with Revelations of Life in the Zenana. Illustrated with Sketches from Nature*, 2 vols. (London: Pelham Richardson, Cornhill, 1850). Because of the scarcity of the original, I have used the *Oxford in Asia Reprint*, 2 vols., ed. by Esther Chawner (Karachi: Oxford University Press, 1975), henceforth P. in text (P. II. 455). I have failed to track down any contemporary reviews, which suggests that the eccentricity and maybe high price of Parks's *Wanderings* (compared to Emma Roberts, or Emily Eden's *Up the Country*) prevented any wide circulation.   [74] Suleri, p. 84.

श्री गणेशः

SRI GÚNÉSHÚ

12. Fanny Parks, 'Sri Gunesha', *Wanderings of a Pilgrim* (1850), I, frontispiece.

"Prag"',[75] at which place it came into my possession' (P. I. xxv). Despite the book's title, the real object of this pseudo-pilgrim's 'wanderings', it quickly becomes clear, is not so much the picturesque proper (had not Southey insisted that there was nothing 'more anti-picturesque . . . than the mythological personages of the Brahmins'?)[76] as the *curious*. Ganesha's object-status as a 'curiosity' is granted more importance than his mythographical meaning as a deity of violent hybridization and writing. The orientalist vagueness underpinning 'the pilgrim's' self-description as 'the Haji of the East', and the Islamic 'Salam! Salam!' which sounds her praise to a Hindu deity, only betray her text's devotion to the god of a random, syncretizing, and accumulative curiosity.

Whereas male travellers such as Francis Buchanan, John Barrow, or Humboldt mapped out distant space by means of the universal graticules of imperial geography, Parks's collection is assembled within the enclosing (although equally totalizing) bower of the female cabinet of curiosities. Later in her narrative, she melodramatically describes her 'Bottle of Horrors' in which are contained living specimens of 'cobra de capello, scorpions, lizards, millepieds, centipiedes, grillus monstrosus, and I know not what. Mephistopheles himself would be affrighted; and I, the Faust of this Margaret, am sitting in quiet unconcern, smoking my cigar, as happy as if I was one of the party in the bottle, the daily object of admiration' (P. I. 243). Assuming the role of a cigar-smoking Faust (and *not* Marguerite), she transmutes the tedium of Anglo-Indian domesticity into the space of the collection, with her own masculinized self as the final, missing curiosity. (Unlike other European women in India, she frequently dressed in native clothing and enjoyed smoking opium.) She thus inoculates herself against colonial threats 'on the outside' by her Faustian contract with the proscribed horrors which she has collected in her bottle/narrative. *Wanderings of a Pilgrim* staves off the tedium of her 'four and twenty years' in India by perpetuating an 'archaic' culture of Anglo-Indian curiosity within the bloodless genre of the Victorian female picturesque.[77] At the same time, like Emma Roberts's moonlight 'scenes', Fanny Parks's own 'guiltless spoliations' stand as metonyms for a social reality rendered untouchable by the colonial situation. In this sense indeed her Indian idols are 'desacralized' as allegories of colonial ownership.[78]

In contrast to Emma Roberts's narrative self-effacement, Parks aspires to the swashbuckling, egotistical style of 'military tourists' such as Mundy, Skinner,

---

[75] Parks uses a form of the Sanskrit name for Allahabad (Prayaga), her place of residence.

[76] *Southey's Poetical Works, Complete in One Volume* (London: Longman, 1876), p. 543.

[77] The associations between 'archaic curiosity' in Kames's sense (see Introduction) and the 'creolized' culture of Anglo-India are numerous, as in the telling title of (the Anglo-Indian) Seely's *The Wonders of Elora* (my emphasis), quite distinct from the reformist imperialism of the 'survey' and 'picturesque' modalities. A later literary example of the same phenomenon is Lurgan Sahib's 'curious' shop at Simla in Kipling's novel *Kim* (1901), ed. with intro. by Alan Sandison (Oxford University Press, 1987), 152–61.   [78] See Suleri, p. 85.

and Archer. Her recently deceased father, Col. William Archer (not to be confused with Edward Archer, ADC to Lord Combermere and author of *Tours
in Upper India*)[79] had served in the 16th Lancers and distinguished himself in
the Revolutionary and Napoleonic wars. Fanny's husband, Charles Parks, a
shadowy figure in her text, was also a Collector, but of customs duties rather
than curiosities. After a short residence in Calcutta, Charles was posted to
Allahabad where the Parks (who remained childless) lived from 1826 until 1839,
with a four-year spell in Kanpur. After her return to England in 1839, Fanny
Parks spent three years in Europe, rejoining her invalid husband in South Africa
in 1843. They returned to Allahabad for a brief spell thereafter, but ill-health
forced Charles Parks to retire to England in 1845.

Anglo-Indian domesticity, with all its social privileges of thermantidotes,
imported American ice, and a staff of fifty-seven household retainers, was clearly
penury to Parks, particularly in the hot season; in 1828 she complained that 'a
novel and a sofa is all one is equal to during such intense heat' (P. I. 84). As the
sheer accumulation of domestic details which forms a kind of intermittent base-
line to her thousand-page account goes to show, the banal modernity of the
Anglo-Indian household is literally unnarratable: as she wrote in August 1837,
'why should I keep a journal? there is nothing to relate in the monotony of an
Indian life at home' (P. II. 124). As in the case of Emma Roberts, travel provided
the only relief, substituting for some of the pleasures she had forfeited by leaving
England:

> How weary and heavy is life in India, when stationary! Travelling about the country
> is very amusing; but during the heat of the rains, shut up in the house, one's mind
> and body feel equally enervated. I long for a bracing sea-breeze, and a healthy walk
> through the green lanes of England; the lovely wild flowers,—their beauty haunts me.
> Here we have no wild flowers . . .'.   (P. II. 57)[80]

For Parks (in contrast to Elizabeth Eastlake) domesticity acts like a gravitational
pressure, against which the woman traveller must struggle to achieve happiness
and narrative agency.

It is precisely the drive of collection which gives movement to Parks's text as
a corrective both to the dead weight of domestic detail and the dead stasis of
the female picturesque. 'The wandering life is very delightful' she writes; 'I shall
never again be content "to sit in a parlour sewing a seam"; which the old song
gives forth as the height of female felicity! Much sooner would I grope through
a dark alley idol hunting' (P. II. 452). (So much for Eastlake's 'seamstress's
vision'.) Groping through dark alleys is hardly what one would expect from a
'pilgrim in search of the picturesque', but there again neither is joy in the

[79] As Suleri, following K. K. Dyson, mistakenly asserts (p. 83).
[80] Although occasionally (as here) Parks indulges 'centripetal' nostalgia for England, more often her
'curious' imagination works by a reverse, 'centrifugal' movement.

description of mutilated mendicants or the bottling of venomous reptiles. Even Parks's picturesque desideratum of sketching the Indian landscape is compared (by an 'unladylike' analogy) with the hunting world of Mundy and Skinner:

roaming about with a good tent and a good Arab, one might be happy for ever in India: a man might possibly enjoy this sort of life more than a woman; he has his dog, his gun, and his beaters . . . I have a pencil instead of a gun, and believe it affords me satisfaction equal, if not greater than the sportsman derives from his Manton [a brand of sporting gun].   (P. II. 191)

Parks's snobbish discomfort with the role of picturesque tourist (a contrast here with Emma Roberts) is evident in her December 1834 trip to the Taj Mahal. Parks marked her difference from other Europeans bound for the Taj by travelling 'solo' upriver from Allahabad in her boat 'The Seagull' (in fact, she had a 22-man crew and was accompanied by a 'cook-boat') (P. I. 322).[81] The vulgarity of short-stay Britons dancing quadrilles in front of the resplendent tomb is contrasted with her own aristocratic attitude of 'deep devotion' to the memory of the Mughals (P. I. 356). (This exemplifies an Anglo-Indian version of James Buzard's 'cultural economy' 'in which upper class "travellers" competed for pre-eminence by displaying their imaginative capacities, and by attacking that always available enemy, the tourist'.[82]) Whereas picturesque viewing constructed its object through the medium of distance, the 'curiosity hunter' is more concerned with the close-up view, as is evident from the plates representing Parks's collection published in *Wanderings of a Pilgrim* (Ill. 13).

Returning from Europe up-river to Allahabad in 1844, Parks's view of 'Gangescape' was now mediated by a picturesque guidebook, the *Calcutta Directory*, an index of the rise of European-style tourism in India by mid-century. Parks's account of the Ganges is (predictably) a set of skirmishes with the prescribed view. Although dutifully citing the heroic story of Augustus Cleveland at Bhagalpur (P. II. 401) verbatim from the *Directory*,[83] by Benares her patience has run out: 'So much for the "Directory" from which I differ. So far from the distant view of the city giving you the best idea of it,—it is not until you are in the midst of and close to the various beautiful ghats and temples just beyond the minars that you can have an idea of the beauty of Benares' (P. II. 441).[84] Parks's preference for the proximate view develops Maria Graham's but breaks with Emma Roberts's aesthetic as discussed above. In part a gendered

---

[81] Note here her eroticized description of the nearly naked men who composed her 'cannibal crew'.

[82] Buzard, *The Beaten Track*, p. 114.

[83] For the colonial consecration of Cleveland's career in 'taming' the Santhals and the construction of his monument as a tourist site, see Teltscher, *India Inscribed*, pp. 121–4.

[84] Parks's resistance to her guidebook qualifies Inderpal Grewal's rather functionalist account of the genre in *Home and Harem*, pp. 90–104.

On Stone by Major Parlby.

JUGUNNATHU.

13. Fanny Parks, 'Juggunathu', *Wanderings*, II, facing p. 385.

response to the prescriptions of the 'female picturesque', it may also reflect the influence of male artists like George Chinnery and Charles D'Oyly, who had preferred close observation and itimate detail to 'broadcast viewing' of the Hodges and Daniells' stamp. According to Mildred Archer, both these men exerted 'a deep influence on a whole generation of amateur artists in the way they themselves observed India'.[85] At Bindachun, on the same trip, Parks forces her unwilling husband to accompany her onto the steps of the ghat and through the winding streets of the bazaar to the temple (P. II. 452). 'My husband objects to accompanying me . . . because such a crowd collect after me;—he goes along quietly, but with me it is different: the moment I stop to sketch, a crowd collects, and the attendants are obliged to drive them off to enable me to see the objects' (P. II. 455). Here, as elsewhere, Parks revels in her curiosity status as an unveiled 'Bibi Sahib', safe in the knowledge that she has the authority to enforce distance when necessary.

Colonial Politics and Feminism

Fanny Parks had some reason to represent her own hyphenated, Anglo-Indian existence as a kind of freedom. Despite the long stationary years in Allahabad, as a married, childless woman with upper class connections in the European community (she was distantly related to Lady Amherst, wife of the governor-general) and later the Hindu and Muslim communities, she enjoyed a freedom of movement and an access to colonial 'polite society' denied to Emma Roberts.[86] Sara Suleri overstates her case in arguing that Parks was barred from political commentary, turning instead 'to the alternative politics of the picturesque'.[87] On the contrary Parks makes frequent and pointed reference to Company policy, openly criticizing Amherst's adventurist Burmese War in 1824, whilst applauding Lord Combermere's 'resolute' policy in the Upper Provinces against the Marathas. 'We took Bhurtpore [a Maratha stronghold] last night over the whist table, by a *coup de main*; I trust we shall be able to play our cards as well when before it' (P. I. 56), she wrote, wittily domesticating the horrors of

---

[85] *India Observed*, p. 71.

[86] As such, she was personally privy to many of the public events and personalities of her era: she dined with Rammohan Roy in Calcutta, received early news of Reginald Heber's death from her sister in Cuddalore (with whom the bishop had stayed prior to his fatal trip to Trichinopoly); cultivated friendship with the 'picturesque' Col. Gardiner and his Indian family, the royal Begam Hyat-ool-Nissa in the Mughal court at Delhi, and the Maratha Queen Baiza Ba'i, to whom she introduced Emily Eden, sister of Governor-General Lord Auckland during his state visit to Allahabad in Dec. 1837. She also enjoyed the acquaintance of passing celebrities like the Baron von Hugel, the Revd Joseph Wolff, and Ranjit Singh's French *condottiero* Gen Allard; and was enlivened by the periodic scandals which rocked colonial society, such as the murder of William Fraser, British resident in Delhi (friend of Victor Jacquemont), and the execution of the Nawab of Ferosepur, etc.

[87] Suleri, p. 83.

war like a good military daughter. Unlike Emily Eden, whose narrative *Up the Country* remains resolutely silent concerning her brother, Lord Auckland's, disastrous invasion of Afghanistan in 1838 in which 16,000 British soldiers and sepoys were lost,[88] Parks included letters from Afghanistan written by an acquaintance in the 16th Lancers, highly critical of the whole fiasco (P. II. 321–6).[89] As an off-beat Tory who execrated Leigh Hunt and the radicals at home whilst celebrating Lord Byron's romantic spirit of rebellion (P. I. 48), she was openly critical of Amherst's Whig successor, Lord William Bentinck, whose cuts in the vaccination department she blamed for having cost numerous lives (P. II. 110).

Whilst it may be patronizing to Parks, particularly in the teeth of overwhelming evidence to the contrary, to suggest that as a woman she was unable (or unwilling) to comment on politics, it is also true that like other Anglo-Indians she often discussed 'Company policy' as a screen to hide more disturbing questions about the ethics of colonialism. In this respect it would be more accurate to say that 'politics' and the 'picturesque' are *parallel* discourses which served complimentary ideological functions in British India, rather than assuming the latter to be a 'feminized' or aestheticized displacement of the former. Sketching a picturesque Hindu temple at Kanauj in June 1837, Parks was mobbed by a crowd of villagers 'wildly, frantically, and with tears imploring for food; their skeleton forms hideously bearing proof of starvation; the very remembrance makes me shudder' (P. II. 145). Regretting her inability to relieve their sufferings, she apologized that whatever errors appeared in her sketch of the picturesque temple 'must be attributed to the painful scene by which I was surrounded' (P. II. 145). (Contrast this with Lord Valentia's reaction to a similar situation outside Pune in 1805.) (Ill. 14) Parks transmutes her picture from the status of a 'guiltless' into a markedly *guilty* spoliation: an urgent ethical problem (to say the least) is aestheticized into a stylistic blemish in the repose of picturesque representation.[90] Nevertheless it is precisely the *narrative* insistence

[88] The Hon. Emily Eden, *Up the Country: Letters written to her Sister from the Upper Provinces of India*, 2 vols. (1866). With an intro. and notes by Edward Thompson (London and Dublin: Curzon Press, 1978, reprint of Oxford University Press, 1930 edn.). As Indira Ghose points out, it is unclear whether Eden's reticence is a result of the 'evasion of colonial realities or loyalty to her brother' (*Women Travellers*, p. 85).

[89] *Wanderings of a Pilgrim* also played an active role in stoking up the Thug 'information panic', transcribing a lengthy narrative entitled 'Confessions of a Thug' from an official circular in March 1830 (P. I. 122–31). Reversing the recurrent trope of native misrule in independent Awadh, Parks insisted that the 'subjects of his Majesty of Oudh are by no means desirous of participating in the blessings of British Rule. They are a richer, sleeker, and merrier race than the natives in the territories of the Company' (P. I. 184). Like her hero Col. Sleeman (also of Thuggee fame), she was opposed to British annexation of Awadh, in contrast, we might recall, to Emma Roberts.

[90] Parks's comments on the natives of the subcontinent are in general free of the gross racism which mars her account of South Africans, as in her 'picturesque' judgement at the Cape: 'How many of the groups would have formed an admirable picture, in spite of the ugliness of these Malay and Hottentot animals!' (P. II. 359).

ANCIENT HINDU RUIN AT KANAUJ.

14. Fanny Parks, 'Ancient Hindu Ruin at Kanauj', *Wanderings*, II, facing p. 143.

of Parks's book (unlike the disembodied composure of Emma Roberts, whose moonlight picturesque would veil any such disturbance) which permits the bad conscience of the episode to intrude into her text.

Parks is here unable or unwilling to make the connection between the devastating 1837 famine and Lord Auckland's grand march through the Indian countryside (in which she briefly participated) 'accompanied by a train of 12,000 camp followers and their animals, all requiring sustenance'.[91] Emily Eden, travelling with her brother, the governor-general, admitted that 'it seems somehow wicked to move 12,000 people with their tents, elephants, camels, horses, trunks, &c., for so little, but there is no help for it'.[92] She attempted to mitigate the ocean of human misery by adopting 'a miserable little baby, something like an old monkey' and attempting to restore its tiny famished frame to health.[93] Eden's assertion that 'I never ask questions, I hate information' stood her in good stead here, and she solaced herself with the thought that 'we can do no more than give what we do, and the subject is much too shocking'.[94]

An altogether more affirmative instance of Parks's politics is her uncompromising feminism. (She partly modelled herself on Die Vernon in Scott's novel *Rob Roy* (P. I. 62), a female character who dresses and behaves like a man and assumes the unfeminine role of a collector of antiquities, armour, and weaponry.[95]) Parks is particularly vocal on the subject of woman's oppression in England during her reported conversations with another female figure with whom she strongly identified, the deposed Maratha queen of Gwalior HH Baiza Ba'i ('were I an Asiatic, I would be a Mahratta', she wrote admiringly) (P. II. 38). Parks complained to her friend of the miseries of unhappy marriage and the fact that the rigid English divorce laws prevented the 'emancipat[ion] of the white slaves of England' (P. II. 8). The fact that her interlocutor here is a 'colonized' Asian woman, albeit a martial and aristocratic horse-lover conforming to Parks's Byronic image of 'the East', adds to the poignancy of her coupling of marriage and slavery. Later, in a biting subversion of the 'liberal colonial' British critique of sati (banned by Bentinck in 1828), she described 'the lives of some few [English wives] in the higher, and of thousands in the lower ranks of life, [as] one perpetual sati, or burning of the heart, from which they have no refuge but the grave, or the cap of liberty,—i.e. the widow's, and either is a sad consolation' (P. II. 420). The association of widowhood here with a symbol of revolutionary liberty (despite the qualifier, and the ethically questionably

[91] Ghose, p. 48.   [92] *Up the Country*, p. 65.   [93] Ibid., p. 66.
[94] Ibid., pp. 62, 65. As Edward Thompson comments, 'Miss Eden considered that their presence was a blessing rather than a difficulty, since it was good for trade. She never came to suspect the extent to which dependants of an [Imperial] Indian official pillage a country through which they pass' (ibid., p. xi).
[95] See Alexander Welsh, *The Hero of the Waverley Novels, with New Essays on Scott* (Princeton, NJ: Princeton University Press, 1992), pp. 126, 233.

metaphorization of the burning of Hindu women)[96] draws the readers' attention away from sati as a local problem of 'Company policy' to question the hegemonic liberal ideology which oppressed women in Britain and colonial India alike.

The quality of Parks's feminism is put to the test in her visits to the Indian zenana, the 'revelations' promised in her title. As C. A. Bayly has indicated, areas of colonial ignorance such as the zenana, sati, human sacrifice, or 'Thuggee' were breeding grounds for orientalist fantasy (particularly, in this case, erotic fantasy), 'evidence of the limitations of colonial power and knowledge [rather than] the effectiveness of its projection on society'.[97] In this light it is significant that Parks's orientalist account of the zenana is at its most emphatic *before* she has achieved access; her description of the 'minaret view' in Benares, whilst superficially resembling Emma Roberts's discussed above, differs inasmuch as it identifies with male voyeurism rather than female abjection: 'Young men prefer ascending [the minarets] at early dawn, having then a chance of seeing the females of some zenana, who often sleep on the flat roof of the house, which is surrounded by a high wall . . . I thought of Hadji Baba and the unfortunate Zeenab . . .' (P. I. 67).[98] Yet her account of the Mulka Begam, which, as Indira Ghose has indicated, contains a number of intertextual echoes of Lady Mary Wortley Montagu's description of 'Fatima',[99] loses her initial, moralizing tone in its spellbound admiration for Asian beauty: 'I felt no surprise when I remembered the wondrous tales told by the men of Eastern women' (P. I. 383).

Although Parks again invokes male orientalism, but only to internalize her own homoerotic attraction (her dreams are haunted that night by the 'beautiful Begam'), she employs her desire for Mulka as an opportunity for comparing European and Asian women, to the advantage of the latter: 'In Europe, how rarely—how very rarely does a woman walk gracefully! bound up in stays, the body is as stiff as a lobster in its shell; that snake-like, undulating movement,—the poetry of motion—is lost, destroyed by the stiffness of the waist and hip, which impedes the free movement of the limbs' (P. I. 383). Reversing Graham's moralizing perspective, Parks's zenana becomes a touchstone for her feminist analysis of the European negation of womanly freedom (although elsewhere she can sound more negative about Asian women). In contrast to Montagu, she

---

[96] Parks certainly cannot be accused though of having romanticized sati like a number of male travellers (including Hodges). Early in her first volume she relates the gruesome tale of a woman who has escaped from sati, half burned, into the Ganges, as an instance of female heroism (I. 92).

[97] Bayly, *Empire and Information*, p. 171.

[98] Parks's reference here to James Morier's 1828 orientalist novel (set in Persia, not India) heightens the links between male erotic curiosity and orientalism as a 'textual attitude', in contrast to the sort of de-eroticized, socialized vision of the nude female oriental body in Lady Mary Wortley Montagu's *Letters*.

[99] Ghose, p. 58.

excludes personal reference to her own dress in this rather abstract reference to European female stays, although she does remark that 'to the slave girls I was myself an object of curiosity . . . the arrival of an English lady was a novelty' (P. I. 387).[100] Her own reactions seem to internalize the moral ambivalence of the zenana itself, which she describes as 'a place of intrigue' in which 'many conflicting passions are called forth' (P. I. 391).

Curiosity, Collecting, Narrating

'All day long I sit absorbed in modelling little temples, or ghats, or some folly or another, in khuree, a sort of soap-stone. I can scarcely put it aside, it fascinates me so much. I cannot quit my soap stone. Any thing I see, I try to imitate' (P. I. 343). Like many Europeans abroad Parks's struggle against colonial listlessness takes the form of a compulsive mimetic desire, as if internalizing the epistemological imperative of a century of male travel narrative in the absence of any real narrative *content*. Although stationary in Allahabad for much of her time in India, her journal is punctuated by accounts of her 'wanderings', short trips in search of curiosities, the memory of which is solicited by the souvenirs arranged around her as she writes. Susan Stewart argues that 'the souvenir must remain impoverished and partial so that it can be supplemented by a narrative discourse . . . which articulates the play of desire'.[101] A miniaturized, female rewriting of Belzoni's mock-epic of antiquarian acquisition in another 'antique land', Parks's *Wanderings* restores a prodigious narrative existence to her decontextualized metonyms of 'authentic India'. Brass puja vessels, Hindu and Buddhist 'idols' which allegedly contained gems within their heads, 'Thug dice' (illustrated, like 'Juggunathu' in her own hand in 'amateur-ethnographic' fashion as contextless objects dependent upon the accompanying text for their meaning), a huge stuffed albatross, shot Ancient Mariner-style on board ship on the voyage out,[102] 'skulls of alligators, crocodiles, hyenas, and tigers beautifully prepared, to add to my cabinet of curiosities' (P. I. 134), and 'a pair of the most magnificent cow-tails, of the yak or cow of Thibet . . . great curiosities, and shall go with my collection to England' (P. I. 238): the list accumulates throughout her long narrative.

[100]   In this respect Ghose underestimates the degree of influence of Montagu on Parks's text, arguing that Parks, unlike her literary model, fails to 'produce herself as the object of the other's gaze and locate herself firmly in the viewing process' (pp. 58–9). Ghose suggests that 'Parks' gaze serves the colonial policy of "knowing" the other, a strategy to implement an improved surveillance of the colonised' (p. 60).
[101]   Stewart, *On Longing*, p. 136.
[102]   Suleri reads the albatross as a convenient Coleridgean symbol for the guilt of all Parks's future expropriations, albeit a guilt never acknowledged in the text, pp. 86–8.

Arriving back in England on leave in 1839, accompanied by her first cargo of idols, stuffed birds, and buffalo horns, Parks visited the British Museum to compare collections. Despite the improvements since her previous visit nearly two decades before, she was unimpressed by the South Asian collection:

the new rooms that have been added are handsome, and well filled with Egyptian curiosities; mummies in crowds, and very fine ones. The Elgin Marbles . . . are also shown to great advantage. My collection of Hindoo idols is far superior to any in the Museum; and as for Gunesh, they never beheld such an one as mine, even in a dream! Nor have they any horns that will compare with those of my buffalo, or birds to vie with my eagles, which are superb.   (P. II. 334)

Arranged without reference to context and provenance, the museum's Indian specimens lack narrative, as well as the private collector's increment of nostalgia which seem to bring her souvenirs to life.[103] Parks's challenge to the British Museum anticipates Walter Benjamin's remark (in 'Unpacking My Library') that 'the phenomena of collecting loses its meaning as it loses its personal owner. Even though public collections may be less objectionable socially and more useful academically than private collections, the objects get their due only in the latter.'[104] As Nicholas Thomas writes of an earlier epoch, to which Fanny Parks's collecting mentality is nostalgically linked (in contrast to the nineteenth-century 'museum order'), 'the relationship between exotic objects and knowing subject was profoundly hermeneutic—a thing could not be considered a curiosity without reference to the knower's intellectual and experiential desire'.[105]

In contrast to the standard 'Hindu Pantheon' which was a common feature of earlier Indian travelogues, Parks's mythography simply itemizes the attributes of her collection. To quote Stewart again, the 'souvenir reduces the public, the monumental, and the three-dimensional into the miniature, that which can be enveloped by the body, or into the two-dimensional representation, that which can be appropriated within the privatized view of the individualized subject'.[106] Asked by an English correspondent for information concerning Hindu deities, she replied 'Shall I send them the names of the three hundred gods which are interwoven in silk and gold on the janéo I wear around my neck, to which is appended the key of my cabinet [of curiosities]?' (P. II. 147). Orientalist scholarship (and she cites Thomas Maurice, William Jones, and Edward Moore with learned authority) is miniaturized and safeguarded next to her skin

[103] Compare with Bernard Cohn's analysis of Rakhal Das Halder's account of visiting the India Museum at Fife House in 1862, and his viewing the empty throne of Ranjit Singh. *Colonialism and its Forms of Knowledge*, p. 105.
[104] *Illuminations*, p. 67.
[105] Thomas, 'Licenced Curiosity', in *The Cultures of Collecting*, ed. by John Elsner and Roger Cardinal, p. 122.
[106] Stewart, pp. 137–8.

as a token of desire, like a love-locket. Only she possesses the key which will open the secrets of her cabinet. In common with the popularizing 'presentism' of Belzoni and Bullock, Parks's discourse is based upon a metonymic, rather than metaphorical (philological or historicist), trope of curiosity based upon personal possession and contact.

Like other European travellers in India, Parks frequently bought or stole statues and carvings from their original sites in or around temples. Although Forbes, Valentia, Mackenzie, Mackintosh, Heber, and others all succeeded in licitly or illicitly acquiring such curiosities, the collection of antiquities was not as common in India as in Egypt, Italy, or Greece, partly because many temples were still sites of worship supervised by Brahmins who kept a watchful eye on European visitors.[107] Moreover, as the fate of Mackenzie's 'Amaravati Marbles' goes to show, aesthetic interest in Hindu, Jain, and Buddhist antiquities was limited, and there was still little demand for Indian sculpture in the great metropolitan collections.[108] In the acquisition of such objects, Parks by her own account showed all the stealth and ingenuity of a tiger-hunter. At Kanauj, for example, despite being nearly mobbed by starving villagers, she managed to 'pick up a curious piece of ancient sculpture, Mahadeo, with Parvati in the centre, and a devi on each side, which I brought to my tent on the elephant' (P. III. 145). As with Belzoni's account of the smiling bust of Rameses at Thebes, Parks employs *prosopopoeia* in describing her idols: burying the Kanauj sculpture under a peepal tree, she planned to pick it up on her return journey 'if it will please to remain' (P. II. 145). On her 1844 trip upriver to Allahabad she accumulated numerous 'Kalsas' (clay ornaments from the top of sati tombs) and two 'idols in black stone' which she exchanged for a gift, rather than bought, from an old fisherman under cover of night, so that he could not reproach himself for 'selling his gods' (P. II. 418). Parks's colonial curiosity here appears as a strange double of the sort of Hindu 'superstition' and idolatry censured in European discourse, based as it is on an 'irrational' mania for collecting, animating, and fetishizing the identical objects worshipped by 'heathen' colonial subjects.

The declining appeal of 'picturesque' India for the Victorian imagination— exacerbated by the events of 1857—ensured that 'the literature of India produced in England now became even more what to some extent it always had been, a literature intended for that specialist public which had lived and worked

---

[107] As described in Seely's *Wonders of Elora*, p. 192.

[108] Two of the most famous virtuosi of the Regency period, Charles Townley and Richard Payne Knight, both possessed Indian sculpture groups and other objects connected with Hindu worship. But, as Partha Mitter points out, they were less interested in their aesthetic than their iconographic value, particularly their relation to erotic lingam and yoni worship which Payne Knight and d'Hancarville supposed to be the origin of all religious symbolism (*Much-Maligned Monsters*, pp. 84–104).

in India, and learned to love it'.[109] It is perhaps ironic that the self-portrait with which Fanny Parks closes her long, thousand-page narrative evokes the stasis of domesticity against which she has struggled so vigorously during her Indian years:

And now the pilgrim resigns her staff and plucks the scallop-shell from her hat,—her wanderings are ended—she has quitted the East, perhaps for ever;—surrounded in the quiet home of her native land by the curiosities, the monsters, and the idols that accompanied her from India, she looks around and dreams of days that are gone. (P. II. 496)

Like travel narrative itself, the exorbitant objects in her collection now assume a completeness and an order which they never could have done in India, having successfully recalled 'days that are gone', in the bourgeois retirement of St Leonard's by the Sea. In a bold reversal of the sort of nostalgia frequently evoked by the Indian picturesque, Parks's 'unhomely' curiosities still have the power to undo the binding spell of British domesticity and (albeit privately) connect the collector with the freedoms of her wandering, 'creolized' past. In contrast to the threatening role of Indian curios in much Victorian fiction (Wilkie Collins's *Moonstone*, or the trophies of 'Pondicherry Lodge' in Arthur Conan Doyle's *The Sign of Four*), Parks's objects signify a private liberty, albeit one contingent upon privileges of social class and collusion in the project of colonial acquisitiveness. At least Fanny Parks's narrative of collection, in deploying the unlicensed, libidinous, and unfeminine discourse of curiosity, resists the blank and deadly detachment enjoined by the *Quarterly Review* upon the domesticated British woman abroad.

[109] Lightbown, *India Observed*, p. 125. As Lightbown indicates, the orientalist artist David Roberts (author of the highly successful *Picturesque Sketches in Spain* (1837) and *The Holy Land* (1842–9)) was commissioned to work on a lavish volume of Indian lithographs entitled *The Oriental Portfolio*, which collapsed after only two numbers in 1840 due to lack of public interest (ibid., pp. 122–5). This perhaps signals the fading of the Indian picturesque, heralding, over the next twenty-five years, 'the substitution of more truthful and more photographic but also more prosaic illustrations in true Victorian spirit' (ibid., p. 128).

6

Alexander von Humboldt and the
Romantic Imagination of America:
The Impossibility of Personal Narrative

> America began to be richer for us the other day, when Humboldt came
> back and told us of its luxuriant and gigantic vegetation; of the myriads
> of shooting lights, which revel at evening in the southern sky; and of that
> great constellation, at which Dante seems to have made so remarkable a
> guess.
>
> Leigh Hunt, 'On the Realities of Imagination'

On 1 August 1804 the ship *La Favorita* anchored off Bordeaux after a 27-day
Atlantic crossing from Philadelphia. On board was the Prussian *savant* and
explorer Alexander von Humboldt and his *compagnon de voyage*, French
botanist Aimé Bonpland, returning to wide celebrity in Europe after their
privately financed five-year expedition to the Spanish colonies of tropical
America.[1] Writing to his old friend K. K. Freiesleben from on board the same
day, while awaiting quarantine clearance, Humboldt described his return
journey from Mexico via Cuba and the United States. With uncharacteristic
egotism, he boasted that

> my expedition of nine thousand miles in the two hemispheres [of the Americas] has
> been incomparably felicitous. I have not once suffered illness, and I feel healthier,
> stronger, more industrious, and happier than ever. I bring back thirty-five crates laden
> with botanical, astronomical and geological treasures; it will take me many years to
> publish my great work . . . It is with great sorrow that I have left the splendid world

---

[1] The death of his mother in 1797 left Humboldt (and his brother Wilhelm) heirs to the family
fortune. Alexander consumed the whole of his share in financing his travels and publishing the results
after his return to Europe. For details, see the standard biography by Hanno Beck, *Alexander von
Humboldt* (Wiesbaden, Franz Steiner Verlag, 1959–61). I use the Spanish language translation throughout: *Alexander Von Humboldt* (Mexico City: Fondo de Cultura Económica 1971). Hereafter Beck.
(Translations my own.)

of the Indies, but the idea of seeing you again, of returning to embrace you one day
. . . holds an infinite attraction for me.[2]

Although the travellers had originally hoped to complete a circumnavigation
of the globe, the wear and tear suffered by their formidable array of scientific
instruments, as well as their fear of losing touch with the rapid march of
the physical sciences in Europe, prompted an early return. If Humboldt and
Bonpland's journey had taken nearly five years, the publication of their
textual odyssey would take over thirty.

Humboldt's journey through the tropical rainforests, river systems, and
llanos of Venezuela and Colombia, the Andean *cordilleras* of Ecuador and Peru,
the mountainous mining districts and pre-Hispanic pyramids of Mexico, and
the sugar haciendas of Cuba was only possible due to the support of the Spanish
king, Carlos IV, who had granted a passport to Humboldt in his public role as
chief inspector of mines for Ansbach-Bayreuth to Friedrich Wilhelm III of
Prussia. Shortly after his return to Paris, in August 1804, Humboldt met the 21-
year-old Simón Bolívar, thereby forging an adamantine link with the imminent
cause of Latin American independence.[3] Nevertheless, while in the Americas
he travelled, as David Brading has indicated, 'as the spokesman of the Bourbon
Enlightenment, the approved medium . . . through which the collective inquiries of an entire generation of royal officials and creole savants were transmitted to the European public, their reception assured by the prestige of the
editor'.[4] Humboldt is thus a deeply paradoxical figure: despite his aristocratic
gift of charming royalty (ironically, for the remainder of his life after 1827, bankrupted by his publishing project, he would serve as a chamberlain to the Prussian king), he long retained the revolutionary enthusiasm which had impelled
him to visit Paris in 1790 with his mentor, George Forster, whose *Voyage Around
the World* I discussed in Chapter 1, and who vitally influenced Humboldt's own
travel writing. While in Paris, the young Prussian savant had loaded sand in a
wheelbarrow to help construct the Temple of Liberty (Beck, p. 40).[5] Humboldt
and Bonpland's decision to leave war-torn Europe in 1799 and travel to the New
Continent was also in many ways politically motivated. In *Aspects of Nature*
Humboldt echoed Rousseau's *Reflections of a Solitary Walker* in describing
how the botanizing traveller, 'amidst the unreconciled discord of nations, seeks

---

[2] Alejandro De Humboldt, *Cartas Americanas*, trans. by Marta Traba, compiled, selected, and
edited by Charles Minguet (Caracas, Biblioteca Ayacucho, 1980), p. 119. This is now the most up-to-
state scholarly edition of Humboldt's American correspondence in any language, with excellent
annotations and bibliography. Hereafter CA.

[3] See Beck, p. 244. As Mary Louise Pratt has shown, Humboldt's life and works became a fundamental resource for 19th-century Latin American creole self-fashioning. (*Imperial Eyes*, pp. 172–97.)

[4] David Brading, *The First America: The Spanish Monarchy, Creole Patriots, and the Liberal State,
1492–1867* (Cambridge University Press, 1991), p. 517.

[5] George Forster commemorated this journey in his *Ansichten vom Niederrhein*, inspiration for
Humboldt's own *Ansichten der Natur*. The former is described by Hanno Beck as stimulating a new
form of descriptive, 'geographical' travel writing in Germany (Beck, p. 41).

for intellectual calm, gladly turn[ing] to contemplate the silent life of vegetation, and the hidden activities of forces and powers operating in the sanctuaries of nature'.[6]

Nicholas Rupke has recently argued that the 'local circumstances' of the production and reception of Humboldt's textual *Voyage* resulted in the variations in the meanings and emphases attributed to its constituent parts.[7] It is of great significance that Humboldt elected to return to the Paris of Cuvier, Lagrange, Lalande, Laplace, Gay-Lussac, capital of European science and culture, rather than to Prussia or Spain.[8] His own intellectual personality embodied a rare attempt to synthesize the holistic idealism of Goethe, Schiller, and German *Naturphilosophie* with the quantitative and materialistic approach of late-enlightenment French physics, a fact which has led to conflicting claims from his German and French biographers.[9] Humboldt's neo-classical allegory on the vital force, *Der Rhodische Genius*, had been published in Schiller's journal *Die Horen* in 1797, although (in contrast to his more conservative-minded brother Wilhelm) Alexander enjoyed a closer rapport with Goethe, who could better appreciate his attempt to balance idealism with empirical research. Yet, as Michael Dettelbach has demonstrated, 'Humboldt's global physics appears [rather] at every point attached to a Laplacian agenda [of precision measurement] and to the institutions that embodied it in mathematical and observational practice'.[10] This present chapter is concerned with this constitutive tension in Humboldt's travel writing, a sophisticated version of the struggle between literary modes of travel writing and 'geographical narrative' which has been a recurrent theme of this

[6] *Aspects of Nature, in Different Lands and Different Climates; with Scientific Elucidations*, trans. by Mrs Sabine, 2 vols. (London, 1849), I. 26. (This was the first English translation of Humboldt's popular *Ansichten der Natur*, 1808, unusual in that it was written in German rather than French.) Henceforth AN. Humboldt's letters from America to French colleagues bore the date of the new revolutionary calendar, and well into the era of Bourbon Restoration, his disciple J. B. Boussingault described him defiantly sporting the blue coat, yellow waistcoat, and striped pantaloons which had been fashionable during the Directory (CA, p. 237).

[7] 'A Geography of Enlightenment: The Critical Reception of Humboldt's Mexico Work', in *Geography and Enlightenment*, ed. by David N. Livingstone and Charles Withers (University of Chicago Press, 1999), pp. 319–39.

[8] In so doing, of course, Humboldt and Bonpland courted the displeasure of Napoleon, who resented the fact that the celebrity of the returning travellers, announced in the *Moniteur* for 12 August 1804, was stealing fire from his imperial coronation, scheduled for 2 December.

[9] See Michael Dettelbach, 'Global Physics and Aesthetic Empire: Humboldt's Physical Portrait of the Tropics', in *Visions of Empire: Voyages, Botany, and Representations of Nature*, ed. by David Miller and Peter Reill (Cambridge, 1996), pp. 258–92. The allegorical frontispiece of the German text of Humboldt's *Ideen zu einer Geographie der Pflanzen* (Tübingen, 1807), dedicated to Goethe, depicts Apollo, god of poetry, unveiling the Ephesian Diana, representing Nature. Lying at the foot of Diana's plinth is a stone tablet bearing the title of Goethe's great botanical work, *Metamorphosen der Pflanzen*. 'Hanno Beck ne cite ni Diderot, ni l'Encyclopedie, dans sa biographie de Humboldt', complains Charles Minguet in insisting upon a dominant French rather than German influence on Humboldt's thought, in his *Alexandre de Humboldt: Historien et Geographe de l'Amérique Espagnole* (Paris: Francis Maspero, 1969), p. 65.

[10] Michael Dettelbach, 'Global Physics', p. 280.

book. I argue that Humboldt's work represents the nemesis of the 'curious' travel account in its concern with mapping global uniformities, and bringing wonder under the discipline of the newly formulated aesthetic.

Although, as we saw in Chapter 2, precision instruments were essential prerequisites for the eighteenth-century scientific traveller, Humboldt lent new expertise to the practice of measurement. This Laplacian emphasis on measurement is evident both in his careful account of his instruments in the Introduction to the *Personal Narrative* and the visual representation of his results in the form of isoline maps.[11] In this respect, Humboldt differed greatly from his compatriots: Goethe insisted that the unassisted eye was sufficient to embrace the totality of phenomena, deriding dependence upon what he called 'Kunstliche instrumente'.[12] In a letter of 6 August 1797 Schiller more radically attacked the intrusive rationalism which he saw underlying Humboldt's project of wresting measurements from a nature 'always incommensurable, venerable and unfathomable in all her aspects' (Beck, p. 120). Only in the Paris of the Institut de France, the Observatoire, and the Société d'Arcueil could Humboldt and Bonpland find the technical expertise necessary to execute the monumental task of publishing the results of their five-year expedition. Humboldt's choice of location, as well as his decision to write his travels in French (all the more marked at a moment when his German contemporaries were reinventing a German national identity through language) were more than just gauges of his intellectual cosmopolitanism.[13]

The *Physical Portrait of the Tropics* and *Aspects of Nature*

The publication of Humboldt's thirty-volume *Voyage aux régions équinoxiales du Nouveau Continent, fait en 1799, 1800, 1801, 1802, 1803, 1804* (Paris,

---

[11] See *Personal Narrative of Travels to the Equinoctial Regions of the New Continent, During the Years 1799–1804. Written in French by Alexander De Humboldt and Aimé Bonpland, and translated into English by Helen Maria Williams*, 7 vols. (London, 1814–29), I. 33–9. (Hereafter PN.) For further discussion of Humboldt's instruments, see Ramon Sanchez Flores y Max Seeberger, 'Humboldt y sus instrumentos científicos', in *Alejandro Humboldt en México*, ed. by Frank Holl (Mexico City: INAH, 1997), pp. 55–66. Dettelbach writes that 'Humboldt was the first to use extensively and systematically the techniques of isoline cartography. Upon his return in 1804, he coined the terms *isodynamic, isogonics,* and *isoclines* to denote lines of equal magnetic intensity, declination, and inclination' (Global Physics, p. 261). See also Dettelbach, 'Humboldtian Science', in *Cultures of Natural History*, ed. by N. Jardine, J. A. Secord, and E. C. Spary (Cambridge, 1996), pp. 290–1 for a more qualified account of his debt to Laplace; and Anne Godlewska, 'From Enlightenment Vision to Modern Science? Humboldt's Visual Thinking', in *Geography and Enlightenment*, pp. 236–75.

[12] Minguet, p. 72.

[13] Obliged to return to Berlin in 1805, Humboldt complained in a letter to Delambre of the isolation which he felt 'in the middle of this desert that saw me born!', describing the intellectual life of the Prussian capital as 'bear[ing] the character of northern regions. We extend the hibernal sleep until the summer' (Dettelbach, 'Global Physics', p. 281).

1805–34), accompanied by 1,425 plates and maps, has itself assumed mythic proportions in the history of scientific travel writing. A largely private enterprise, this cost in printing and paper of the 1,300 folio pages of copper-plate illustrations alone came to 840,000 francs, nearly twice that of the state-funded French *Description de l'Égypte*.[14] For Humboldt even more than earlier travellers the ability to 'mobilize' the experience of exotic travel back to his native Europe was as important as the fact of travelling itself. In what follows I propose to examine some of the highlights of the *Voyage*, in chronological sequence, in order to gauge Humboldt's contribution to romantic travel writing and his success or failure in integrating personal narrative with the scientific overview. The ability to represent his experience of tropical lands in visual or verbal form for the benefit of a metropolitan public (what Humboldt called 'giving animated pictures of distant regions')[15] was likewise of fundamental importance. In *Cosmos* (1849–59), Humboldt remembered the impression made upon his youthful mind by tropical representations encountered at large in Europe which had first stimulated his desire to travel further afield; his reading of George Forster's travel account of the South Pacific, William Hodges' picturesque views of the Ganges (seen at the home of Warren Hastings during his visit to England in 1790), and 'a colossal dragon tree in an old tower of the Botanical Gardens in Berlin' (Cosmos II. 372). In all the works he published subsequent to his return from the Americas in 1804, Humboldt sought to create a 'tropical aesthetic' for the European mind, on the grounds that 'the nobler and grander forms of nature' and 'the luxurious fullness of life in the tropical world' create a stronger impression of the interplay between the physical and moral realms, and the occult harmony of nature in all regions of the world (Cosmos II. 454).[16]

Developing the romantic 'cult of the south' promoted by Winckelmann's predilection for sunny Mediterranean skies over northern gloom and, in the Weimar circle by Goethe's *Italian Journey* of 1787, Humboldt's poetic evocations of a luxuriant tropical America sought to supplement the inwardness, rigour, and melancholy which he associated with harsher northern climes. Schiller had argued for a creative equilibrium between 'bracing' and 'melting' beauty in his 1794–5 *Letters on Aesthetic Education* (first published, like Humboldt's *Rhodische Genius* in *Die Horen*). For Humboldt's brother Wilhelm, the eminent Prussian philologist and statesman, Schiller's 'equation of human

---

[14] Karl Bruhns, *Life of Alexander von Humboldt*, 2 vols. (London, 1873), II. 20. The cost of the fully bound *Voyage* was 10,300 francs, again twice that of the *Description*. Douglas Botting, *Humboldt and the Cosmos* (London: Michael Joseph, 1973), p. 213.

[15] *Cosmos: A Sketch of a Physical Description of the Universe*, 5 vols. trans. by E. C. Otte (London: Bohn, 1849), II. 434. Hereafter Cosmos.

[16] For an excellent account of European attitudes to tropical nature in general, and Humboldt's contribution in particular, see Richard Grove, *Green Imperialism: Colonial Expansion, Tropical Island Edens, and the Origins of Environmentalism, 1600–1860* (Cambridge University Press, 1995).

advancement, freedom, and beauty, . . . [led to identification] of the Greeks with the ideal of individual self-cultivation'.[17] Although (as I shall argue below) Alexander's thinking about the development of civilization was also powerfully marked by Weimar Hellenism, initially at least he sought a more inclusive geocultural ideal. The tropics represented the geographical equivalence of Schiller's 'melting' beauty, the sensuous orientation of the playdrive modifying the excessive formalism and rationalism of the modern European subject.[18] Extending aesthetic to geographical equilibrium, Humboldt proposed to Europeans (in the words of Mary Louise Pratt) 'a new kind of planetary consciousness'[19] cognizant of the distinct geographical environments of the world, which might enable them to intuit the invisible harmony guiding the workings of nature. As we shall see, however, such a 'disinterested' cosmopolitanism— itself, of course, a product of European spatial/temporal construction—proved hard to sustain in a world increasingly dominated by the expansion of Western power and capital.

At Jena in 1795, four years before setting out for America, Humboldt had conducted a series of experiments on galvanism and animal electricity, assisted by his lover, a Prussian guardsman named Reinhard von Haeften. Simon Schaffer and Michael Dettelbach have described some of these masochistic self-experiments' arguing that self-experimentation 'patently violated the distance between observer and object so carefully policed by Enlightenment systems of witnessing and authorising [representing] the emergence of a new form of scientific authority, the creative genius'.[20] Humboldt's rigorous South American expedition represented another sort of self-experimentation 'in the field': alongside his constant astronomical and terrestrial measurements and observations made with eudiometers, hygrometers, and cyanometers, he studiously gauged his own sensibility in relation to the ever-varying environmental stimuli of the tropics. In the Humboldtian version of romantic imagination, aesthetic and emotional responses to natural phenomena counted as data about these phe-

---

[17] Suzanne L. Marchand, *Down from Olympus*, p. 26.

[18] *On the Aesthetic Education of Man*, ed. and trans. with an intro. and commentary by Elizabeth Wilkinson and L. A. Willoughby (Oxford: Clarendon Press, 1967), Letter 16, p. 115. 'The man who lives under the constraint of either matter or forms is, therefore, in need of melting beauty; for he is moved by greatness and power long before he begins to be susceptible to harmony and grace.' Reciprocally, 'the man who lives under the indulgent sway of taste is in need of energising beauty' (ibid.); translated into geographical terms, this might be taken to apply to the natives of the torrid rather than the temperate zone.

[19] *Imperial Eyes*, p. 120.

[20] In one such experiment, caustic plasters were applied to Humboldt's back in order to raise large blisters and remove the skin; he then galvanized his wounds and recorded the effects and sensations on his body . . . he reopened the wounds frequently for demonstration. Dettelbach, 'Romanticism and Administration: Mining, Galvanism, and Oversight in Humboldt's Global Physics'. (Unpublished Ph.D. thesis, Cambridge University, 1993), p. 88. See also Schaffer, 'Genius', in *Romanticism and the Sciences*, p. 92.

nomena,[21] in contrast to their rigorous exclusion from contemporary practices of naval and military surveying. This, of course, added an experiential and psychological dimension to Humboldt's practices of travel, the erotics of which Michael Shortland has described as 'a mixture of more or less repressed homosexuality and more or less explicit sado-masochism', citing several episodes in the *Personal Narrative* which seem to dwell upon an indistinguishable congeries of pain and pleasure.[22] Despite his desideratum, Humboldt's *difficulty* in integrating 'personal narrative' with objective observation in the *Voyage* is a major theme of this chapter.

In order to recapture the sublime 'enjoyment' derived from the experience of tropical America (the obverse of the masochistic travail of mobile 'self-experimentation'), to represent the *unseen* nexus of physical laws which harmonized apparently diverse environments, Humboldt's *Aspects of Nature* plundered the aesthetic resources of picturesque travel writing, landscape painting, and popular exotic displays:

Individual plants languishing in our hot-houses can give but a very faint idea of the majestic vegetation of the tropical zone. But the high cultivation of our languages, the glowing fancy of the poet, and the imitative art of the painter, open to us sources whence flow abundant compensations, and from whence our imagination can derive the living image of that more vigorous nature which other climes display. In the frigid North, in the midst of the barren heath, the solitary student can appropriate mentally all that has been discovered in the most distant regions, and can create within himself a world free and imperishable as the spirit by which it is conceived. (AN II. 31)[23]

Although Humboldt had made himself famous as a traveller by his conquest of geographical distance, in his writings he sought to internalize global space in the minds of 'stationary' metropolitan readers. In one sense his project echoes Kant's famous claim for the transcendental ideality of space: 'there is only one space'. As Edward Casey comments, 'whether located outside the human subject or within, [for Kant] space stays the same: absolute and infinite, homogeneous and unitary, regular and striated, isotropic and isometric'.[24] Humboldt's romantic notion of the mirroring of the physical and moral worlds develops the notion of planetary consciousness as a disinterested freedom of spirit which permitted the European subject to transcend the 'accidental' determinations of birth and environment. Decisively breaking with the nostalgic

---

[21] Malcolm Nicholson, 'Alexander von Humboldt and the Geography of Vegetation', in *Romanticism and the Sciences*, ed. by Andrew Cunningham and Nicholas Jardine (Cambridge University Press, 1990), p. 180.

[22] *Eros and Kosmos: Making Knowledge with Alexander von Humboldt*, pre-circulated draft paper for 'New Perspectives on Alexander von Humboldt', International Symposium, Göttingen, 29–31 May 1997.

[23] This was largely reworked from the *Essai sur la géographie des plantes* (Paris, 1807), pp. 34–5.

[24] *The Fate of Place*, p. 193.

associationism characteristic of the British imperial picturesque (as studied in Chapters 4 and 5), Humboldt denied that the imagination of the cultivated individual was 'rivetted to the soil, or confined to any single region' (AN II. 31). Humboldt's own citizenship of Prussia 'which has no direct communication with the colonies of either India' (PN I. 3) seemed to offer the possibility of a disinterested and truly cosmopolitan representation of tropical America. His privately funded travels and travel writings—in contrast to most of the others considered in this book—were not directly connected to European colonial expansion. Nevertheless, such spatial freedom (itself considered as the condition of 'progressive' civilization) was implicitly premised upon the appropriation of Europe's tropical Others for whom such a planetary consciousness was envisaged to be impossible, at least in their current state of cultural development. Although Humboldt openly campaigned against slavery and denounced racism as 'the depressing assumption of superior and inferior races of men' (*Cosmos* I. 368), he nevertheless subscribed to a common nineteenth-century notion of uneven development in which the advancement of the West (defined as the progressive cultural legacy of Hellenic civilization) served to calibrate the backwardness of the rest of the world.

Humboldt boasted in his letter to Freiesleben, quoted above, that he had collected an almost unprecedented number of specimens (even in the first seven months of their expedition, the two men had dried over 4,000 plants, as well as describing 800 new or practically unknown species) (CA p. 119). The Introduction to his *Personal Narrative* describes the pains which he had taken to form duplicate collections to be dispatched to diverse 'centres of calculation' in Paris, Madrid, and London, as well as the problems of carrying his delicate instruments and his mineral, botanical, and ethnographic 'mobiles' across the Andes on the backs of twenty mules (PN I. xii). But Humboldt subordinated the necessary tasks of discovery, measurement, and collection to the project of constructing what he called a new 'physique du monde' or 'global physics'. As he declared in an address to the Berlin Academy in 1806:

Little has been done by travelling naturalists [*reisende Naturforscher*] for the physical description of the earth, or rather for the physics of the globe, because almost all of them are concerned exclusively with the descriptive [*naturbeschreibenden*] sciences and with collecting, and have neglected to track the great and constant laws of nature manifested in the rapid flux of phenomena.[25]

Although Humboldt had already pioneered research in chemistry, galvanism, and geology in his native Germany and later in France, the most immediate and significant achievement of research undertaken in Spanish America was his work on the geography and environmental relations of plants.[26] In a sense Hum-

[25] Quoted in Dettelbach, 'Global Physics', p. 260.
[26] See Malcolm Nicholson, 'Humboldt and the Geography of Vegetation', pp. 169–88.

boldt's manifesto for plant geography (here quoted from the Introduction to the *Personal Narrative*) sums up the holistic and aesthetic programme of his 'global physics' as a critique of singularity and curiosity:

Preferring the connection of facts, which have been long observed, to the knowledge of insulated facts, although they were new, the discovery of an unknown genus seemed to me far less interesting than an observation on the geographical relations of the vegetable world, on the migration of the social plants, and the limits of the height which their different tribes attain on the flanks of the cordilleras.   (PN I. iv)

Replacing the idea of the *botaniste nomenclateur* with that of the *botaniste physicien*, Humboldt defended his study of the spatial distribution of plants against the taxonomies of the Linnaean tradition, as well as developing the ramifications of plant geography for the understanding of zoological, meteorological, and cultural phenomena. His rejection of the singular 'insulated fact' and the itemizing, anecdotal, narrative of the curious traveller (he mischievously associated Linnaean systematics with 'archaic curiosity') represents a sophisticated critique of the 'curious' eighteenth-century travelogue discussed in the early sections of this book. At the same time, his distinctive style of travel writing is radically different from the 'survey modality' of Constantin Volney, Francis Buchanan, or Lord Valentia, in its concern to stimulate the aesthetic sense of the reader. Rather than dwell on isolated forms, Humboldt preferred to consider 'the picturesque character of vegetation over the entire surface of the globe, and the impression produced on the mind of the beholder by the grouping of contrasted forms in different zones of latitude or elevation' (AN II. 205). The aesthetics of planetary consciousness create, in the words of Anthony Pagden, 'stable global contexts for differing cultures'.[27] Transcontinental uniformities of geological formation or barometric isolines, no less than the organized diversities of plant distribution, map the inner freedom of the sensitive romantic psyche onto the physical space of the planet, holistically conceived.

Humboldt described how he had published the *Essai sur la géographie des plantes* as the first fruit of the expedition, rather than a brief résumé in the form of a 'personal narrative', on the grounds that 'I believe that it is more philosophical to opt for nature "en grande" than to recount my own personal adventures. [The *Essai*] indicates what I've achieved . . . proving that my researches have encompassed the totality of phenomena, and above all [it] speaks to the imagination' (CA p. 127). As we shall see below, this marks the beginning of the suppression of anecdotal 'personal' travel narrative in Humboldt's opus. Amidst the welter of comparative observations and the typology of landscapes, there seems little space for the persona of the traveller himself, or for the episodic, dramatic narrative of his travels. Despite his self-conscious scrutiny of his own travelling sensibility, Humboldt is only ever present in the text as a

[27] *European Encounters with the New World* (Yale University Press, 1993), p. 37.

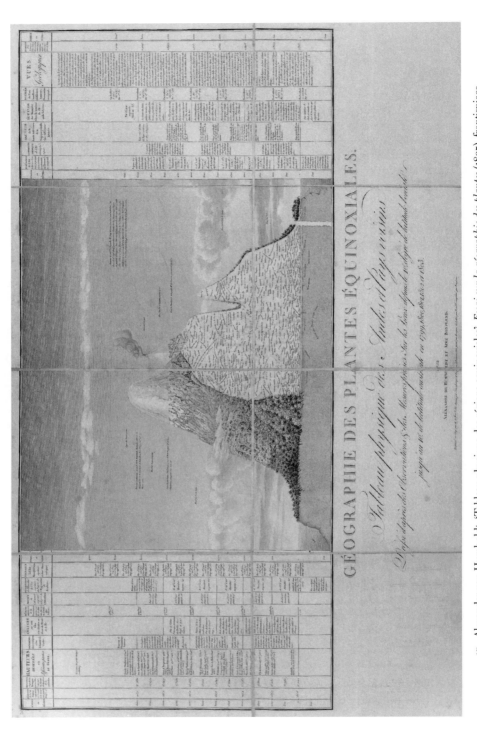

15. Alexander von Humboldt, 'Tableau physique des régions equinoxiales', *Essai sur la géographie des plantes* (1805), frontispiece.

transcendental self, whose own excursive 'planetary consciousness' offers a reflexive history of the holistic relationship between nature and the development of human culture.

This is well exemplified in the *Essai sur la géographie des plantes* by the huge fold-out 'Tableau physique des régions equinoxiales', depicting a cross-sectional profile of the Andes from the Atlantic to the Pacific at the latitude of Chimborazo, which encompasses in graphic form the whole project of the *Voyage* (Ill. 15). Because it has been thoroughly studied by historians of science,[28] I discuss it here only in so far as it offers a visual analogue to some of the representational problems which we shall encounter in discussing Humboldt's personal narrative proper. True to his aim of borrowing from the techniques of landscape painters, Humboldt's 'Tableau physique' ('tableau' translates as 'Ansicht' in German; 'Aspect' in English) depicts the changing vegetational environments from the tropical coastline to the snows on the summit of Chimborazo, as well as (in the more expensive hand-coloured aquatint version) the delicate gradations of green on the mountain slopes and the deepening blue of the tropical skies. True to the desideratum of his idea of 'plant geography', Humboldt images the total environmental distribution of individual plants rather than simply cataloguing species and genera in isolation, the synchronic harmonies and contrasts of which lend a specifically 'local tint' to the Andean mountainscape.

Unlike the huge coloured plate of Chimborazo which appears as the centrepiece of his *Vues des Cordillères*, Humboldt's 'Physical Portrait of the Tropics' breaks the normal conventions of landscape representation (the picturesque or the sublime) in its bid to synchronize 'toutes les recherches dont je me suis occupé pendant mon expédition aux tropiques'.[29] The whole right half of the mountain's surface has been cut away in order to present a *tabula rasa* upon which to record the Linnaean (as well as some indigenous) names of plants growing at different altitudes, entailing a sudden transition from figurative to 'descriptive' representation. Moreover, the mountainous profile is framed by sixteen tabular columns which digest all the results of Humboldt's scientific observations and measurements of Chimborazo, from blueness of the sky, measured by Saussure's cyanometer, to the comparative elevation of other mountain peaks, providing comparative figures which allow the particular case to be generalized on a global scale. In one striking *coup d'oeil*, Humboldt seeks to combine an aesthetic 'tableau' of tropical nature with an encyclopaedic digest of quantitative information which is the result of five years' worth of field observation and measurement, as well as of metropolitan 'combination' in Bruno

[28] See, e.g. Dettelbach, 'Global Physics', pp. 268–72; and Malcolm Nicholson, 'Humboldt', p. 178.
[29] *Essai sur le géographie des plantes, accompagné d'un tableau physique des régions équinoxiales, et servent d'introduction a l'ouvrage* (Paris, 1807), p. 41.

Latour's sense.[30] The 'Physical Portrait' thus aspires to combine aesthetics with a sort of scientific hyper-text, illustrating Humboldt's bid (in Mary Louise Pratt's words) to 'reframe bourgeoise subjectivity, heading off its sundering of objectivist and subjectivist strategies, science and sentiment, information and experience'.[31]

The question remains, however—largely unaddressed by commentators—to what extent Humboldt succeeded in this synthesizing project, or whether the aporetic imposition of botanical graffiti onto the (disfigured) surface of the mountain disrupts rather than harmonizes the visual unity of the whole. Although contemporary maps frequently borrowed figurative elements from topographical drawing, it was unusual for landscape representation to borrow from cartography in this way. Like Wittgenstein's famous duck/rabbit, the 'Physical Portrait' can be only either figurative or schematic at one moment, but never both at once. As Humboldt himself confessed, 'the unbounded riches of Nature occasion an accumulation of separate images; and accumulation disturbs the repose and the unity of impression which should belong to the picture' (AN I. viii). Professor John Leslie, writing in the *Edinburgh Review* in April 1810, was uncertain what to make of this 'very curious and instructive drawing . . . perhaps too much crowded with names and with detached notices; but the originality of the design and the general skilfulness of its execution, deserve high commendation' (ER, 31, (April 1810), 242–3). Ironically, Humboldt's *Tableau* is here praised for its curiosity and novelty rather than its aesthetic or scientific accomplishment.

Humboldt returned to tackle the problem of aesthetic versus scientific representation (albeit this time in the medium of language), in the popularizing work which he published in 1808 entitled *Ansichten der Natur*, simultaneously translated into French as *Tableaux de la Nature*.[32] Based on public lectures given in Berlin in 1806 and 1807, after Napoleon's defeat of the Prussian armies at Jena, each of the 'Ansichten' dilated upon one 'typical' South American topography: 'Steppes and Deserts'; 'The Cataracts of the Orinoco'; or 'The

---

[30] Back in Paris, the astronomer Delambre provided the tables of refraction, Gay-Lussac calculated and corrected Humboldt's hygrometric and eudiometric readings, J.-B. Biot standardized the table of light intensities, whilst the great Laplace himself calculated the scales correlating barometric pressure with elevation' (Dettelbach, pp. 280–1).

[31] Pratt, p. 119.

[32] Robert van Dusen in his *Literary Ambitions and Achievements of Alexander von Humboldt* (Herbert Land Bern, Peter Lang, Frankfurt am Main, 1971), writes that 'the term "Ansichten" implies the concept of intuitive contemplation. We have seen in [George] Forster's work, *Ansichten vom Niederrhein*, a quality of intuitive visualisation ascribed to travel reports. Humboldt uses the same power of visualisation when he evaluates the information gathered from his travels' (p. 36). Van Dusen also indicates the poor quality of contemporary German landscape description 'adhering to artificial idyllic pastoral-romances and didactic poems' (p. 53), which Humboldt set out to reform by drawing upon the scientific study of the earth's surface.

Nocturnal Life of Animals in the Primeval Forests', derived from fragmentary jottings from Humboldt's field journals subsequently 'moulded into a whole' (AN I. vii).[33] Untrammelled by the generic demands of the 'personal narrative', Humboldt could expatiate upon the single 'striking scene' or 'tableau', allowing nature as it were to speak for itself unshackled by authorial egotism. As with Emma Roberts's 'Ganges-scape' discussed in Chapter 5, the kinetic quality of natural description here seems to borrow from popular illusionistic shows like de Loutherbourg's Eidophusikon (1783) or Charles Willson Peale's 'perspective views, with changeable effects, of nature in motion' (Humboldt met Peale and visited his museum in Philadelphia in 1803).[34]

Particular passages of the book (apparently Humboldt's own special favourite among all his publications) (Beck, p. 258) became fundamental to the nineteenth-century's image of South American nature: the coming of the rains to the *llanos*, the dried earth cracking from torpid crocodiles, and water-snakes buried in desiccating mud; the 'picturesque' spectacle of terrified horses rearing, half-stunned by gymnoti (electric eels) at Calabozo; earth-eating Otomac Indians on the banks of the Orinoco; the foaming cataracts of Atures and Maypure; or the cave of Ataruipe 'the burying place of a deceased nation' of Indians (AN I. 228). In the 'Nocturnal Life of Animals in the Primeval Forests' Humboldt analysed the stylistic requirements for this kind of writing, emphasizing 'simplicity in the narration of what we have ourselves beheld or experienced, and by limiting and individualising the locality with which the narration is connected' (AN I. 261). Mary Louise Pratt has insightfully analysed the dynamic prose of *Aspects of Nature*, noting how active verbs are all governed by invisible natural forces rather than human agency, indicating the erasure of the human. Nobody seems to inhabit these 'melancholy and sacred solitudes' apart from the transient 'hypothetical and invisible European traveller himself' (Pratt, p. 125). The traveller internalizes the landscape, rather than being internalized by it.

Nevertheless, the picturesque 'striking scene' is revealed to be a means to an end rather than an end in itself. Humboldt here once again assumes that purely aesthetic enjoyment provides a kind of stimulus to cultivate 'insight into the more hidden connection of the different powers and forces of nature'. To this end each of the 'Aspects' is glossed by endnotes, scientific 'elucidations and

---

[33] Further essays on 'Volcanoes', and the 'Plateau of Caxamarca' were added to the 2nd and 3rd editions, along with reprints of miscellaneous earlier works such as the *Rhodian Genius*. Surprisingly, the work was not translated into English until 1849; Mrs Sabine's translation was based on the 3rd German edition. Another translation was published by Bohme in the following year.

[34] For an account of Peale's moving pictures, see Susan Stewart, 'Death and Life, in that Order, in the Works of Charles Willson Peale', in *The Cultures of Collecting*, ed. by John Elsner and Roger Cardinal (Reaktion, 1994), p. 216. For Humboldt's meeting with Peale in 1804, see Beck, p. 232 (Peale's name is here misprinted as 'Teale').

annotations', as the English translator expressed it. Like the tabular columns flanking the 'Portrait' or the isomorphic maps that synthesized Humboldt's scientific measurements in graphic form, 'generalisation of physical views, and the statement of general results, belong rather to the "study of the Cosmos", which, indeed, must ever continue to be a science of Induction' (AN I. 261). Although the texts of the essays remained essentially the same in successive nineteenth-century editions (subject to the increments mentioned above), the endnotes were revised in accordance with the progress of scientific research; in the third edition Humboldt announced that 'almost all . . . [had] been either enlarged or replaced by new and more comprehensive ones' (AN I. xiii). Dedicated to 'minds oppressed with the cares or sorrows of life' (AN I. ix) at a time of national crisis and humiliation, the *Aspects of Nature*, like Schiller's *Spieltrieb* or aesthetic play-drive, ushers the fragmented, post-enlightenment European subject back to a higher unity with the natural world, conceived as a global totality.[35]

Humboldt and the Dispute of the New World

What justification can there be for concluding 'From an antique land' with a chapter on Humboldt, whose vision of the '*New* Continent' is aptly described by Mary Louise Pratt as 'dramatic, extraordinary nature, a spectacle capable of overwhelming human knowledge and understanding'?[36] Humboldt seemed to endorse such a view of America when he wrote, in the Introduction to his *Personal Narrative*, that 'in the ancient world, nations, and the distinctions of their civilisation formed the principal figures on the canvass; in the new, man and his productions almost disappear amid the stupendous display of wild and gigantic nature' (PN I. xliii–xliv). There is no doubt that Humboldt perceived Columbus's discovery of the New World as a momentous event for the Old, poised as it was 'on that uncertain border where the Middle Ages and the modern age merge with one another'.[37] Pagden has demonstrated Humboldt's appropriation of Columbus as one of his own intellectual ancestors, in bringing the New World home to the Old, and thereby initiating the modern age.[38] But this emphasis on the discovery (and romantic *re*discovery) of America as nature

---

[35] For the 'Spieltrieb', see Schiller's *Aesthetic Education*, Letter 14, pp. 95–9. Humboldt's 'planetary consciousness' in a sense resembles his brother Wilhelm's plan for the University of Berlin in which the external role of the state was limited to providing the organizational framework for nurturing the individual's aesthetically based 'bildung'. See Elinor Schaffer, 'Romantic Philosophy and the Organisation of the Disciplines: The Founding of the Humboldt University of Berlin', in *Romanticism and the Sciences* (eds.), A. Cunningham and N. Jardine (Cambridge University Press, 1990).

[36] Pratt, p. 120.

[37] *Examen critique de l'histoire de la géographie du Nouveau Continent*, 5 vols. (Paris, 1836–9), III. 9.

[38] Pagden, pp. 107–8. See also Anne Godlewska, *Geography Unbound: French Geographic Science from Cassini to Humboldt* (University of Chicago Press, 1999), pp. 276–7.

rather than culture,[39] its sole historical importance lying in its role as a catalyst for European renaissance and modernity, overlooks a crucial aspect of Humboldt's account of America. As a characteristically romantic traveller, it might indeed have been hard for Humboldt to see America as anything other than an 'antique land', which everywhere bore the material traces of indigenous high cultures violently destroyed in the holocaust of the Spanish conquest, but whose survivors still composed a significant proportion of the American population. In positing Humboldt's travels as the historical *ricorso* of Columbus's voyage of discovery,[40] we should not overlook their more immediate historical context, the enlightenment polemic described by Antonello Gerbi as 'the dispute of the New World'.[41]

As Gerbi's erudite study makes clear, Humboldt's opus was partly aimed at vindicating the American continent and its inhabitants from criticisms made by enlightenment savants. The Comte de Buffon, the Abbe Raynal, and William Robertson had all insisted that America was more recently formed and immature than the rest of the planet, whilst Cornelius de Pauw, in *Recherches philosophiques sur les Américains* (Berlin, 1768), had described its inhabitants as degenerate and debilitated. Buffon's thesis was particularly influential, building on the error which seemed to confuse the 'recent' discovery of America by Europeans in a relative sense with its 'novelty' in an absolute sense:

the greater part of the American continent [is] a new land, in which nature has not had time to carry out all her plans . . . the men are cold and the animals small, because the ardour of the men and the size of the animals are dependent on the healthiness and the warmth of the air . . .[42]

Leaving his concern with the inhabitants of the New Continent and the antiquity of their culture to one side for a moment, Humboldt's account of the dynamism and sublimity of American nature alone takes on considerable

[39] Pratt stresses this aspect of Humboldt's identification with Columbus by quoting the latter's famous letter to the Spanish monarchs in 1493 describing the natural wonders of the island of Juana (p. 126).

[40] Perhaps the most famous statement of the Humboldt/Columbus identification was that of the German geographer Karl Ritter who, in 1844, hailed him as the 'scientific rediscoverer of the New World . . . for the cultivated European world' (Beck, p. 237). As Jaime Labastida rightly stresses, rather than being a 'discoverer' in the Renaissance sense, Humboldt was more interested in establishing a scientific evaluation of the planet as whole, a project which would culminate in *Cosmos* ('Humboldt y La Antropología en México', in *Alejandro De Humboldt en México*, ed. by Frank Holl (INAH/Instituto Goethe, Mexico City, 1997), p. 138. In the *Personal Narrative*, Humboldt wrote that 'being a man of the 15th century, [Columbus] was not always so humane, as he is said to be in the 18th century from hatred of his detractors' (PN VI. pt. 1, 34).

[41] Antonello Gerbi, *The Dispute of the New World: The History of a Polemic, 1750–1900*. Revised and enlarged edn. trans. by Jeremy Moyle (Pittsburgh: Pittsburgh University Press, 1973). For an account of the role of America in the development of the Scottish Enlightenment 'Four Stage theory', of social development, see Ronald Meek, *Social Science and the Ignoble Savage* (Cambridge University Press, 1976).

[42] *Ouevres complètes*, XV. 455–6. Quoted in Gerbi, p. 14.

polemical significance when seen in the context of 'the dispute of the New World'. Before we denounce Humboldt for complicity in dehumanizing and deterritorializing America's indigenous inhabitants by 'naturalizing' the New Continent, we should first acknowledge his crucial role in constructing a more positive image of Spanish American nature *and* culture in post-enlightenment Europe. In doing so he made common cause with American creole intellectuals like José Granados y Gálvez, Francisco Clavigero, or Pedro José Márquez, a fact which explains his (continuing) lionization in Latin America.[43]

In a passage often repeated throughout his various publications, Humboldt described how 'after a long voyage, we tread for the first time the soil of a tropical land, we experience a certain feeling of surprize and gratification in recognizing, in the rocks that surround us, the same inclined schistose strata, and the same columnar basalt . . . that we had left in Europe . . . But these rocky masses of schist and of basalt are covered with vegetation of a character with which we are unacquainted' (Cosmos I. 5).[44] For Pagden, this description of the geological structure of the continent illustrates Humboldt's 'principle of attachment'; like his isolines, isotherms, and global uniformities, it represents the triumph of uniformity over differences between tropical and temperate nature.[45] In what follows I shall argue for an analogous balancing act in Humboldt's description of American high cultures, a desire at once to grant America parity with Europe and Asia as an 'antique land' but also to insist upon its cultural *difference* from, and hierarchical subordination to, Europe.

An analogous but now anthropological 'principle of attachment' is evident in Humboldt's description of Carib Indians observed in Cumana: 'the strongest and most muscular people I have ever seen; sufficient alone to refute Raynal and De Pauw's strictures concerning the weakness and degeneration of the human species in the New World. An adult Carib resembles a Hercules cast in bronze' (CA p. 72).[46] Whilst the aesthetic comparison resembles the temporal-

---

[43] It is only to fair to the creole intelligentsia to acknowledge that the exiled Mexican Jesuit Clavigero's *Storia Antica del Messico* (1780–1) had already, long before Humboldt, related the 'cult of Aztec antiquity to the social problems of the contemporary Indians' and contributed to 'liquidate the influence of [de Pauw's] *Recherches philosophiques*'. Benjamin Keen, *The Aztec Image in Western Thought* (New Brunswick, NJ: Rutgers University Press, 1971), pp. 299–300.

[44] Humboldt's geological 'principal of attachment' doubtless served to rationalize the wonder which (conventionally enough) overpowered the travellers upon first landing at Cumana: 'Bonpland assures me that he will go mad if these marvels don't stop presenting themselves to us soon', he wrote to his brother on 16 July 1799 (CA p. 14).

[45] Pagden, *European Encounters*, pp. 26–7.

[46] Cf. also his 'temporalizing' account of his first sight of a canoe full of Guayqueria Indians (PN II. 41). Humboldt had a particular predilection for Caribs, whose 'confederated tribes' he likened to 'ancient Germany', imbued with 'the spirit of liberty' (PN VI. pt. 2, 40), and who are favourably contrasted to other indigenous societies of the Orinocan region like the Otomacs and Chaymas. This selective idealization conforms with Peter Hulme's account of the 'good versus bad Indian' binary in his chapter 'Caribs and Arawaks', although interestingly with the Caribs now in the positive rather than

izing trope of European travellers in India studied in Chapters 4 and 5, it also manifestly requires to be understood in specific relation to the 'dispute of the new world'. Temporalization 'attaches' the unfamiliar to the familiar, and in so doing legitimizes American culture as 'classical' rather than primitive, against the censures of the philosophes. The statuesque, bronze, metaphor for classical culture here serves an analogous function to the description of the geological substructure in the natural world. This is also evident in Humboldt's complex allegorical frontispiece to the 1814 *Atlas géographique et physique . . . du Nouveau Continent*, engraved by Barthelemy Roger after a drawing by François Gerard (Ill. 16). Mercury, the god of commerce, helps a fallen Aztec prince to his feet while Minerva, goddess of letters, proffers the olive branch of peace and prosperity. The motto of this strange, eclectic image is a quotation from Pliny's 'Letters': 'Humanitas. Literae. Fruges'. Global equilibrium, achieved through the restoration of America by European (that is to say neo-Hellenic) commerce, husbandry, and learning, is here represented in a classical, temporalized idiom which embraces both hemispheres, although Europe's gift seems to allow for little reciprocity, obscuring the enormous historical dependence of the Old World upon indigenous American crops and agriculture in the wake of the conquest.

Gerbi argues (in an unintentionally revealing turn of phrase) that Humboldt's writings performed the 'peaceful conquest and intellectual annexation' of America by 'Western Thought', for which it had hitherto been merely 'an object of curiosity, amazement, or derision'.[47] We have seen how for Humboldt (like Schiller, whose poem 'Auf den Bergen ist Freiheit' he quotes in the Introduction to *Aspects of Nature*)[48] the aesthetic insight into the global uniformity of nature was conceived as a refuge from the political conflict which was currently dismembering Europe (and its overseas colonies), and its envisaged resolution by peaceful means. In a letter to Caroline von Wolzogen of 14 May 1806 Humboldt attributed to Goethe and the spirit of Jena romanticism the informing insight that, whether in the heart of the Amazon rainforests or the slopes of the Andes, 'the same breath animates the same life-force from one pole to another in rocks, plants and animals, as well as in the dilated breast of man' (CA p. 143). Humboldt's planetary consciousness thus 'matched Schiller's vision of an

negative position (*Colonial Encounters: European and the Native Caribbean 1492–1797* (London and NY: Methuen 1986), pp. 45–87).

[47] Gerbi, p. 408. Pratt's claim that Humboldt 'by no means saw his work as grounded in the debate [about America] or subsumed by it' rests on Gerbi's statement (which she quotes) that his position in the dispute is 'anomalous' and 'somewhat marginal', exercising only a 'belated and lateral influence' (p. 120). But Gerbi seems to contradict himself in the statement quoted above: Humboldt's position can only be seen as anomalous in comparison with that of Hegel, of much greater importance to Gerbi's book.

[48] See Dettelbach, 'Global Physics', pp. 272–7.

Voy. de Humb. et Bonpl.

HUMANITAS. LITERÆ. FRUGES.

Plin. jun. l. VIII. Ep. 24.

16. Alexander von Humboldt, 'Humanitas. Literae. Fruges.' *Atlas géographique et physique . . . du Nouveau Continent* (1814), frontispiece.

aesthetic empire, where men will be led to a new and most lasting union beyond the state'.[49]

Thanks to the sophisticated techniques of quantification developed by French science, Humboldt was able to plot in systematic manner the lawfulness of the planetary life-force in isoline maps, just as he was able to evoke the imaginative qualities of the tropics in poetic prose. Humboldt attacked the primitivism and anthropomorphism of the supposedly 'enlightened' detractors of America, such as Buffon, De Pauw, and Robertson, identified here with the *curiosi* of a prescientific age more concerned with the singularity and wonder than the harmonious lawfulness of the globe.[50] He was equally impatient with Hegel, who in the *Encylopaedia* and in *Lectures on the Philosophy of History* argued that

the existence of the new world became actual through the connection created when it was discovered, and so brought into the general system of peoples. This discovery was fortuitous however, and its recency is not the only factor in the newness of the continent, for everything within it is new. No continent of the old world has been coerced by another, while America is merely part of Europe's booty.[51]

Writing to Varnhagen in July 1837 Humboldt admired the 'world of ideas' offered to him by Hegel's *Philosophy of History*, but added 'to a man like me, who has examined the earth and the differences of nature with minute attention, such an abstract statement of facts and completely false opinions concerning America and the Indies depresses me and robs me of spiritual freedom' (CA p. 207).

In his striking evocation of the dense, uninhabited rainforests between the Cassiquiare and the Atabapo in 'Steppes and Deserts', Humboldt comments that 'figures graven on the rocks shew that even these deserts too were once the seat of some degree of intellectual cultivation' (AN I. 25). Consistently critical of attempts (such as Rousseau's, in his *Discourse on the Origin of Inequality*) to interpret Carib and Cheyma Indians—not to mention the 'high cultures' of Mexico and Peru—as noble savages at the dawn of civilization, he preferred to describe them as 'wandering hordes, separated by the differences of languages

---

[49] Pagden, p. 115.

[50] In a note to 'Steppes and Deserts', Humboldt criticized the primitivism of the supposedly enlightened detractors of America: 'Fantastic images of . . . terrestrial youth, and unrepose . . . on the one hand, and on the other . . . of increasing dryness, and inertia in maturer age, — could only have presented themselves to minds more inclined to draw ingenious and striking contrasts between the two hemispheres, than to strive to comprehend, in one general view, the construction of the entire globe . . . There exists no reason for assuming one entire side of our planet to be older or newer than the other' (AN I. 137–8).

[51] *Enzyklopedie*, pp. 350–1. Trans from Hegel's *Philosophy of Nature*, ed. and trans. by M. J. Petry (London: Allen and Unwin, 1970), III. 24. For Hegel's belated involvement in the 'dispute of America', see Gerbi, ch. 7.

and manners, and scattered like the remains of a vast shipwreck' (PN III. 209). Not only were they *not* children of nature, but the complex structure of native American languages showed them to be descendants of a much higher civilization, of which their language was the sole remaining monument (PN III. 242; VI. Pt 1. 14). In contrast to his description of America as the 'New Continent' in the title of his *Personal Narrative*, Humboldt rather sought to represent it as an 'antique land' bearing everywhere the same traces of classical culture as other hemispheres, as well as traces of a nature which had undergone transformations and convulsions identical to those of the rest of planet. This historical uniformitarianism is manifest in Humboldt's next two publications to be discussed here: the *Essai politique sur le royaume de la Nouvelle Espagne . . . avec un atlas de 20 cartes* (1808–11); and the *Vues des Cordillères et monumens des peuples indigènes de l'Amérique* (1810), principally dedicated to the social, cultural, and historical aspects of equinoctial America.

The *Political Essay on New Spain*

Both the *Essai politique* and the *Vues des Cordilleres* are represented by Humboldt as outgrowths of the *Personal Narrative*, which (in 1810) he still seemed reluctant to write, for reasons which will be considered below. In his Preface to the *Essai politique*, Humboldt confessed that the geographical and statistical materials which he had gathered during his sojourn in the capital of New Spain—much of it originally collected by order of the reformist Spanish viceroy Count de Revillagigedo during the years 1789–94[52]—had swelled to too great a volume to be included in the long-promised personal narrative of his travels. Nicholas Rupke's recent bibliometric analysis of Humboldt has shown that the *Essai* was the most widely reviewed and (in immediate terms) the most influential of all his writings, appealing directly to European political and economic interests[53] in the half-century after its publication, in part due to the unforeseen event of Latin American independence, which opened a window of opportunity for European and N. American capital. But Rupke's extrapolation from his analysis that 'the sanitized image of Humboldt as a cosmopolitan universalist

---

[52]   For a detailed account of these sources, see José Miranda, '*El Ensayo Político sobre el Reino de la Nueva España*: Razón, Entidad, Transcendencia', in *Ensayos sobre Humboldt* (UNAM: Mexico, 1962), p. 38. Brading points out that 'the weakest section of the *Essai politique* dealt with agriculture and domestic industry, areas of activity on which the Bourbon bureaucracy had collected few statistics . . . Humboldt depended heavily on the availability of systematic documentation and, where such sources were not forthcoming, he was reduced to the general observations and personal impressions of any traveller' (*The First America*, p. 531). See Humboldt's *Political Essay on the Kingdom of New Spain*, trans. by John Black, 4 vols. (London, 1811), i. 2. Henwforth PE in text.

[53]   Rupke, p. 335.

is of a later date and does not fit the original Humboldt'[54] is not entirely fair to the published text. The first sketch of Humboldt's *Essai*, 'Tablas geografi-copolíticos del reino de la Nueva España', was published in Mexico in December 1803 and dedicated to the Viceroy Iturrigaray.[55] John Black, English translator of the *Political Essay* (1811), criticized Humboldt's frank admission of dependence upon Mexican sources on the (dubious) grounds of prepossession in favour of his subject-matter: 'even Dr Johnson . . . would have hesitated to read his Tour to the Hebrides to his Scotch landlords' (I. vi). Seen from the perspective of Anglo-Saxon capitalist expansionism, this compromised Humboldt's authority. The *British Review*, in its essay on the American explorer Major Montgomery Pike's *Expedition to the Source of the Mississippi and the Interior Parts of New Spain* (1810) preferred Pike's wildly inaccurate data on Mexico to Humboldt's because it was not dependent on mendacious Hispanic sources.[56] Nevertheless, Humboldt's *Political Essay* was the fundamental inter-text for all British and North American travel accounts concerned with Mexico both in the 1820s mining investment boom and thereafter well into mid-century.

Humboldt's early training in the Hamburg Commercial Academy and as a state bureaucrat for the Prussian king had certainly familiarized him with a statistical approach to geography, but he disliked the term and regretted the fact that his 'sterile tables' of Mexican commercial and mining statistics were considered of more value than 'all that imagination or science could offer', especially in Britain, Napoleon's 'nation of shopkeepers' (CA p. 140). In the book's Introduction Humboldt strove to distinguish his *Essai* from statistical surveys (such as Francis Buchanan's *Journey through Mysore*, although the book is not mentioned by name) which depended on war and colonial annex-ation (PE I. iv). Although subsequent abridgements of the *Essai* reduced the ethnographical, social, and historical sections in order to highlight its com-mercial and mining information, in fact the original *Essai* aspired to be a qual-itative analysis of the cultural, as well as a quantitative analysis of the economic condition of Spain's wealthiest colony.[57] On the one hand, Humboldt sought, contra Raynal and Robertson, to emphasize the sophistication, modernity, and wealth of New Spain, praising the stylish neo-classical buildings of the capital, its Academy of Arts, and recently founded Mining Academy. The achievements of Novohispanic savants like José de Alzate, Miguel Velásquez de León, and

---

[54] Ibid.   [55] *Ensayos sobre Humboldt*, p. 259.
[56] In his Introduction to the *Personal Narrative*, Humboldt later censured Pike's inaccuracy (PN I. xxix–xxx).
[57] Miranda, p. 40. Jorgé A. Vivo Escoto describes it as 'the first work of modern regional geogra-phy referring to a single country', examining its links with the geographical principles of Varenius, Kant, and Ritter. 'La Obra de Humboldt en México, Fundamento de la Geografía Regional Moderna', in *Ensayos sobre Humboldt* (Mexico City: UNAM, 1962), p. 170. Escoto perhaps overlooks Sir John Sinclair's *Statistical Survey of Scotland*.

Antonio de León y Gama demonstrated that 'Mexico participated in the universal culture of the Enlightenment'.[58] As a producer of silver Mexico had outstripped Peru and in the 1770s nearly doubled its production, its whole mining industry propelled forward by a combination of entrepreneurial skill, capital input, and a well-paid work-force, so that by 1803 it exported some 10 million pesos a year to Spain in fiscal tribute, and as such was easily Spain's most prosperous colony.[59] Little wonder that such a flourishing picture encouraged aspirations to independence among creole élites as well as whetting the appetite of European and North American capitalists. As we saw in Chapter 4, much British travel writing about India in this period was ideologically opposed to a creolized Anglo-Indian identity. Humboldt's travel writing about Spanish America had exactly the reverse effect in empowering 'creole self-fashioning' and stimulating nationalism in colonial Mexico.

The British East India Company were possibly cognizant of this fact when in 1821 they refused Humboldt's request to be allowed to study Sanskrit texts in Banares and mount a scientific expedition to the Himalayas (Beck, pp. 279–88). They also, doubtless, feared that Humboldt would expose the negative side of British rule in India as he had done Spanish rule in America. For, alongside its praise for the prosperity and reformist energy of New Spain, the *Essai* was deeply critical of the social and political arrangements that had prevailed since the conquest: 'Mexico is the country of inequality. No where does there exist such a fearful difference in the distribution of fortune, civilisation, cultivation of the soil, and population' (PE I. 184). Although, as in the *Aspects*, Humboldt's narrative persona is minimized amidst the plethora of statistical information, his sympathy for the plight of the indigenous inhabitants as victims of European imperialism, offering everywhere 'a picture of extreme misery' (PE I. 185), at times breaks the surface. 'The inhabitants of Mexico and Peru, and the Indians of the Ganges', he wrote, 'attract in a very different manner from the Chinese and Japanese the attention of an observer endowed with sensibility. Such is the interest which the misfortunes of a vanquished people inspires, that it renders us frequently unjust towards the descendants of the conquerors' (PE I. 140). Humboldt refuted the (still evergreen) European prejudice that few members of the 'copper-coloured race' had survived the Spanish conquest, showing that on the contrary the indigenous population numbered over two and a half million, had been on the increase for the previous half-century, and currently formed two-fifths of the entire population of New Spain (PE I. 131). The low state of intellectual cultivation among them, however, he attributed to

---

[58] Brading, p. 527. 'In Mexico City there have been two translations of Lavoisier's *Elements of Chemistry*, in Madrid, not one . . . Mexico City resembles Berlin but is more beautiful, with a severer style of architecture', Humboldt wrote on 17 May 1808 to Conrad Malte-Brun (CA p. 149).

[59] Brading, p. 529.

the surviving legacy of the conquest, which had simply wiped out the educated classes of the Aztec Empire, and the ill-treatment which they had suffered since. 'If all that remained of the French or German nation', he wrote, 'were a few poor agriculturists, could we read in their features that they belonged to nations which had produced a Descartes and Clairaut, a Kepler and a Leibnitz?' (PE I. 157). Citing the example of Tupac Amaru's Andean revolt of 1781 in which the indigenous peasantry had nearly deprived the king of Spain of all his mountainous regions (PE I. 200) and cleared the region of Europeans, in the same decade as Britain lost her American colonies, he warned of the pressing need to liberalize the social and economic conditions of the Mexican *indígenas* and integrate them with the rest of Novohispanic society. Regrettably, of all the sections of the *Essai* this would prove the least influential, although similar complaints concerning the conditions of the *castas*, the mixed-race strata of Mexican society, and the inferiority of the American-born *criollos* to the Spanish *peninsulares*, would resonate more strongly during the coming independence struggle.[60]

Researches Concerning the Institutions and Monuments of the Ancient Inhabitants of America

In the *Political Essay* Humboldt had declared his original intention of presenting his researches into American antiquities in 'the historical account of our expedition to the tropics' (PE I. 140).[61] Only as part of 'the narrative of my journey' (he later explained) can they be meaningful 'since, as the nations to whom these edifices and sculptures are attributed still exist, their character, and the knowledge of their manners, will throw light on the history of their migrations' (Res. I. 38). Humboldt's own personal interactions as a traveller with modern native Americans are here credited with providing deeper insight into the meaning of pre-hispanic culture and antiquities than any consideration based on purely scholarly or comparativist criteria. This desideratum, as well as the *Essay*'s powerful indictment of the condition of contemporary Mexican *indigenas*, must qualify Mary Louise Pratt's blanket statement that 'the

---

[60] Writing in the 1820s, he argued that whereas African-Americans had taken an active part in the Independence Wars, 'the copper-coloured race [i.e. the Indians] in its timid distrust, and mysterious passiveness, has remained a stranger to the movements from which it must profit in spite of itself' (PN VII. 268). This completely ignores the fact that many combatants in the independence struggle were conscripted Indians who gained little (and sometimes lost out) in the transition from Spanish to *Criollo* rule.

[61] Note that Black here chooses to translate the French 'rélation historique' as 'historical account', whilst the approved English translation of the *Rélation historique du voyage* (1814–25) by Helen Maria Williams rendered it as 'personal narrative'.

European imagination produces archeological subjects by splitting contemporary non-European peoples off from their precolonial, and even their colonial, pasts'.[62] Humboldt's appreciation of the inventive syncretism of Mexican culture and the adaptability of indigenous traditions is exemplified by his marvellous, Gibbonesque, description of the great prehispanic *teocalli* at Cholula, now topped by the church of the Virgin of Remedios:

from [the platform of the pyramid] the eye ranges over a magnificent prospect; Popocatapetl, Iztaccihautl, the peak of Orizaba, and the Sierra de Tlascalla, famous for the tempests which gather around its summit. We view at the same time three mountains higher than Mont Blanc, two of which are still burning volcanoes . . . An ecclesiastic of the Indian race celebrates mass every day on the top of this antique monument.   (Res. I. 97)[63]

Yet in the end Humboldt did fail to integrate his scholarly observations on the antiquities of pre-hispanic American with his ethnographic account of modern native Americans in his travel account. Lamentably, the volume of the *Personal Narrative* describing Humboldt's travels in Ecuador, Peru, and Mexico, the principal 'high cultures' of America, was never published and subsequently destroyed, and the format of the account which did appear supports Pratt's charge. Humboldt's antiquarian observations were published in 1810 in the form of a picturesque atlas, comprising sixty-nine plates (some coloured) accompanied by prose descriptions, supplementary to the still unpublished *Personal Narrative*.[64] The original French *Vues des Cordillères, et Monumens des peuples indigènes de l'Amérique* appeared in an English translation by Humboldt's friend and collaborator Helen Maria Williams in 1814 (published as an inexpensive one-volume octavo, reduced to sixteen plates), entitled *Researches Concerning the Institutions and Monuments of the Ancient Inhabitants of America, with Descriptions and Views of Some of the most Striking Scenes in the Cordilleras!*[65] The use of sixteen different type founts, gothic black letters for 'striking scenes', and an exclamation mark after 'Cordilleras' on the title page

---

[62] Pratt, p. 134.

[63] Humboldt may have been aware that the topos of the 'four volcanoes' of Cholula was a classic configuration in Mexican codices, such as the Tepexic Annals (?1273). See Gordon Brotherston, *The Book of the Fourth World: Reading the Native Americas through their Literature* (Cambridge University Press, 1992), colour plate 15.

[64] As early as February 1805 Humboldt wrote to M. A. Pictet describing the tenth volume of his planned opus as 'Voyage to the Tropics, observations made in the Atlantic ocean, the interior of the New Continent, and part of South America (1799–1804), comprising at least four folio volumes, with an atlas of American antiquities, a view of Chimborozo, and the pyramid of Cholula' (CA p. 127).

[65] The English translation was actually based on the French two-volume octavo edition of 1813 which reduced the original 69 plates to 20 for the sake of economy (Letter to Jomard, 26 July 1813, CA p. 159). Although Humboldt here claimed that he had 'tried to re-establish the order of the objects [represented] by describing successively Mexican and Peruvian monuments' (ibid., pp. 159–60), there is no evidence of reordering in the English translation at least. I have not seen the French 1813 edition.

of the English translation must have sensationalized the contents of Humboldt's book for its audience. The unavoidable connection made with the culture of popular exoticism—with Humboldt as showman—was picked up by the *Monthly Magazine*'s review, which described Humboldt's travel writing as 'a philosophical phantasmagoria . . . a rapid succession of images which [he] causes to disappear or appear again without any natural connections'.[66] As we shall see in the conclusion, the sensationalist British reception of Humboldt's antiquarianism was capitalized upon by the showman/traveller William Bullock in his 1824 London exhibition 'Mexico Ancient and Modern'. Despite his sustained critique of 'vulgar' curiosity, Humboldt's representations of tropical America were easily appropriated by a commercially orientated culture of popular exoticism.

The 'picturesque atlas' format once again allowed Humboldt to develop the successful 'striking scenes' formula of the 'Physical Portrait' and the *Aspects of Nature*, obviating the need for the auto-narrative of the conventional travelogue. The plates contained in the original French text are of three main types: illustrations of Mexican, and some Peruvian, antiquities either collected by the author or sketched 'in the field', many based on drawings by colonial antiquarians like Márquez, León y Gama, and Dupaix;[67] Mexican and Maya codices copied either in Mexico City or in the great renaissance libraries of Paris, Vienna, Dresden, and Rome (many of them fully coloured, even in the octavo translation) which Humboldt had been avidly studying since his return from America; and, lastly, topographical, picturesque, or sublime mountain scenes which evoked an aesthetic response to the physical totality of tropical America.[68] In his Introduction, Humboldt apologized for the work's want of geographical order, which he blamed upon the difficult logistics of marshalling engravers in Italy, Germany, and France, although he felt that it was 'less reprehensible in the descriptions of a Picturesque Atlas, than in a regular Treatise' (Res. I. 6).[69]

[66] *Monthly Magazine*, 88 (March 1819), 235.
[67] It is a myth that indigenous antiquities had been neglected during the Spanish colonial era. Carlos III of Spain, as former king of the Two Sicilies, had been responsible for resuming excavations in Pompeii and Herculaneum, and took a keen interest in the archaeological investigation of his American colonies. In 1787 Antonio del Río had been sent to investigate the ruins of Palenque, Guillermo Dupaix headed the Real Expedición Anticuaria patronized by Carlos IV in 1805–9, José Antonio Alzate studied the ruins of Xochicalco near Cuernavaca, and León y Gama the Calendar Stone and Coatlicue statues dug up in the Plaza Mayor in 1790. The publication of the results of these investigations was severely impeded by the War of Independence.
[68] The Mexican emphasis—four-fifths of the antiquarian sections of *Researches* are dedicated to Mexico, only one-fifth to Peru—is partly explained by the fact that in Mexico Humboldt was able to collaborate, to a greater extent than in Ecuador or Peru, with creole antiquarians like Don José Antonio Pichardo, and had access to the researches and collections of Boturini, León y Gama, and Alzate (Res. I. 187).
[69] The *Monthly Magazine*'s review of *Personal Narrative* capriciously interpreted the apparent 'disorder' of Humboldt's work as endorsing Buffon's theory of America as an immature continent recently

However, a method does emerge from this seemingly random juxtaposition of 'rude monuments of the indigenous tribes of America, and the picturesque views of the mountain countries which they inhabited' (Res. I. 39). Harking back to the concerns of the *Essai sur le géographie des plantes*, Humboldt insisted that

the climate, the nature of the soil, the physiognomy of the plants, the view of beautiful or of savage nature, have great influence on the progress of the arts, and on the style which distinguishes their productions. This influence becomes the more perceptible, the farther man is removed from civilisation.   (Res. I. 40)

Although Humboldt constantly noted traces of 'high culture' in the Orinocan rainforests and along the coastal regions of South America, he subscribed to the conventional climatological belief that 'high' civilization can only prosper in a harsh landscape and a temperate climate. His theory that the aboriginal inhabitants of America had originally crossed over from the temperate latitudes of north-east Asia and settled in the cooler mountain regions of the American continent supported his thesis that the only indigenous societies which produced 'remarkable monuments' were those of the mountains in Anahuac (Mexico), Cundinamarca (Highland Colombia), and Peru, for 'their productions bear the stamp of the savage nature of the cordilleras' (Res. I. 40).[70]

On a superficial level this was demonstrated by the great *teocallis*, or pyramids, at Cholula, Xochicalco, Teotihuacan, and El Tajín, the architecture of which echoed the surrounding mountains, as well as providing platforms for the 'sublime and awful' practice of human sacrifices (Res. I. 103). In so far as Mexican or Peruvian monuments mirrored the physical environment of the high cordilleras, they were stamped with a 'savagery' which Humboldt only occasionally (as here) equated with the European aesthetic of the sublime.[71]

emerged from primordial chaos. 'The New Continent, indeed, which M. de Humboldt presents to our notice, appears as if it were not yet risen from an indigested state; and the materials are so jumbled and broken, that they resemble truly the elements of the poetic chaos, the "Non bene junctarum discordia semina rerum" ' (MM, 88 (March 1819), 234).

[70] Cf. also (PN VI. pt 1, 14). Humboldt here distinguished Mexico as 'a vast monarchy enclosing small republics' from the 'real theocracies' of Cundinamarca and Peru. The pattern of civilization in the New World, he observed, stretched from north to south along the Andean range, whereas in the Old World it stretched rather from east to west.

[71] The discovery of the ruins of the Maya cities in Central America and the flat limestone plains of the Yucatan in the coming decades would completely undercut Humboldt's thesis. Antonio del Río's *Description of the Ruins of an Ancient City, discovered near Palenque* (London, 1822), which recorded the findings of an archaeological investigation (sponsored by the Spanish authorities) of the Maya city in 1787, was known to Humboldt (Palenque—unlike Chichen Itza or Uxmal—was perhaps too close to the mountains to effect his theory). But Humboldt would have balked at del Río's insistence that the original builders had 'some analogy to, and intercourse with, the Romans, from the similarity in the choice of situation as well as a subterranean stone aqueduct' (p. 5). Del Río's text was accompanied by Dr Pablo Cabrera's *Teatro Crítico Americano*, which, defending a Biblical version of diffusionism, argued for an Egyptian provenance for the Maya in order to combat Isaac La Peyrère's

However, as we shall see below, the environmental determinism which determined the juxtaposition of images in the 'picturesque atlas' turns out to be an inadequate principal for evaluating the artworks of ancient cultures, despite Humboldt's suggestion that such cultures are more influenced by environment than more developed ones. It is precisely the habit of 'slavish imitation' of pre-established symbolic forms, rather than a mimetic sensitivity to the beauty or sublimity of the natural environment, which Humboldt diagnoses as the severe limitation of native American art.

The question which Humboldt set out to answer in *Researches* was how it could be that 'towards the end of the 15th century, in a world which we call new' Europeans had encountered 'those ancient institutions, those religious notions, and that style of building, which seem in Asia to indicate the very dawn of civilisation'? (Res. I. 2). In other words, how could America be simultaneously a 'new continent' and an 'antique land'? Aztec and Inca civilizations, leaping straight from a 'nomadic' to a 'polished' state of social organization without appearing to pass through the intermediate stage of 'pastoral', had raised a problem for the stadial theory of social development embraced by William Robertson in his influential *History of America* (1777). (This account, of course, chose to ignore the fact that agriculture—albeit not of a pastoral kind—was tropical America's greatest gift to the Old World.) The Scots historian was forced to blame this anomaly on the 'gloomy and atrocious' nature of Aztec religion which had counterbalanced social progress, thereby producing 'an effect that is singular in the history of the human species'.[72] This was clearly an evasion, as Humboldt archly suggested in his critique of Robertson (Res. I. 408), revealing the limitations of the 'abrupt distinctions into barbarous and civilised nations' which characterized the stadial model, ignoring the influence of environmental factors and the organic germ or 'primitive type' of specific civilizations. Alert to the relativistic nature of societal development, Humboldt warned that we should not be surprised to learn that the Mexican historical records upon which Francisco Clavigero had based his influential *Historia antica de Messico* (1784) did not go back any further than AD 700. Schloezer had recently demonstrated that the historical records of northern Europe reached no higher than the *tenth*: 'an epocha when Mexico was in a more advanced state of

polygeneticist argument about 'preadamite men' (p. 28). This old chestnut was, of course, little different from the polemical targets of Anglican mythographers like Jacob Bryant, Thomas Maurice, and Francis Wilford. See my essay 'Mythology', in *An Oxford Companion to the Romantic Age*, ed. by Iain McCalman (Oxford University Press, 1999), pp. 338–44.

[72] William Robertson, *History of America*, 2 vols. (London, 1777), ii. 302. Kames, who also accepted Buffon's thesis of American enfeeblement in developing the stadial theory, made a similar comment in his *Sketches of the History of Man* (1774): 'America is full of political wonders . . . We are not sufficiently acquainted with the natural history of America, nor with that of its people, to attempt an explanation of these wonders', quoted in Meek, *Social Science and the Ignoble Savage*, p. 160.

civilisation than Denmark, Sweden, and Russia' (Res. I. 83). The relationship between the Old and the New Worlds is not so much one of incommensurability, as of uneven development.

Unhappy with the stadial model which represented the most sophisticated enlightenment thinking about societal development, Humboldt was even more critical of older diffusionist models which still dominated thinking about the origins of advanced American civilizations. In the very years when Humboldt and Bonpland were travelling through Spanish America, Robert Southey was revising his imperialist epic poem 'Madoc', the initial draft of which had identified the Welsh prince Madoc ap Gwyneth with the Inca law-giver Mango Capac, based on contemporary reports of a tribe of Welsh-speaking Indians encountered within the North American interior.[73] Humboldt was quick to demolish such Eurocentric myths which attributed the high American civilizations to bearded white gods—Quetzalcoatl, Bochica, or Mango Capac—deriving ultimately from Europe or, in the various biblical versions, Semitic western Asia (Res. I. 30). Rejecting diffusionism and the crude etymological method which supported it,[74] Humboldt approached the question of origins with cautious scepticism. Although he felt that properly speaking it was no more the province of history than cosmogony was the province of natural history (Res. I. 13), he was nevertheless willing to speculate that 'the American race bears a very striking resemblance to that of the Mongul nations, which include the descendants of the Hiong-Nu, known heretofore by the name of Huns, the Kalkas, the Kalmucks, and the Burats' (Res. I. 14). At the same time, anticipating modern scholars, he supposed that native Americans had been long isolated from other cultures and had developed along quite autochthonous lines. Benjamin Keen correctly sums up Humboldt's programme when he writes that the 'main thrust of [his] thinking on the subject is not diffusionist, [in] that he believed most of the similarities to which he himself called attention resulted from parallel evolution'.[75]

In the several scholarly treatises on languages, religious myths, and astronomy scattered through the *Researches*, Humboldt sought to substantiate this affinity between America and East Asia, whilst never losing sight of his belief that ultimately cultures develop in tune with their physical and geographical environments, as well as via the organic principle of what he called the 'primi-

---

[73] Humboldt offered a plausible explanation for this in his account of meeting a Spanish sailor who claimed to have heard Basque spoken on Tahiti, and an English sailor who had heard Irish spoken in Hawaii. In both cases metropolitan travellers confuse the relatively unfamiliar languages of their own peripheries with those of the completely unfamiliar languages of Pacific peoples (PN VI. pt 1, 326).

[74] In his attack on cultural comparison based on etymologies, Humboldt argued that 'the study of words should always be accompanied by that of the structure of languages, and a complete knowledge of grammatical forms' (PN VI. pt 1, 353). The influence of Volney, important in this respect, is studied by Martin Thom, in *Republics, Nations and Tribes*, pp. 145-9.

[75] *The Aztec Image*, p. 334.

tive type' of race (Res. I. 2). His fascination in *Researches* with the writing systems of Mexican codices and screen-fold books in particular countered a pervasive myth of America as an oral rather than a scriptural culture, sustained in our own times by as prestigious a thinker as Claude Lévi-Strauss.[76] Humboldt was sceptical about Vater's theory that affinities could be shown to exist between the languages of America and Asia (Res. I. 147) but dedicated many pages of the *Researches* to examining the 'hieroglyphic' writing of the Aztec codices. Only the Mexicans, the most 'advanced' civilization of America, he argued, had begun the process of 'decomposing words' into phonetic elements, the precondition for alphabetical writing, but he cautioned that 'ages would have elapsed' before the authoritarian, tradition-bound cultures of Anahuac could have developed a fully fledged alphabet (Res. I. 162).[77] Humboldt's complex, dialectical approach to the comparison of high cultures avoided the twin pitfalls of an over-simplistic dependence on either diffusionism or environmental determinism. It is necessary to consider Humboldt's writings on American antiquities in their historical context in order to measure his achievement, which Modern Mexican scholars like Paul Kirchhoff and Jaime Labastida present as a programme for a still-unrealized comparative study of high cultures.

It would, however, be a grave mistake to see in Humboldt a twentieth-century cultural relativist *avant le lettre*, who, in his anxiety to defend America against the criticisms of prejudiced enlightenment *philosophes*, placed the societies of Moctezuma II or Atahualpa on a par with the Athens of Pericles. So much is clear from a startling passage in the introduction to the *Researches*, which I quote in full because it touches on so many themes of the present book:

Since the end of the last century, a happy revolution has taken place in the manner of examining the civilisation of nations, and the causes which impede or favour its

---

[76] See Brotherston, *The Book of the Fourth World*, pp. 40–81. 'Philosophically [Lévi-Strauss] continues a long-standing aversion to the idea of script that is traceable back to Plato and that in French found telling expression in Montaigne's remark on the same tropical-forest dweller studied by [him], the denizen of a world "so new and infantine, that he is yet to learn his ABC."' (p. 41). Derrida makes much of this point in *Of Grammatology*.

[77] Conventionally enough, Humboldt argued that for many ages alphabetic writing 'was unknown except in Egypt, in the Phoenician and Grecian colonies, and in the small space lying between the Mediterranean, the Oxus, and the Persian Gulf' (Res. I. 156). As Brotherston points out, this ethnocentric distinction between phonetic and pictorial script is 'undermined by the fact that degrees of phoneticism vary between scripts, and even alphabets can never register sounds entirely, while even the most rudimentary-seeming pictography will always imply a kind of language' (ibid., p. 42). *Tlacuilolli*, the Mesoamerican writing system discussed by Humboldt here, is 'among the scripts of the world . . . the one that has perhaps the most defied definition and analysis. Nonphonetic, it may register sound-concepts and does so in Nahautl, Mixtec, and other Mesoamerican languages. Highly flexible in layout, it may conform by turns to a chronicled narrative, an icon or map, or a mathematical table. Indeed, integrating into one holistic statement what for us are the separate concepts of letter, picture, and arithmetic, it positively flouts received Western notions of writing' (p. 50). It was precisely this holism which Humboldt blamed for having impeded the development of alphabetical writing and naturalistic visual expression, as we shall see below. See also Pagden, pp. 134–40.

progress. *We have become acquainted with countries, the customs, institutions, and arts of which differ almost as widely from those of the Greeks and Romans, as the primitive forms of extinct races of animals differ from those of the species, which are the objects of descriptive natural history.* The society at Calcutta has thrown a luminous ray over the history of the people of Asia. The monuments of Egypt, which are at present delineated with singular precision, have been compared with the monuments of countries the most remote; and my own recent investigations on the natives of America appear at an epocha, in which we no longer deem unworthy of attention whatever is not conformable to that style, of which the Greeks have left such inimitable models'.   (Res. I. 5–6) (emphasis mine)

Humboldt the 'private' traveller and scholar here makes common cause with colonial projects like Napoleon's *Description de l'Égypte*[78] and the researches of Sir William Jones and the Asiatic Society of Bengal. Yet his desire that American, African, and Asian high cultures be judged by criteria independent of those derived from Greek antiquity at first glance seems progressive, departing from a tradition of 'temporalized' historiography descending from Las Casas through J. L. Lafitau to Francisco Clavigero.[79] In the *Personal Narrative* he blamed the sixteenth-century navigators and chroniclers for reading the Americas according to 'all that the Greeks have taught us of the first age of the world' so that, 'led by those travellers into another hemisphere, we fancy ourselves going over past times' (PN V. 389–90). As we shall see, this was in fact little different from his own practice, although the analogon had changed.

What is troubling, however, about Humboldt's 'happy revolution' in comparative ethnology is the steering analogy, derived from Georges Cuvier's new science of palaeontology and comparative anatomy, upon which it is based.[80] In a 1798 paper to the Société d'Histoire Naturelle de Paris, Cuvier had urged the naturalist (*physicien*) to

do for the history of nature what antiquarians do for the history of the techniques and customs of people: the former will have to go and search among the ruins of the globe for the remains of organisms that lived at its surface, just as the latter dig in the ruins

[78] Humboldt had originally planned to travel to Egypt, and followed Napoleon's expedition with avid interest. His preparatory reading, on Egyptian antiquities, proved 'useful, when I examined the relations between the barbarous monuments of Mexico and those belonging to the nations of the old world' (PN I. 5–6).

[79] Brading argues that Clavigero, like the 17th-century Inca humanist Garcilaso de la Vega, 'followed Las Casas in framing a comparison no matter how moderate, with the Romans and Greeks', in order to 'establish the image of Incas and Aztecs as civilised nations'. Clavigero's barbs were aimed at De Pauw, Robertson, and Buffon, just as Garcilaso's had been directed at the tradition of Spanish imperial historiography represented in the work of Oviedo, Sepúlveda, and Gómara, upon which the *philosophes* were (ironically) often dependent (*The First America*, p. 461). Humboldt to some extent repudiated both traditions.

[80] For a study of the epistemic links between Cuvier's comparative anatomy and Franz Bopp's comparative linguistics, see M. Foucault, *The Order of Things: An Archaeology of the Human Sciences* (London: Tavistock Publications, 1970), pp. 263–302.

of cities in order to unearth the monuments of taste, the genius, and the customs of the men who lived there.[81]

In his major antiquarian work, Humboldt now repaid the compliment, by adapting Cuvier's theory that 'several animal species have been entirely destroyed by the revolutions that our planet has undergone', and his painstaking comparative method in piecing together the fragments of 'primitive, extinct cultures'.[82] Although, as we have seen, Humboldt was keenly aware of the ways in which the contemporary peoples of the New World were connected with their pre-hispanic traditions, he implicitly denies them vitality and progressive force by likening them (in common with Hindu or Egyptian cultures) to the fossilized remains of extinct animal species.[83] By contrast, the methodology for studying Hellenic antiquity and its inheritance is likened to 'descriptive natural history', the science of organic and evolving species. An attentive reader of Kant's *Critique of Judgement*, Humboldt here develops Kant's idea of affinity between aesthetic and teleological judgement, in the first case addressing the subjective finality of art; the second the organic finality of nature. He thereby legitimized Cuvier's notion of palingenesis as a Kantian analogon for a judgement of taste in discriminating Hellenic from oriental artworks.[84] We can see here (at the very moment when traditional diffusionism is rejected in favour of a more complex, comparativist understanding of cultural development) the first

[81] 'Extract from a memoir on an animal of which the bones are found in the plaster stone around Paris, and which appears no longer to exist today', published in Martin J. Rudwick, *Georges Cuvier, Fossil Bones, and Geological Catastrophe: New Translations and Interpretations of the Primary Texts* (Chicago and London: University of Chicago Press, 1997), pp. 33–41. (A summary of this 1798 paper was published in the bulletin of the Société Philomathique.) Cuvier's own 'antiquarian' credentials were considerable, having himself contributed to the 1805 French 'translation' of *Asiatic Researches* and examined his colleague Geoffroy Sainte-Hilaire's collection of ancient Egyptian animal mummies gathered during Napoleon's expedition (ibid., pp. 80, 229).

[82] Cuvier's theory of extinction was deeply opposed to his rival J.-B. Lamarck's theory of transformism, or evolution. It seems that Humboldt was willing to borrow analogies from Cuvier when discussing 'oriental' civilizations, and from Lamarck when lauding the achievements of the European Hellenic heritage. Cuvier's major work was published in 1812, as *Recherches sur les ossemens fossiles de quadrupèdes*, full of praise for Humboldt's 'excellent and magnificent work on the Mexican Monuments' (Rudwick, *Georges Cuvier*, p. 245). For a fully contextualized study, see Martin Rudwick, *The Meaning of Fossils: Episodes in the History of Paleontology* (New York: Neale Watson Academic Publications, 1976), 2nd edn. revised, ch. 3.

[83] Humboldt never makes its clear whether (in common with the external catastrophes which for Cuvier rendered species extinct) this was a result of the holocaust of Spanish conquest as much as any intrinsic defect inherent in these cultures themselves, which did by his own admission manifest some 'progressive' tendencies.

[84] Of course, it is more common to see Kant's notion of teleological judgement—the second section of the *Critique of Judgement*—as deriving from his aesthetic theory as expounded in the first part, rather than vice versa. Kant stresses that 'Judgement's concept of a finality of nature falls . . . under the head of natural concepts, but only as a regulative principle of the cognitive faculties—although the aesthetic judgement on certain objects (of nature or of art) which occasions that concept, is a constitutive principle in respect of the feeling of pleasure or displeasure' (Kant, *The Critique of Judgement*, trans. with an analytical index by James Creed Meredith (Oxford: Clarendon Press, 1952), p. 39).

vestiges of a comparative scale of value which smuggles the teleology of the natural sciences into the comparative study of civilizations. Humboldt's analogy between extinct and living species, replacing classical temporalization as a model for comparing cultures, thus established the precedent for an *ontological* difference between American and Hellenic cultures, between Europe and its others.

Humboldt continued by arguing that it was permissible to trace 'internal' comparisons between the Hindoos, the Tibetans and Chinese, the ancient Egyptians, and the Mexica or Inca, but not between any of these respective civilizations and the Greeks or Romans. 'The same causes have produced similar effects', he concluded, 'in ancient Egypt, in India, in China, in Mexico, and in Peru; wherever men were merely masses animated by a sameness of will' (Res. I. 184–5).[85] The great epistemological divide is not between peoples who possess a history and those who do not (as in the terms of a recent critique of the ethnocentric *cordon sanitaire*),[86] so much as between those whose culture demands a hermeneutic understanding based on aesthetic judgement, and those whose artworks merely document the history of mankind understood in an anthropological sense. In this respect, by invalidating the traditional 'classical' interpretation of pre-hispanic American civilization, Humboldt was simply replacing it with an 'orientalist' model which now conformed to the beginnings of an alteritist anthropology.[87] In contrast to the Greek 'aesthetic state',

the monuments of those nations . . . which have attained no high degree of intellectual cultivation, which either from religious or political causes, or the nature of their organisation, have never been affected by the beauty of forms, can be considered only as memorials of history.   (Res. I. 36)

It is notable that Humboldt has *already* departed from his declared intention of considering American 'monuments' by criteria independent of those derived from the study of Greek culture, by applying the classical aesthetic as an eval-

[85] In one respect Humboldt preferred Mexican over Hindu religion: the absence of phallic worship of the sort which fascinated impious mythographers like Dupuis, D'Hancarville, and Payne Knight. Amusingly enough, the account of the *absence* of phallic worship in America is left in the original French in H. M. Williams's English translation! (II. 228–9).

[86] See Eric Wolf, *Europe and the People Without History* (Princeton, NJ: Princeton University Press, 1982).

[87] This accords with the new metaphysical cosmology of the *Naturphilosophen* and their reaction against Kant's notion of orientation. As Helmut Muller-Sievers points out in his essay 'From Geography to *Erdkunde*: Strategies of Orientation in 18th and 19th century Science and Philosophy', in Schelling and Ritter, 'the compass bearings are turned 90 degrees towards west: the conflict between north and south that had dominated the debates in the 18th century ever since Winckelmann . . . gave way to a focus on the orient as geographical, historical, and cultural origin and the west as the direction of dispersal and decline' (p. 25). Humboldt's Weimar background nevertheless reasserts itself here in his insistence on subordinating the world-historical east–west axis to the normative north–south criterion of post-Winckelmannian Hellenism. Thanks to Simon Schaffer for making this unpublished essay available to me. For Humboldt on Schelling, see Dettelbach, 'Global Physics', pp. 278–9.

uative absolute.[88] Humboldt here writes as a disciple of Weimar classicism, in terms quite similar to the exclusive Hellenism of F. A. Wolf, founder of modern German *Altertumswissenschaft*.[89]

Humboldt's refusal to consider American antiquities aesthetically is all the more flagrant in the context of a 'picturesque atlas' dedicated to stimulating an aesthetic response to tropical American scenery among European readers. Although Humboldt had argued that medieval northern Europe was 'backward' in relation to American high cultures in the same period, modern European romanticism (he argued) has transcended its historical limitations by means of the dialectical engagement of enlightenment rationality and aesthetic idealism. Both, of course, were ultimately legacies of the Renaissance, with its simultaneous *re*covery of Europe's Hellenic roots and *dis*covery of America, unknown to the ancients. As I mentioned above, Humboldtian 'planetary consciousness'—closely linked to Kantian and Schillerian aesthetics—served to demarcate 'progressive' civilizations from unprogressive, the latter subject only to consideration from an anthropological perspective. In a telling passage in the *Political Essay*, Humboldt proposed that the Mexican Academy of Arts should exhibit 'the remains of the Mexican sculpture, which are covered with Aztec hieroglyphs, and bear some resemblance to the Egyptian and Hindoo style' alongside its extensive collection of Graeco-roman castes: 'it would be curious to see these monuments of the first cultivation of our species, the works of a semibarbarous people inhabiting the Mexican Andes, placed beside the beautiful forms produced under the sky of Greece and Italy' (PE I. 212). The totality of human civilization could be represented simultaneously, the aesthetic juxtaposed with the anthropological, as a lesson in social and artistic progress, and the distinction between organic and 'fossilized' cultures.

The merits and demerits of Humboldt's approach to pre-hispanic antiquities are well illustrated by his treatment in *Researches* of two of the monuments excavated in the Plaza Mayor in Mexico City in late 1790: the famous 'Aztec Calendar' stone; and a gigantic statue of the goddess 'Teoyamiqui'. The appearance of these monuments in the colonial city which (unlike today, after the 1970s excavations of the Templo Mayor) contained few visible relics of pre-hispanic Tenochtitlan, was seized upon by colonial savants to vindicate the antiquity and

---

[88] Humboldt made a very similar point in his Introduction to Carl Nebel's splendidly illustrated *Voyage pittoresque et archaeologique sur la partie la plus intéressante du Mexique* (Paris, 1836). 'Ce n'est pas le beau ideal, ni le sentiment de la perfection des formes, que l'on cherche dans les monumens des peuples du Nouveau-Monde, chez ceux qui vivent, soit a l'est de l'Euphrate et de la Pentapotamide, soit dans l'Archipel asiatique ou a pénétré avec le Boudhisme, la culture intellectuelle de l'Indoustane. L'étude de l'art de ces régions lointaines offre un interêt historique d'un genre grave et élevé . . .' (np). Benjamin Keen also points out Humboldt's failure to honour his own strictures against evaluating Mexican art by the standards of Greek culture (*Aztec Image*, p. 331).

[89] See Suzanne L. Marchand, *Down from Olympus*, pp. 16–24.

the achievements of Mexican culture against the attacks of the likes of Raynal, Robertson, and De Pauw. To this end Antonio de León y Gama had in 1792 published *Descripcíon historica y cronológica de las dos piedras*, a work hailed as the founding text of modern Mexican archaeology.[90] Although the discovery gave a new presence to indigenous history at a time of mounting ideological pressure, the two monuments embodied the characteristic ambivalence of romantic culture towards the Aztec past, evident in Gama's account. If the calendar seemed to represent the mathematical, astronomical, and cosmological achievements of Mexican civilization, the Teoyamiqui statue on the other hand seemed to represent its 'backwardness' in aesthetic terms, evidence of the 'ridiculous and superstitious rituals' which detracted from its material achievements.[91]

Humboldt devoted over 130 pages of *Researches* to the explication of plate 23, the 'relief in basalt, representing the Mexican Calendar', the longest single dissertation in the whole book (Ill. 17). Paul Kirchoff comments that this dissertation represents Humboldt's only really sustained attempt to demonstrate links between Mexican and Asiatic high cultures.[92] Because he uncritically accepted León y Gama's theory of a supposed intercalation in the Mexican calendar (the existence of which he could not prove), and because his ignorance of the as-yet unstudied Olmec and Mayan calendars profoundly skewed his judgement about its actual antiquity, his interpretation was of limited archaeological value in the long term.[93] Humboldt correctly indicated that the discovery of the calendar had rendered obsolete the earlier scholarship of William Robertson and J.-S. Bailly, revealing the profound links between the Mexican cosmogonic tradition of the four ages and the 'yougs' and 'calpas' of the Hindus recently elaborated in the pages of the *Asiatic Researches*. Indigenous monuments like the calendar, as well as the Mexican codices explicated elsewhere in *Researches*, could themselves be employed to reconstruct pre-hispanic history, a possibility doubted by Robertson.[94] 'It is by collecting and comparing the different systems of American chronology', Humboldt asserted, 'that we can judge of the communications, which appear to have existed, in very remote times, between the nations of India and Tartary, and those of the New Continent' (Res. I. 281).

Much of the dissertation demonstrates mythographic syncretism of the sort associated with Sir William Jones, Charles Dupuis, and Richard Payne Knight, and there are moments when Humboldt's scepticism about making easy

[90] Benjamin Keen, *The Aztec Image*, p. 303. Gama's essay was reprinted in an extended edition with notes by Carlos Bustamante in 1832 after Mexican independence, this time as a vindication of creole identity against Spanish colonialism. See Keen, pp. 312–27 on the nationalistic revival of the Aztec past.

[91] *Descripción histórica y cronológica de las dos piedras . . . por don Antonio de León y Gama*, (1792) ed. by Carlos María de Bustamante, 2nd edn. (Mexico City, 1832) (facsimile edition, Mexico City: INAH, 1990), p. 44.

[92] *Ensayos sobre Humboldt*, p. 94.   [93] Ibid., pp. 94–5.   [94] See Brading, p. 523.

Relief en basalte, représentant le Calendrier Mexicain.

17. Alexander von Humboldt, 'Calendaire mexicaine', *Vues des Cordillères* (1810), facing p. 125.

transcultural links is swamped by his syncretist enthusiasm. In discussing the design and iconography of the calendar stone itself, for example, he likened the central image of the yawning mouth and protruding tongue of the Mexican solar deity Tonatiuh to the Hindu god Kala (Time), supported by quotation from Wilkins's translation of the *Bhagvat-Gheeta*. Tonatiuh, he continued in true romantic syncretist vein, 'is Krishna assuming the form of Kala, it is Chronos devouring his children, whom we imagine we find under the name of Moloch amongst the Phoenicians' (Res. I. 400). Humboldt even found some artistic taste 'in the repetition of the same forms, that attention to order and feeling of symmetry, which among half-civilised nations is a substitute for the feeling of the beautiful' (Res. I. 399). He concluded that on the material evidence of the calendar alone the Mexica 'had no doubt reached a degree of civilisation superior to that which has been allowed by Pauw, Raynal, and even Robertson' (Res. I. 408).

By contrast, the 'Aztec Idol of Basaltic Porphyry' (Ill. 18) which, following Gama, Humboldt identified as the goddess Teoyamiqui, by dint of its 'total ignorance of the proportions of the human body' illustrated 'the barbarism of the arts and the taste for incorrect and hideous forms' (Res. II. 42). The statue (actually representing another Mexica goddess, Coatlicue, or 'snake-belt') appeared to European eyes as a grotesque female figure with two serpent heads and birds claws, bedecked with a belt of snakes and dismembered human hands, hearts, and skulls. After its discovery, the statue was displayed in the cloisters of the university, where it soon attracted the attention of Indians resident in the Mexican capital. As a disgusted Bishop Moxo y Francoly wrote in 1805: 'the Indians, who contemplate European art-works with stupid indifference, showed a worrying curiosity to contemplate their famous statue'.[95] An indigenous cult began to form around it and candles and offerings were left in the university cloisters, a remarkable enough fact when one considers that aboriginal Mexicans had been nominally converted to Catholicism for two and a half centuries. The ecclesiastical authorities had the statue reburied, only disinterring it briefly to allow Humboldt to study and draw it in April 1803. (Pre-hispanic antiquities would only achieve legitimacy after independence, when the Mexican Museo Nacional was established by presidential decree in 1825, and the government finally took measures to stem the exportation of antiquities overseas.)

Citing Gama's theory that the statue, with its 'united heads of two monsters' represented Huitzilopochtli and his wife, Teoyamiqui, Humboldt avoided any temptation to render it sublime by dismissing it as a 'shapeless mass' (echoing his earlier description of Aztec society as 'merely masses animated by sameness of will') (Res. I. 185). Deflecting attention from its disturbing iconographic qualities by a display of mineralogical expertise, Humboldt described it as com-

---

[95] See Gama's *Descripción*, introduction by Eduardo Matos Moctezuma, np.

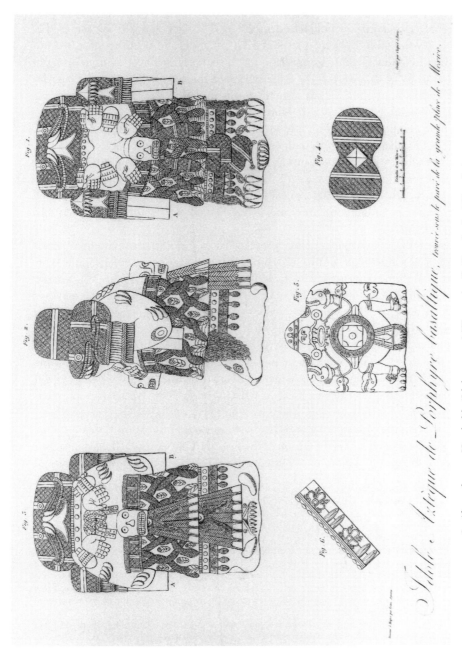

18. Alexander von Humboldt, 'Idole azteque' ('Teoyamiqui'), *Vues des Cordillères* facing p. 215.

posed of 'bluish grey basaltic wakke, cleft, and filled with vitreous feldspar'
(Res. II. 48). Humboldt's interpretation of the statue is functionalist in the
extreme, associating it with blood sacrifice. The fact that the bottom of the
statue represented the fanged jaws of Mictlantecuhtli, lord of the underworld,
led him to follow Gama's supposition that it had originally been raised on high
columns, its head towered 5 or 6 metres above the temple floor, so that sacrificial victims might be dragged to their deaths under an appropriately terrifying
image of death (Res. II. 47). As Jaime Labastida has pointed out, this rationalist interpretation is based on a total misunderstanding of Aztec *mentalité*: the
image of Mictlantecuhtli was sculpted on the ground-facing surface of Coatlicue
not so that it could be seen, but as a magical guarantee of the earth goddess's
contact with the underworld.[96] Humboldt's blindness to Mesoamerican
aesthetics, evident in the light of subsequent research, ironically mirrors that of
contemporary indigenous Mexicans to the Hellenistic 'beauty of forms' in his
own account.

True to his commitment to interpret American antiquities as evidentiary documents in a historical anthropology of art rather than as aesthetic objects in
their own right, Humboldt's essay on Teoyamiqui is the occasion for a searing
denunciation of the limited achievements of Mesoamerican culture. Human sacrifice, priestcraft, the 'chimerical dreams of astrology', and hieroglyphic writing
combined to impede the development of a naturalistic aesthetic along the lines
of ancient Greece.[97] As we saw above, Humboldt believed that the Mexica had
failed to develop an alphabetic writing system which would decompose sounds
rather than visual signs, a fact which is blamed for the poverty of their visual
and plastic arts, an extreme case of what Derrida calls Western 'phonocen-
trism'.[98] In contrast to the 'solemn simplicity' of Egyptian hieroglyphics,
Mexican hieroglyphics are marked by 'a viciousness of imitation, this taste for
the minutest details, this repetition of the most ordinary forms' (Res. II. 43). But
it is not the minute imitation of Dutch painting, rather a grotesque hybridity of

[96] Jaime Labastida, 'Humboldt y la antropología en México', in *Alejandro de Humboldt en México*,
pp. 144–5. Labastida here develops Paul Westheim's interpretation in *Ideas fundamentales del arte
preshispánico en México* (Mexico, 1957). On the Coatlicue statue (now located, like the 'Calendar
Stone', in Mexico City's Museum of Anthropology), see Westheim's *Art of Ancient Mexico*, trans. by
Ursula Bernard (New York: Doubleday, 1965), pp. 226–31; and Justino Fernández, *Coatlicue, estética
del arte indígena antiguo* (Mexico City: Centro de Estudios Filosóficos, 1954).
[97] In his essay on Plate 32, 'The Hieroglyphic History of the Aztecs', Humboldt does, however,
suggest that progress is evident if we look over hieroglyphic manuscripts of different periods 'the
stunted figures become more proportionate . . . symbolic painting . . . is insensibly transformed into
an animated painting, which employs only a few phonetic hieroglyphics, to indicate the names of
persons and sites' (Res. II. 62).
[98] In fact, phonetic writing was abundant 1,000–2,000 years earlier in Zapotec, Olmec, and Maya
cultures, suggesting that Mexican writing systems might rather be seen as the results of political choice
than as developmental 'failure'. Thanks to Gordon Brotherston for this communication.

representations which confounded European ideas of mimesis. Thus, the jux-taposition of composed picturesque views of American landscapes with plates representing pre-hispanic antiquities in Humboldt's *Atlas* is intended to under-line the contrast between the aesthetics of European naturalism and the rebar-bative semiotics of indigenous art.

The power of the ritual calendar in a culture marked by 'a languid unifor-mity of customs and superstitions' (Res. I. 184) has resulted, Humboldt argues, in a highly abstract, non-mimetic system of representation in which

each event seemed to be at the same time under the influence of the hieroglyphics which presided over the day, the half-decade, or the year; and hence arose the idea of coupling signs, and creating those merely fantastic beings, which we find so often repeated in the astrological paintings which have reached us.   (Res. II. 42)

'Dwarfish' human figures of the sort discussed in relation to the Vatican Codex (Plate 13), far beneath the lowest products of Hindu, Chinese, or Japanese art (I. 165) are inspired only by slavish repetition and religious terror, gathering up 'all that is strange in nature' (II. 42). At times such as this the mask of Hum-boldt's scientific detachment slips to reveal the aesthetic disgust which seemed to accompany (as a good disciple of Weimar classicism) his researches in Aztec culture. The reward for applying one's self to this mass of 'shapelessness' (and Humboldt at least deserves credit for pioneering the European study of Aztec codices) is an insight into 'the first unfolding of the faculties of man' (II. 152). But in his remarks on American antiquities one easily senses the aesthetic equivalent of the masochistic self-experimentation to which Humboldt had martyred himself as a young man in the name of scientific progress.

Personal Narrative of Travels to the Equinoctial Regions of the New Continent

So far this long chapter has surveyed some of the tension between scientific overview and aesthetic affect in Humboldt's representation of tropical America, in both the visual medium of the 'Physical Portrait of the Tropics' and the textual medium of the *Tableaux de la Nature*; the rigorous exclusion of personal witness in the 'statistical' *Essai politique*; and the incongruity between 'pic-turesque' landscapes and 'shapeless' Aztec antiquities in the *Researches*. In his Introduction to the *Personal Narrative*, the first volume of which finally appeared in 1814 (the first volume of H. M. Williams's excellent English trans-lation, supervised by Humboldt himself, from which I quote throughout this chapter, was published in the same year), Humboldt frankly confessed that

I had left Europe with the firm intention of not writing what is usually called the historical narrative of a journey, but to publish the fruit of my inquiries in works merely descriptive; and I had arranged the facts, not in the order in which they successively presented themselves, but according to the relation they bore to each other. Amidst the overwhelming majesty of Nature, and the stupendous objects she presents at every step, the traveller is little disposed to record in his journal what relates only to himself, and the ordinary details of life.   (PN I. xxxviii)

I turn now in this closing section to consider Humboldt's travel writing proper, a body of writing which sums up many of the literary achievements of the genre studied in previous chapters, at the same time as it brought the idea of 'personal narrative' to crisis point.

Given that Humboldt's distrust of narrative (manifest in these introductory remarks) problematized the whole project of the *Personal Narrative*, it is remarkable that it has recently been accredited with having 'created a new genre [of travel writing] . . . explicitly followed by Charles Darwin, Henry Bates, Thomas Belt, A. R. Wallace and Louis Agassiz through to Redmond O' Hanlon today'.[99] In a brief analysis of some of the textual strategies of the *Personal Narrative*, I shall suggest that, on the contrary, Humboldt's book, although today probably the most famous part of his canon, represented the *terminus* of the 'integrated' travel account of the late enlightenment and romantic period discussed in Chapter 1, rather than a new beginning. After Humboldt readers would not expect scientific information from travel books so much as literary amusement, or else (as in the case of Charles Darwin's 1845 *Journal of Researches*),[100] a popularizing supplement to the specialist scientific records of an expedition. (Darwin indicated in his 1845 Preface that 'I trust that naturalists will remember, that they must refer for details to the larger publications, which comprise the scientific results of the Expedition'.[101]) To be sure, as Humboldt himself acknowledged in an 1839 letter to the young English naturalist, Darwin's *Journal of Researches* represented the most significant development of his own project, by Darwin's own admission consciously modelled

---

[99] Jason Wilson, Introduction to Humboldt's *Personal Narrative* (Harmondsworth: Penguin Books, 1994), p. lxii.

[100] The first edition of Darwin's travelogue was published in 1839 as the third volume of Robert FitzRoy's *Narrative of the Surveying Voyages of HMS Adventure and Beagle*. The 1845 second edition was published as a separate volume and Darwin made considerable changes to transform what had originally been a rather specialized record of 'Geology and Natural History' into a more popular travelogue. This was published in John Murray's best-selling 'Home and Colonial Library', the aim of which was to 'produce a Series of Works as entertaining as romances, yet not frivolous, but abounding in sound information'. See John Tallmadge, 'From Chronicle to Quest: The Shaping of Darwin's *Voyage of the Beagle*', *Victorian Studies*, 3:23 (Spring 1980), 328. Thanks to Jim Secord for this reference.

[101] *Journal of Researches into the Natural History and Geology of the Countries visited during the Voyage round the World of H.M.S Beagle*, 2nd edn. (1845) (London: John Murray, 1905), p. vii.

on the *Personal Narrative*.[102] For instance, marvelling at the coral reefs of the Cocos and Keeling Islands, Darwin struck a Humboldtian note when he wrote

It is not a wonder, which at first strikes the eye of the body, but rather, after reflection, the eye of reason. We feel surprised, when travellers relate accounts of the vast extent of certain ancient ruins; but how utterly insignificant . . . when compared to the pile of stone here accumulated by the work of various minute animals.[103]

Yet Darwin's *Journal*, particularly in its 1845 version, is inflected with the confident, expansionist mood of British imperialism rather than Humboldtian 'planetary consciousness', which in the end gives it a very different feel.[104] In his adaptation of the 'genre' of Humboldtian personal narrative to the very different conditions of Victorian popular science, Darwin skilfully translated the global romanticism of his model into the popularizing idiom of the British 'civilizing mission', untramelled by the sort of scruples about form and narrative which dogged Humboldt. As I hope will become evident in my ensuing discussion, only an interpretation of Humboldt's work based on the many nineteenth- and twentieth-century selective abridgements of the *Personal Narrative* (rather than the whole work in its original published form), could establish it as such a seminal influence on the 'literary' form of much subsequent travel writing.

Like Humboldt's later account of the economy of losses and gains which in his view characterized nineteenth-century travel writing (cited in my Introduction), his methodological scruples concerning 'personal narrative' suggest why he was so reluctant to embark on composition, and also help to explain the difficulties which dogged him once he began (albeit belatedly, for by 1814, much of the scientific content of the *Voyage* had already been published).[105]

[102] Paul Barrett and Alain Corcos, 'A Letter from Humboldt to Charles Darwin', *Journal of the History of Medicine* (April 1972), 159–72. The passages of Darwin's travelogue which Humboldt singled out for particular praise were, unsurprisingly, those which represented Darwin at his most 'Humboldtian' (see ibid., pp. 171–2).

[103] *Voyage of the Beagle* (1839), ed. with intro. by Janet Browne and Michael Neve (Harmondsworth: Penguin, 1989), p. 342. This Humboldtian *aperçu*, transcribed from Darwin's *Diary* entry for 12 April, has vanished in the 1845 popular edition which attempts a more strategic use of wonder.

[104] Even Humboldtian plant geography now seemed to be based on competition and struggle rather than harmony, a perception which would, of course, provide the basis for Darwin's later theory of natural selection. See Janet Browne, 'Biogeography and Empire', in *Cultures of Natural History*, pp. 312–15; and Susan Cannon, *Science in Culture: The Early Victorian Period* (New York: Dawson and SHP, 1978), pp. 86–92 on Darwin as 'Humboldtian Scientist'.

[105] Humboldt was disingenuous about the genesis of his *Personal Narrative*. In a letter of 21 Feb. 1801, he had declared his intention of dividing his *Voyage* into separate volumes, given that not all of its various scientific concerns could be of equal interest to all readers: 'My travel narrative, properly speaking . . . will only contain matter of interest to all cultivated readers; physical and moral observations, general conditions, the character of indigenous peoples, languages, manners, the commercial relations of cities and colonies, the aspect of the landscape, agriculture, the altitude of mountains (only the results), meteorology' (CA p. 64). On 3 Feb. 1805, after his return to Paris, he wrote of his intention to

Acknowledgement of these problems might help to solve the great mystery of Humboldt studies, why the *Personal Narrative* terminated abruptly at the end of the third volume (seventh in the English translation), as Humboldt and Bonpland headed down the Magdalena river in Colombia in March 1801, bound for Ecuador, Peru, and Mexico, leaving over half of their expedition unnarrated. As is clear from a letter written to Willdenow on 17 March 1810, the manuscript of the fourth and final volume was ready, but was suddenly destroyed on Humboldt's orders. It was a costly decision, as Humboldt had to remit 9,500 francs to his editors.[106]

Humboldt's preference for describing the facts of his journey not in the order in which they successively presented themselves (i.e. in the form of an itinerary narrative) but rather 'according to the relation which they bore to each other' suggests why he preferred either the synchronic image/table of the 'Physical Portrait' or the 'Picturesque Atlas', or the descriptive 'prose poetry' of *Aspects of Nature*, to travel writing in the more conventional sense. In presenting the results of his travels in graphic or synchronic form he could reveal the relationship of objects to each other whilst preserving the role of the traveller/observer as a form of transcendental consciousness shaping and uniting scientific and aesthetic ways of seeing and understanding. He could at least *pretend* to preserve unity between disparate modes of perception, albeit a unity (as I have been arguing) more wished-for than achieved. But how could the narrative of a traveller bent on minute, frequent, and widely disparate 'scientific observations' be expected to encompass entertaining pictures of manners or the 'great phenomena of nature' in a single view? (PN I. xl). Humboldt's Introduction to the *Personal Narrative* evinces nostalgia for the old style of travel book in which observation of places and people assumed a concrete and dramatic form in the narratives of relatively 'unlettered men'. For this reason the Introduction needs to be read as quite different in intention from the conventional disclaimer in which travel writers excused their incapacity to provide an adequate relation of their experiences, often on account of their amateur status. Humboldt's problem was rather that he was *too* learned, and learned over too wide a range of fields.

The first casualties of the multifaceted scientific travel account would be anecdote and narrative drama. 'The most faithful picture of manners is that', Humboldt wrote 'which best displays the relations of men toward each other. The character of savage or civilized nations is portrayed either in the obstacles

---

complete the personal narrative (as volume 10 of a projected 11-volume work) in two and a half years at the outermost (CA p. 127). On 24 Dec. 1805 he wrote to Cuvier 'it would be useless to write a travel narrative after so much time had passed because both the public and the author become equally lukewarm' (CA p. 138). This was only about a year after his return!

[106] Minguet, p. 105.

which a traveller meets with, or in the sensations which he feels' (PN I. xl–xli]. The personal narratives of earlier travellers had stressed human interactions rather than detached observation, for 'it is the man himself that we continually desire to see in contact with the objects that surround him; and his narration interests us the more, when a local tint is spread over the description of the country and its inhabitants' (ibid.). Humboldt praised the writings of the early navigators Vespucci and Columbus, of Gemelli Carreri,[107] and most recently the 'irresistable charm' of Mungo Park for achieving this combination of 'dramatic' interaction and 'local tint'.

But this style of writing could not keep up with the rapid advance of modern science. We saw in Chapters 3 and 4 how 'progressive' thinkers like Constantin Volney and James Mill mounted an epistemological critique of travel writing on the grounds that it was based on fleeting first impressions rather than 'philosophical' analysis and comparison. In 1807 George Cuvier (who, as discussed above, would later complement Humboldt on his *non*-narrative atlas *Monuments of the Ancient Inhabitants of America*) mounted a very similar attack on scientific travellers in his review of Humboldt's *Tableaux de la Nature*, arguing that 'it is really only in one's study that one can roam freely throughout the universe'.[108] Writing in his capacity as director of the Muséum National d'Histoire Naturelle, Cuvier argued that although the travelling naturalist had the advantage of observing objects in their natural environments, he could only devote a few moments to each, and was deprived of the opportunity to compare each specimen with others in different contexts, as well as books which might allow him to consider the relevant comments of previous observers. By contrast, 'if the sedentary naturalist does not see nature in action, he can yet survey all her products spread before him', manifesting a 'different sort of courage' from the doughty explorer, 'courage which comes from unlimited devotion to the truth'.[109] As Dorinda Outram has argued, whereas field naturalists were 'validated by their heroism in physically encountering and overcoming distance from metropolitan centres . . . sedentary naturalists were forced to argue that their *psychic* distance from the object . . . guaranteed the superior truth value of their brand of natural history'.[110] Like the abstract universalism of the imperial museum order (in contrast to the sensationalism and presentism of the popular exhibition), the sedentary naturalist rejected the traveller's fleeting experiential contact with the exotic object 'in the field'.

---

[107] 'Gemelli's descriptions have that local tint, which is the principal charm of the narratives of travel, written by the most unlettered men' (Res. II. 59). He is compared with 'a celebrated traveller, who, in our own times, has been treated with so much severity' (surely James Bruce?); both 'contain an inextricable mixture of errors and well-observed facts' (ibid., II. 60).

[108] Quoted by Dorinda Outram, 'New Spaces in Natural History', in *Cultures of Natural History*, pp. 249–65, p. 249.

[109] Ibid., pp. 260–1.   [110] Ibid., p. 263.

In setting up an opposition of this kind between Cuvier and Humboldt, however, Outram perhaps underestimates the extent to which Humboldt succeeded in internalizing the 'enclosure' of the museum while in the field, subjecting his body and its affective responses to a severe epistemological control. It is also necessary to consider the extent to which Humboldt struggled with Cuvier's (or Volney's) objection in the composition of his *Personal Narrative*. Perhaps Humboldt was influenced by Cuvier's strictures when he feared that the 'unity of composition' necessary to produce interesting and amusing travel writing had become practically impossible on account of the increasing diversification and specialization of knowledge. Encyclopaedic geographical and antiquarian archives like the *Asiatic Researches* and the *Description de l'Égypte* had not even attempted to represent such unity, publishing their multi-authored investigations in multi-volumed series each aimed at a different public of specialist readers. The narrative 'itinerary' has been replaced by the objective paradigm of the 'map', because, as Humboldt wrote, it is 'scarcely possible to connect so many different materials with the narration of events; and that part which we may call dramatic gives way to dissertations merely descriptive' (PN I. xlii).

However, there was a strong contemporary counter-argument which championed Humboldt as a heroic travelling philosopher against objections such as those of Cuvier. Rousseau had famously complained, in the tenth note to his *Discourse on the Origin of Inequality*, that 'individuals go here and there in vain; it seems that philosophy doesn't travel and that the philosophy of one nation proves little suited to another'.[111] Taking this passage as his text, John Playfair commented in his glowing 1814 review of *Researches* that

the philosopher of Geneva . . . would have retracted the assertion . . . if he had lived to see the great work, of which a part is now before us . . . we congratulate the present age on having produced a traveller, armed at all points, and completely accomplished for the purpose of physical, moral and political observations.[112]

In his *Physical Geography*, Kant had argued that 'more is needed for knowledge of the world than just seeing it. He who wants to profit from his journey must have a plan beforehand, and must not merely regard the world as an object of the outer sense',[113] a view which we saw being endorsed by George Forster in Chapter 1. Humboldt also complied with this transcendentalist programme, whilst at the same time he acknowledged the difficulties faced by the travelling polymath, and the danger of being considered a jack of all trades and master of

---

[111] J.-J. Rousseau, *A Discourse on Inequality*, trans. with an intro. and notes by Maurice Cranston (Harmondsworth: Penguin Books, 1984), p. 159.

[112] ER, 24 (Nov. 1814), 134.

[113] Quoted in Margarite Bowen, *Empiricism and Geographical Thought from Francis Bacon to Humboldt* (Cambridge University Press, 1981), p. 208.

none.[114] The problem remained, however, as to whether it was any longer possible, or even desirable, to represent this act of aesthetic and epistemological synthesis in the narrative form of the conventional travel account. Certainly those general readers who preferred literary amusement to instruction would be the losers; there could be small temptation to 'follow those travellers in their expeditions who drag along with them a considerable apparatus of instruments and collections' (PN I. xlii).

In his letter to Pictet of 3 February 1805 Humboldt already envisaged the narrative 'Voyage to the Tropics' as an important component of his magnum opus, stating that it would be based on seven volumes of hurriedly written travel diaries which he wanted time to edit and polish in order 'to attract people of good taste' (CA p. 127). In his Introduction to the *Personal Narrative* he described these diaries as 'brief itineraries' which he had written 'to the moment' during land or river journeys or ascending Chimborazo and other mountains; while stationary in cities or preoccupied with scientific collection and measurement he had not bothered to keep them up. A random collection of 'fugitive ideas', 'unclassifiable facts', and 'first impressions . . . received from nature or from man', they represented the residue of his fieldwork and certainly had not been intended as the basis of 'an extensive work to be offered to the public' (I. xxxix). Above all, these were the jottings of a man of science, which Humboldt had doubted would 'present very few of these incidents, the recitals of which give the principal charm to an itinerary' (I. xxxix). Clearly, Humboldt was far from wishing to suggest that his *Personal Narrative* be 'merely entertaining'.

Given these difficulties, why had Humboldt proceeded with the *Personal Narrative* at all? In the Introduction he gives the odd motive that the difficulties of writing the technical treatises which made up the bulk of the *Voyage* 'insensibly overcame my reluctance to write the narrative of my journey' (I. xxxix). A more plausible motive was his sense that scientists had not really 'fulfilled their engagements with the public' until they had written their 'itineraries', a genre which currently enjoyed tremendous popularity (PN I. xl). We saw above how Humboldt's public lectures in Berlin in 1806 provided the nucleus for the *Ansichten der Natur*, which remained one of his most widely read works. The image of Humboldt in the 1810s as a lonely workaholic buried in his study at the École Polytechnic, struggling to complete his thirty-volume *Voyage*, is belied by the American visitor George Ticknor's description of his stellar

---

[114] See his letter to Pictet, 3 Jan. 1806 (CA p. 141). It is interesting to compare this with his statement in his 1805 *Confessions*, where Humboldt suggested that his polymathic energy was a psychopathological trait: 'unquiet, agitated, and without the ability to enjoy anything which I have completed, I am only happy when I am initiating new projects and doing three things at the same time' (CA p. 233).

performances in the Parisian salons. Visiting Madame de Staël's salon (run by her daughter, the Duchesse de Broglie) in May 1817, Ticknor met Benjamin Constant, Lacratelle, and A. W. Schlegel 'assembled to hear the Baron de Humboldt read some passages out of an unpublished volume of his travels'. Ticknor was overwhelmed by Humboldt's 'genius and modesty, and his magical descriptions of the scenery of the Orinoco, and the holy solitudes of nature, and the missionaries'.[115] (The 'unpublished volume' from which Humboldt read was probably the fifth volume of the *Personal Narrative*, not published in English until 1821).

I have elsewhere speculated that the *Personal Narrative* was at least in part the fruit of Humboldt's friendship with the English poet and travel writer Helen Maria Williams, at whose Paris salon he also 'performed' and who co-owned (with her lover, John Hurford Stone) the English Press, one of several Parisian publishing houses bankrupted by the expense of printing Humboldt's multi-volume *Voyage*.[116] Williams recouped some of her lost fortune by dedicating the last decade of her life to producing an outstanding English translation of both *Researches* and the *Personal Narrative*. Her translator's Preface (her own writings were associated with the late eighteenth-century culture of radical sensibility) championed Humboldt's travelogue on the grounds that whereas 'he appears only to address himself to our reason, he has the secret of awakening the imagination, and of being understood by the heart' (PN I. ix). Humboldt was encouraged by his friends (although probably not by Georges Cuvier) to make one more attempt to produce a publicly accessible and 'aesthetic' narrative of his travels, associated with the social space of the female-dominated salon or lecture hall, alongside the 'private', scientific space of the study or the laboratory. To this end Humboldt's Introduction argues, as an article of faith, that 'one of the noblest privileges, which distinguishes modern civilization from that of remoter times', is 'having thrown a more general interest over objects, which heretofore occupied only a small number of scientific men, because these objects were contemplated separately, and from a narrower point of view' (PN I. xix). 'General interest' here needs to be distinguished from 'popular interest', given Humboldt's reluctance to popularize his travels. Nevertheless, the faith expressed here in a 'disinterested' intellectual public sphere militates against a more common contemporary perception (expressed by thinkers as diverse as Adam Smith, Goethe, Schiller, and Coleridge) that public culture was becoming increasingly fragmented by the intellectual division of labour. The question remains: how far did Humboldt succeed in what might be considered in this

---

[115] *Life, Letters and Journals of George Ticknor* (Boston, 1876), 2 vols., I. 134.
[116] 'Salons, Alps and Cordilleras: Helen Maria Williams, Alexander Von Humboldt, and the Discourse of Romantic Travel', in *Woman, Writing and the Public Sphere, 1700–1830*, ed. by C. Grant, E. Eger, C. O'Gallchoir, and P. Warburton (Cambridge University Press, 2001), pp. 217–38.

light as a quixotic bid to unite fragmented bourgeois subjectivity in presenting his travels and researches in the 'New Continent' under a 'single point of view'?

When approaching the *Personal Narrative* it must be remembered that the details of his American expedition, including many highlights such as his canoe journey down the Orinoco and Casiquiare canal, the capturing of electric gymnoti on the *llanos* of Venezuela, and the spectacular ascent of Chimborazo (thought to be the highest mountain in the world), were already in the public domain and enjoyed the status of 'popular curiosities'. Garbled newspaper reports, his own popular evocations of South America in the Berlin lectures, and detailed narratives of his travels in the periodicals[117] had aroused popular interest in the voyage to an unprecedented pitch. The lack of reliable information on Spanish America, combined with the outbreak of the massive continental rebellion against the Spanish crown, enhanced the already considerable allure of Humboldt's descriptive prose, making the narrative marketable in the extreme. Humboldt considered such publicity to be a mixed blessing at best. At the beginning of the 1814 volume, for instance, he took the opportunity of disassociating himself from a pirate narrative, published in Hamburg, inauspiciously entitled 'A Voyage Round the World, and in South America, by A. de Humboldt', based on newspaper reports and notes from his lectures (PN I. 3).

The three grand quarto French volumes of the *Relation historique* were published in 1814, 1819, and 1825, respectively: their English translation, the *Personal Narrative*, divided into seven volumes (in six lengthy books) were published in 1814 (vols. 1–2), 1818 (vol. 3), 1819 (vol. 4), 1821 (vol. 5), 1826 (vol. 6, parts 1 and 2), and 1829 (vol. 7). The 1814, 1818, 1819, and 1829 English publications each averaged around 600 pages in length, whilst the 1821 and 1826 books ran to about 860 pages. The total of roughly 4,000 pages (in the reduced octavo English translation at least) makes it the longest of all Humboldt's publications, and indeed one of the longest single travel books ever written, vying with the *Travels* of James Bruce and E. D. Clarke. The fact that this enormous quantity of text covered only the period between June 1799 and April 1801 (leaving the rest of the expedition, up to August 1804, unnarrated) makes it all the more monumental. In his study of Humboldt's reception, Nicholas Rupke notes the difficulty of gaining a European-wide overview of the maximum periods of reviewing intensity on account of the spread of dates of publication of different volumes and their various translations. Humboldt was notorious for delaying the publication of promised writings and dragging out their completion, and when the final part of the English translation was published in 1829, its translator, H. M. Williams, had been dead for three years.

Rupke's chart of reviewing intensities, however, reveals that interest in the

---

[117] See, for example, John Leslie's long article in the *Edinburgh Review* in April 1810 (ER, 31 (April 1810), 223–53).

Relation historique, although considerable in the decade 1815–25, was never equivalent to the *Essai politique*, or indeed *Cosmos* in the years after 1845. Reviewers' fatigue appears to have set in by the mid-1820s, and he concludes that 'in our sample of [British, French and German] periodicals no reviews appeared of volume three of the *Relation historique*'.[118] Nevertheless, the admiration of contemporary British men of letters is perhaps exemplified by Robert Southey's enthusiastic comment in December 1821 that '[Humboldt] is among travellers what Wordsworth is among poets. The extent of his knowledge and the perfect command which he has of it are truly surprising; and with this he unites a painter's eye and a poet's feelings'.[119] The critical reception of the *Personal Narrative* in British periodicals was predictably dominated by partisan politics: the Whig *Edinburgh Review* was euphoric in its praises; whilst the Tory *Quarterly Review* was damning.[120] In an 1823 letter to the geologist Charles Lyell, Humboldt complained that 'I was roughly handled by the Quarterly, but still more injured by the extravagant praises of the Edinburgh. For when they paid me such insidious compliments as to say I was the first of savants etc., they could not fail to make me enemies.'[121]

Why had public interest in the *Personal Narrative* peaked by the early mid-1820s? To answer this question we need to examine the intrinsic qualities of the book itself, as well as extrinsic factors such as authorial procrastination and public over-exposure. As we have seen, Humboldt formulated the problem of writing his *Personal Narrative* in terms of achieving an equilibrium between the general and the particular: 'I have not always succeeded in separating the observations of detail from those general consequences, which interest every enlightened mind' (PN I. xviii–xix).[122] The method which he adopted, and fairly successfully sustained in the earlier volumes at least, was to begin by narrating the itinerary in temporal sequence and with some acknowledgement of his own affective reaction to phenomena observed, and then to consider such objects of interest in their general, scientific, relations. He had no scruples about simply suppressing personal incidents (of the sort often noted in his diaries) which were not susceptible of this sort of generalization, and 'which can be rendered amusing only by the perfection of style' (PN I. xliii). This method is well exemplified in his account of an expedition to the summit of the volcano of Tenerife in the first volume (Book 1, Chapter 2).

---

[118]   Rupke, 'Geography of Enlightenment', p. 326.

[119]   *New Letters of Robert Southey*, ed. by K. Curry, 2 vols. (New York and London, 1965), p. 231.

[120]   See Calvin P. Jones, 'The Spanish-American Works of Alexander von Humboldt as Viewed by Leading British Periodicals, 1800–1830', *The Americas*, XXIX, 4 (April 1973), 442–8.

[121]   Quoted in Jean Theodorides, 'Humboldt and England', *British Journal for the History of Science*, III 3:9 (1966), 39–55.

[122]   In her translator's Preface, H. M. Williams on the contrary praised Humboldt's faculty of 'raising the mind to general ideas, without neglecting individual facts' (PN I. ix).

Describing in passing his impressions of the town of Orotava and its famous 'dragon tree', Humboldt restrains his temptation to dissert on the botanical and geological features of the ascent, complains in conventional terms about the laziness and truculence of his guides, and describes his odd physical sensations— simultaneously burning feet and freezing hands on account of the hot ash on the ground at an altitude well above the snow level. Scientific generalization is again forestalled by description of the 'picturesque beauties' experienced on the summit, but even here Humboldt rejects the egotistical focus conventionally communicated by a rhetoric of emotional intensity (such as Bruce's account of Gish).

[The author] is exposed to the danger of fatiguing his readers by the monotonous expression of his admiration. It appears to be more conformable to the plan, which I have proposed to myself in this narrative, to indicate the peculiar character that distinguishes each zone. We exhibit with more clearness the physiognomy of the landscape, in proportion as we endeavour to sketch the individual features, to compare them with each other, and discover by this kind of analysis the sources of these enjoyments, which are offered us by the great picture of nature.   (I. 178)

The Humboldtian picturesque here urges a 'phenomalism' quite distinct from the associative intensity of more conventional formulations, as discussed in Chapter 4.

The catalogue of 'typical landscapes' presented throughout the *Personal Narrative* details the characteristic physiognomy of each as a precondition for comparison with others. Aesthetics are in this way mediated through the overview of Humboldtian 'planetary consciousness'. The eye first *passively* enjoys the harmonious activity of landscape: 'our eyes hovered over an inhabited world; we enjoyed the striking contrast between the bare sides of the Peak, its steep declivities covered with scoriae, its elevated plains destitute of vegetation, and the smiling aspect of the cultured country beneath' (PN I. 180). As in the *Views of Nature*, the objective configuration of landscape here takes precedence over subjective affect, the traveller's observation being expressed by the use of weak verbs whilst nature takes dynamic (often metaphoric) adjectives. At the end of his description of the excursion to climb the Pico de Teide, Humboldt reminds the reader that he deliberately avoided interrupting his narrative in order to present the general results of his geological observations, which he now sets about doing. 'Before we quit the Archipelago of the Canaries, I shall delay a moment, and bring into one point of view what relates to the physical picture of these countries' (I. 196–7).

The illusion of narrative time is here sustained by the fiction that the 'general' or scientific view is a divagation which holds up the narrative progress of the travel account, whereas we know that (if anything) it is the prior motive for having made the ascent in the first place. But Humboldt's desire to defend the aesthetics of travel writing here resurfaces at the end of his vulcanological dissertation when he again apologizes for interrupting the 'rapidity' of the itinerary, which is excused by quite a different rationale for travel narrative, 'the principal end of which is the progress of physical knowledge, [so] every other consideration ought to be subservient to those of instruction and utility' (I. 230). But in now preferring scientific to narrative progress, Humboldt seems to embrace Cuvier's critique of traditional travelogues which, by 'isolating facts' embedded in itinerary narratives, 'have given birth to so many false ideas of the pretended contrasts, which Nature offers in Africa, in New Holland, and on the ridge of the Cordilleras. The great geological phenomena are subject to the same laws, as well as the forms of plants and animals' (I. 230). 'Personal narratives' of travels, by their very nature, seem to embody the discursive form of a culture of curiosity which privileges singularities and contrasts over laws and uniformities. To see nature holistically, in a single point of view, is precisely *not* to see her with the fleeting glance of the traveller who can see only one thing at a time.

As I mentioned in an earlier section, the *Personal Narrative*'s failure to describe the 'antique lands' of Peru and Mexico has resulted in a skewed impression that Humboldt was interested in natural history to the exclusion of historical and antiquarian researches. Certainly its most memorable passages are concerned with evoking the aesthetics of tropical nature, rather than describing human transactions or adventures (apart from the constant stress on the travellers' physical privations): the first sight of the Southern Cross (which Humboldt associates with the description in Bernardin de St Pierre's *Paul et Virginie*) (II. 21–2), the screaming nocturnal birds in the Cueva del Guachero (III. 122–7), the canoe journey along the Orinoco, Casiquiare, and Rio Negro rivers, and the Ature rapids, the cavern of Ataruipe, the 'place of sepulchre of a whole nation destroyed' (V. 615). As in his narrative of the ascent of Pico del Teide, Humboldt is more concerned with a 'phenomenalist' delineation of objects than with picturesque affect; at the rapids of Atures, for example, he insists that 'I shall endeavour to paint, not the sensations we felt, but the aspect of a spot so celebrated amongst the scenes of the new world' (V. 7). But in his description of the 'unexpected aspect of the forests of South America', it transpires that phenomenalism may perform double duty as a rhetoric of sublime inarticulacy:

If [the traveller] feel[s] strongly the beauty of picturesque scenery, he can scarcely define the various emotions, which crowd upon his mind; he can scarcely distinguish what most excites his admiration, the deep silence of those solitudes, the individual beauty and contrast of forms, or that vigour and freshness of vegetable life, which characterise the climate of the tropics.   (PN III. 36)

(The affective confusion which responds to the sheer abundance of tropical nature, subverts the possibility of 'personal narrative' just as it confounds the taxonomical habits of the botanist, 'by a continual interlacing of parasite plants, the botanist is often led to confound the flowers, the fruits, and leaves, which belong to different species' (III. 37).) This, of course, rhetorically evokes the fecundity and diversity of the tropics better than any simply paratactic itemization of species or genus. Elsewhere, Humboldt does employ parataxis in boldly combining scientific and aesthetic registers of description, as in this account of the savannahs of Atures:

Where springs gush from the bosom of these rocks, verrucarias, psoras, and lichens are fixed on the decomposed granite, and have there accumulated mould. Little euphorbias, peperomias, and other succulent plants, have taken the place of the cryptogamous tribes; and evergreen shrubs, rhexias, and purple-flowered melastomas, form verdant islands amidst desert and rocky plains.   (PN V. 45)

Forbidding as this is to the non-botanist, the syntax, active verbs, and island metaphor at least represent nature as a dynamic process—a holistic geography of plants—rather than an itemized catalogue of Linnaean species.

The reader of the *Personal Narrative* looks in vain for the sort of dramatic, interactive account of the human inhabitants found in James Bruce or Mungo Park, and this can only partly be attributed to the fact that Humboldt and Bonpland never leave Spanish colonial territory. As Mary Louise Pratt indicates, Humboldt 'naturalises colonial relations and racial hierarchy, representing Americans, above all, in terms of the quintessential colonial relationship of *disponibilité*' (Pratt, p. 130). True, Bonpland is attacked and injured by a 'zambo' with a club at Cumana (III. 308–9), but Humboldt describes the incident as Bonpland's 'accident'; the travellers are horrified when their Indian servant confesses that the meat of the marimonde monkey is nearly as good as that of human flesh (V. 428). But, as in *Researches*, much of Humboldt's ethnography (such as, memorably, the cavern of Ataruipe) (V. 617) is devoted to demolishing the myth of the American Indian as 'noble savage', situated at the dawn of humankind.[123] More generally, Humboldtian ethnography is presented as a series of 'separate treatises', some of which, he mentions in the Introduction, had actually been

[123] At Ataruipe the travellers find a parrot which still speaks the language of the extinct community whose bodies are buried in the cave. Humboldt digresses on the power of 'remembrances of time past' in a country 'where the traveller is tempted to regard human society as a new institution . . . Those remembrances were not indeed of a distant date; but in all that is monumental antiquity is a relative idea, and we easily confound what is ancient with what is obscure and problematic. The Egyptians considered the historical remembrances of the Greeks as very recent' (PN V. 623).

'prepared during my journey' (I. xxxvii).[124] Amidst his erudite study of American languages and social manners (Humboldt supplied eminent comparativist linguists like his brother Wilhelm and Vater with linguistic materials he had gathered), a habit of generalization emerges which, again echoing the method of *Researches*, situates Amerindians within the history of world civilizations, whilst relegating them to a subordinate position in moral and aesthetic terms. 'We observe in the men of copper hue, a moral inflexibility, a steadfast perseverance in habits and manners which, though modified in each tribe, characterise essentially the whole race' (III. 218). It is precisely this lack of 'mobility' which distinguishes the sullen, melancholy Indian from the 'feeling' European. Humboldt's own extreme 'mobility' as a traveller and his sensitive, aesthetic response to American nature provide an implicit endorsement of this racist and ethnocentric stereotyping throughout the *Personal Narrative*.

Unlike James Bruce in Abyssinia, Humboldt had little interest in discovering the 'source' of the Orinoco; he was more interested in establishing the nature of the whole river system of the region. His engagement with the human geography of South America is conducted in the same *esprit de système*, unconcerned with wonder-hunting. Given that all exotic travel writing in this period is to a greater or lesser extent indebted to 'curious' discourse (however much it may protest to the contrary), Humboldt's narrative is punctuated by anecdotes which bring to mind the magic realism of Gabriel García Márquez's *One Hundred Years of Solitude*. But in conformity with his systematizing approach he parades anecdotal singularities only to disenchant and generalize them. For example, the case of Francisco Lozano, a Venezuelan campesino who has suckled his own child, becomes the occasion for a dissertation on male animals which suckle their young, and the function of the male nipple. Citing examples from as far afield as Cork and Syria, he argues (against Buffon and De Pauw, for whom the lactiferous nature of Amerindian males was a sign of their natural effeminacy) that the phenomenon is no more prevalent in the New than in the Old World (III. 47–51). But legends encountered in the heart of the Orinocan rainforest, such as the 'hairy man of the woods' and the lost Amazonian republic of women, rather than being dismissed out of hand, are given 'higher-critical' validity as testifying to some 'ill-observed' physical or historical truth. The 'man of the woods' (Humboldt digresses to tell the tale of a woman who married such a creature and bore it a brood of hirsute children) is probably simply a capuchin monkey or a large bear; in 'treating [such stories] with disdain, the traces of a discovery may often be lost in natural philosophy, as well as in zoology' (V. 84).

---

[124] These include a dissertation 'on the races of men in S. America; on the missions of the Orinoco; on the obstacles to progress of society in the torrid zone' (I. xxxvii) as well as essays on 'the physical constitution and manners of the Cheymas' (Vol. III, chap. 9) and 'Antiquities of the Aboriginal Inhabitants of America' (VI. pt 1, Note A).

Humboldt's claim that in the mission of the Uruana he had met 'geophagous' Otomac Indians who dined on earth caused nearly as much controversy in the Paris salons as had Bruce's claim to have witnessed Abyssinians cutting beef off live cows in 1770s London. But Humboldt's credit was now indisputable as he analysed the chemical constitution of the yellowish-grey clay which they ate, and its physiological effects in producing a comfortable feeling of satiety (two young French scientists, he announced, have tried a diet of 'laminar talc' and have found it effective in assuaging hunger). Moreover, he is able to 'generalize' the phenomenon by citing geographical parallels: earth-eating negroes in Guinea and savage New Caledonians, Mexicans mixing lime with their maize flour in preparing tortillas, and even (nearer home) German miners who spread clay on their bread to make 'steinbutter' (V. 639–60). Humboldt, ever anxious to turn curiosity into utility, concludes by speculating that with the progress of chemistry, Europeans will soon be able to transform timber into 'alimentary substances' to alleviate famine (V. 661).

'When we have followed the traveller step-by-step in a long series of observations modified by the localities of a place, we love to stop, and raise our views to general considerations' (PN III. 138). Even his admirers sensed the tendency of Humboldt's 'general considerations' to choke 'personal narrative', like some virulent tropical parasite smothering its host. As John Leslie wrote in an otherwise laudatory review of the 1814 volumes:

every object recalls so many others with which it is connected, that the exuberance of illustration sometimes overpowers the reader, and withdraws his attention from the main object. Examples and comparisons . . . do by their number and variety, impair the unity, perhaps in some instances the perspicuity, of the descriptions, and present the collateral objects without a sufficient subordination to the principal.[125]

In his damning review of the same work in the *Quarterly Review*, the voice of the Tory exploration establishment, John Barrow, praised Humboldt's lack of 'egotism' but lambasted his

constant attempt at generalisation, a species of philosophy the more likely to become fashionable from its lying at so little depth beneath the surface . . . a single word or a name suggests a hundred different ideas, and transports him to as many different places . . . in the meanwhile, the subject under immediate discussion is lost sight of.[126]

Those commentators supportive of a 'literary' definition of travel writing tended to criticize this sort of textual diffuseness, as in the *Monthly Review*'s complaint that 'the part which may properly be intitled [*sic*] travels constitute

---

[125] ER, 25 (June 1815), 111.

[126] QR, 14 (Jan. 1816), 401–2. Barrow's description of Bonpland as Humboldt's 'sleeping partner' (p. 369), alluding to his slight contribution to the volumes bearing his name as co-author, suggests also that he was aware of Humboldt's homosexuality, but I have found no other references of this kind in contemporary commentary.

the smallest part of the work . . . so intermixed with disquisitions on various branches of science, that we often lose sight of the progress of the traveller'.[127] Others, like the *British Critic*, considered Humboldt as a naturalist rather than a traveller proper, and therefore found that the book's itinerary format (like Francis Buchanan's *Journey from Madras*, discussed in Chapter 4) interfered with the task of scientific description and comparison, introducing a 'want of arrangement' whereby '[he] treats his subjects not in any logical order but in the order of time and place'.[128] It appeared that the fate of Humboldt's travel account, rather than achieving synthesis, was to fall between the stools of scientific and literary discourse.

A feature of the *Personal Narrative* which has not attracted the critical notice that it deserves is the fact that generalized description gradually overtook 'personal narrative' as the work progressed. In the words of Douglas Botting: 'the first thing to be said about the *Personal Narrative* is that it is neither strictly personal nor strictly narrative'.[129] The English volume of 1814 is largely a conventional travel narrative, albeit one which included lengthy dissertations on volcanoes and ocean currents, as noted above. In the 1818 sequel, pages 1–207, 307–419, and 470–536 are all personal narrative (out of a total of 575 pages), as are pages 56–256, 263–573 (out of a total of 573 pages) in 1819; whilst the 1821 volume contains 636 out of 864 pages of personal narrative. A dramatic shift is noticeable, however, in the 1826 and 1829 volumes (corresponding to the third, and final, volume of the French original). The 1826 volume (English vol. 6, parts 1 and 2) contains only 146 out of 845 pages of travel account; whilst 1829 (English vol. 7) preserves only 120 out of 482 pages. What these quantitative analyses reveal is that Humboldt's *Personal Narrative* was gradually transforming itself, in the course of its protracted and painful delivery, into a 'geographical narrative', a digest of scientific, statistical, and anthropological information which backgrounded the traveller and his itinerary. As if conscious of the metamorphosis that the work was undergoing, and of the problems attendant upon a scientific treatise ordered only by the contingency of an itinerary, in the Preface to the 1826 volume the author promised to give a 'methodological index, for the facility of reference'(VI. pt 1, iii).[130] The final volume, in which the transformation is most obvious, was published separately under the title *Essai politique sur l'île de Cuba*, by Gide in 1826. Only the last chapter of this volume picks up the thread of the narrative, taking us from Cuba back to Colombia bound for Peru, but the narrative is abruptly terminated shortly thereafter.

Humboldt never seems to have explicitly discussed his change of heart con-

[127] MR, 88 (March 1819), 244.   [128] BC, 12 (Oct. 1819), 339.
[129] Douglas Botting, *Humboldt and Cosmos*, p. 211.
[130] Exactly as Francis Buchanan had done in the Preface to his *Travels through Mysore*, discussed in Chap. 4.

cerning the *Personal Narrative*, his reasons for having come over to Cuvier's point of view about travel writing, although (as we saw above) he had been sceptical from the beginning. Clearly the amount of time that had elapsed since the voyage itself—raised by Humboldt as an obstacle to the viability of personal narrative as early as 1805—was a contributing factor. Also, the liberal politics of his book, particularly the anti-slavery sentiments of the Cuban volume, earned him little favour in the reactionary political climate of the late 1820s.[131] In 1829 Humboldt set out on another expedition, to Russian Central Asia, the interest of which would to some extent eclipse the American voyage, even if his claim that he still intended to complete the *Personal Narrative* was true. (But this seems unlikely given his claim to have burnt a completed fourth volume in 1810.[132])

One can only speculate as to the reasons for Humboldt's failure to complete his great work. Charles Minguet suggests that he was deeply embarrassed by the scandal in Ecuador caused by his passing over the brilliant young naturalist Francisco José de Caldas in favour of the aristocratic Carlos Montúfar to join his expedition, for reasons determined either by social snobbery or homosexual attraction to the young nobleman. He would doubtless have had to justify publicly this decision in the completed final section of the *Personal Narrative*.[133] Conversely, Claudio Greppi has hypothesized that Humboldt's growing scholarly interest in the early chroniclers of America, particularly Vespucci and Columbus, inspired by his reading of Spanish historian Martin de Naverette's *Coleccion de los viajes y discubrimientos que hicieron por mar los Españoles desde fines del siglo xv*, published between 1825 and 1837, had overtaken his will to complete his own travel narrative.[134] Greppi indicates the extent to which the latter volumes of the *Personal Narrative* are increasingly burdened with

[131] Margarita Bowen, *Empiricism and Geographical Thought*, pp. 240–1.

[132] The Russian Tsar warned Humboldt to avoid commenting on social conditions in his travelogue, a warning with which he complied (Bowen, p. 242). Minguet points out that Humboldt's thirteen original American travel diaries can still be consulted in the Staatsbibliothek in Berlin, although many are barely legible on account of the astronomical measurements and calculations scrawled over notes filled with geographical and historical details: 'Les journaux sont donc difficilement exploitables, pour ne pas dire inutilisables' (p. 106). Nevertheless, Margot Faak has edited a German text of those diaries which would have provided the basis for the missing fourth volume of *Personal Narrative* (*Alexander von Humboldt: Reise auf dem Rio Magdalena, durch die Anden und Mexico*) (Berlin, 1986). Of course, the original field diaries would have looked quite different after redaction.

[133] See Minguet, p. 105. Caldas was recommended by the eminent Bogotan scientist Celestino Mutis. Montúfar, financed by Humboldt for the rest of the journey, was son of the Marquis of Selva Alegre, one of Quito's premier families; although less skilled in science than Caldas, Montúfar was Humboldt's social peer. Jason Wilson guesses that the choice was homosexually motivated, although in the absence of any evidence on a par with Humboldt's homosexual letters to Reinhard von Haeften, he remains speculative. This theory does, however, have the advantage of explaining why Humboldt claimed to have *burned* the manuscript of the fourth volume. See Introduction to Humboldt's *Personal Narrative* (Penguin), p. xliv.

[134] 'Alejandro De Humboldt y La Invención del Nuevo Mundo', in *Tierra Firma* (Caracas), no: 58, ano 15, vol. XV (1997). My thanks to Felix Driver for this reference.

historical references to the early Spanish chroniclers, to the extent that Humboldt's scholarly odyssey could no longer be contained in notes to his own travelogue. The advantage of this theory is that it explains why Humboldt's major work of the 1830s, which bridges the gap between the *Personal Narrative* and the all-embracing, objectivist *Cosmos*, was the *Examen critique de l'histoire de la géographie du Nouveau Continent* (5 vols., 1836–9). But it does not do justice to the fact that the final volume of the *Personal Narrative* is just as concerned with the contemporary political economy of Cuba, the problem of slavery, and the independence struggles of Spanish America as with the history of early exploration.

I have referred to the unfortunately one-sided image of tropical America as nature rather than culture which resulted from Humboldt's failure to include his account of Peru and Mexico in his *Personal Narrative*, in contrast to the attention devoted to the antiquities of these countries in the *Picturesque Atlas*. Whilst accepting the plausibility of the various explanations on offer for the suppression of the second part of Humboldt's journey, it appears that the seeds for his failure might have been already sown at the book's inception. One need look no further than Humboldt's Introduction, with its innate scepticism about personal narrative, and its gradual textual metamorphosis away from the itinerary format in the conventional sense, to understand the reasons for its abrupt truncation. Humboldt's bid to unite the two hemispheres, to place America within the same time and space as the Old World, ended up sundering literary-aesthetic and scientific narrative modes, as well as to some extent subject-matter. It was clear that no writer after Humboldt was going to succeed where he had failed; the art of travel writing would increasingly be subsumed within the literary field, shorn of its scientific pretensions, just as the professionalization of scientific and geographical discourse would dispense with the taint of the traveller's personal narrative. Humboldt's remarks about travel writing in *Cosmos* (discussed in my Introduction) reveal his personal nostalgia for the old style 'curious' travel account which still bridged the two registers, whilst at the same time he seems to be expressing admiration for the gains in scientific terms, which might compensate for the loss of aesthetic unity.

Conclusion: William Bullock's Mexico and the Reassertion of 'Popular Curiosity'

In the closing pages of his *Personal Narrative*, Humboldt insisted that despite the 'tardy publication' of his book, and the political changes which had seen the Spanish colonies metamorphosed into the independent republics of Latin America, it was still unsurpassed by the myriad of British, American, and European travelogues which had been rushed out in the 1820s. Over-hasty publication to satisfy the craving for information about Mexico and the other republics, ignorance of the Spanish language, inadequate topographical information, 'unjust and disdainful' accounts of the natives, and trivial, anecdotal 'personal narrative' damned most of the new pretenders in his eyes. Whereas Humboldt had sought to 'preserve for the narrative of my travels . . . independence of passing circumstances' and therefore the disinterested character of 'a work of science' (*Personal Narrative* VII. 472), the new travelogues were motivated by sensationalism and commercial greed rather than curiosity. For Humboldt, the narratives of the 'capitalist vanguard' (in Pratt's words)[1] represented a regressive tendency: 'renew[ing] in our days, those enumerations of vice and virtue which disfigured the ancient treatises of geography, and which are founded on vague popular belief' (VII. 470).

Humboldt himself planned to settle in Mexico in 1822 as the president of a projected Latin American institute for the sciences under the patronage of the new republican government of Lucas Alamán (CA p. 177). As popular European interest in Mexico boomed during the post-independence decade, however, he abstained from any personal involvement in 'Mexicomania'. Humboldt's professional training as a mining engineer and his unsurpassed knowledge of Mexican mines could have been turned to lucrative ends, but his ruling attitude of Jena 'disinterestedness' and his distaste for British commercialism prohibited it. In the words of John Taylor (a director of the British-owned Real del Monte silver-mining company) in his Introduction to his *Selections*

---

[1] Pratt, pp. 146–55.

from Humboldt's Works: '[Humboldt] has consistently refused the most advantageous offers to engage himself in any concerns connected with Mexico, that his mind might remain unbiased by any consideration of personal interest'.[2]

Humboldt might well have been dismissive of the hand-in-pocket attitude of the new wave of European and American travellers, but they, by contrast regarded his *Essai politique* with awed reverence—at least until the 'silver bubble' burst in the late 1820s, when the Prussian traveller was frequently criticized for having duped the investing public by painting too rosy a picture of Mexico and its resources. The American traveller Joel Poinsett, in his *Notes on Mexico, Made in 1822*, lamented that 'when I turn to the work of this extraordinary man, I am disposed to abandon any journal. He has seen more of the country, and described it better, than any other can hope to do, and has left almost nothing for the future traveller, but the narrative of his own adventures, and a record of his own feelings and impressions'.[3] The British diplomat Henry Ward reiterated Poinsett's anxiety of belatedness in 1829: 'to write a book about Mexico, without referring to Baron Humboldt at almost every page, is almost impossible . . . [he] traced, with the hand of a master, the outline of that vast picture, which present and future travellers can only assist in filling up'.[4] None the less, it is perhaps ironic that it was the vacuum left by the non-appearance of Humboldt's 'personal narrative' of Mexico which quickly drew in the egotistical, commercially orientated narratives of the 'capitalist vanguard' as they retrod Humboldtian territory.

Although he is never named in person, Humboldt's strictures may have been directed in particular at William Bullock, Pickwickian entrepreneur, showman, naturalist, antiquarian, and proprietor of the Egyptian Hall, Piccadilly; and also one of the first British travellers to visit independent Mexico, where he spent six months in 1822–3.[5] In previous chapters of this book, I have

[2] John Taylor, *Selections from the Works of the Baron de Humboldt, relative to the Climate, Inhabitants, Productions, and Mines of Mexico* (London, 1824) p. iii. Taylor admitted, in contrast, that he was 'deeply interested in the success of these adventures . . . a partial adviser' (p. xxviii). The first 100 pages of Taylor's abridgement deal with topography, climate, agriculture, population, etc., but pp. 110–308 (two-thirds of the book) are solely concerned with mining. Cf. Beck, pp. 298–9 for details of Humboldt's refusal to involve himself in the 1824 mining scheme.

[3] Joel Roberts Poinsett, *Notes on Mexico, Made in 1822, Accompanied by a Historical Sketch of the Revolution, and Translations of Official Reports on the Present State of that Country* (1824) (New York, Washington, London: Praeger Scholarly Reprints, 1969), p. 43.

[4] *Mexico, by Henry G. Ward, Esq., His Majesty's Chargé d'Affaires in that Country during the Years 1825, 1826, and part of 1827. Second Edition enlarged, with an account of the Mining Companies, and of the Political Events in that Republic, to the Present Day*, 2 vols. (London, 1829), ii. 397. Ward copied the Humboldtian formula by presenting 'statistical' information about Mexico in his first volume, reserving the second for what he called his 'Personal Narrative'. This, however, breaks down around p. 200 and is replaced by detached information about various Mexican mines.

[5] There is little scholarship on Bullock, but see Jonathan King, 'William Bullock, Showman', in *Viajeros Europeos del Siglo XIX on México* (Comisión Europea en Mexico/Fomento Cultural Banamex, 1996) pp. 117–26 and E. P. Alexander, 'William Bullock: Little-Remembered Museologist and Showman', in *Curator*, 28 (1985), ii. 117–47.

traced the aesthetics of travel writing from the 'curious' narratives of Hawkesworth and Bruce, via the magisterial overview of Napoleon's savants in Egypt, and the 'carnivalesque' appropriation of polite antiquarianism by Belzoni the circus man, to the rise of the picturesque in British India and the 'stabilization' of imperial sensibility. One recurrent theme (announced in the Introduction and Chapter 1) has been the complex relationship between élite and popular exoticism in the transformation of travel writing. The symbiosis as well as the tension between vulgar and rational curiosity has been indicated in the relationship between works like Denon's *Travels* and Belzoni's *Narrative*; between Valentia's *Voyages and Travels* and Fanny Parks's *Wanderings of a Pilgrim*; survey modality versus picturesque modality, scientific description versus personal narrative; travel books written for the library shelf versus travel books for the parlour table. Given Humboldt's difficulties with personal narrative studied in the previous chapter, and the increasing prevalence of popular curiosity in nineteenth-century travel writing, it seems opportune to conclude with William Bullock, who perhaps more than any other single individual in Britain, capitalized on the commercial opportunities offered by popular exoticism. Bullock, rather than Humboldt, reflects the discursive pressures on the genre in the coming decades of the nineteenth century, as the 'egotistical' travel account, and the popular exhibition order meshed with a mass culture of empire.

In many respects Bullock's book and exhibition about Mexico represented a conscious attempt to emulate the successful formula of Belzoni's Egyptian exhibition and travel narrative, but this time with Bullock single-handedly travelling, collecting, exhibiting, and narrating (he was accompanied in Mexico by his son in the capacity of draftsman).[6] In the spring of 1824 Bullock mounted an enormously popular exhibition entitled 'Ancient and Modern Mexico' in the Egyptian Hall, Piccadilly. He followed this up, later in the same year, with the publication of *Six Months Residence and Travels in Mexico*, which he claimed was the first British travel account of Mexico since the reign of Charles I.[7] Bullock's book, in its racy, popular style reminiscent of Belzoni's, was also published by John Murray; like the exhibition, it capitalized on the massive success of Humboldt's *Essai politique* and the contemporary craze for information about Mexico which accompanied the 'mining boom' of 1824 as British capital poured into the new republic.

[6] Altick, *Shows of London*, pp. 246–9. In the interim, Bullock had mounted an exhibition of Laplanders, complete with a polar panorama, a real-life Sani family, and live reindeer, capitalizing on popular interest in Ross and Parry's Arctic expeditions. (Ibid., pp. 273–4).

[7] *Six Months Residence and Travels in Mexico, Containing Remarks on the Present State of New Spain, its natural productions, state of society, manufactures, trade, agriculture, and Antiquities, etc.* (London: John Murray, 1824), p. vi. Hereafter SMR. Bullock here refers to Thomas Gage's book (based on a visit made in 1625) from which he quotes liberally in SMR, pp. 135–42.

Although not reviewed in either the *Edinburgh Review* or the *Quarterly Review*, presumably on account of what the weekly *Literary Gazette* (8 pence a copy) called its 'popular form',[8] the same periodical noted that *Six Months Residence* was in such demand that the entire first edition of 1,500 copies was bought up by the London booksellers on the first day of publication.[9] Bullock had travelled to Mexico on a semi-official British trades mission carrying samples of British manufactures (SMR p. 27) and copies of Rudolph Ackermann's *Repository of Arts, Literature, Fashions, etc.* to stimulate an appetite for British manufactures and consumer goods among the independent Mexicans.[10] In return he investigated the conditions of the mines for his sponsors while avidly collecting the natural and antiquarian curiosities of Mexico; as the *Literary Gazette* reported in 1824, like a second Hernan Cortéz, Bullock 'arrived when the flood-gates were opened for the first time during centuries . . . our most innovating Countryman was allowed to ransack the superb Capital of Mexico'.[11]

Bullock's Mexican exhibition in some respects echoes Humboldt's concern to provide a visual and aesthetic representation of his travels in the *Ansichten* and *Vues des Cordillères*, using the latest techniques of illusionistic museum display, but translated into the popular idiom of the 'shows of London'. The links between nineteenth-century travel writing and the popular, commercial 'exhibitory order' discussed in Chapter 3 (with reference to Belzoni and Layard) are again laid bare. During his proprietorship of the London Museum (which in 1819 became simply 'the Egyptian Hall', dispensing with its permanent collection in favour of temporary exhibitions and auction rooms) Bullock had pioneered the use of habitat displays in which stuffed animals and birds were situated in 'typical landscapes'.[12] The highlight of the London Museum was the so-called 'Pantherion', into which visitors were ushered via a basaltic cavern into an Indian hut in tropical forest surrounded by an illusionistic panorama 'in which are displayed the whole of the known quadrupeds, in a manner that will convey a more perfect idea of their haunts and modes of life than has hitherto been done' (Bullock boasted that the illusion did not, however, forfeit

[8] LG (19 June 1824), p. 390.   [9] LG (3 July 1824), 422.

[10] Both Bullock and his brother George, one of Britain's leading cabinet-makers, had close links with the Saxon-born Ackermann, and the fact that he sailed to Mexico on a ship chartered by the 'Rhenish Company of Merchants', suggests further links with Ackermann's Anglo-German business empire.

[11] *Literary Gazette*, 10 Jan. 1824, p. 25. The 'permission' granted to Bullock to make casts and remove precious Aztec codices is an index of the desperation of the republican government to encourage British investment. The depredations which occurred, however, eventually prompted Carlos Bustamante's 'Ley de Protección Patrimoniale' presented to the Mexican Congress in 1828, which denounced the sale of antiquities as unpatriotic. See Elena Isabel Estrada de Gerlero, 'El Tema Anticuario en Los Pintores Viajeros', in *Viajeros Europeos*, pp. 184–5.

[12] The idea for such displays may have been borrowed from the Philadelphia Museum of Charles Willson Peale.

Exhibition of Ancient Mexico at the Egyptian-Hall, Piccadilly
Drawn, and Printed by A~~~que~~ 30 Mortimer St. C. Hullmandel

19. William Bullock's 'Exhibition of Ancient Mexico at the Egyptian Hall, Piccadilly'.

Linnaean principles of arrangement and nomenclature). Bullock's catalogue proudly claimed that 'the illusion produced [is] so strong, that the surprised visitor finds himself suddenly transported from a crowded metropolis to the depths of an Indian forest'.[13]

Following the successful formula of his earlier Egyptian and Lapp exhibitions, Bullock now extended the illusionistic treatment to Mexico, ancient and modern. As his guide book to the exhibition boasted, 'the Egyptian Hall has been fitted up, so as to convey some idea of the Temple of Mexico, and in it is disposed whatever relates to the ancient religion'.[14] As his frontispiece illustration shows (Ill. 19) the Egyptian decor of the Hall provided an appropriate (if to the modern eye anatopic) setting for members of the public to examine casts of the Aztec Calendar Stone ('Montezuma's watch'), the Stone of Sacrifices, the 'Great Serpent', the Teoyamiqui statue (Coatlicue), a scale model of the Teotihuacan pyramid, and other Mexican antiquities familiarized to European eyes by Humboldt's *Researches*.[15] At the same time the syntagmatic arrangement of the objects in the 'habitat' context of the Egyptian Hall gave palpable life to the disaggregated antiquarian objects represented in Humboldt's 'picturesque atlas', casting (for example) a sensationalist 'gothic' aura over the cruelties of Aztec sacrifice. Around the walls were displayed copies and originals of Mexican codices, some of which Bullock had acquired on loan from the Boturini Collection in Mexico City, with the permission of the new government (Des p. 51).

In another room was displayed a panorama of modern Mexico City, with an Indian hut surrounded by model agaves and other objects of ethnological, botanical, and zoological interest.[16] A young Mexican Indian called José Cayetano Ponce de León, from Texcoco, who had volunteered to return to England with Bullock, sat in the hut and chatted to the visitors (SMR p. 442), explaining the meaning of the exhibits and even claiming to interpret the pic-

---

[13] *A Companion to the London Museum and Pantherion, Constituting a Brief Description of upwards of 15,000 Natural and Foreign Curiosities, Antiquities, and Productions of the Fine Arts; now open for inspection in the Egyptian Temple, Piccadilly* . . . 15th edn. (London, 1813), pp. 109–10.

[14] *A Description of the Unique Exhibition, called Ancient Mexico; Collected on the Spot in 1823, by the Assistance of the Mexican Government, and now open for public inspection, at the Egyptian Hall, Piccadilly* (London, 1824), p. 30. Hereafter Des.

[15] Bullock's transcultural juxtaposition was by no means simply a feature of the popular exhibition order. Ian Jenkins describes a 'similar clustering' of Mexican antiquities in the Egyptian sculpture gallery of the British Museum. 'By the same reasoning the arts of oriental civilisations were displayed side by side with "curiosities" from Africa and Oceania', *Archaeologists and Aesthetes in the Sculpture Gallery of the British Museum 1800–1839* (London, 1992), p. 62. Many of the BM's Mexican antiquities referred to here were purchased from Bullock after the closure of the 'Mexican Exhibition'.

[16] The following year, John and Robert Burford's panorama of Mexico City, based on Bullock's drawings, was exhibited at the Rotunda in Leicester Square. As with the Egyptian Hall exhibition, the descriptive pamphlet took the opportunity of stressing the commercial advantages of the young republic for interested investors. See Scott Wilcox, 'El Panorama de Leicester Square', in *Viajeros Europeos*, pp. 134–5.

tographic symbols on the Aztec codices.[17] Far from providing the link between the diverse chronotopes of ancient and modern Mexico, the presence of Ponce de León, whom the *Literary Gazette* hailed as the 'first [Mexican Indian] who has visited Europe since the days of Cortez',[18] furthered the sense of Mexico as a time-capsule which was now being unsealed for the delectation of the British public.[19]

Bullock's 51-page descriptive catalogue of 'Ancient Mexico'[20] (presumably 'Modern Mexico' was self-explanatory in the light of what the booklet said about 'Ancient Mexico', as no equivalent catalogue seems to have been available for the former) set the scene by hailing the exhibition as a triumph of the combined forces of creole political virtue and British enterprise over the 'jealous policy of Old Spain' which had kept Mexico in the dark since the conquest (Des p. 2). Bullock provided a very watered-down version of Humboldt's syncretist account of the affinities between Mexican, Egyptian, and Hindu antiquity, indicating points of similarity with 'the Dome of Jugghernaut [and] the Caves of Elephanta or Ellora', but vulgarizing the complexity of his source by supposing that 'their kindred origin can hardly be doubted'[21] (Des p. 3). Bullock's diffusionism was, of course, enforced by the 'Egyptian' setting of the London

---

[17] In April 1824 Dorothy Wordsworth visited the exhibition with her niece, her brother William, and Henry Crabb Robinson. Although she dismissed the antiquities as 'a collection of ugly monstrous things', she enjoyed the modern Mexico section and Robinson showed off his Spanish by chatting to Sr Ponce de León, *Letters of William and Dorothy Wordsworth: The Later Years IV, Part I, 1821–28*, 2nd edn., revised, arranged, and edited by Alan G. Hill (Oxford: Clarendon Press, 1978), p. 260.

[18] LG (3 Jan. 1824), p. 9.

[19] Human exhibits of this kind were common, and continued in the Victorian 'exhibitory order'. As Felix Driver points out, however, 'there was always the possibility that the exhibits themselves would offer unexpected visions and unscripted meanings'. See 'Geography, Empire and Visualisation: Making Representations', in *Royal Holloway, Dept of Geography Research Papers*, General Series No. 1 (1994), p. 6, which discusses the polemic about two African boys exhibited in the 'Stanley and Africa' exhibition of 1890.

[20] Bullock's *Description* challenges Benjamin Keen's assertion that the Louvre's 1851 *Notice des monumens exposés dans la Salle d'Antiquités* was 'the first monograph on Aztec archaeology issued by a European museum' (*Aztec Image*, p. 340). His statement that 'Bullock's own few comments were superficial' is, however, undeniable (p. 348).

[21] In *Six Months Residence* Bullock darkly hinted that Mexican antiquity 'strongly resembled [that] of an enlightened nation of Africa, which may be said to have ceased to exist twenty centuries before this continent was discovered—Who can now solve this difficulty' (p. 395). Fortunately Bullock was too preoccupied with his business affairs to pursue this further. But his comments here anticipate the theories of the colourful Baron Frederick de Waldeck, who believed that the builders of the Maya city of Palenque (in the ruins of which he lived with his Lacendon mistress, Nicte-Tac, for a year in 1832–3) were Africans or Phoenicians. In the *Voyage pittoresque et archéologique dans la province de Yucatán (Amérique Centrale)* (Paris and London, 1838), Waldeck interpreted the Chac-Mool masks at Uxmal as African elephant heads (p. 71). Waldeck was financed by the eccentric Irish nobleman Lord Kingsborough (1795–1837), who spent 32,000 pounds on publishing the lavish nine-volume *Mexican Antiquities* (1832); although the book published all known Mexican codices, the third volume sought to establish the author's pet theory that Mexico had been colonized by the Jews. Kingsborough died in a debtor's prison in Dublin in 1837, ruined by the publication costs. Until the publications of John Stephens and Frederick Catherwood, *Incidents of Travel in Central America and the Yucatan* in 1841, most accounts of American antiquities were regressive in relation to the 'sceptical diffusionist' argument propounded by Humboldt's *Researches*.

exhibition. Humboldt's nuanced analysis of Mexican colonial society was like-wise collapsed back into the terms of the traditional 'black legend' of Spanish rapine. The bloody priestcraft of Moctezuma's reign and the equally bloody policy of Spanish *encomienderos* and inquisitors were represented by Bullock as macabre equivalents both finally transcended in the struggle for republican independence, which had opened a window of opportunity for British capital, liberalism, and free trade (Des p. 4).

Quoting long passages from Cortéz and Bernal Díaz, Bullock established an eyewitness picture of ancient Mexico which provided visitors with the neces-sary grounding for observing the exhibits, uniformly presented here as anti-quarian curiosities rather than as ethnographic specimens or aesthetic objects. Although his description of the exhibits was heavily dependent on the text of Humboldt's *Researches*, Bullock took considerable licence in translating his col-lection into the popular idiom of the 'shows of London', quite distinct from the historical 'grand narrative' which was beginning to transform the syntagmatic arrangement of the contemporary British Museum. His attempt to elicit wonder and the sublime of terror from Mexican antiquities is illustrated in his sensa-tionalization of the iconography of the cast of the Teoyamiqui statue ('the goddess of war'), whose body he described as resembling a 'deformed human frame'; 'the still-palpitating hearts of the unfortunate victims were rubbed', he claimed, 'on the fangs hanging out of the [statue's] mouth'. (This must have been difficult, given the fact stated later in the text that the 'head of the idol was probably elevated five or six metres above the pavement of the temple' (Des. pp. 41–3).[22]) Bullock hoped that the cast of the 'colossal idol', or Great Serpent, crushing a woman in its jaws, despite the fact that it has been 'divested of some of the most offensive parts', would 'serve to give the public an idea of the mon-strous deities of these people, the inspection of which so strongly excited the feelings of Bernal Dias, when he visited the temple with Cortes' (Des p. 31).[23] Despite the 'black legend', the nineteenth-century British viewer was still invited to see indigenous Mexico through the eyes of the first Spanish conquerors.

Ironically, in his *Aspects of Nature* Humboldt had argued for the efficacy of illusionistic exoticism in the construction of European 'planetary conscious-ness', and, in the second volume of *Cosmos* (1849), championed the construc-tion of panoramic displays to complement museums in all great European cities.

[22] Like Gama, Humboldt, and later Carl Nebel, Bullock supposed that the relief of Mictlantecuhtli on the statue's base was intended to be seen by sacrificial victims dragged beneath it.

[23] Capt. G. F. Lyon, in his 1828 *Journal of a Residence and a Tour in the Republic of Mexico in the Year 1826*, 2 vols. (Port Washington, New York and London: Kennikat Scholarly Reprints, 1971) com-pared Bullock's 'somewhat embellished casts' with the originals displayed in the University of Mexico, and regretted that, of the 'Great Serpent' statue, 'the original is nowhere to be found, except in Mr Bullock's exhibition' (II. 120–1). Thanks to Ángel Gurría Quintana for this reference.

Panoramas and dioramas might 'substitute for travelling through different regions', he wrote, as 'the spectator, enclosed as it were within a magic circle, and wholly removed from all the disturbing influences of reality, may more easily fancy that he is actually surrounded by a foreign scene' (*Cosmos* II. 457). At the same time, the spectator's absorption would be generalized and rationalized by his or her ability to locate the spectacle in relation to an internalized 'planetary consciousness'. We saw in Chapter 6 how this conformed (in Humboldt's publications) to tabular hypertexts or scientific end-notes; but it might have been more difficult to enforce in the commercial context of the 'entertaining' panorama or exotic exhibition.[24] It is intriguing to know what Humboldt would have made of Bullock's exhibition, in many ways as much a popularization of his own representation of Mexico as of the country itself. Bullock's museology, in its concern to make the distant object 'present' for a metropolitan public, conforms to only one side of the Humboldtian 'tableau'. Although the popular exhibition, like the popular travelogue, certainly maintained a sense of educational purpose (witness the Linnaean labelling in Bullock's Pantherion, or the descriptive booklets on sale to visitors at the Mexico exhibition), the fact that both were commercial speculations inevitably ensured the prioritization of entertainment over instruction. Filtered through the medium of the popular exhibition, and the rampant commercialism of early nineteenth-century Britain, Humboldt's transcendental aesthetic appears very fragile. Mexico ancient and modern appear here in commodified form, their mobiles—antiquarian casts, stuffed animals, even an indigenous inhabitant—combined at the metropolitan centre with the exclusive aim of stimulating the *commercial* curiosity of potential British investors. The 'antique' Mexico on exhibition feeds a desire which is a necessary precondition for metropolitan capital investment in the new republic, a clear example of what I have termed the 'temporal exchange' of romanticism.

Above all, the exhibition's 'presentism' (like much contemporary travel writing) becomes a vicarious form of travelling, a substitute for the perils of 'the real thing'. The *Literary Gazette* hailed 'Mr Bullock's Mexico in Piccadilly' as in every respect superior to the troubled post-independence reality: 'a country free from the agitation of factions, and the bloodshed of revolutions; where we love to roam and contemplate, at peaceful leisure, almost as much of Mexico as we could see by crossing the Line, and enduring the swamps of Vera Cruz'.[25]

---

[24] On the 'absorptive' qualities of panoramic viewing, see my essay 'Wandering through Eblis: Absorption and Containment in Romantic Exoticism', in *Romanticism and Colonialism: Writing and Empire 1780–1830*, ed. by Tim Fulford and Peter Kitson (Cambridge University Press, 1998).

[25] LG (14 August 1824), p. 521. The ultimate example of mobilization on the grand scale was John L. Stephens's plan to buy the ruined Mayan city of Copan: 'to remove the monuments of a by-gone people from the desolate region in which they were buried, set them up in the "great commercial emporium" [New York], and found an institution to be the nucleus of a great national museum of American

The fever-ridden, politically unstable torrid zone is frozen into a safe spectacle for consumption by the stay-at-home British public. Bullock as 'heroic' traveller has overcome personal dangers to prospect new geopolitical spaces/markets so that the dangerous heterogeneity of the world might be processed and consumed in the centre without risk, even offering a token encounter with indigenous peoples whose surplus labour would be massively expropriated by European capital over the following decades. The magnanimous Humboldtian ideal of planetary consciousness here contracts into the panoptic and one-dimensional European world-view which Timothy Mitchell has called the 'exhibitory order'.[26] The *Literary Gazette*'s review of the Mexico exhibition foreshadows the style of nineteenth-century exotic travel famously exemplified by Flaubert in Egypt, evoked by Maxime du Camp: 'had it been possible for him, he would have preferred to travel stretched out motionless on a divan, watching the landscapes, ruins and cities pass by before him like the canvas of a mechanically-unfolding panorama'.[27]

If Humboldt's *Voyage* had represented the traveller as a transcendental consciousness whose manifest presence gradually dissolved into a totally *impersonal* narrative, Bullock's Pickwickian travelling personality, his commercial transactions with Mexicans, and artisanal 'mobilization' of antiquities and natural historical specimens are the main concerns of *Six Months Residence*. Whilst Poinsett and Ward deferred to their precursor at every point, Bullock unabashedly ticks off Humboldt for his inaccurate representation of sites like Cholula (SMR p. 115) boasting of his success in obtaining a rare Aztec map of Tenochtitlan which Humboldt had failed to locate. Humboldt's geological 'principle of attachment' upon first setting foot on the New Continent is burlesqued in Bullock's narrative into pure unrefined John Bullism: landing on the pier at Vera Cruz, he is gratified to see that

it was partially paved with pigs of iron, each bearing the broad arrow of the king of England . . . the first step an Englishman takes in New Spain is upon what was once English property. May this be an auspicious omen of the future good understanding and commercial intercourse between the two countries.   (SMR p. 15)

Dispensing, then, with the Humboldtian transcendental self, Bullock adopts a low-brow version of the egotistical, anecdotal, episodic, transactive narrative of the Bruce, Denon, or Belzoni style. Like Belzoni's *Narrative*, Bullock's *Six Months Residence* exposes the fetishized relationship between the metropolitan

antiquities . . . they belonged of right to us'. Stephens's plan was never fulfilled. *Incidents of Travel in Central America, Chiapas, & Yucatan (1841)* (London: Century Books, 1988), p. 57.

[26] 'Orientalism and the Exhibitory Order', in *Colonialism and Culture*, ed. by Nicholas Dirks (Ann Arbor: University of Michigan Press, 1992), pp. 289–318.

[27] Quoted by Roger Cardinal in 'Romantic Travel', in *Rewriting the Self: Histories from the Renaissance to the Present*, ed. by Roy Porter (London: Routledge, 1997), p. 150.

spectator and the exotic object as 'a definite social relationship between men', although it is less easy to sympathize with Bullock's proactive John Bullism. Everywhere Bullock travels he dispels the gloom, idleness, and ignorance of centuries of Spanish misrule, filling the vacuum with commercial modernity. Those Mexicans still ignorant enough to consider Britons as mere filibusters in the Francis Drake and Walter Ralegh mould, 'viewed with surprise my walking-stick gun, my portable chair and table, my camera lucida, and other little specimens of English ingenuity' (p. 54). Bullock as 'commercial traveller' is as keen to promote distant Britain among future Mexican clients as he is to 'realize' distant Mexico for British investors and manufacturers in *Six Months Residence*. The fact that Bullock could not speak a word of Spanish further prompts his obsession with money as a universal language with the power to traverse all cultural barriers.

Bullock's account continues the obsession with detail characteristic of the tradition of travel writing noted throughout this book; the only difference here is that the conventional separation of 'curiosity' from 'utility' is thrown to the winds. Every particular has a price tag attached, belying Bullock's claim to General Santa Anna that the purpose of his visit was 'solely to acquire scientific information' (SMR p. 28). The absence of knives at the Mexican table hints at a potential market for Sheffield cutlers (SMR p. 58); the observation that the chairs in fashionable households are of American rather than Mexican manufacture suggests another opportunity for British enterprise (SMR p. 210). Bullock even redesigned the dye of the Mexican eagle for the mint in Mexico City, 'copied from a fine specimen of the Falco Chrysaetos, which I killed in Scotland, and is well etched by Howett, in my catalogue of the late London Museum' (SMR p. 202). For Bullock the circulation of better designed silver coinage (and he greedily estimated that a total of 2,250 million dollars had been struck in the mint and circulated over the globe) would have 'contributed to improve the taste of mankind, by diffusing a knowledge of the arts' (SMR p. 202). The intimate relationship between travel, curiosity, and capitalism often concealed in the scientific or antiquarian tradition of travel writing is here laid bare.

Despite his claim to have been debarred from female company, Bullock manifested a keen interest in women's fashions: observing the black Spanish dress and mantillas of the ladies of Jalapa, he handed out copies of Ackermann's fashion plates, and upon returning six months later was delighted to note that 'instead of appearing in black as formerly, many were now to be seen in the last fashions of England, in white muslins, printed calicos, and other manufactures of Manchester and Glasgow' (p. 484). 'The revolution in dress and fashion will probably be as great as that in politics', Bullock wrote complacently, archly adding 'and I hope [fashions] will change more frequently' (p. 485). On this point he showed a remarkable lack of foresight concerning the future of

Mexican politics; its debilitating instability exacerbated by the fluctuating caprice of nineteenth-century capital.

The climax of Bullock's narrative is his 'taking possession' of the Del Bada silver mine at Temascaltepec, the rights to which he had been granted by the Mexican government as a reward for his entrepreneurial activities. In a symbolic anticipation of the shape of Anglo-Mexican relations over the next decade, Bullock enthuses over the picturesque situation of his mine, the perfection of the climate, the fecundity of the vegetation, the richness of the agricultural productions, the *disponibilité* of the local Indians (SMR p. 432). Leaving his son to manage the mine while he returned to England, he successively raised (via the Mexican exhibition and travel book) 15,000–20,000 pounds of capital to invest in the project. Visiting Temascaltepec a few years later, Henry Ward noted the splendid house built by Bullock, but recorded the collapse of the 'unfortunate speculation' due to the fact that 'in the mine itself . . . there was no vestige of a vein!' He regretted that Bullock 'should have been influenced rather by the beauties of the scenery, than by the intrinsic value of the mine' itself (*Mexico* II. 152). His son had died of yellow fever.[28]

If Bullock visited Mexico as a harbinger of commercial modernity, the Mexico which he appropriated (by a selective reading or misreading of Humboldt) and brought back to Britain was sealed in the historical time of the Spanish Conquest. Cortéz, rather than Humboldt, is Bullock's presiding genius, albeit a Cortéz scaled down from the heroic, epic stature of conqueror to that of a particularly enterprising nineteenth-century commercial traveller. When he visited Cortéz's tomb in the Hospital of Jesus, Bullock was allowed to touch his bones and subject his cranium to phrenological examination, but noted (in an anthropomorphized version of Bruce's diminishment of the Nile at Gish) that 'I saw nothing to distinguish it—I should judge from it that his person was small' (SMR p. 159). Bullock's first view of Mexico City (a climactic moment in the narratives of Cortéz and Bernal Díaz) was one of disappointment: 'the country in its immediate vicinity resembled the worst parts of Lincolnshire . . . have I then for such a place left my home and all that is dear to me . . . what have I gained in the exchange?' (SMR p. 123).[29] Bullock instead

---

[28] Stymied in Mexico, Bullock's next project was the establishment of a utopian community called 'Hygeia' outside Cincinnati, which he publicized in his *Sketch of a Journey through the Western States of North America ... with a description of the new and flourishing city of Cincinnati by Messrs. Drake and Mansfield, containing useful information to persons desirous of settling in America* (London: John Miller, 1827). See Fanny Trollope's amusing account of meeting Bullock in Cincinnati in 1828 in ch. 5 of her *Domestic Manners of the Americans* (1832) (Gloucester: Alan Sutton Publishing, 1984), pp. 35–6.

[29] Compare my discussion of Fanny Calderón's first sight of Mexico City in 'The Ghost in Chapultepec: Fanny Calderón de la Barca, William Prescott and 19th-Century Mexican Travel Accounts', in *Voyages and Visions*, pp. 197–8.

identifies with Cortéz in adversity, viewing the Aztec armies from atop the pyramid before the Battle of Otumba, after his expulsion from Tenochtitlan on the *noche triste* (SMR p. 413), yet filled with resolve to overcome all obstacles.

Bullock asserted that Mexico is 'three hundred years behind Europe in every species of refinement' due to Spanish misrule (SMR p. 203). Again and again Mexico and its inhabitants are presented in Radcliffean picturesque terms; their strangeness familiarized by reference to feudal, pre-reformation English history, in the by-now familiar idiom of romantic temporalization. In Puebla, he suggested that

the antiquarian will . . . find himself removed to the period of our Henrys and Edwards, not only in the style of building of those times, but even in the similarity of customs and manners, the same religion and ceremonies, the same observance of holydays, with the religious processions that at once were the solace and amusement of our ancestors.   (SMR p. 82)

Yet 'the very dresses and accoutrements of the country gentlemen strongly remind us of the period of the discovery of America, the costumes having undergone very little alteration from their first introduction by the Spaniards' (SMR pp. 82–3). By wiping three hundred years of Spanish colonial history off the slate, Bullock tacitly associates Cortéz's Mexico with the manners of feudal England, thereby providing an imaginative template for the new conquest of Mexico by British capital. Although he nowhere mentions Robert Southey's epic poem *Madoc* (1804), Bullock is thus performing a similar ideological task in reimagining the conquest of Mexico as a British rather than a Hispanic achievement, and as a process of commercial reciprocation rather than of rapine and destruction.[30]

Romantic temporalization here is, however, easily burlesqued as historical farce. Bullock's chapter 24, 'Ancient Mexico', is largely composed of lengthy quotations from the Abbe Clavigero's history, which offers, among other things, to reconstruct the contemporary 'feel' of Moctezuma's court (including, obviously enough, detailed descriptions of the museologically-minded Aztec emperor's botanical garden, zoo, and collection of human freaks). But in chapter 26, passing through the village of S. Miguel de los Ranchos, en route for Temascaltepec, Bullock describes a fiesta featuring a pantomimic recreation of the court of Moctezuma staged by the fully costumed Indians (SMR p. 356). When the actor impersonating Moctezuma receiving the homage of his prisoners momentarily forgot his protocol, 'he was gently reminded of the error by getting a smart stroke on the cheek with the fiddlestick of the high priest'

---

[30] On the employment of Southey's poem in later Anglo-American writings on Mexico, see ibid., pp. 191, 198.

(SMR p. 357). This comic humiliation domesticates the more *unheimlich* aspects of Aztec history—war, mutilation, and human sacrifice—narrated in chapter 24, as the indigenous descendants of Moctezuma parody their own tragic history.

One attractive feature of Bullock's popular, egotistical style (again like Belzoni and in contrast to Humboldt) is his willingness to describe his own mockery at the hands of local Mexicans. One of the clowns at the Indian fiesta in Temascaltepec mimics the future proprietor of the town's mine, making 'several pointed allusions to a stranger who had arrived . . . from the other side of the world, to feast on humming-birds, beetles, butterflies, and lizards'. This satire on natural history collecting as alimentary perversion in some ways balances Bullock's earlier account of Mexican Indians as 'descendants of cannibal ancestors' (SMR p. 50). Bullock—in the spirit of reciprocity—adds that he was obliged to join in the laughter at his own expense (SMR pp. 368–9). Yet the Indian mimic had correctly noted Bullock's obsessive desire to copy, model, and collect. True to his vocation as a museum curator and member of the Linnaean Society, for Bullock to observe specimens was also to acquire, preserve, and transport them. Author of an influential treatise on taxidermy, he was concerned to make his mobiles as lifelike as possible in order to enhance the illusionistic 'presentism' of his exhibitions. Like Belzoni's narrative (and in stark contrast to Humboldt's), *Six Months Residence* is a chronicle of collecting, a supplement to the objects on display in the Egyptian Hall (needless to say, the narrative is frequently interrupted in order to advertise the Mexico exhibition). The 'real' Mexico of the travelogue always has a slight edge over the Piccadilly Mexico, however: for example, Bullock confessed that although 'he had carefully preserved about two hundred species [of humming-birds] in the best possible manner, yet they are still but the shadow of what they were in life' (SMR p. 273). As well as collecting and stuffing numerous species of animals such as axolotls, 'armadilloes, deers, parrots, currassow-birds, quans [*sic*], tiger-cats, etc. etc.' (SMR p. 483), he made plaster casts of a wide variety of exotic fruit which he bought in the market. Bullock's narrative of his artesanal techniques of mimicry is always in the end more interesting than the plaster copies exhibited in Piccadilly.

The account of Bullock's acquisition of Mexican antiquities (or their casts) in chapter 25 of *Six Months Residence* provides a fuller context for the objects exhibited in the Egyptian Hall—as well as their collector's overdetermined relationship to them—than the impersonal, itemizing account in the descriptive catalogue. As such, it looks back to Belzoni's *Narrative*, and forward to A. H. Layard's *Ninevah and its Remains* (1849) (also discussed in Chapter 3) which provided a similar narrative 'context' for the Egyptian and Assyrian antiquities exhibited in the British Museum. Compared to many of the other European antiquarians who flocked to Mexico in the wake of independence,[31] Bullock was clearly an amateur, more interested in collecting curiosities for his museum than in scholarly antiquarian or comparativist research. Like Belzoni, he emphasized the artisanal effort necessary to procure his casts: the laborious process of erecting a scaffold in order to mould a cast of the Aztec Calendar, for example, which he praised as 'this fine specimen of Aztec skill' (SMR p. 334), acknowledging the co-operation and generosity of the Mexican minister, Lucas Alamán.

Describing the Stone of Sacrifices in its original location, he noted the abhorrence with which it was still regarded by modern Mexicans: 'I once saw a boy jump upon it, clench his fist, stamp with his foot, and use other gesticulations of the greatest abhorrence' (SMR p. 335). In general, lower class Mexicans are represented (like the Egyptian or Indian peasants of Denon, Belzoni, and Heber's narratives) as being utterly ignorant of the value or meaning of their own antiquities.[32] Yet, untrammelled by Humboldtian concerns about aesthetic hierarchy, the showman in Bullock admired the efficacy of the Teoyamiqui (Coatlicue) statue as an object of popular sublime terror: 'the united talents and imagination of Brughel and Fuseli would in vain have attempted to improve it' (SMR p. 340). Following Humboldt's example, he had caused the statue's disinterral from under the gallery of the university in order to make a cast. Bullock described the divergent reactions on the part of the watching Mexicans as the 'hideous' statue came to light: whereas the criollos 'expressed the most decided anger and contempt', the Indians watched with silence and attention, one old man remarking 'It is true that we have three very good Spanish gods, but we might still have been allowed to keep a few of those of our ancestors!' (SMR pp. 341–2). Subaltern disquiet here feeds Bullock's 'temporalizing' myth, allowing ancient Mexico to obtrude through centuries of colonial misrule, feeding the desire of the British public for unmediated possession of such 'curious' monuments of an 'antique land' in exchange for commerce, reason, and modernity. But Bullock's hyperbolic picture of Mexico seems to have been just as susceptible of 'boom and bust' as the new capitalist economy which it promoted. When Capt. Lyon (agent, it should be said, of a rival mining company) met Bullock in 1826, he reported that the latter 'now finds how mistaken he was in the grand ideas which he had formed of [Mexico] . . . against which and its whole population he now rails most unmercifully'.[33]

[31] See Isabel Estrada de Gerlero, 'El Tema Antićuario en los Pintores Viajeros', in *Viajeros Europeos*, pp. 183–201.

[32] As mentioned above, Mexican nationalism constructed a romanticized version of the indigenous past as a foundation for independent Mexican identity, although by mid-century it seemed to carry little weight. See 'The Ghost in Chapultepec', pp. 190–1; and Anthony Pagden 'Identity Formation in Spanish America', in *Colonial Identity in the Atlantic World*, ed. by Nicholas Canny and Anthony Pagden (Princeton University Press, 1987), pp. 51–94, particularly pp. 66–8.

[33] *Journal of a Residence*, ii. 125–6.

Bullock's Mexico is at once the travesty, and the inevitable translation into the language of commodity capitalism, of Humboldtian 'planetary consciousness'. Hans Blumenberg reminds us that Humboldt himself 'most nearly typifies curiosity [*theoretische Neugierde*] for the first half of the nineteenth century'. (Blumenberg here celebrates 'curiosity' as the key term in a grand emancipatory narrative which legitimated the modern age, more akin to the 'rational' as opposed to the 'vulgar' sense defined by Lord Kames, discussed in Chapter 1.[34]) At the same time, Blumenberg cites the Prussian traveller in a letter of December 1849 asking

Is it not enough to drive one to despair, to have to see how all our efforts to disseminate accurate geographical data amongst the people are in vain? How an object of curiosity is botched, you can see from the issue of the *Illustrated News* that I have enclosed.[35]

The two styles of curiosity have a disconcerting tendency to converge, undermining the transcendental overview of Humboldt's programme, its desire to emancipate romantic world-consciousness from vulgar interest. The Prussian savant's irritated bid to salvage the distinction between an appetite for legitimate knowledge (*Wissbegierde*) and vulgar curiosity (*Neugier*), contrasted with William Bullock's indifference to any such distinction, illuminates the ongoing ambivalence of the term, which, in its intimate relationship with travel writing, has been a guiding thread of this book.

[34] See pp. 25–9 above, and Neil Kenny's critique of the Blumenbergian grand narrative in *Curiosity in Early Modern European Word Histories*, pp. 45–9.
[35] Hans Blumenberg, *The Legitimacy of the Modern Age*, trans. by Robert M. Wallace (Cambridge, Mass.: Harvard University Press, 1983), pp. 438–9.

Bibliography

Primary Sources

Periodicals Cited

Analytical Review	AR
Annals of the Fine Arts	
Asiatic Register	A Reg
Asiatic Researches	A Res
British Critic	BC
Edinburgh Review	ER
Examiner	
Literary Gazette	LG
London Magazine	LM
Monthly Magazine	MM
Monthly Review	MR
Quarterly Review	QR

Books and Articles

Abu Taleb Khan, Mirza, *The Travels of, in Asia, Africa, and Europe, during the years 1799, 1800, 1801, 1802, and 1803. Written by himself, in the Persian Language*, trans. by Charles Stewart, 2 vols. (London, 1810).

Al-Jabarti, *Chronicle of the First Seven Months of the French Occupation of Egypt*, ed. and trans. by S. Moreth (Leiden: E. J. Brill, 1975).

Bacon, Lt. Thomas, *First Impressions and Studies from Nature in Hindostan . . . from 1831–34*, 2 vols., illus. with lithographic plates (London: William Allen, 1837).

Banks, Joseph, *The Endeavour Journal*, ed. by J. C. Beaglehole, 2 vols. (Sydney: Angus & Roberston, 1962).

Bartram, William, *Travels through North and South Carolina, Georgia, East and West Florida . . .* (1791), ed. by Mark van Doren (New York: Dover Publications, 1928).

Belzoni, Giovanni, *Narrative of the Operations and Recent Discoveries within the Pyramids, Temples, Tombs and Excavations, in Egypt and Nubia; and of a Journey to the coast of the Red Sea, in search of the Ancient Berenice; and another to the Oasis of Jupiter Ammon* (1820), 2nd edn. (London: John Murray, 1821).

——*Description of the Egyptian Tomb, Discovered by G. Belzoni* (London: John Murray, 1821).

Bougainville, Louis de, *Voyage Round the World*, trans. by J. R. Forster, 2 vols. (London, 1772).

Browne, William G., *Travels in Africa, Egypt and Syria, from the year 1792 to 1798* (London, 1799).

Bruce, James, *Travels to Discover the Source of the Nile*, 5 vols. (Edinburgh: J. Ruthven, 1790).

—— *Travels to Discover the Source of the Nile, 3rd edition, to which is prefixed a life of the Author*, 8 vols. (Edinburgh, 1813).

Bruce's Travels to Discover the Source of the Nile, selected and edited by C. F. Beckingham (Edinburgh University Press, 1964).

Brydone, Patrick, *A Tour through Sicily and Malta*, 2 vols. (Dublin, 1774).

Buchanan, Francis, *Journey from Madras through the Countries of Mysore, Canara, and Malabar*, 2 vols. (London, 1807).

Bullock, William, *A Companion to the Liverpool Museum, Containing a Brief Description of Two Thousand of its Curiosities; the Natural History arranged according to the System of Linnaeus*, 4th edn. (Liverpool, 1805).

—— *A Companion to the London Museum and Pantherion, Constituting a Brief Description of upwards of 15,000 Natural and Foreign Curiosities, Antiquities, and Productions of the Fine Arts; now open for inspection in the Egyptian Temple, Piccadilly . . .* , 15th edn. (London, 1813).

—— *A Concise and Easy Method of Preserving Subjects of Natural History, Intended for the Use of Sportsmen, Travellers, etc.* (London, 1817).

—— *A Description of the Unique Exhibition, called Ancient Mexico; Collected on the Spot in 1823, by the Assistance of the Mexican Government, and now open for public inspection, at the Egyptian Hall, Piccadilly* (London, 1824).

—— *Six Months Residence and Travels in Mexico, Containing Remarks on the Present State of New Spain, its natural productions, state of society, manufactures, trade, agriculture, and antiquities, etc.* (London: John Murray, 1824).

—— *Sketch of a Journey through the Western States of North America . . . with a description of the new and flourishing city of Cincinnati by Messrs. Drake and Mansfield, containing useful information to persons desirous of settling in America* (London, John Miller, 1827).

Burckhardt, John Lewis, *Travels in Nubia, Published by the Association for Promoting the Discovery of the Interior Parts of Africa* (1820), 2nd edn. (London: John Murray, 1822).

Burke, Edmund, *Correspondence*, ed. by Thomas Copeland, 10 vols. (Cambridge University Press and Chicago University Press, 1958–78).

Burney, Fanny, *The Early Journals and Letters of*, Vol. II (1774–7), ed. by Lars E. Troide (Oxford: Clarendon Press, 1990).

Calderón de la Barca, *Life in Mexico (1843): The Letters of Fanny Calderón de la Barca with new material from the Author's Private Journals*, ed. and annotated by Howard T. Fisher and Marion H. Fisher (New York: Doubleday, 1966).

Chandra [Chunder], Bholanath, *The Travels of a Hindoo to Various Parts of Upper India*, intro. by J. Talboys Wheeler, 2 vols. (London, 1869).

Clarke, Edward Daniel, *Travels in Various Countries of Europe, Asia, and Africa; Part 1, Russia, Tartary, and Turkey*, 6 vols. (Cambridge and London, 1810). *Part II, Greece, Egypt and the Holy Land* (London, 1812).

Clavigero, Francisco, *The History of Mexico, Collected from Spanish and Mexican Histories, from Manuscripts, and Ancient Paintings of the Indians . . . To which are added Critical Dissertations on the Land, the Animals, and the Inhabitants of Mexico*. (1780–1), trans. by Charles Cullen, 2 vols. (London, 1787).

Coleridge, S. T., *Poetical Works*, ed. by E. H. Coleridge (Oxford University Press, 1912).

—— *Table Talk*, ed. by Carl Woodring, 2 vols. (Princeton, NJ and London: Princeton University Press, 1990), ii. 57.

—— *Biographia Literaria*, ed. by Nigel Leask (London: J. M. Dent, 1997).

Combe, William, *The Tour of Dr Syntax, in Search of the Picturesque: A Poem*, 5th edn. with new plates (1813) (London, nd).

Cuvier, Georges, *Recherches sur les ossemens fossiles de quadrupèdes (1812)*, in Martin J. Rudwick, *Georges Cuvier, Fossil Bones, and Geological Catastrophe: New Translations and Interpretations of the Primary Texts* (Chicago and London: University of Chicago Press, 1997), pp. 33–41.

Daniell, Thomas, and Daniell, William, RA, *Oriental Scenery* (144 aquatint engravings), (London, 1795–1808).

—— —— *A Picturesque Voyage to India, by the Way of China* (London, 1810).

Darwin, Charles, *Journal of Researches into the Natural History and Geology of the Countries visited during the Voyage round the World of H.M.S Beagle*, 2nd edn. (1845), (London: John Murray, 1905).

De Quincey, Thomas, *Works*, ed. by David Masson, 14 vols. (Edinburgh, 1890).

Degérando, J.-M., *The Observation of Savage People*, trans. by F. C. T. Moore, Preface by E. E. Evans-Pritchard (London: RKP, 1969).

Del Río, Antonio, *Description of the Ruins of an Ancient City, discovered near Palenque* (London, 1822).

Denon, Vivant, *Travels in Upper and Lower Egypt, in Company with Several Divisions of the French Army, during the Campaigns of Gen. Bonaparte in that Country* (1801), trans. by Arthur Aikin, 3 vols. (London, 1803).

De Pauw, Cornelius, *Recherches philosphiques sur les Américaines, ou mémoires intéressants pour servir a l'histoire de l'espèce humaine*, 2 vols. (Berlin, 1768).

Description de l'Égypte, 22 vols. (Paris, 1809–22).

—— Fourier, J. B., 'Préface historique', *Description de l'Égypte* (Paris, 1809).

—— *Antiquités, Planches*, Tome Deuxième (Paris, 1812).

Eastlake, Lady Elizabeth, 'Lady Travellers', *Quarterly Review*, 76 (June–Sept. 1845), 98–137.

Edmonstone, Sir Archibald, Brt., *A Journey to Two of the Oases of Upper Egypt* (London: John Murray, 1822).

Elphinstone, Mountstuart, *Account of the Kingdom of Caubul, and its Dependencies in Persia, Tartary, and India* (London, 1815).

Faak, Margot, *Alexander von Humboldt: Reise auf dem Rio Magdalena, durch die Anden und Mexico* (Berlin, 1986).

Fay, Eliza, *Original Letters from India (1779–1815), Containing a Narrative of a Journey through Egypt, and the Author's Imprisonment at Calicut by Hyder Ali* (1817), new edn. with intro. and notes by E. M. Forster (London: Hogarth Press, 1925).

Fitzclarence, Lt.-Col. (Earl of Munster), *Journal of a Route across India, through Egypt, to England, in the latter end of 1817 and the beginning of 1818* (London: John Murray, 1819).

Forbes, James, *Oriental Memoirs: Selected and Abridged from a Series of Familiar Letters written during 17 years residence in India*, 4 vols. (London, 1813).

Forster, George, *A Journey from Bengal to England, Through the North Part of India, Kasmire, Afghanistan, and Persia . . .* 2 vols. (London, 1798).

Forster, George, [Georg] *A Voyage Round the World in his Brit. Majesty's Sloop Resolution, commanded by Capt. Cook, during the years 1772, 1773, 1774, and 1775*, 2 vols. (London, 1777).

Forster, J. R., *Observations made during the Voyage round the World, on Physical Geography, Natural History, and Ethic Philosophy* (London, 1778), new edn. by N. Thomas, H. Guest, and M. Dettelbach (University of Hawaii Press, 1996).

Fraser, James Baillie, *Journal of a Tour through Part of the Snowy Range of the Himala Mountains, and to the Sources of the Rivers Jumna and Ganges* (London, 1820).

—— *Views in the Himala Mountains*, engraved by Robert Havell & Sons (London, 1820).

Gilpin, William, *Three Essays on Picturesque Beauty*, 'Essay 1 on Picturesque Beauty', in Malcolm Andrews (ed.), *The Picturesque: Literary Sources and Documents*, 3 vols. (E. Sussex: Helm Information, 1994).

Gordon, George, Lord Byron, *Letters and Journals*, ed. by Leslie Marchand, 12 vols. (London: John Murray, 1978).

Graham, Maria, *Journal of a Residence in India*, 2nd edn. (Edinburgh, 1813).

J. J. Halls, *Life and Correspondence of Henry Salt*, 2 vols. (London, 1834).

Hamilton, William, *Remarks on Several Parts of Turkey. Pt 1 Aegyptiaca, or Some Account of the Antient and Modern State of Egypt, as obtained in the Years 1801, 1802* (London, 1809).

Hawkesworth, John, *An Account of the Voyages Undertaken by the Order of his Present Majesty for Making Discoveries in the Southern Hemisphere, and successively performed by Comm. Byron, Capt. Wallis, Capt. Carteret, and Capt. Cook . . . Drawn up from the Journals which were kept by the several Commanders and from the Papers of Joseph Banks, Esq.*, 3 vols. (London: W. Strahan and T. Cadell, 1773).

Haydon, Benjamin, R., *Autobiography* (Oxford University Press, 1927).

Hazlitt, William, *Complete Works*, ed. by P. P. Howe, 21 vols. (London and Toronto: Dent, 1930–4).

Heber, the Late Right Revd Reginald, DD, Lord Bishop of Calcutta, *Narrative of a Journey through the Upper Provinces of India, from Calcutta to Bombay, 1824–1825 (with Notes upon Ceylon). An Account of a Journey to Madras, and the Southern*

Provinces, 1826, and Letters written in India, ed. by Amelia Heber, 2 vols. (London: John Murray, 1828).

Hegel, G. W. F., *Lectures on the Philosophy of World History: Introduction*, trans. by H. B. Nisbet, intro. by Duncan Forbes (Cambridge University Press, 1975).

Hemans, Felicia, 'The Traveller at the Source of the Nile' (1829), in Andrew Ashfield (ed.), *Romantic Women Poets, 1770–1838: An Anthology* (Manchester University Press, 1995), pp. 190–1.

Hobhouse, John Cam, *A Journey through Albania, and other Provinces of Turkey in Europe and Asia, to Constantinople, during the years 1809–10*, 2 vols., 2nd edn. (London, 1813).

Hodges, William, *Select Views in India*, 2 vols. (London, 1785–88).

—— *Travels in India* (London, 1793).

Home, Henry [Lord Kames], *Elements of Criticism* (1762), 11th edn. with the author's last corrections and additions (London, 1839).

—— *Sketches of the History of Man* (1774), 2 vols. 3rd edn. (Dublin, 1779).

Humboldt, Alexander von, *Aspects of Nature, in Different Lands and Different Climates; with Scientific Elucidations*, trans. by Mrs Sabine, 2 vols. (London, 1849).

—— *Cartas Americanas*, trans. by Marta Traba, compiled, selected, and ed. by Charles Minguet (Caracas: Biblioteca Ayacucho, 1980).

—— *Atlas pittoresque du voyage, plus connu sous le titre: vues des Cordillères, et monumens des peuples indigènes de l'Amérique*, 2 vols., avec 69 planches (Paris, 1810) (Vols. 15–16 of *Voyage*).

—— *Political Essay on New Spain*, 4 vols., trans. by John Black (London, 1811).

—— *Researches Concerning the Institutions and Monuments of the Ancient Inhabitants of America, with Descriptions and Views of Some of the most Striking Scenes in the Cordilleras*, trans. by H. M. Williams (London, 1814).

—— *Rélation historique du voyage aux regions équinoxiales du Nouveau Continent, fait en 1799–1804*, 3 vols. (Paris) (Vol. I, 1814; Vol. II, 1819; Vol. III, 1825) (Vols. 28–30 of *Voyage*).

—— *Personal Narrative of Travels to the Equinoctial Regions of the New Continent, During the Years 1799–1804. Written in French by Alexander de Humboldt and Aimé Bonpland, and translated into English by Helen Maria Williams*, 7 vols. (London, 1814–29) (Vols. 1–2, 1814; Vol. 3, 1818; Vol. 4, 1819; Vol. 5, 1821; Vol. 6 pts 1 and 2, 1826; Vol. 7, 1829).

—— *Examen critique de l'histoire de la géographie du Nouveau Continent*, 5 vols. (Paris, 1836–9) (Vol. 19 of *Voyage*).

—— *Cosmos: A Sketch of a Physical Description of the Universe*, 5 vols., trans. by E. C. Otte (London: Bohn, 1849).

—— and Bonpland, Aimé, *Essai sur la geógraphie des plantes, accompagné d'un Tableau Physique des régions equinoxiales, et servent d'introduction à l'ouvrage* (Paris, 1807). (Vol. 27 of *Voyage aux régions equinoxiales du Nouveau Continent, fait en 1799–1804 par Alexandre du Humboldt et Aimé Bonpland*, 30 vols., Grande édition (Paris: Schoell, Dufour, Maze et Gide), 1807–34).

Hume, David, *Enquiries Concerning Human Understanding and Concerning the*

Principles of Morals, reprinted from 1777 edition, with intro and Analytical Index by L. A. Selby-Bigge, 3rd edn., with text revised and notes by P. H. Nidditch (Oxford: Clarendon Press, 1975).

Hume, David, *A Treatise of Human Nature,* ed., with an analytical index, by L. A. Selby-Bigge, 2nd edn., with text rev. by P. H. Nidditch (Oxford: Clarendon Press, 1978).

Jacquemont, Victor, *Letters from India; Describing a Journey in the British Dominions of India, Tibet, Lahore, and Cashmere, during the years 1828, 9, 30, 31. Undertaken by Order of the French Government,* 2 vols., (trans. by anon.) (London, 1834).

—— *Voyage dans l'Inde . . . pendant les années 1828–1832,* 6 vols. (Paris: Firmin Didot Frères, 1841).

Johnson, Samuel, *A Voyage to Abyssinia* (trans. from the French), ed. by Joel J. Gold, Vol. XV of *The Yale Edition of the Works of Samuel Johnson* (New Haven and London: Yale University Press, 1985).

Jones, Sir William, *Letters,* ed. by Garland Cannon, 2 vols. (Oxford: Clarendon Press, 1970).

Kant, Immanuel, *The Critique of Judgement,* trans. with an analytical index by James Creed Meredith (Oxford, Clarendon Press, 1952).

—— 'What is Orientation in Thinking?', in *Kant: Political Writings,* ed. with intro. and notes by Hans Reiss, trans. by H. B. Nisbet (Cambridge University Press, 1970).

Kindersley, Jemima, *Letters from the Island of Teneriffe, Brazil, The Cape of Good Hope, and the East Indies* (London, 1777).

Kinglake, A. W., *Eothen, or Traces of Travel Brought Home from the East* (1843) (London: John Ollivier, 1844).

Knight, Richard Payne, *An Analytical Inquiry into the Principles of Taste,* 4th edn. (London, 1808).

Knox, Vicesimus, *Essays, Moral and Literary* (1778), a new edn., 2 vols. (Dublin, 1786).

Landon, Letitia, *The Zenana, and Minor Poems of L.E.L., With a Memoir by Emma Roberts* (London and Paris, nd).

Lane, Edward William, *An Account of the Manners and Customs of the Modern Egyptians* (London, 1836).

Layard, A. H., *Ninevah and its Remains,* 2 vols. (London, 1850).

—— *A Popular Account of Discoveries at Ninevah arranged from his larger work* (London: J. Murray, 1854).

León y Gama, don Antonio de, *Descripción histórica y cronológica de las dos piedras . . . dada a luz por Carlos María de Bustamante,* 2nd edn. (Mexico City, 1832), facsimile edn. (Mexico City: INAH 1990).

Leyden, Dr John, *Poetical Remains,* ed. by the Revd James Morton (London, 1819).

Long, G., *The British Museum: Egyptian Antiquities,* Vol. I (London, 1832).

Longinus, *On the Sublime* (1739), trans. and ed. by William Smith, 4th edn. (London, 1770).

Lyon, Capt. G. F., *Journal of a Residence and a Tour in the Republic of Mexico in the year 1826*, 2 vols., 1828 (Port Washington, New York and London: Kennikat Scholarly Reprints, 1971).

Mill, James, Review of 'Voyage aux Indes Orientales, par Le P. Paulin de S. Barthelemy', *Edinburgh Review*, 15 (Jan. 1810), 363–84.

—— *The History of British India* (1817), ed. by John Clive (Chicago: University of Chicago Press, 1975).

Mir Hasan Ali, Mrs, *Observations on the Mussulmauns of India* (1832), reprint (Karachi: Oxford University Press, 1974).

Murray, the Revd Alexander, *Account of the Life and Writings of James Bruce* (Edinburgh, 1808).

Nebel, Carl, *Voyage pittoresque et archaeólogique sur la partie la plus intéressante du Mexique* (Paris, 1836).

Niebuhr, Carsten, *Travels through Arabia, and Other Countries in the East*, trans. by Robert Heron with notes, 2 vols. (Dublin, 1792).

Park, Mungo, *Travels in the Interior District of Africa, Performed under the Direction and Patronage of the Africa Association, in the years 1795, 6, and 7* (London, 1799).

[Parks, Fanny], *Wanderings of a Pilgrim in Search of the Picturesque, during four and twenty years residence in the East; with Revelations of Life in the Zenana. Illustrated with Sketches from Nature*, 2 vols. (London: Pelham Richardson, Cornhill, 1850). *Oxford in Asia Reprint*, 2 vols., ed. by Esther Chawner (Karachi: Oxford University Press, 1975).

Pinkerton, John (ed.), *A General Collection of the Best and Most Interesting Voyages and Travels*, 17 vols. (London, 1814).

Pococke, Richard, *A Description of the East, and Some Other Countries*, 2 vols. (London, 1743).

Poinsett, Joel Roberts, *Notes on Mexico, Made in 1822, Accompanied by a Historical Sketch of the Revolution, and Translations of Official Reports on the Present State of that Country* (1824) (New York, Washington, London: Praeger Scholarly Reprints, 1969).

Price, Uvedale, *An Essay on the Picturesque, as Compared with the Sublime and the Beautiful*, new edn. (London, 1796).

Raspe, R. E. et al., *Singular Travels, Campaigns and Adventures of Baron Munchausen*, intro. by John Carswell (New York: Dover Publications, 1960).

Raynal, G. T. F., *A Philosophical and Political History of the Settlements and Trade of the Europeans in the East and West Indies*, trans. by J. Justamond, 4 vols. (London, 1776).

Roberts, Emma, *Oriental Scenes, Sketches, and Tales* (London, 1832).

—— *Scenes and Characteristics of Hindostan, with Sketches of Anglo-Indian Society*, 3 vols. (London: William Allen, 1835).

Robertson, William, *History of America*, 2 vols. (London, 1777).

Rousseau, J.-J., *A Discourse on Inequality*, trans. with an intro. and notes by Maurice Cranston (Harmondsworth: Penguin Books, 1984).

Salt, Henry, *A Voyage to Abyssinia, and Travels into the Interior of that Country, 1809–10* (London, 1814).

Salt, Henry, 'Egypt, a Descriptive Poem, with Notes', published in The *Life and Cor-respondence of Henry Salt, Esq.*, FRS, 2 vols. (London, 1834).

Schiller, F., *On the Aesthetic Education of Man*, ed. and trans. with an intro. and com-mentary by Elizabeth Wilkinson and L. A. Willoughby (Oxford: Clarendon Press, 1967).

Seely, Capt. John, *The Wonders of Elora: or, The Narrative of a Journey to the Temples and Dwellings excavated out of a Mountain of Granite* (London, 1824).

Shelley, Mary, *Journal*, ed. by Frederick L. Jones (Norman: University of Oklahoma Press, 1947).

Shelley, P. B., *Poems*, Vol. 2, 1817–19, ed. by Kelvin Everest and Geoffrey Matthews (Harlow, England: Longman, 2000).

Smith, Adam, *Lectures on Rhetoric and Belles Lettres*, ed. by J. Bryce (Oxford: Clarendon Press, 1983).

——'The Principles which Lead and Direct Philosophical Enquiries; illustrated by the History of Astronomy', in *The Essential Adam Smith*, ed. by Robert Heilbroner and Lawrence J. Malone (Oxford University Press, 1986).

Solvyns, Balthazard, *A Collection of Two Hundred and Fifty Coloured Etchings descrip-tive of the Manners, Customs, and Dresses of the Hindoos* (Calcutta, 1796–9).

——*Les Hindous*, 4 vols. (Paris, 1808–12).

Sonnerat, Pierre, *A Voyage to the East Indies and China; Performed by Order of Lewis XV, Between the Years 1774 and 1781*, trans. by Francis Magnus, 3 vols. (Calcutta, 1788–9).

Southey, Robert, *Commonplace Book*, 4th series, ed. by J. Warter (London, 1851).

——*New Letters*, ed. by K. Curry, 2 vols. (New York and London, 1965).

Stephens, John Lloyd, *Incidents of Travel in Egypt, Arabia Petraea, and the Holy Land* (1837) ed. with intro. by Victor von Hagen (San Francisco: Chronicle Books, 1991).

——and Catherwood, Frederick, *Incidents of Travel in Central America, Chiapas, & Yucatan* (1841) (London: Century Books, 1988).

Taylor, John, *Selections from the Works of the Baron de Humboldt, relating to the Climate, Inhabitants, Productions, and Mines of Mexico* (London, 1824).

The Hon. Emily Eden, *Up the Country: Letters written to her Sister from the Upper Provinces of India*, 2 vols. (1866), with an intro. and notes by Edward Thompson (London and Dublin: Curzon Press, 1978) reprint of Oxford University Press 1930 edn.

Trial for Adultery. The Whole Proceedings in the Trial of J. B. Gawler, Esq., for Criminal Conversation with Lady Valentia, in the Court of the King's Bench, before Lord Kenyon (London, 1799).

Trollope, Fanny, *Domestic Manners of the Americans* (1832) (Gloucester: Alan Sutton Publishing, 1984).

Valentia, George Annesley, Viscount, *Voyages and Travels to India, Ceylon, the Red Sea, Abyssinia, and Egypt, in 1802, 3, 4, 5, and 6*, 3 vols. (London, 1809).

Volney, Constantin, *Travels through Syria and Egypt, in the Years 1783–85, Contain-ing the present Natural and Poltical State of those Countries, their Productions,*

Arts, Manufactures, and Commerce; with Observations on the Manners, Customs, and Government of the Turks and Arabs, 2 vols. (London, 1787).

—— *The Ruins, or a Survey of the Revolutions of Empires* (1791) 2nd edn. (London, 1795).

—— *Simplification des langues orientales ou méthode nouvelle et facile d'apprendre les langues arabes, persannes, et turques avec des caractères européens* (Paris, 1794–5).

Waldeck, Baron Frederick de, *Voyage pittoresque et archéologique dans la province de Yucatán (Amérique Centrale)* (Paris and London, 1838).

Walpole, Horace, *Correspondence* (The Yale Edition), ed. by W. S. Lewis, 48 vols. (London and New Haven: Oxford University Press and Yale University Press, 1937–83).

Ward, Henry G., *Mexico, by His Majesty's Chargé d'Affaires in that Country during the Years 1825, 1826, and part of 1827. Second Edition enlarged, with an account of the Mining Companies, and of the Political Events in that Republic, to the Present Day*, 2 vols. (London, 1829).

Weber, Henry, *Popular Romances: Consisting of Imaginary Voyages . . . Including Gulliver's Travels . . . and the Adventures of Robinson Crusoe* (Edinburgh, 1812).

White, Lt. George Francis, *Views in India, chiefly among the Himalaya Mountains*, ed. by Emma Roberts (London and Paris, 1838).

Williamson, Capt. Thomas, *The East India Vade-Mecum; or, Complete Guide to Gentlemen intended for the Civil, Military, or Naval Services of the Hon. East India Company* (London, 1808).

Wolcot, John, 'Complimentary Epistle to James Bruce, Esq.', in *The Works of Peter Pindar, Esq., in 2 vols.* (London, 1801).

Wollstonecraft, Mary, *A Short Residence in Sweden*, ed. with intro. and notes by Richard Holmes (Harmondsworth: Penguin, 1987).

Wordsworth, William, and Wordsworth, Dorothy, *Letters: The Middle Years. Part 1, 1806–1811*, ed. by E. de Selincourt, rev. by Mary Moorman (Oxford: Clarendon Press, 1969).

———— *Letters: The Later Years IV, Part I, 1821–28*, 2nd edn., revised, arranged, and ed. by Alan G. Hill (Oxford: Clarendon Press, 1978).

Suggested Further Reading

Adams, Percy, *Travellers and Travel Liars 1660–1800* (New York: Dover Publications, 1980).

—— *Travel Literature and the Evolution of the Novel* (Lexington: University Press of Kentucky, 1983).

Altick, Richard, *The Shows of London* (Cambridge, Mass., 1978).

Archer, Mildred, and Lightbown, Ronald, *India Observed: India as Viewed by British Artists, 1760–1860* (London: Trefoil Books, V&A Museum, 1982).

Bann, Stephen, *The Clothing of Clio: A Study of the Representation of History in 19th-century Britain and France* (Cambridge University Press, 1984).

Bann, Stephen, *Under the Sign: John Bargrave as Collector, Traveller, and Witness* (Ann Arbor: University of Michigan Press, 1994).

Barrell, John, 'The Dangerous Goddess: Masculinity, Prestige, and the Aesthetic in Early 18th-century Britain', in *The Birth of Pandora and the Division of Knowledge* (London: Macmillan, 1992), pp. 63–87.

Batten, Charles, *Pleasurable Instruction: Form and Convention in 18th Century Travel Literature* (Berkeley, London: University of California Press, 1978).

Bayly, C. A., *Imperial Meridian: The British Empire and the World, 1780–1830* (London: Longman, 1989).

—— *Empire and Information: Intelligence Gathering and Social Communication in India, 1780–1870* (Cambridge University Press, 1996).

Benedict, Barbara, 'The Curious Attitude in 18th-Century Britain: Observing and Owning', *Eighteenth-Century Life*, 14 (1990), 59–98.

Bennett, Tony, *The Birth of the Museum: History, Theory, Politics* (London and New York: Routledge, 1995).

Blumenberg, Hans, *The Legitimacy of the Modern Age* (1966), trans. by Robert Wallace (Cambridge, Mass.: Harvard University Press, 1983).

Bopp, Marianne, O. de, Miranda, José et al., *Ensayos Sobre Humboldt* (México: UNAM, 1962).

Brading, David, *The First America: The Spanish Monarchy, Creole Patriots, and the Liberal State, 1492–1867* (Cambridge University Press, 1991).

Bravo, Michael, 'Precision and Curiosity in Scientific Travel: James Rennell and the Orientalist Geography of the New Imperial Age (1760–1830)', in *Voyages and Visions*, ed. by J. Elsner and J.-P. Rubiés (London: Reaktion Books, 1999).

Bunn, David, '"Our Wattled Cot": Mercantile and Domestic Spaces in Thomas Pringle's African Landscapes', in W. J. T. Mitchell (ed.), *Landscape and Power* (Chicago and London: University of Chicago Press, 1994).

Bunn, James, 'The Aesthetics of British Mercantilism', *NLH*, 11: 2 (Winter 1980), 303–21.

Buzard, James, *The Beaten Track: European Tourism, Literature, and the Ways to 'Culture'* (Oxford: Clarendon Press, 1993).

Casey, Edward S., *The Fate of Place: A Philosophical Study* (Berkeley, Calif., and London: University of California Press, 1984).

Catalogue of English Travel Literature in the Micro-Edition of the Fürstliche Biblio-thek Corvey (Olms Neue Medien, 1998).

Chard, Chloe, *Pleasure and Guilt on the Grand Tour: Travel Writing and Imagina-tive Geography, 1600–1830* (Manchester and New York: Manchester University Press, 1999).

Clark, Steve (ed.), *Travel Writing and Empire: Postcolonial Theory in Transit* (London and New York: Zed Books, 1999).

Cohn, Bernard, *Colonialism and Its Forms of Knowledge: The British in India* (Princeton, NJ: Princeton University Press, 1996).

Cox, Edward G., *A Reference Guide to the Literature of Travel*, 3 vols. (Seattle: University of Washington Press, 1935–49).

Crone, G. R., and Skelton, R. A., 'English Collections of Voyages and Travels 1625–1846', in Edward Lynam (ed.), *Richard Hakluyt and his Successors* (London: Hakluyt Society, 1946), pp. 65–140.

Daston, Lorraine, 'Curiosity in Early Modern Science', *Word & Image*, II, 4 (Oct.–Dec. 1995), 391–404.

—— and Park, Katherine, *Wonder and the Order of Nature, 1150–1750* (New York: Zone Books, 1998).

Davis, Lennard, *Factual Fictions: The Origins of the English Novel* (New York: Columbia University Press, 1983).

de Certeau, Michel, *The Practice of Everyday Life*, trans. by Stephen Rendall (Berkeley, Calif. and London, 1984).

Dettelbach, Michael, 'Global Physics and Aesthetic Empire: Humboldt's Physical Portrait of the Tropics', in *Visions of Empire: Voyages, Botany, and Representations of Nature*, ed. by David Miller and Peter Reill (Cambridge University Press, 1996).

Dirks, Nicholas, 'Guiltless Spoliations: Picturesque Beauty, Colonial Knowledge, and Colin Mackenzie's Survey of India', in *Perceptions of South Asia's Visual Past*, ed. by Catherine B. Asher and Thomas R. Metcalf (New Delhi, Bombay, Calcutta: Oxford and IBH Publishing, 1994).

Dolan, Brian, *Exploring European Frontiers: European Travellers in the Age of Enlightenment* (Basingstoke, Macmillan, 2000).

Dyson, K. K., *A Various Universe: A Study of the Journals and Memoirs of British Men and Women in the Indian Subcontinent, 1765–1856* (Delhi: Oxford University Press, 1978).

Edney, Matthew, *Mapping an Empire: The Geographical Construction of British India, 1765–1843* (Chicago and London: University of Chicago Press, 1998).

Elsner, John, and Cardinal, Roger (eds.), *The Culture of Collecting* (London: Reaktion Books, 1994).

Elsner, Jas, and Rubiés, Joan-Pau (eds.), *Voyages and Visions: Towards a Cultural History of Travel* (London: Reaktion Books, 1999).

Fabian, Johannes, *Time and the Other: How Anthropology Makes its Object* (New York: Columbia University Press, 1983).

Gascoigne, John, *Joseph Banks and the English Enlightenment: Useful Knowledge and Polite Culture* (Cambridge University Press, 1997).

Gerbi, Antonello, *The Dispute of the New World: The History of a Polemic, 1750–1900*, revised and enlarged edn. trans. by Jeremy Moyle (Pittsburgh: Pittsburgh University Press, 1973).

Ghose, Indira, *The Power of the Female Gaze: Women Travellers in Colonial India* (New Delhi: Oxford University Press, 1998).

Godlewska, Anne, 'Map, Text and Image: The Mentality of Enlightened Conquerors. A New Look at the *Description de l'Égypte*', *Transactions of the Institute of British Geographers*, ns, 20, (1995), 5–28.

—— *Geography Unbound: French Geographic Science from Cassini to Humboldt* (University of Chicago Press, 1999).

Holl, Frank (ed.), *Alejandro De Humboldt on México* (Mexico City: INAH/Instituto Goethe, 1997).

Jenkins, Ian, *Archaeologists and Aesthetes in the Sculpture Galleries of the British Museum 1800–1839* (London: British Museum Press, 1993).

Jonathan, Crary, *Techniques of the Observer: On Vision and Modernity in the 19th Century* (Cambridge, Mass., and London: MIT Press, 1990).

Keen, Benjamin, *The Aztec Image in Western Thought* (New Brunswick, NJ: Rutgers University Press, 1971).

Kenny, Neil, *Curiosity in Early Modern Word Histories*, Wolfenbütteler Forschungen, Band 81 (Wiesbaden: Harrassowitz Verlag, 1998).

Klonk, Charlotte, *Science and the Perception of Nature: British Landscape Art in the late 18th and Early 19th Centuries* (New Haven and London: Yale University Press, 1996).

Latour, Bruno, *Science in Action: How to Follow Scientists and Engineers Through Society* (Milton Keynes: Open University Press, 1987).

Leask, Nigel, 'Kubla Khan and Orientalism: The Road to Xanadu Revisited', in *Romanticism*, 4:1 (1998).

—— 'Wandering Through Eblis: Absorption and Containment in Romantic Exoticism', in *Romanticism and Colonialism: Writing and Empire 1780–1830*, ed. by Tim Fulford and Peter Kitson (Cambridge University Press, 1998).

—— 'The Ghost in Chapultepec: Fanny Calderón de la Barca, William Prescott and 19th Century Mexican Travel Accounts', in *Voyages and Visions*, ed. by J. Elsner, and J.-P. Rubiés (London: Reaktion Books, 1999).

—— 'Francis Wilford and the Colonial Construction of Hindu Geography, 1799–1822', in *Romantic Geographies: Discourses of Travel 1775–1844*, ed. by Amanda Gilroy (Manchester and New York: Manchester University Press, 2000).

—— 'Salons, Alps and Cordilleras: Helen Maria Williams, Alexander Von Humboldt, and the Discourse of Romantic Travel', in *Woman, Writing and the Public Sphere, 1700–1830*, ed. by C. Grant, E. Eger, C. O'Gallchoir, and P. Warburton (Cambridge University Press, 2001).

Livingstone, D. N., and Withers, C. W. J. (eds.), *Geography and the Enlightenment* (Chicago: University of Chicago Press, 1998).

Majeed, Javed, *Ungoverned Imaginings: James Mill's History of British India and Orientalism* (Oxford University Press, 1992).

Marshall, P. J., 'The Whites of British India, 1780–1830: A Failed Colonial Society?', in *Trade and Conquest: Studies on the Rise of British Dominance in India* (Aldershot and Brookfield, Vt: Ashgate Publishing, 1993).

—— and Williams, Glyndwr, *The Great Map of Mankind: British Perceptions of the World in the Age of Enlightenment* (London and Melbourne: J. M. Dent and Sons, 1982).

Mayes, Stanley, *The Great Belzoni* (London: Putnam, 1959).

Meek, Ronald, *Social Science and the Ignoble Savage* (Cambridge University Press, 1976).

Miller, David, and Reill, Peter, *Visions of Empire: Voyages, Botany and Representations of Nature* (Cambridge University Press, 1996).

Miller, Edward, *That Noble Cabinet: A History of the British Museum* (London: Andre Deutsch, 1973).

Minguet, Charles, *Alexandre de Humboldt: historien et géographe de l'Amérique Espagnole* (Paris: Francis Maspero, 1969).

Mitchell, Timothy, *Colonising Egypt* (Cambridge University Press, 1988).

—— 'Orientalism and the Exhibitory Order', in *Colonialism and Culture*, ed. by Nicholas Dirks (Ann Arbor: University of Michigan Press, 1992).

Mitter, Partha, *Much Maligned Monsters: History of European Reactions to Indian Art* (Oxford: Clarendon Press, 1977).

Obeyesekere, Gananath, *The Apotheosis of Captain Cook: European Mythmaking in the Pacific, With a New Afterword* (Princeton, NJ: Princeton University Press, 1997).

Outram, Dorinda, 'New Spaces in Natural History', in *Cultures of Natural History*, ed. by N. Jardine, J. A. Secord, and E. C. Spary (Cambridge University Press, 1996).

Pagden, Anthony, *European Encounters with the New World, From Renaissance to Romanticism* (New Haven and London: Yale University Press, 1993).

—— 'Identity Formation in Spanish America', in *Colonial Identity in the Atlantic*, ed. by Nicholas Canny and Anthony Pagden (Princeton, 1993).

Pomian, Krzysztof, *Collectors and Curiosities: Paris and Venice, 1500–1800* (1987), trans. by Elizabeth Wiles-Porter (Cambridge: Polity Press, 1990).

Prakash, Gyan, *Another Reason: Science and the Imagination of Modern India* (Princeton, NJ: Princeton University Press, 1999).

Pratt, Mary Louise, *Imperial Eyes: Travel-Writing and Transculturation* (London and New York: Routledge, 1992).

Rennie, Neil, *Far-Fetched Facts: The Literature of Travel and the Idea of the South Seas* (Oxford: Clarendon Press, 1995).

Sahlins, Marshal, *How 'Natives' Think: About Captain Cook, For Example* (Chicago and London: University of Chicago Press, 1996).

Said, Edward, *Orientalism* (Harmondsworth: Penguin, 1985).

Schaffer, Simon, 'Self-Evidence', *Critical Inquiry*, 18 (Winter 1992), 327–62.

—— and Shapin, Steven, *Leviathan and the Air Pump: Hobbes, Boyle, and the Experimental Life* (Princeton, NJ: Princeton University Press, 1985).

Smith, Bernard, *European Vision and the South Pacific, 1768–1850: A Study in the History of Art and Ideas* (1960), 2nd edn. (New Haven, 1985).

St Clair, William, *Lord Elgin and the Marbles* (Oxford and New York: Oxford University Press, 1998).

Stafford, Barbara Maria, 'Towards Romantic Landscape Perception: Illustrated Travels and the Rise of "Singularity" as an Aesthetic Category', *Art Quarterly*, ns, 1 (1977), 89–124.

—— *Voyage into Substance: Art, Science, Nature, and the Illustrated Travel Account 1760–1840* (Cambridge, Mass., and London: MIT Press, 1984).

Stewart, Susan, *On Longing: Narratives of the Miniature, the Gigantic, the Souvenir, the Collection* (Durham and London: Duke University Press, 1993).

Suleri, Sara, *The Rhetoric of English India* (Chicago and London: University of Chicago Press, 1992).

Taussig, Michael, *The Devil and Commodity Fetishism in South America* (Chapel Hill: University of North Carolina Press, 1980).

—— *Mimesis and Alterity: A Particular History of the Senses* (New York and London: Routledge, 1993).

Teltscher, Kate, *India Inscribed: European and British Writing on India 1600–1800* (Oxford and New Delhi: Oxford University Press, 1995).

Thomas, Nicholas, *Colonialism's Culture: Anthropology, Travel and Government* (Princeton, NJ: Princeton University Press, 1994).

—— 'Licenced Curiosity: Cook's Pacific Voyages', in *The Culture of Collecting*, ed. by John Elsner and Roger Cardinal (London: Reaktion Books, 1994), pp. 116–36.

—— *Entangled Objects: Exchange, Material Culture, and Colonialism* (Cambridge, Mass. and London: Harvard University Press, 1991).

Viajeros Europeos del Siglo XIX en México (Comisión Europea en México/Fomento Cultural Banamex, 1996), intro. by Elías Trabulse.

Whale, John, 'Romantic Explorers, Picturesque Travellers', in *The Politics of the Picturesque: Literature, Landscape and Aesthetics since 1770*, ed. by Stephen Copley and Peter Garside (Cambridge University Press, 1994).

Index

Italic page-references indicate illustrations.